DAILY LIGHT

from the Holy Bible,
New International Version

Hodder & Stoughton
LONDON SYDNEY AUCKLAND

Introduction

Daily Light on the Daily Path is probably the most widely read collection of daily readings from the Bible ever published. For three generations this set of readings from the King James Bible has been a classic religious work, and the number of its printings has long been forgotten. Its compilation was the work of the descendants of the London bookseller, Samuel Bagster.

His grandson, Robert, who died in 1924, wrote of the origins of this book, '*Daily Light on the Daily Path* was prepared entirely within the family. Few are able to appreciate the heart-searching care with which every text was selected, the days, nay the weeks of changes, alterations and improvements, until at last each page was passed to the printer.'

This devotional book offers two selections of Bible readings from the NIV for every day in the year, morning and evening. A single daily theme helps to emphasize a particular Bible truth so that as we progress through the book we complete a Bible teaching course to help us in our daily Christian walk. Also, readings for a selection of *Special Occasions* appear at the back.

This edition gives new expression to the cherished readings of *Daily Light on the Daily Path* by its use of the Inclusive Language Edition of the (NIV) or New International Version of the Bible, a contemporary translation of distinctive clarity and beauty of language.

But as for you, continue in what you have learned and have become convinced of, because you know those from whom you learned it, and how from infancy you have known the holy Scriptures, which are able to make you wise for salvation through faith in Christ Jesus. All Scripture is God-breathed and is useful for teaching, rebuking, correcting and training in righteousness, so that God's servant may be thoroughly equipped for every good work.

2 Timothy 3:14–17
New International Version
Inclusive Language Edition

Morning

But one thing I do: Forgetting what is behind . . . I press on towards the goal to win the prize for which God has called me heavenwards in Christ Jesus.

'Father, I want those you have given me to be with me where I am, and to see my glory, the glory you have given me.'—I know whom I have believed, and am convinced that he is able to guard what I have entrusted to him for that day.—He who began a good work in you will carry it on to completion until the day of Christ Jesus.

Strict training
Do you not know that in a race all the runners run, but only one gets the prize? Run in such a way as to get the prize. Everyone who competes in the games goes into strict training. They do it to get a crown that will not last; but we do it to get a crown that will last for ever.

Let us throw off everything that hinders and the sin that so easily entangles, and let us run with perseverance the race marked out for us. Let us fix our eyes on Jesus.

> Philippians 3:13–14. John 17:24. 2 Timothy 1:12. Philippians 1:6.
> 1 Corinthians 9:24–25. Hebrews 12:1–2.

Evening

The LORD himself goes before you and will be with you; he will never leave you nor forsake you.

If your Presence does not go with us, do not send us up from here.—I know, O LORD, that a man's life is not his own; it is not for man to direct his steps.

The LORD makes firm the steps of those who delight in him; though they stumble, they will not fall, for the LORD upholds them with his hand.

You hold me
I am always with you; you hold me by my right hand. You guide me with your counsel, and afterwards you will take me into glory.—For I am convinced that neither death nor life, neither angels nor demons, neither the present nor the future, nor any powers, neither height nor depth, nor anything else in all creation, will be able to separate us from the love of God that is in Christ Jesus our Lord.

> Deuteronomy 31:8. Exodus 33:15. Jeremiah 10:23.
> Psalms 37:23–24; 73:23–24. Romans 8:38–39.

January 2

Morning

Sing to the Lord a new song.

Sing for joy to God our strength; shout aloud to the God of Jacob! Begin the music, strike the tambourine, play the melodious harp and lyre . . . He put a new song in my mouth, a hymn of praise to our God. Many will see and fear and put their trust in the Lord.

'Be strong and courageous. Do not be terrified; do not be discouraged, for the Lord your God will be with you wherever you go.'—'For the joy of the Lord is your strength.'—Paul thanked God and was encouraged.

Put on the armour of light
Let us put aside the deeds of darkness and put on the armour of light. Let us behave decently, as in the daytime, not in orgies and drunkenness, not in sexual immorality and debauchery, not in dissension and jealousy. Rather, clothe yourselves with the Lord Jesus Christ, and do not think about how to gratify the desires of the sinful nature.

Isaiah 42:10. Psalms 81:1–2; 40:3. Joshua 1:9. Nehemiah 8:10.
Acts 28:15. Romans 13:12–14.

Evening

May my prayer be set before you like incense; may the lifting up of my hands be like the evening sacrifice.

Make an altar of acacia wood for burning incense . . . Put the altar in front of the curtain that is before the ark of the Testimony—before the atonement cover that is over the Testimony—where I will meet with you.

The prayer of the saints
[Jesus] is able to save completely those who come to God through him, because he always lives to intercede for them.—The smoke of the incense, together with the prayers of the saints, went up before God from the angel's hand.

You also, like living stones, are being built into a spiritual house to be a holy priesthood, offering spiritual sacrifices acceptable to God through Jesus Christ.

Pray continually.

Psalm 141:2. Exodus 30:1, 6–8. Hebrews 7:25. Revelation 8:4.
1 Peter 2:5. 1 Thessalonians 5:17.

Morning

He led them by a straight way.

In a desert land he found him [Jacob], in a barren and howling waste. He shielded him as the apple of his eye, like an eagle that stirs up its nest and hovers over its young, that spreads its wings to catch them and carries them on its pinions. The LORD alone led him; no foreign god was with him.

'Even to your old age and grey hairs I am he, I am he who will sustain you. I have made you and I will carry you; I will sustain you and I will rescue you.'

I will fear no evil
He restores my soul. He guides me in paths of righteousness for his name's sake. Even though I walk through the valley of the shadow of death, I will fear no evil, for you are with me; your rod and your staff, they comfort me.

The LORD will guide you always; he will satisfy your needs in a sun-scorched land and will strengthen your frame. You will be like a well-watered garden, like a spring whose waters never fail.

> Psalm 107:7. Deuteronomy 32:10–12. Isaiah 46:4. Romans 23:3–4.
> Isaiah 58:11.

Evening

'What do you want me to do for you?' . . . 'Lord, I want to see.'

Open my eyes that I may see wonderful things in your law.

Then he opened their minds so they could understand the Scriptures—'But the Counsellor, the Holy Spirit, whom the Father will send in my name, will teach you all things.'—Every good and perfect gift is from above, coming down from the Father of the heavenly lights.

The eyes of your heart
The God of our Lord Jesus Christ, the glorious Father, may give you the Spirit of wisdom and revelation, so that you may know him better. I pray also that the eyes of your heart may be enlightened in order that you may know the hope to which he has called you, the riches of his glorious inheritance in the saints, and his incomparably great power for us who believe.

> Luke 18:41. Psalm 119:18. Luke 24:45. John 14:26. James 1:17.
> Ephesians 1:17–19.

January 4

Morning

This is not your resting place.

Many rooms
'In my Father's house are many rooms; if it were not so, I would have told you. I am going there to prepare a place for you. And if I go and prepare a place for you, I will come back and take you to be with me that you also may be where I am.'—With Christ, which is better by far.

[God] will wipe every tear from their eyes. There will be no more death or mourning or crying or pain, for the old order of things has passed away.—There the wicked cease from turmoil, and there the weary are at rest.

Treasures in heaven
'But store up for yourselves treasures in heaven, where moth and rust do not destroy, and where thieves do not break in and steal. For where your treasure is, there your heart will be also.'—Set your minds on things above, not on earthly things.

> Micah 2:10. John 14:2–3. Philippians 1:23. Revelation 21:4. Job 3:17.
> Matthew 6:20–21. Colossians 3:2.

Evening

'Where, O death, is your victory? Where, O death, is your sting?'

The sting of death is sin.—Then Christ would have had to suffer many times since the creation of the world. But now he has appeared once for all at the end of the ages to do away with sin by the sacrifice of himself. Just as people are destined to die once, and after that to face judgment, so Christ was sacrificed once to take away the sins of many people; and he will appear a second time, not to bear sin, but to bring salvation to those who are waiting for him.

Free those held in slavery
Since the children have flesh and blood, he too shared in their humanity so that by his death he might destroy him who holds the power of death—that is, the devil—and free those who all their lives were held in slavery by their fear of death.

The crown of righteousness
For I am already being poured out like a drink offering, and the time has come for my departure. I have fought the good fight, I have finished the race, I have kept the faith. Now there is in store for me the crown of righteousness.

> 1 Corinthians 15:55, 56. Hebrews 9:27–28; 2:14–15. 2 Timothy 4:6–8.

Morning

We who have believed enter that rest.

They weary themselves with sinning.—I see another law at work in the members of my body, waging war against the law of my mind and making me a prisoner of the law of sin at work within my members. What a wretched man I am! Who will rescue me from this body of death?

'Come to me'
'Come to me all you who are weary and burdened, and I will give you rest.'— Therefore, since we have been justified through faith, we have peace with God through our Lord Jesus Christ, through whom we have gained access by faith into this grace in which we now stand. And we rejoice in the hope of the glory of God.

For those who enter God's rest also rest from their own work.—Not having a righteousness of my own that comes from the law, but that which is through faith in Christ—the righteousness that comes from God and is by faith.

Hebrews 4:3. Jeremiah 9:5. Romans 7:23–24. Matthew 11:28.
Romans 5:1–2. Hebrews 4:10. Philippians 3:9.

Evening

Set a guard over my mouth, O Lord; keep watch over the door of my lips.

If you, O Lord, kept a record of sins, O Lord, who could stand? . . . For they rebelled against the Spirit of God, and rash words came from Moses' lips.

'What goes into your mouth does not make you "unclean", but what comes out of your mouth, that is what makes you "unclean".'

Gossips
Gossips separate close friends. . . . Reckless words pierce like a sword, but the tongue of the wise brings healing. Truthful lips endure for ever, but a lying tongue lasts only a moment.—But no-one can tame the tongue. It is a restless evil, full of deadly poison. . . . Out of the same mouth come praise and cursing. My brothers and sisters, this should not be.

But now you must rid yourselves of all such things as these: anger, age, malice, slander and filthy language from your lips. Do not lie to each other, since you have taken off your old self with its practices.

Psalms 141:3; 130:3; 106:33. Matthew 15:11. Proverbs 16:28; 12:18–19.
James 3:8, 10. Colossians 3:8–9.

January 6

Morning

May the favour of the Lord our God rest upon us; establish the work of our hands for us.

And we, who with unveiled faces all reflect the Lord's glory, are being transformed into his likeness with ever-increasing glory, which comes from the Lord, who is Spirit.—The Spirit of glory and of God rests on you.

Walk in his ways
Blessed are all who fear the LORD, who walk in his ways. You will eat the fruit of your labour; blessings and prosperity will be yours.—Commit to the LORD whatever you do, and your plans will succeed.

Eternal encouragement
Continue to work out your salvation with fear and trembling, for it is God who works in you to will and to act.—May our Lord Jesus Christ himself and God our Father, who loved us and by his grace gave us eternal encouragement and good hope, encourage your hearts and strengthen you in every good deed and word.

> Psalm 90:17. 2 Corinthians 3:18. 1 Peter 4:14. Psalm 128:1–2.
> Proverbs 16:3. Philippians 2:12–13. 2 Thessalonians 2:16–17.

Evening

The apostles gathered round Jesus and reported to him all they had done and taught.

There is a friend who sticks closer than a brother or sister.

'I have called you friends'
'You are my friends if you do what I command. I no longer call you servants, because servants do not know their master's business. Instead, I have called you friends, for everything that I learned from my Father I have made known to you.'

The Spirit of adoption
For you did not receive a spirit that makes you a slave again to fear, but you received the Spirit of adoption. And by him we cry, '*Abba*, Father.'

In everything, by prayer and petition, with thanksgiving, present your requests to God.—The prayer of the upright pleases him.

> Mark 6:30. Proverbs 18:24. John 15:14–15. Romans 8:15.
> Philippians 4:6. Proverbs 15:8.

Morning

Remember me with favour, O my God.

'I remember the devotion of your youth, how as a bride you loved me and followed me through the desert, through a land not sown.'—'Yet I will remember the covenant I made with you in the days of your youth, and I will establish an everlasting covenant with you.'—'I will come to you and fulfil my gracious promise to bring you back to this place. For I know the plans I have for you,' declares the LORD, 'plans to prosper you and not to harm you, plans to give you hope and a future.'

Many are the wonders you have done
'As the heavens are higher than the earth, so are my ways higher than your ways and my thoughts than your thoughts.'—Many, O LORD my God, are the wonders you have done. The things you planned for us no-one can recount to you; were I to speak and tell of them, they would be too many to declare.

Nehemiah 5:19. Jeremiah 2:2. Ezekiel 16:60. Jeremiah 29:10–11.
Isaiah 55:9. Psalm 40:5.

Evening

'I will never leave you or forsake you.'

Not one of all the LORD's good promises to the house of Israel failed; every one was fulfilled.—Know therefore that the LORD your God is God; he is the faithful God, keeping his covenant of love to a thousand generations of those who love him and keep his commands.—He remembers his covenant for ever.

 'Can a mother forget the baby at her breast and have no compassion on the child she has borne? Though she may forget, I will not forget you! See, I have engraved you on the palms of my hands.'

'He will quiet you with his love'
'The LORD your God is with you, he is mighty to save. He will take great delight in you, he will quiet you with his love, he will rejoice over you with singing.'

Joshua 1:5; 21:45. Deuteronomy 7:9. Psalm 111:5. Isaiah 49:15–16.
Zephaniah 3:17.

January 8

Morning

Those who know your name will trust in you, for you, LORD, have never forsaken those who seek you.

The name of the LORD is a strong tower; the righteous run to it and are safe.— 'I will trust and not be afraid. The LORD, the LORD, is my strength and my song; he has become my salvation.'

He will deliver us
For the sake of his great name the LORD will not reject his people, because the LORD was pleased to make you his own.—He has delivered us from such a deadly peril, and he will deliver us. On him we have set our hope that he will continue to deliver us.

Be content
Be content with what you have, because God has said, 'Never will I leave you; never will I forsake you.' So we say with confidence, 'The Lord is my helper; I will not be afraid.'

Psalm 9:10. Proverbs 18:10. Isaiah 12:2. 1 Samuel 12:22.
2 Corinthians 1:10. Hebrews 13:5–6.

Evening

He has freely given us in the One he loves.

Who is a God like you, who pardons sin and forgives the transgression of the remnant of his inheritance? You do not stay angry for ever but delight to show mercy. You will again have compassion on us; you will tread our sins underfoot and hurl all our iniquities into the depths of the sea.

Free from accusation
To present you holy in his sight, without blemish and free from accusation.

To keep you from falling
To him who is able to keep you from falling and to present you before his glorious presence without fault and with great joy—to the only God our Saviour be glory, majesty, power and authority, through Jesus Christ our Lord, before all ages, now and for evermore! Amen.

Ephesians 1:6. Micah 7:18–19. Colossians 1:22. Jude 24–25.

Morning

The Lord is my Banner.

We will shout for joy when you are victorious and will lift up our banners in the name of our God.—'The Lord has vindicated us; come, let us tell in Zion what the Lord our God has done.'

More than conquerors
No, in all these things we are more than conquerors through him who loved us.—But thanks be to God! He gives us the victory through our Lord Jesus Christ.

Be strong in the Lord
Finally, be strong in the Lord and in his mighty power.—'Fight the battles of the Lord.'—'Be strong, all you people of the land,' declares the Lord, 'and work. For I am with you.'—'Open your eyes and look at the fields! They are ripe for harvest.'—For in just a very little while, 'He who is coming will come and will not delay.'

Exodus 17:15. Psalm 20:5. Jeremiah 51:10. Romans 8:37.
1 Corinthians 15:57. Ephesians 6:10. 1 Samuel 18:17. Haggai 2:4.
John 4:35. Hebrews 10:37.

Evening

'Only one thing is needed.'

Many are asking, 'Who can show us any good?' Let the light of your face shine upon us, O Lord. You have filled my heart with greater joy than when their grain and new wine abound.

Earnestly I seek you
As the deer pants for streams of water, so my soul pants for you, O God. My soul thirsts for God, for the living God . . . O God, you are my God, earnestly I seek you; my soul thirsts for you, my body longs for you, in a dry and weary land where there is no water.

One thing I will ask of the Lord
Mary . . . sat at the Lord's feet listening to what he said.—One thing I ask of the Lord, this is what I seek: that I may dwell in the house of the Lord all the days of my life, to gaze upon the beauty of the Lord and to seek him in his temple.

Luke 10:42. Psalms 4:6–7; 42:1–2; 63:1. Luke 10:39. Psalm 27:4.

January 10

Morning

May your whole spirit, soul and body be kept blameless at the coming of our Lord Jesus Christ.

Christ loved the church and gave himself up for her . . . to present her to himself as a radiant church, without stain or wrinkle or any other blemish, but holy and blameless.—We proclaim him, admonishing and teaching everyone with all wisdom, so that we may present everyone perfect in Christ.

Let the peace of Christ rule in your hearts, since as members of one body you were called to peace.

You will be blameless
May our Lord Jesus Christ himself and God our Father, who loved us and by his grace gave us eternal encouragement and good hope, encourage your hearts and strengthen you in every good deed and word.—He will keep you strong to the end, so that you will be blameless on the day of our Lord Jesus Christ.

> 1 Thessalonians 5:23. Ephesians 5:25, 27. Colossians 1:28; 3:15.
> 2 Thessalonians 2:16–17. 1 Corinthians 1:8.

Evening

'Then the nations will know that I the LORD make Israel holy, when my sanctuary is among them for ever.'

'Then have them make a sanctuary for me, and I will dwell among them.' . . . 'There also I will meet with the Israelites, and the place will be consecrated by my glory. . . . Then I will dwell among the Israelites and be their God.'

Temples of the Holy Spirit
For we are the temple of the living God. As God has said: 'I will live with them and walk among them, and I will be their God, and they will be my people.'— Your bodies are temples of the Holy Spirit, who is in you.

A dwelling in which God lives
And in him you too are being built together to become a dwelling in which God lives by his Spirit.

My sanctuary is among them
'Then the nations will know that I the LORD make Israel holy, when my sanctuary is among them for ever.'

> Ezekiel 37:28. Exodus 25:8; 29:43, 45. 2 Corinthians 6:16.
> 1 Corinthians 6:19. Ephesians 2:22.

Morning

Praise awaits you, O God, in Zion.

For us there is but one God, the Father, from whom all things came and for whom we live; and there is but one Lord, Jesus Christ, through whom all things came and through whom we live.—'That all may honour the Son just as they honour the Father. Whoever does not honour the Son does not honour the Father, who sent him.'

Through Jesus, therefore, let us continually offer to God a sacrifice of praise—the fruit of lips that confess his name.

A great multitude that no-one could count
After this I looked and there before me was a great multitude that no-one could count, from every nation, tribe, people and language, standing before the throne and in front of the Lamb. They were wearing white robes and were holding palm branches in their hands. And they cried out in a loud voice: 'Salvation belongs to our God, who sits on the throne, and to the Lamb.' . . . 'Amen! Praise and glory and wisdom and thanks and honour and power and strength be to our God for ever and ever. Amen!'

Psalm 65:1. 1 Corinthians 8:6. John 5:23. Hebrews 13:15.
Revelation 7:9–10, 12.

Evening

Who redeems your life from the pit.

Yet their Redeemer is strong; the LORD Almighty is his name.—'I will ransom them from the power of the grave; I will redeem them from death. Where, O death, are your plagues? Where, O grave, is your destruction?'

Since the children have flesh and blood, he too shared in their humanity so that by his death he might destroy him who holds the power of death—that is, the devil—and free those who all their lives were held in slavery by their fear of death.

'Those who believe in the Son have eternal life, but those who reject the Son will not see life, for God's wrath remains on them.'

Your life is now hidden with Christ
For you died, and your life is now hidden with Christ in God. When Christ, who is your life, appears, then you also will appear with him in glory.

Psalm 103:4. Jeremiah 50:34. Hosea 13:14. Hebrews 2:14–15.
John 3:36. Colossians 3:3–4.

January 12

Morning

The only God our Saviour

Christ Jesus . . . has become for us wisdom from God—that is, our right-eousness, holiness and redemption.

'Can you fathom the mysteries of God? Can you probe the limits of the Almighty? They are higher than the heavens—what can you do? They are deeper than the depths of the grave—what can you know?'

God's secret wisdom

No, we speak of God's secret wisdom, a wisdom that has been hidden and that God destined for our glory before time began.

The wisdom that comes from heaven

If any of you lacks wisdom, you should ask God, who gives generously to all without finding fault, and it will be given to you. . . . But the wisdom that comes from heaven is first of all pure; then peace-loving, considerate, submissive, full of mercy and good fruit, impartial and sincere.

Jude 25. 1 Corinthians 1:30. Job 11:7–8. 1 Corinthians 2:7.
James 1:5; 3:17.

Evening

'Watchman, what is left of the night?' The watchman replies, 'Morning is coming.'

For in just a little while, 'He who is coming will come and will not delay.'—He is like the light of morning at sunrise on a cloudless morning.

'I am coming back to you'

'I am going there to prepare a place for you. And if I go and prepare a place for you, I will come back and take you to be with me that you also may be where I am.' . . . 'Do not let your hearts be troubled and do not be afraid. You heard me say, "I am going away and I am coming back to you." '

There will be no night there

'So may all your enemies perish, O Lord! But may they who love you be like the sun when it rises in its strength.'—You are all children of the light and children of the day. We do not belong to the night or to the darkness.—There will be no night there.

Isaiah 21:11–12. Hebrews 10:37. 2 Samuel 23:4. John 14:2–3, 27–28.
Judges 5:31. 1 Thessalonians 5:5. Revelation 21:25.

Morning

Cast all your cares on the LORD and he will sustain you; he will never let the righteous fall.

'I will trust and not be afraid. The LORD, the LORD, is my strength and my song; he has become my salvation.'

Do not be anxious about anything, but in everything, by prayer and petition, with thanksgiving, present your requests to God. And the peace of God, which transcends all understanding, will guard your hearts and your minds in Christ Jesus.—In quietness and trust is your strength.

'My peace I give to you'
The effect of righteousness will be quietness and confidence for ever.—'Peace I leave with you; my peace I give you. I do not give to you as the world gives. Do not let your hearts be troubled and do not be afraid.'—Grace and peace to you from him who is, and who was, and who is to come.

> Psalm 55:22. Isaiah 12:2. Philippians 4:6–7. Isaiah 30:15; 32:17.
> John 14:27. Revelation 1:4.

Evening

Do not let the sun go down while you are still angry.

'If your brother or sister sins against you, go and show them their fault, just between the two of you. If they listen to you, you have won them over.' . . . 'Lord, how many times shall I forgive someone who sins against me? Up to seven times?' Jesus answered, 'I tell you, not seven times, but seventy-seven times.'—'When you stand praying, if you hold anything against anyone, forgive them, so that your Father in heaven may forgive you your sins.'

Forgive as the Lord forgave you
Therefore, as God's chosen people, holy and dearly loved, clothe yourselves with compassion, kindness, humility, gentleness and patience. Bear with each other and forgive whatever grievances you may have against one another. Forgive as the Lord forgave you.

> Ephesians 4:20. Matthew 18:15, 21–22. Mark 11:25. Colossians 3:12–13.

January 14

Morning

'The Father is greater than I.'

'I do exactly what my Father has commanded me.' . . . 'The words that I say to you are not just my own. Rather, it is the Father, living in me, who is doing his work.'

'The Father loves the Son and has placed everything in his hands.' . . . 'For you granted him authority over all people that he might give eternal life to all those you have given him.'

'I am in the Father'
'Lord, show us the Father and that will be enough for us.' Jesus answered: 'Don't you know me, Philip, even after I have been among you such a long time? Anyone who has seen me has seen the Father. How can you say, "Show us the Father"? Don't you believe that I am in the Father, and that the Father is in me?' . . . 'I and the Father are one.'

'As the Father has loved me, so have I loved you. Now remain in my love. If you obey my commands, you will remain in my love, just as I have obeyed my Father's commands and remain in his love.'

John 14:28, 31, 10; 3:35; 17:2; 14:8–10; 10:30; 15:9–10.

Evening

'He will crush your head, and you will strike his heel.'

But he was pierced for our transgressions, he was crushed for our iniquities; the punishment that brought us peace was upon him, and by his wounds we are healed.

'But this is your hour—when darkness reigns.'—'You would have no power over me if it were not given to you from above.'

To destroy the devil's work
The reason the Son of God appeared was to destroy the devil's work.—He also drove out many demons, but he would not let the demons speak because they knew who he was.

The God of peace will soon crush Satan under your feet.

Genesis 3:15. Isaiah 53:5. Luke 22:53. John 19:11. 1 John 3:8.
Mark 1:34. Romans 16:20.

Morning

Set your minds on things above, not on earthly things. For you died, and your life is now hidden with Christ in God.

But our citizenship is in heaven. And we eagerly await a Saviour from there, the Lord Jesus Christ, who, by the power that enables him to bring everything under his control, will transform our lowly bodies so that they will be like his glorious body.

For the sinful nature desires what is contrary to the Spirit, and the Spirit what is contrary to the sinful nature. They are in conflict with each other, so that you do not do what you want.—Therefore, brothers and sisters, we have an obligation—but it is not to the sinful nature, to live according to it. For if you live according to the sinful nature, you will die; but if by the Spirit you put to death the misdeeds of the body, you will live.

Abstain from sinful desires
I urge you, as aliens and strangers in the world, to abstain from sinful desires, which war against your soul.

> Colossians 3:2–3. Philippians 3:20–21. Galatians 5:17. Romans 8:12–13.
> 1 Peter 2:11.

Evening

The measure of faith

Those whose faith is weak. . . . Strengthened in his faith and gave glory to God.—'You of little faith,' he said, 'why did you doubt?' . . . 'Woman, you have great faith! Your request is granted.'

'According to your faith'
'Do you believe that I am able to do this?' 'Yes, Lord,' they replied. . . . 'According to your faith will it be done to you.'

'Increase our faith!'—Build yourselves up in your most holy faith.—Rooted and built up in him, strengthened in the faith as you were taught, and overflowing with thankfulness.

The God of all grace
Now it is God who makes both us and you stand firm in Christ.—And the God of all grace, who called you to his eternal glory in Christ, after you have suffered a little while, will himself restore you and make you strong.

> Romans 12:3; 14:1; 4:20. Matthew 14:31; 15:28; 9:28–29. Luke 17:5.
> Jude 20. Colossians 2:7. 2 Corinthians 1:21. 1 Peter 5:10.

January 16

Morning

For God was pleased to have all his fulness dwell in him.

'The Father loves the Son and has placed everything in his hands.'—God exalted him to the highest place and gave him the name that is above every name, that at the name of Jesus every knee should bow, in heaven and on earth and under the earth, and every tongue confess that Jesus Christ is Lord, to the glory of God the Father.

For by him all things were created: things in heaven and on earth, visible and invisible, whether thrones or powers or rulers or authorities; all things were created by him and for him.

Lord of both the dead and the living
Christ died and returned to life so that he might be the Lord of both the dead and the living.—You have been given fulness in Christ, who is the Head over every power and authority.—From the fulness of his grace we have all received one blessing after another.

Colossians 1:19. John 3:35. Philippians 2:9–11. Colossians 1:16.
Romans 14:9. Colossians 2:10. John 1:16.

Evening

'Write, therefore, what you have seen, what is now and what will take place later.'

Prophets, though human, spoke from God as they were carried along by the Holy Spirit.—We proclaim to you what we have seen and heard, so that you also may have fellowship with us. And our fellowship is with the Father and with his Son, Jesus Christ.

So that you also may believe
'Look at my hands and my feet. It is I myself! Touch me and see; a ghost does not have flesh and bones, as you see I have.' When he had said this, he showed them his hands and feet.—The man who saw it has given testimony, and his testimony is true. He knows that he tells the truth, and he testifies so that you also may believe.

We did not follow cleverly invented stories when we told you about the power and coming of our Lord Jesus Christ, but we were eye-witnesses of his majesty.—So that your faith might not rest on human wisdom, but on God's power.

Revelation 1:19. 2 Peter 1:21. 1 John 1:3. Luke 24:39–40. John 19:35.
2 Peter 1:16. 1 Corinthians 2:5.

Morning

In your love you have kept me from the pit of destruction.

He sent his one and only Son into the world that we might live through him. This is love: not that we loved God, but that he loved us and sent his Son as an atoning sacrifice for our sins.

Who is a God like you, who pardons sin and forgives the transgression of the remnant of his inheritance? You do not stay angry for ever but delight to show mercy. You will again have compassion on us; you will tread our sins underfoot and hurl all our iniquities into the depths of the sea.

I waited patiently for the Lord
'When my life was ebbing away, I remembered you, LORD, and my prayer rose to you, to your holy temple.'—I waited patiently for the LORD; he turned to me and heard my cry. He lifted me out of the slimy pit.

Isaiah 38:17. 1 John 4:9–10. Micah 7:18–19. Jonah 2:7. Psalm 40:1–2.

Evening

Now we see but a poor reflection.

At present we do not see everything subject to him.

Your word is a lamp to my feet
And we have the word of the prophets made more certain, and you will do well to pay attention to it, as to a light shining in a dark place, until the day dawns and the morning star rises in your hearts.—Your word is a lamp to my feet and a light for my path.

But, dear friends, remember what the apostles of our Lord Jesus Christ foretold. They said to you, 'In the last times there will be scoffers who will follow their own ungodly desires.'—The Spirit clearly says that in later times some will abandon the faith and follow deceiving spirits and things taught by demons.

Dear children, this is the last hour.—The night is nearly over; the day is almost here. So let us put aside the deeds of darkness and put on the armour of light.

1 Corinthians 13:12. Hebrews 2:8. 2 Peter 1:19. Psalm 119:105.
Jude 17–18. 1 Timothy 4:1. 1 John 2:18. Romans 13:12.

January 18

Morning

The one to come.

Jesus, who was made a little lower than the angels, now crowned with glory and honour because he suffered death, so that by the grace of God he might taste death for everyone.—One died for all.—For just as through the disobedience of the one man the many were made sinners, so also through the obedience of the one man the many will be made righteous.

The Son is the radiance of God's glory
'The first Adam became a living being'; the last Adam became a life-giving spirit. The spiritual did not come first, but the natural, and after that the spiritual.—But in these last days he has spoken to us by his Son, whom he appointed heir of all things, and through whom he made the universe. The Son is the radiance of God's glory and the exact representation of his being.—'For you granted him authority over all people.'

> Romans 5:14. Hebrews 2:9. 2 Corinthians 5:14. Romans 5:19.
> 1 Corinthians 15:45–46. Hebrews 1:2–3. John 17:2.

Evening

'What is yet to come.'

He is coming with the clouds
Look, he is coming with the clouds, and every eye will see him, even those who pierced him; and all the peoples of the earth will mourn because of him. So shall it be! Amen.

With the Lord for ever
Brothers and sisters, we do not want you to be ignorant about those who fall asleep, or to grieve like the rest, who have no hope. We believe that Jesus died and rose again and so we believe that God will bring with Jesus those who have fallen asleep in him. . . . For the Lord himself will come down from heaven, with a loud command, with the voice of the archangel and with the trumpet call of God, and the dead in Christ will rise first. After that, we who are still alive and are left will be caught up together with them in the clouds to meet the Lord in the air. And so we will be with the Lord for ever.

> John 16:13. Revelation 1:7. 1 Thessalonians 4:13–14, 16–17.

Morning

'I served the Lord with great humility.'

'Whoever wants to become great among you must be your servant, and whoever wants to be first must be your slave—just as the Son of Man did not come to be served, but to serve, and to give his life as a ransom for many.'

Unworthy servants
If any of you think you are something when you are nothing, you deceive yourselves.—'When you have done everything you were told to do, [you] should say, "We are unworthy servants; we have only done our duty." '

This all-surpassing power
Now this is our boast: . . . we have conducted ourselves in the world . . . in the holiness and sincerity that are from God. We have done so not according to worldly wisdom but according to God's grace. . . . But we have this treasure in jars of clay to show that this all-surpassing power is from God and not from us.

Acts 20:19. Matthew 20:26–28. Galatians 6:3. Luke 17:10.
2 Corinthians 1:12; 4:7.

Evening

For the transgression of my people he was stricken.

Noah, a man of the soil, proceeded to plant a vineyard. When he drank some of its wine, he became drunk.—And rash words came from Moses' lips.

The men of Israel did not inquire of the LORD
The men of Israel sampled their provisions but did not inquire of the LORD. Then Joshua made a treaty of peace with them.—For David had done what was right in the eyes of the LORD and had not failed to keep any of the LORD's commands all the days of his life—except in the case of Uriah the Hittite.

All commended for their faith
These were all commended for their faith.—And are justified freely by his grace through the redemption that came by Christ Jesus.

Isaiah 53:8. Genesis 9:20–21. Psalm 106:33. Joshua 9:14–15.
1 Kings 15:5. Hebrews 11:39. Romans 3:24.

January 20

Morning

And he will be called Wonderful.

The Word became flesh and made his dwelling among us. We have seen his glory, the glory of the One and Only, who came from the Father, full of grace and truth.—For you have exalted above all things your name and your word.

'They will call him Immanuel'—which means, 'God with us.' . . . 'Jesus, because he will save his people from their sins.'

The name that is above every name
All may honour the Son just as they honour the Father.—Therefore God exalted him to the highest place and gave him the name that is above every name.—Far above all rule and authority, power and dominion, and every title that can be given, not only in the present age but also in the one to come. And God placed all things under his feet.—He has a name written on him that no-one knows but he himself . . . KING OF KINGS AND LORD OF LORDS.

> Isaiah 9:6. John 1:14. Psalm 138:2. Matthew 1:23, 21. John 5:23.
> Philippians 2:9. Ephesians 1:21–22. Revelation 19:12, 16.

Evening

The LORD's portion is his people.

You are of Christ, and Christ is of God.—The Son of God, who loved me and gave himself for me.

Honour God with your bodies
You are not your own; you were bought at a price. Therefore honour God with your bodies.—But as for you, the LORD took you and brought you out of the iron-smelting furnace, out of Egypt, to be the people of his inheritance, as you now are.

For we are God's co-workers; you are God's field, God's building.—A spiritual house to be a holy priesthood.

'Glory has come to me through them'
'They will be mine,' says the LORD Almighty, 'in the day when I make up my treasured possession.'—'All I have is yours, and all you have is mine. And glory has come to me through them.'—The riches of his glorious inheritance in the saints.

> Deuteronomy 32:9. 1 Corinthians 3:23. Galatians 2:20.
> 1 Corinthians 6:19–20. Deuteronomy 4:20. 1 Corinthians 3:9.
> 1 Peter 2:5. Malachi 3:17. John 17:10. Ephesians 1:18.

Morning

'He cuts off every branch that bears no fruit.'

But we also rejoice in our sufferings, because we know that suffering produces perseverance; perseverance, character; and character, hope. And hope does not disappoint us, because God has poured out his love into our hearts by the Holy Spirit, whom he has given us.

A harvest of righteousness
Endure hardship as discipline; God is treating you as children. For what children are not disciplined by their parents? If you are not disciplined (and everyone undergoes discipline), then you are illegitimate and not true children. . . . No discipline seems pleasant at the time, but painful. Later on, however, it produces a harvest of righteousness and peace for those who have been trained by it. Therefore, strengthen your feeble arms and weak knees!

John 15:2. Romans 5:3–5. Hebrews 12:7–8, 11–12.

Evening

The LORD detests all the proud of heart.

Better to be lowly in spirit and among the oppressed than to share plunder with the proud.

'Blessed are the poor in spirit'
'Blessed are the poor in spirit, for theirs is the kingdom of heaven.'
   There are six things the LORD hates, seven that are detestable to him: haughty eyes, a lying tongue, hands that shed innocent blood.

Search me, O God
Search me, O God, and know my heart; test me and know my anxious thoughts. See if there is any offensive way in me, and lead me in the way everlasting.

Proverbs 16:5, 19. Matthew 5:3. Proverbs 6:16–17. Psalm 139:23–24.

January 22

Morning

For this God is our God for ever and ever; he will be our guide even to the end.

O Lord, you are my God; I will exalt you and praise your name, for in perfect faithfulness you have done marvellous things, things planned long ago.

He guides me in paths of righteousness for his name's sake. Even though I walk through the valley of the shadow of death, I will fear no evil, for you are with me; your rod and your staff, they comfort me. . . . You hold me by my right hand.

God is my portion for ever
You guide me with your counsel, and afterwards you will take me into glory. Whom have I in heaven but you? And earth has nothing I desire besides you. My flesh and my heart may fail, but God is the strength of my heart and my portion for ever. . . . The Lord will fulfil his purpose for me; your love, O Lord, endures for ever—do not abandon the works of your hands.

Psalm 48:14. Isaiah 25:1. Psalms 23:3–4; 73:23–26; 138:8.

Evening

When anxiety was great within me, your consolation brought joy to my soul.

I call as my heart grows faint; lead me to the rock that is higher than I.
    I am troubled; O Lord, come to my aid!

Perfect in weakness
And who is equal to such a task?—I know that nothing good lives in me.—'My grace is sufficient for you, for my power is made perfect in weakness.'—'Take heart, son; your sins are forgiven.'—'Take heart, daughter,' he said, 'your faith has healed you.'

My soul will be satisfied as with the richest of foods; . . . On my bed I remember you through the watches of the night.

Psalms 94:19; 61:2. Isaiah 38:14. 2 Corinthians 2:16. Romans 7:18.
2 Corinthians 12:9. Matthew 9:2, 22. Psalm 63:5–6.

Morning

Hope does not disappoint us.

'I am the LORD; those who hope in me will not be disappointed.'

Find rest, O my soul, in God alone; my hope comes from him. He alone is my rock and my salvation; for he is my fortress, I shall not be shaken.

I am not ashamed, because I know whom I have believed.

An anchor
Because God wanted to make the unchanging nature of his purpose very clear to the heirs of what was promised, he confirmed it with an oath. God did this so that, by two unchangeable things in which it is impossible for God to lie, we who have fled to take hold of the hope offered to us may be greatly encouraged. We have this hope as an anchor for the soul, firm and secure. It enters the inner sanctuary behind the curtain, where Jesus, who went before us, has entered on our behalf.

> Romans 5:5. Isaiah 49:23. Psalm 62:5–6. 2 Timothy 1:12.
> Hebrews 6:17–20.

Evening

The offence of the cross.

'Those who would come after me must deny themselves and take up their cross and follow me.'

Many hardships
Don't you know that friendship with the world is hatred towards God: Anyone who chooses to be a friend of the world becomes an enemy of God.—'We must go through many hardships to enter the kingdom of God.'

'The one who trusts in him will never be put to shame.'

I have been crucified with Christ
May I never boast except in the cross of our Lord Jesus Christ, through which the world has been crucified to me, and I to the world. . . . I have been crucified with Christ . . . Those who belong to Christ Jesus have crucified the sinful nature with its passions and desires.

If we endure, we will also reign with him. If we disown him, he will also disown us.

> Galatians 5:11. Matthew 16:24. James 4:4. Acts 14:22. Romans 9:33.
> Galatians 6:14, 2:20; 5:24. 2 Timothy 2:12.

January 24

Morning

The Lord is near.

For the Lord himself will come down from heaven, with a loud command, with the voice of the archangel and with the trumpet call of God, and the dead in Christ will rise first. After that, we who are still alive and are left will be caught up together with them in the clouds to meet the Lord in the air. And so we will be with the Lord for ever. Therefore encourage each other with these words.

'I am coming soon'
He who testifies to these things says, 'Yes, I am coming soon.' Amen. Come, Lord Jesus.

Avoid every kind of evil
Avoid every kind of evil. May God himself, the God of peace, sanctify you through and through. May your whole spirit, soul and body be kept blameless at the coming of our Lord Jesus Christ. The one who calls you is faithful and he will do it.

You, too, be patient and stand firm, because the Lord's coming is near.

Philippians 4:5. 1 Thessalonians 4:16–18. Revelation 22:20.
1 Thessalonians 5:22–24. James 5:8.

Evening

'This is my Father's glory, that you bear much fruit, showing yourselves to be my disciples.'

'I had planted you like a choice vine of sound and reliable stock. How then did you turn against me into a corrupt, wild vine?'

The fruit of the Spirit
The acts of the sinful nature are obvious: sexual immorality, impurity and debauchery; . . . and envy; drunkenness, orgies, and the like. I warn you, as I did before, that those who live like this will not inherit the kingdom of God. But the fruit of the Spirit is love, joy, peace, patience, kindness, goodness, faithfulness, gentleness and self-control.

'Remain in me'
'I am the true vine, and my Father is the gardener. He cuts off every branch in me that bears no fruit, while every branch that does bear fruit he prunes so that it will be even more fruitful. . . . Remain in me, and I will remain in you.'

John 15:8. Jeremiah 2:21. Galatians 5:19, 21–23. John 15:1–2, 4.

Morning

This righteousness from God comes through faith in Jesus Christ to all who believe.

God made him who had no sin to be sin for us, so that in him we might become the righteousness of God.—Who has become for us wisdom from God—that is, our righteousness, holiness and redemption.

Renewal by the Holy Spirit
He saved us, not because of righteous things we had done, but because of his mercy. He saved us through the washing of rebirth and renewal by the Holy Spirit, whom he poured out on us generously through Jesus Christ our Saviour.

I consider everything a loss compared to the surpassing greatness of knowing Christ Jesus my Lord, for whose sake, I have lost all things. I consider them rubbish, that I may gain Christ and be found in him, not having a righteousness of my own that comes from the law, but that which is through faith in Christ—the righteousness that comes from God and is by faith.

Romans 3:22. 2 Corinthians 5:21. 1 Corinthians 1:30. Titus 3:5–6.
Philippians 3:8–9.

Evening

The Spirit of adoption. And by him we cry, '*Abba*, Father.'

After Jesus said this, he looked towards heaven and prayed: 'Father, . . . Holy Father, . . . Righteous Father.'—'*Abba*, Father,' he said.—Because you are sons, God sent the Spirit of his Son into our hearts, the Spirit who calls out, '*Abba*, Father.'—For through him we both have access to the Father by one Spirit. Consequently, you are no longer foreigners and aliens, but fellow-citizens with God's people and members of God's household.

He went to his father
'I will set out and go back to my father and say to him: Father, I have sinned against heaven and against you. I am no longer worthy to be called your son; make me like one of your hired servants.' So he got up and went to his father.

Be imitators of God, therefore, as dearly loved children.

Romans 8:15. John 17:1, 11, 25. Mark 14:36. Galatians 4:6.
Ephesians 2:18–19. Luke 15:18–20. Ephesians 5:1.

January 26

Morning

If you are insulted because of the name of Christ, you are blessed, for the Spirit of glory and of God rests on you.

Dear friends, do not be surprised at the painful trial you are suffering, as though something strange were happening to you. But rejoice that you participate in the sufferings of Christ, so that you may be overjoyed when his glory is revealed.—As you share in our sufferings, so also you share in our comfort.

Suffering disgrace for the Name
The apostles left the Sanhedrin, rejoicing because they had been counted worthy of suffering disgrace for the Name.—He chose to be ill-treated along with the people of God rather than to enjoy the pleasures of sin for a short time. He regarded disgrace for the sake of Christ as of greater value than the treasures of Egypt, because he was looking ahead to his reward.

1 Peter 4:14, 12–13. 2 Corinthians 1:7. Acts 5:41. Hebrews 11:25–26.

Evening

The Lord Jesus Christ . . . will transform our lowly bodies so that they will be like his glorious body.

Above the expanse over their heads was what looked like a throne of sapphire, and high above on the throne was a figure like that of a man. I saw that from what appeared to be his waist up he looked like glowing metal, as if full of fire, and that from there down he looked like fire; and brilliant light surrounded him. Like the appearance of a rainbow in the clouds on a rainy day, so was the radiance around him.

Being transformed
And we, who with unveiled faces all reflect the Lord's glory, are being transformed into his likeness with ever-increasing glory, which comes from the Lord, who is the Spirit.

'Never again will they hunger; never again will they thirst.' . . . 'And [they] sang the song of Moses the servant of God and the song of the Lamb.

Philippians 3:20–21. Ezekiel 1:26–28. 2 Corinthians 3:18.
Revelation 7:16; 15:3.

Morning

But you know that he appeared so that he might take away our sins. And in him is no sin.

But in these last days he has spoken to us by his Son, whom he appointed heir of all things, and through whom he made the universe. The Son is the radiance of God's glory and the exact representation of his being, sustaining all things by his powerful word. After he had provided purification for sins, he sat down at the right hand of the Majesty in heaven.

Live as strangers

Live your life as strangers here in reverent fear. For you know that it was not with perishable things such as silver or gold that you were redeemed from the empty way of life handed down to you from your ancestors, but with the precious blood of Christ, a lamb without blemish or defect.

For Christ's love compels us, because we are convinced that one died for all, and therefore all died. And he died for all, that those who live should no longer live for themselves but for him who died for them and was raised again.

1 John 3:5. Hebrews 1:2–3. 1 Peter 1:17–19. 2 Corinthians 5:14–15.

Evening

I have set before you life and death, blessings and curses. Now choose life, so that you and your children may live.

For I take no pleasure in the death of anyone, declares the Sovereign LORD. Repent and live!

'If I had not come and spoken to them, they would not be guilty of sin. Now, however, they have no excuse for their sin.'

Eternal life

The wages of sin is death, but the gift of God is eternal life in Christ Jesus our Lord.—'Those who believe in the Son have eternal life, but those who reject the Son will not see life, for God's wrath remains on them.'—Don't you know that when you offer yourselves to someone as obedient slaves, you are slaves to the one whom you obey—whether you are slaves to sin, which leads to death, or to obedience, which leads to righteousness?

Deuteronomy 30:19. Ezekiel 18:32. John 15:22. Romans 6:23. John 3:36.
Romans 6:16.

January 28

Morning

And your strength will equal your days.

'Whenever you are arrested and brought to trial, do not worry beforehand about what to say. Just say whatever is given you at the time, for it is not you speaking, but the Holy Spirit.'

The God of Israel gives power and strength to his people. Praise be to God!—He gives strength to the weary and increases the power of the weak.

When I am weak, then I am strong
'My grace is sufficient for you, for my power is made perfect in weakness.' Therefore I will boast all the more gladly about my weaknesses, so that Christ's power may rest on me. That is why, for Christ's sake, I delight in weaknesses, in insults, in hardships, in persecutions, in difficulties. For when I am weak, then I am strong.—March on, my soul; be strong!

> Deuteronomy 33:25. Mark 13:11. Psalm 68:35. Isaiah 40:29.
> 2 Corinthians 12:9–10. Judges 5:21.

Evening

As parents have compassion on their children, so the LORD has compassion on those who fear him.

No discipline seems pleasant at the time, but painful. Later on, however, it produces a harvest of righteousness and peace for those who have been trained by it.—The fruit of the Spirit.

Inwardly renewed
Though outwardly we are wasting away, yet inwardly we are being renewed day by day. For our light and momentary troubles are achieving for us an eternal glory that far outweighs them all. So we fix our eyes not on what is seen but on what is unseen. For what is seen is temporary, but what is unseen is eternal.

Although he [Jesus] was a son, he learned obedience from what he suffered. . . . But we have one who has been tempted in every way, just as we are—yet was without sin.

> Psalm 103:13. Hebrews 12:11. Galatians 5:22. 2 Corinthians 4:16–18.
> Hebrews 5:8; 4:15.

Morning

'You are the God who sees me.'

O LORD, you have searched me and you know me. You know when I sit and when I rise; you perceive my thoughts from afar. You discern my going out and my lying down; you are familiar with all my ways. Before a word is on my tongue you know it completely, O LORD. . . . Such knowledge is too wonderful for me, too lofty for me to attain.

'God knows your hearts'
The eyes of the LORD are everywhere, keeping watch on the wicked and the good. . . . For your ways are in full view of the LORD, and he examines all your paths.—'God knows your hearts. What is highly valued by people is detestable in God's sight.'
  'Lord, you know all things; you know that I love you.'

> Genesis 16:13. Psalm 139:1–4, 6. Proverbs 15:3; 5:21. Luke 16:15.
> John 21:17.

Evening

I will praise you, O Lord my God, with all my heart; I will glorify your name for ever.

Those who sacrifice thank-offerings honour me. . . . It is good to praise the LORD and make music to your name, O Most High, to proclaim your love in the morning and your faithfulness at night.
  Let everything that has breath praise the LORD.

Always giving thanks
Through Jesus, therefore, let us continually offer to God a sacrifice of praise—the fruit of lips that confess his name.—Always giving thanks to God the Father for everything, in the name of our Lord Jesus Christ.
  'Worthy is the Lamb, who was slain, to receive power and wealth and wisdom and strength and honour and glory and praise!'

> Psalms 86:12; 50:23; 92:1–2; 150:6. Hebrews 13:15. Ephesians 5:20.
> Revelation 5:12.

January 30

Morning

Let us run with perseverance the race marked out for us. Let us fix our eyes on Jesus, the author and perfecter of our faith.

'Those who would come after me must deny themselves and take up their cross daily and follow me.' . . . 'In the same way, those of you who do not give up everything you have cannot be my disciples.'

Put on the armour of light
Let us put aside the deeds of darkness and put on the armour of light.

A crown that will last for ever
Everyone who competes in the games goes into strict training. They do it to get a crown that will not last; but we do it to get a crown that will last for ever. . . . No, I beat my body and make it my slave so that after I have preached to others, I myself will not be disqualified for the prize.

Let us acknowledge the LORD; let us press on to acknowledge him.

Hebrews 12:1–2. Luke 9:23; 14:33. Romans 13:12.
1 Corinthians 9:25, 27. Hosea 6:3.

Evening

Before I was afflicted I went astray, but now I obey your word.

God disciplines us for our good
We have all had human parents who disciplined us and we respected them for it. How much more should we submit to the Father of our spirits and live! Our parents disciplined us for a little while as they thought best; but God disciplines us for our good, that we may share in his holiness.

It was good for me to be afflicted so that I might learn your decrees.

'I know the plans I have for you,' declares the LORD, 'plans to prosper you and not to harm you.'—Humble yourselves, therefore, under God's mighty hand, that he may lift you up in due time.

Psalm 119:67. Hebrews 12:9–10. Psalm 119:71. Jeremiah 29:11.
1 Peter 5:6.

Morning

Fight the good fight of faith.

The weapons we fight with are not the weapons of the world. On the contrary, they have divine power to demolish strongholds. . . . And we take captive every thought to make it obedient to Christ.

More than conquerors
For the sinful nature desires what is contrary to the Spirit, and the Spirit what is contrary to the sinful nature. They are in conflict with each other, so that you do not do what you want.—But I see another law at work in the members of my body, waging war against the law of my mind and making me a prisoner of the law of sin at work within my members. . . . We are more than conquerors through him who loved us.

1 Timothy 6:12. 2 Corinthians 10:4–5. Galatians 5:17. Romans 7:23; 8:37.

Evening

What, then, shall we say in response to this: If God is for us, who can be against us?

The Righteous One
If anybody does sin, we have one who speaks to the Father in our defence—Jesus Christ, the Righteous One. He is the atoning sacrifice for our sins, and not only for ours but also for the sins of the whole world.

God presented him as a sacrifice of atonement, through faith in his blood. He did this to demonstrate his justice, because in his forbearance he had left the sins committed beforehand unpunished—he did it to demonstrate his justice at the present time, so as to be just and the one who justifies those who have faith in Jesus.

At the right hand of God
It is God who justifies. Who then can condemn? Christ Jesus, who died—more than that, who was raised to life—is at the right hand of God and is also interceding for us.

Romans 8:31. 1 John 2:1–2. Romans 3:25–26. Romans 8:33–34.

February 1

Morning

You have not seen him.

We live by faith, not by sight. We love because he first loved us. . . . And so we know and rely on the love God has for us. God is love. Those who live in love live in God, and God in them.

Included in Christ
And you also were included in Christ when you heard the word of truth, the gospel of your salvation. Having believed, you were marked in him with a seal, the promised Holy Spirit.

If we say we love God yet hate a brother or sister, we are liars. For any of us who do not love his brother or sister, whom we have seen, cannot love God, whom we have not seen.

Then Jesus told him, 'Because you have seen me, you have believed; blessed are those who have not seen and yet have believed.'—Blessed are all who take refuge in him.

1 Peter 1:8. 2 Corinthians 5:7. 1 John 4:19, 16. 1 John 4:20. John 20:29.
Psalm 2:12.

Evening

The LORD Our Righteousness.

All of us have become like one who is unclean, and all our righteous acts are like filthy rags.

I will come and proclaim your mighty acts, O Sovereign LORD; I will proclaim your righteousness, yours alone.—I delight greatly in the LORD; my soul rejoices in my God. For he has clothed me with garments of salvation and arrayed me in a robe of righteousness, as a bridegroom adorns his head like a priest, and as a bride adorns herself with her jewels.

'Bring the best robe and put it on him.'

The righteousness that comes from God
I consider everything a loss compared to the surpassing greatness of knowing Christ Jesus my Lord, for whose sake I have lost all things. I consider them rubbish, that I may gain Christ and be found in him, not having a righteousness of my own that comes from the law, but that which is through faith in Christ—the righteousness that comes from God and is by faith.

Jeremiah 23:6. Isaiah 64:6. Psalm 71:16. Isaiah 61:10. Luke 15:22.
Philippians 3:8–9.

Morning

'The spirit is willing, but the body is weak.'

Give me only my daily bread

'Two things I ask of you, O LORD; do not refuse me before I die: Keep falsehood and lies far from me; give me neither poverty nor riches, but give me only my daily bread. Otherwise, I may have too much and disown you and say, "Who is the LORD?" Or I may become poor and steal, and so dishonour the name of my God.'

The LORD will keep you from all harm—he will watch over your life.—'I will save you from the hands of the wicked and redeem you from the grasp of the cruel.'—The one who was born of God keeps them safe, and the evil one cannot harm them.

Since you have kept my command to endure patiently, I will also keep you from the hour of trial that is going to come upon the whole world to test those who live on the earth.—The Lord knows how to rescue the godly from trials.

Matthew 26:41. Proverbs 30:7–9. Psalm 121:7. Jeremiah 15:21.
1 John 5:18. Revelation 3:10. 2 Peter 2:9.

Evening

Those who are wise will shine like the brightness of the heavens, and those who lead many to righteousness, like the stars for ever and ever.

On the way they had argued about who was the greatest. Sitting down, Jesus called the Twelve and said, 'Anyone who wants to be first must be the very last, and the servant of all.'—Clothe yourselves with humility towards one another, because, 'God opposes the proud but gives grace to the humble.' Humble yourselves, therefore, under God's mighty hand, that he may lift you up in due time.

God exalted him

Your attitude should be the same as that of Christ Jesus: Who, being in the very nature God, did not consider equality with God something to be grasped, but made himself nothing, taking the very nature of a servant, being made in human likeness. . . . Therefore God exalted him to the highest place and gave him the name that is above every name, that at the name of Jesus every knee should bow.

Daniel 12:3. Mark 9:34–35. 1 Peter 5:5–6. Philippians 2:5–7, 9–10.

February 3

Morning

'The joy of the LORD is your strength.'

'I am the vine; you are the branches. If you remain in me and I you, you will bear much fruit; apart from me you can do nothing.'—I can do everything through him who gives me strength.—Be strong in the Lord and in his mighty power.

Be strong
This is what the LORD Almighty says: 'You who now hear these words spoken by the prophets . . . let your hands be strong.'—Strengthen the feeble hands, steady the knees that give way; say to those with fearful hearts, 'Be strong, do not fear.'—The LORD turned to him and said, 'Go in the strength you have.'

If God is for us, who can be against us?—Therefore, since through God's mercy we have this ministry, we do not lose heart.

Let us not become weary in doing good, for at the proper time we will reap a harvest if we do not give up.

> Nehemiah 8:10. John 15:5. Philippians 4:13. Ephesians 6:10. Zechariah
> 8:9. Isaiah 35:3–4. Judges 6:14. Romans 8:31. 2 Corinthians 4:1.
> Galatians 6:9.

Evening

The darkness will not be darkness to you.

The LORD watches over you
You will not fear the terror of night . . . nor the pestilence that stalks in the darkness. . . . If you make the Most High your dwelling—even the LORD, who is my refuge—then no harm will befall you, no disaster will come near your tent . . . he who watches over you will not slumber . . . The LORD watches over you—the LORD is your shade at your right hand; the sun will not harm you by day, nor the moon by night. The LORD will keep you from all harm.

The valley of the shadow of death
Even though I walk through the valley of the shadow of death, I will fear no evil.

> Psalm 139:12. Psalms 91:5–6, 9–10; 121:3, 5–7; 23:4.

Morning

He who began a good work in you will carry it on to completion until the day of Christ Jesus.

If they had been thinking of the country they had left, they would have had opportunity to return. Instead, they were longing for a better country—a heavenly one.

Moses
He chose to be ill-treated along with the people of God rather than to enjoy the pleasures of sin for a short time. He regarded disgrace for the sake of Christ as of greater value than the treasures of Egypt.

'My righteous one will live by faith'
'But my righteous one will live by faith. And I take no pleasure in the one who shrinks back.' But we are not of those who shrink back and are destroyed, but of those who believe and are saved.—'No-one who takes hold of the plough and looks back is fit for service in the kingdom of God.'

May I never boast except in the cross of our Lord Jesus Christ, through which the world has been crucified to me, and I to the world.

> Philippians 1:6. Hebrews 11:15–16, 25–26; 10:38–39. Luke 9:62.
> Galatians 6:14.

Evening

Encourage the timid, help the weak, be patient with everyone.

Brothers and sisters, if someone is caught in a sin, you who are spiritual should restore that person gently. But watch yourself, or you also may be tempted.

Those who turn sinners from the error of their ways will save them from death and cover over a multitude of sins.

Bear with the failings of the weak
Therefore let us stop passing judgment on one another. Instead, make up your mind not to put any stumbling-block or obstacle in another believer's way. . . . We who are strong ought to bear with the failings of the weak and not to please ourselves.

Be careful that you don't fall!
Love does not delight in evil.—So, if you think you are standing firm, be careful that you don't fall!

> 1 Thessalonians 5:14. Galatians 6:1. James 5:20. Romans 14:13; 51:1.
> 1 Corinthians 13:6; 10:12.

February 5

Morning

'I have come that they may have life, and have it to the full.'

'When you eat of it you shall surely die.' . . . She took some of it and ate it. She also gave some to her husband, who was with her, and he ate it.

The gift of God is eternal life
For the wages of sin is death, but the gift of God is eternal life in Christ Jesus our Lord.—For since death came through a human being, the resurrection of the dead comes also through a human being. For as in Adam all die, so in Christ all will be made alive.—Our Saviour, Christ Jesus, who has destroyed death and has brought life and immortality to light through the gospel.

God has given us eternal life, and this life is in his Son. Those who have the Son have life; those who do not have the Son of God do not have life.—'For God did not send his Son into the world to condemn the world, but to save the world through him.'

John 10:10. Genesis 2:17; 3:6. Romans 6:23. 1 Corinthians 15:21–22.
2 Timothy 1:10. 1 John 5:11–12. John 3:17.

Evening

When we are judged by the Lord, we are being disciplined so that we will not be condemned with the world.

Now we know that God's judgment against those who do such things is based on truth.

'When the Son of Man comes in his glory, and all the angels with him, he will sit on his throne in heavenly glory. All the nations will be gathered before him, and he will separate the people one from another as a shepherd separates the sheep from the goats.'

'The righteous will shine like the sun'
'Then the righteous will shine like the sun in the kingdom of their Father.'— Who will bring any charge against those whom God has chosen? It is God who justifies. Who then can condemn? Christ Jesus, who died—more than that, who was raised to life—is at the right hand of God and is also interceding for us.

1 Corinthians 11:32. Romans 2:2. Matthew 25:31–32; 13:43.
Romans 8:33–34.

Morning

But when sin increased, grace increased more.

For you know the grace of our Lord Jesus Christ, that though he was rich, yet for your sakes he became poor, so that you through his poverty might become rich.

His kindness to us in Christ Jesus
In order that in the coming ages he might show the incomparable riches of his grace, expressed in his kindness to us in Christ Jesus. For it is by grace you have been saved, through faith—and this not from yourselves, it is the gift of God—not by works, so that no-one can boast.—Know that a person is not justified by observing the law, but by faith in Jesus Christ. So we, too, have put our faith in Christ Jesus that we may be justified by faith in Christ and not by observing the law, because by observing the law no-one will be justified.

He saved us . . . because of his mercy. He saved us through the washing of rebirth and renewal by the Holy Spirit, whom he poured out on us generously through Jesus Christ our Saviour.

Romans 5:20. 2 Corinthians 8:9. Ephesians 2:7–9. Galatians 2:16.
Titus 3:5–6.

Evening

'I am . . . the bright Morning Star.'

'A star will come out of Jacob.'—The night is nearly over; the day is almost here. So let us put aside the deeds of darkness and put on the armour of light.
'Watchman, what is left of the night? Watchman, what is left of the night?' The watchman replies, 'Morning is coming, but also the night. If you would ask, then ask; and come back yet again.'
'I am the light of the world.'—I will also give them the morning star.

'Keep watch'
'Be on your guard! Be alert! You do not know when that time will come. It's like a man going away: He leaves his house and puts his servants in charge, each with an assigned task, and tells the one at the door to keep watch. Therefore keep watch. . . . If he comes suddenly, do not let him find you sleeping. What I say to you, I say to everyone: "Watch!"'

Revelation 22:16. Numbers 24: 17. Romans 13:12. Isaiah 21:11–12.
John 8:12. Revelation 2:28. Mark 13:33–37.

February 7

Morning

Be careful that you do not forget the LORD your God.

One of them, when he saw he was healed, came back, praising God in a loud voice. He threw himself at Jesus' feet and thanked him—and he was a Samaritan. Jesus asked, 'Were not all ten cleansed? Where are the other nine? Was no-one found to return and give praise to God except this foreigner?'

Received with thanksgiving
For everything God created is good, and nothing is to be rejected if it is received with thanksgiving, because it is consecrated by the word of God and prayer.— Those who eat meat, eat to the Lord, for they give thanks to God.—The blessing of the LORD brings wealth, and he adds no trouble to it.

Praise the LORD, O my soul; all my inmost being, praise his holy name. Praise the LORD, O my soul, . . . who forgives all your sins . . . and crowns you with love and compassion.

Deuteronomy 8:11. Luke 17:15–18. 1 Timothy 4:4–5. Romans 14:6.
Proverbs 10:22. Psalm 103:1–4.

Evening

Jesus . . . had compassion on them.

Jesus Christ is the same yesterday and today and for ever. . . . For we do not have a high priest who is unable to sympathise with our weaknesses, but we have one who has been tempted in every way, just as we are—yet without sin . . . He is able to deal gently with those who are ignorant and are going astray.

He returned to his disciples and found them sleeping. 'Simon,' he said to Peter, 'are you asleep? Could you not keep watch for one hour? Watch and pray so that you will not fall into temptation. The spirit is willing, but the body is weak.'

The LORD has compassion
As parents have compassion on their children, so the LORD has compassion on those who fear him; for he knows how we are formed, he remembers that we are dust.

Matthew 14:14. Hebrews 13:8; 4:15; 5:2. Mark 14:37–38.
Psalms 103:13–14; 86:15.

Morning

'I no longer call you servants, because servants do not know their master's business. Instead, I have called you friends.'

God has revealed it to us by his Spirit. The Spirit searches all things, even the deep things of God. . . . We speak of God's secret wisdom, a wisdom that has been hidden and that God destined for our glory before time began.

Blessed are those you choose and bring near to live in your courts! We are filled with the good things of your house, of your holy temple.

'I gave them the words you gave me'
The LORD confides in those who fear him; he makes his covenant known to them.—'For I give them the words you gave me and they accepted them. They knew with certainty that I came from you, and they believed that you sent me.'
'You are my friends if you do what I command.'

> John 15:15. 1 Corinthians 2:10, 7. Psalms 65:4; 25:14. John 17:8; 15:14.

Evening

'But you will call your walls Salvation and your gates Praise.'

Fellow-citizens with God's people
You are no longer foreigners and aliens, but fellow-citizens with God's people and members of God's household, built on the foundation of the apostles and prophets, with Christ Jesus himself as the chief cornerstone. In him the whole building is joined together and rises to become a holy temple in the Lord. And in him you too are being built together to become a dwelling in which God lives by his Spirit.

Offering spiritual sacrifices
Now that you have tasted that the Lord is good. As you come to him, the living Stone—rejected by human beings but chosen by God and precious to him—you also, like living stones, are being built into a spiritual house to be a holy priesthood, offering spiritual sacrifices acceptable to God through Jesus Christ.

> Isaiah 60:18. Ephesians 2:19–22. 1 Peter 2:3–5.

February 9

Morning

He will swallow up death for ever. The Sovereign LORD will wipe away the tears from all faces; he will remove the disgrace of his people from all the earth.

'Your sun will never set again, and your moon will wane no more; the LORD will be your everlasting light, and your days of sorrow will end.'

'God will wipe away every tear'
'These are they who have come out of the great tribulation; they have washed their robes and made them white in the blood of the Lamb. Therefore, "they are before the throne of God and serve him day and night in his temple and he who sits on the throne will spread his tent over them. Never again will they hunger; never again will they thirst. The sun will not beat upon them, nor any scorching heat. For the Lamb at the centre of the throne will be their shepherd; he will lead them to springs of living water. And God will wipe away every tear from their eyes."'

Isaiah 25:8; 60:20. Revelation 7:14–17.

Evening

'Blessed are the dead who die in the Lord from now on.'

There the wicked will cease from turmoil, and there the weary are at rest.

    Whatever your hand finds to do, do it with all your might, for in the grave, where you are going, there is neither working nor planning nor knowledge nor wisdom.—It is not the dead who praise the LORD, those who go down to silence.

I have fought the good fight
For I am already being poured out like a drink offering, and the time has come for my departure. I have fought the good fight, I have finished the race, I have kept the faith. Now there is in store for me the crown of righteousness, which the Lord, the righteous Judge, will award to me on that day.

    There remains, then, a Sabbath-rest for the people of God; for those who enter God's rest also rest from their own work, just as God did from his.

Revelation 14:13. Job 3:17. Ecclesiastes 9:10. Psalm 115:17.
2 Timothy 4:6–8. Hebrews 4:9–10.

Morning

'When your eyes are good, your whole body also is full of light.'

The person without the Spirit does not accept the things that come from the Spirit of God but considers them foolishness, and cannot understand them because they are spiritually discerned.—Open my eyes that I may see wonderful things in your law.

Ever-increasing glory

'I am the light of the world. Whoever follows me will never walk in darkness, but will have the light of life.'—And we, who with unveiled faces all reflect the Lord's glory, are being transformed into his likeness with ever-increasing glory, which comes from the Lord, who is the Spirit. . . . For God, who said, 'Let light shine out of darkness,' make his light shine in our hearts to give us the light of the knowledge of the glory of God in the face of Christ.

God of our Lord Jesus Christ, the glorious Father, . . . give you the Spirit of wisdom and revelation, so that you may know him better.

Luke 11:34. 1 Corinthians 2:14. Psalm 119:18. John 8:12.
2 Corinthians 3:18; 4:6. Ephesians 1:17.

Evening

'You refuse to come to me to have life.'

Our ancestors were all under the cloud and . . . they all passed through the sea. They were all baptised into Moses in the cloud and in the sea. They all ate the same spiritual food and drank the same spiritual drink; for they drank from the spiritual rock that accompanied them, and that rock was Christ.—One of the soldiers pierced Jesus' side with a spear, bringing a sudden flow of blood and water.—But he was pierced for our transgressions, he was crushed for our iniquities; the punishment that brought us peace was upon him, and by his wounds we are healed.

Two sins

'My people have committed two sins: They have forsaken me, the spring of living water, and have dug their own cisterns, broken cisterns that cannot hold water.'—'Let anyone who is thirsty come to me and drink.'—Let all who wish take the free gift of the water of life.

John 5:40. 1 Corinthians 10:1–4. John 19:34. Isaiah 53:5. Jeremiah 2:13.
John 7:37. Revelation 22:17.

February 11

Morning

A scroll of remembrance was written in his presence concerning those who feared the LORD and honoured his name.

As they talked and discussed these things with each other, Jesus himself came up and walked along with them.—'For where two or three come together in my name, there am I with them.'—My co-workers, whose names are in the book of life.

Let the word of Christ dwell in you richly as you teach and admonish one another with all wisdom, and as you sing psalms, hymns and spiritual songs with gratitude in your hearts to God.—But encourage one another daily, as long as it is called Today, so that none of you may be hardened by sin's deceitfulness.

The day of judgment
'People will have to give account on the day of judgment for every careless word they have spoken. For by your words you will be acquitted, and by your words you will be condemned.'

Malachi 3:16. Luke 24:15. Matthew 18:20. Philippians 4:3.
Colossians 3:16. Hebrews 3:13. Matthew 12:36–37.

Evening

The trees of the LORD are well watered.

'I will be like the dew to Israel; he will blossom like a lily. Like a cedar of Lebanon he will send down his roots; his young shoots will grow. His splendour will be like an olive tree, his fragrance like a cedar of Lebanon.'

'I make the dry tree flourish'
'I the LORD bring down the tall tree and make the low tree grow tall. I dry up the green tree and make the dry tree flourish.'

They will still bear fruit in old age
The righteous will flourish like a palm tree, they will grow like a cedar of Lebanon; planted in the house of the LORD, they will flourish in the courts of our God. They will still bear fruit in old age, they will stay fresh and green.

Psalm 104:16. Hosea 14:5–6. Ezekiel 17:24. Psalm 92:12–14.

Morning

'They will be mine,' says the LORD Almighty, 'in the day when I make up my treasured possession.'

'I have revealed you to those whom you gave me out of the world. They were yours; you gave them to me and they have obeyed your word. . . . Father, I want those you have given me to be with me where I am, and to see my glory, the glory you have given me because you loved me before the creation of the world.'

A crown of splendour in the LORD's hand
'I will come back and take you to be with me.'—On the day he comes to be glorified in his holy people and to be marvelled at among all those who have believed.—We who are still alive and are left will be caught up together with them in the clouds to meet the Lord in the air. And so we will be with the Lord for ever.—You will be a crown of splendour in the LORD's hand, a royal diadem in the hand of your God.

> Malachi 3:17. John 17:6, 24; 14:3. 2 Thessalonians 1:10.
> 1 Thessalonians 4:17. Isaiah 62:3.

Evening

'Now show me your glory.'

For God, who said, 'Let light shine out of darkness,' made his light shine in our hearts to give us the light of the knowledge of the glory of God in the face of Christ.—The Word became flesh and made his dwelling among us. We have seen his glory, the glory of the One and Only, who came from the Father, full of grace and truth. . . . No-one has ever seen God, but God the One and Only, who is at the Father's side, has made him known.

Transformed into his likeness
And we, who with unveiled faces all reflect the Lord's glory, are being transformed into his likeness with ever-increasing glory, which comes from the Lord, who is the Spirit.—'Father, I want those you have given me to be with me where I am, and to see my glory, the glory you have given me because you loved me before the creation of the world.'

> Exodus 33:18. 2 Corinthians 4:6. John 1:14, 18. 2 Corinthians 3:18.
> John 17:24.

February 13

Morning

Above the expanse over their heads was what looked like a throne of sapphire, and high above on the throne was a figure like that of a man.

Christ Jesus, himself human.—Being made in human likeness. And being found in appearance as a human being.

'I am alive for ever and ever!'
'I am the Living One; I was dead, and behold I am alive for ever and ever!'—For we know that since Christ was raised from the dead, he cannot die again; death no longer has mastery over him. The death he died, he died to sin once for all; but the life he lives, he lives to God.—He raised him from the dead and seated him at his right hand in the heavenly realms.

He was crucified in weakness, yet he lives by God's power. Likewise, we are weak in him, yet by God's power we will live.

Ezekiel 1:26. 1 Timothy 2:5. Philippians 2:7–8. Revelation 1:18.
Romans 6:9–10. Ephesians 1:20. 2 Corinthians 13:4.

Evening

Your promise preserves my life.

'The first Adam became a living being'; the last Adam, a life-giving spirit.

'For as the Father has life in himself, so he has granted the Son to have life in himself.' . . . 'I am the resurrection and the life. Those who believe in me will live, even though they die; and whoever lives and believes in me will never die.'

Yet to all who received him, to those who believed in his name, he gave the right to become children of God—children born not of natural descent, nor of human decision or a husband's will, but born of God.

'The Spirit gives life'
'The Spirit gives life; the flesh counts for nothing. The words I have spoken to you are spirit and they are life.'—The word of God is living and active. Sharper than any double-edged sword, it penetrates even to dividing soul and spirit, joints and marrow; it judges the thoughts and attitudes of the heart.

Psalm 119:50. 1 Corinthians 15:45. John 5:26; 11:25–26; 1:12–13; 6:63.
Hebrews 4:12.

Morning

'I desire to do your will, O my God; your law is within my heart.'

'Do not think that I have come to abolish the Law or the Prophets; I have not come to abolish them but to fulfil them. I tell you the truth, until heaven and earth disappear, not the smallest letter, not the least stroke of a pen, will by any means disappear from the Law until everything is accomplished.' . . . 'Unless your righteousness surpasses that of the Pharisees and the teachers of the law, you will certainly not enter the kingdom of heaven.'

Christ is the end of the law

For what the law was powerless to do in that it was weakened by the sinful nature, God did by sending his own Son in the likeness of sinful humanity to be a sin offering. And so he condemned sin in our sinful nature, in order that the righteousness of the law might be fully met in us, who do not live according to the sinful nature but according to the Spirit . . . Christ is the end of the law so that there may be righteousness for everyone who believes.

Psalm 40:8. Matthew 5:17–18, 20. Romans 8:3–4; 10:4.

Evening

'I am your share and inheritance.'

Whom have I in heaven but you? And earth has nothing I desire besides you. My flesh and my heart may fail, but God is the strength of my heart and my portion for ever.

A delightful inheritance

LORD, you have assigned me my portion and my cup; you have made my lot secure. The boundary lines have fallen for me in pleasant places; surely I have a delightful inheritance.

I say to myself, 'The LORD is my portion; therefore I wait for him.'—Your statutes are my heritage for ever; they are the joy of my heart.

O God, you are my God, earnestly I seek you; my soul thirsts for you, my body longs for you, in a dry and weary land where there is no water . . . Because you are my help, I sing in the shadow of your wings.

Numbers 18:20. Psalms 73:25–26; 16:5–6. Lamentations 3:24.
Psalms 119:111; 63:1, 7.

February 15

Morning

Who can say, 'I have kept my heart pure'?

Those controlled by the sinful nature cannot please God. . . . I know that nothing good lives in me, that is, in my sinful nature. For I have the desire to do what is good, but I cannot carry it out. For what I do is not the good I want to do; no, the evil I do not want to do—this I keep on doing.—All of us have become like one who is unclean, and all our righteous acts are like filthy rags; we all shrivel up like a leaf, and like the wind our sins sweep us away.

A prisoner of sin
But the Scripture declares that the whole world is a prisoner of sin, so that what was promised, being given through faith in Jesus Christ, might be given to those who believe.—That God was reconciling the world to himself in Christ, not counting people's sins against them.

If we confess our sins
If we claim to be without sin, we deceive ourselves and the truth is not in us. If we confess our sins, he is faithful and just and will forgive our sins and purify us from all unrighteousness.

Proverbs 20:9. Romans 8:8; 7:18–19. Isaiah 64:6. Galatians 3:22.
2 Corinthians 5:19. 1 John 1:8–9.

Evening

Mightier than the thunder of the great waters, mightier than the breakers of the sea—the LORD on high is mighty.

O LORD God Almighty, who is like you? You are mighty, O LORD, and your faithfulness surrounds you. You rule over the surging sea; when its waves mount up, you still them.

'Should you not tremble in my presence?'
'Should you not fear me?' declares the LORD. 'Should you not tremble in my presence? I made the sand a boundary for the sea, an everlasting barrier it cannot cross.'—'When you pass through the waters, I will be with you; and when you pass through the rivers, they will not sweep over you.'

Peter got down out of the boat, walked on the water and came towards Jesus. But when he saw the wind, he was afraid and, beginning to sink, cried out, 'Lord, save me!' Immediately Jesus reached out his hand and caught him. 'You of little faith,' he said, 'why did you doubt?'

Psalms 93:4; 89:8–9. Jeremiah 5:22. Isaiah 43:2. Matthew 14:29–31.

Morning

Christ loved us and gave himself up for us as a fragrant offering and sacrifice to God.

Therefore God exalted him to the highest place and gave him the name that is above every name, that at the name of Jesus every knee should bow.

God has poured out his love
'If you love me, you will obey what I command.'—God has poured out his love into our hearts by the Holy Spirit, whom he has given us.
    And the house was filled with the fragrance of the perfume.—They took note that these men had been with Jesus.

'God with us'
O LORD, our Lord, how majestic is your name in all the earth! . . . 'Immanuel'—which means, 'God with us.'—And he will be called Wonderful Counsellor, Mighty God, Everlasting Father, Prince of Peace.

Ephesians 5:2. Philippians 2:9–10. John 14:15. Romans 5:5. John 12:3.
Acts 4:13. Psalm 8:1. Matthew 1:23. Isaiah 9:6.

Evening

All my longings lie open before you, O Lord: my sighing is not hidden from you.

My guilt has overwhelmed me like a burden too heavy to bear.—What a wretched man I am! Who will rescue me from this body of death?
    We know that the whole creation has been groaning as in the pains of childbirth right up to the present time. Not only so, but we ourselves, who have the firstfruits of the Spirit, groan inwardly as we wait eagerly for our adoption, the redemption of our bodies.—For a little while you may have had to suffer grief in all kinds of trials.

'Death has been swallowed up in victory'
For the perishable must clothe itself with the imperishable, and the mortal with immortality. When the perishable has been clothed with the imperishable, and the mortal with immortality, then the saying that is written will come true: 'Death has been swallowed up in victory.'

Psalm 38:9, 4. Romans 7:24; 8:22–23. 1 Peter 1:6.
1 Corinthians 15:53–54.

February 17

Morning

The fellowship in sharing in his sufferings.

So the soldiers took charge of Jesus. Carrying his own cross, he went out to the place of the Skull (which in Aramaic is called Golgotha). Here they crucified him.

Jesus also suffered outside the city gate
The high priest carries the blood of animals into the Most Holy Place as a sin offering, but the bodies are burned outside the camp. And so Jesus also suffered outside the city gate to make the people holy through his own blood. Let us, then, go to him outside the camp, bearing the disgrace he bore.

But rejoice that you participate in the sufferings of Christ, so that you may be overjoyed when his glory is revealed.—For our light and momentary troubles are achieving for us an eternal glory that far outweighs them all.

Philippians 3:10. John 19:16–18. Hebrews 13:11–13.
1 Peter 4:13. 2 Corinthians 4:17.

Evening

We know that when he appears, we shall be like him, for we shall see him as he is.

God, who is rich in mercy, made us alive with Christ even when we were dead in transgressions.

We are God's handiwork
For we are God's handiwork, created in Christ Jesus to do good works, which God prepared in advance for us to do.—For those God foreknew he also predestined to be conformed to the likeness of his Son, that he might be the firstborn among many brothers and sisters.

We are heirs
Those who overcome will inherit all this, and I will be their God and they will be my children.—Now if we are children, then we are heirs—heirs of God and co-heirs with Christ.

1 John 3:2. Ephesians 2:4–5, 10. Romans 8:29. Revelation 21:7.
Romans 8:17.

Morning

You are my refuge in the day of disaster.

Many are asking, 'Who can show us any good?' Let the light of your face shine upon us, O LORD. . . . But I will sing of your strength, in the morning I will sing of your love; for you are my fortress, my refuge in times of trouble.

'O LORD, be my help'
When I felt secure, I said, 'I shall never be shaken.' . . . To you, O LORD, I called; to the Lord I cried for mercy: 'What gain is there in my destruction, in my going down into the pit? Will the dust praise you? Will it proclaim your faithfulness? Hear, O LORD, and be merciful to me: O LORD, be my help.'

Rejoicing comes in the morning
'You will grieve, but your grief will turn to joy.'—Weeping may remain for a night, but rejoicing comes in the morning.

Jeremiah 17:17. Psalms 4:6; 59:16; 30:6, 8–10. John 16:20. Psalm 30:5.

Evening

As for you, you were dead in your transgressions and sins.

Like the rest, we were by nature objects of wrath.—I am unspiritual, sold as a slave to sin. I do not understand what to do. For what I want to do I do not do, but what I hate I do . . . I know that nothing good lives in me, that is, in my sinful nature.

God's grace
Sin entered the world through one man, . . . Through the disobedience of one man the many were made sinners, . . . For if many died by the trespass of the one man, how much more did God's grace and the gift that came by the grace of one man, Jesus Christ, overflow to the many!

The Spirit of life
The law of the Spirit of life set me free from the law of sin and death.—But thanks be to God! He gives us the victory through our Lord Jesus Christ.

Ephesians 2:1, 3. Romans 7:14–15, 18; 5:12, 19, 15; 8:2.
1 Corinthians 15:57.

February 19

Morning

For the LORD gives wisdom, and from his mouth come knowledge and understanding:

Trust in the LORD with all your heart and lean not on your own understanding.—If any of you lacks wisdom, you should ask God, who gives generously to all without finding fault, and it will be given to you.—For the foolishness of God is wiser than human wisdom, and the weakness of God is stronger than human strength.

The unfolding of your words gives light; it gives understanding to the simple. . . . I have hidden your word in my heart that I might not sin against you.

Wisdom from God
All spoke well of him and were amazed at the gracious words that came from his lips.—It is because of him that you are in Christ Jesus, who has become for us wisdom from God—that is, our righteousness, holiness and redemption.

> Proverbs 2:6; 3:5. James 1:5. 1 Corinthians 1:25. Psalm 119:130, 11.
> Luke 4:22. 1 Corinthians 1:30.

Evening

Yet their Redeemer is strong; the LORD Almighty is his name.

Your dead will live
But your dead will live; their bodies will rise. You who dwell in the dust, wake up and shout for joy. Your dew is like the dew of the morning; the earth will give birth to her dead.

For the Lord himself will come down from heaven, with a loud command, with the voice of the archangel and with the trumpet call of God, and the dead in Christ will rise first. After that, we who are still alive and are left will be caught up together with them in the clouds to meet the Lord in the air. And so we will be with the Lord for ever.

'I will redeem them from death'
'I will ransom them from the power of the grave; I will redeem them from death. Where, O death, are your plagues: Where, O grave, is your destruction?'

> Jeremiah 50:34. Isaiah 26:19. 1 Thessalonians 4:16–17. Hosea 13:14.

Morning

Jesus said, 'It is finished.' With that, he bowed his head and gave up his spirit.

God made him who had no sin to be sin for us, so that in him we might become the righteousness of God.

'The people I formed for myself that they may proclaim my praise.'—His intent was that now, through the church, the manifold wisdom of God should be made known to the rulers and authorities in the heavenly realms, according to his eternal purpose which he accomplished in Christ Jesus our Lord.

A people belonging to God
Having believed, you were marked in him with a seal, the promised Holy Spirit, who is a deposit guaranteeing our inheritance until the redemption of those who are God's possession—to the praise of his glory.—But you are a chosen people, a royal priesthood, a holy nation, a people belonging to God, that you may declare the praises of him who called you out of darkness into his wonderful light.

John 19:30. 2 Corinthians 5:21. Isaiah 43:21.
Ephesians 3:10–11; 1:13–14. 1 Peter 2:9.

Evening

The time of testing in the desert.

When tempted, no-one should say, 'God is tempting me.' For God cannot be tempted by evil, nor does he tempt anyone; but each of you is tempted when, by your own evil desire, you are dragged away and enticed. Then, after desire has conceived, it gives birth to sin.

In the desert
In the desert they gave way to their craving; in the wasteland they put God to the test.

Jesus, full of the Holy Spirit, returned from the Jordan and was led by the Spirit in the desert, where for forty days he was tempted by the devil. He ate nothing during those days, and at the end of them he was hungry. The devil said to him, 'If you are the Son of God, tell this stone to become bread.'

He himself suffered when he was tempted, he is able to help those who are being tempted.—'Simon, Simon, Satan has asked to sift you as wheat. But I have prayed for you, Simon, that your faith may not fail.'

Hebrews 3:8. James 1:13–15. Psalm 106:14. Luke 4:1–3. Hebrews 2:18.
Luke 22:31–32.

Morning

'I am the LORD, who makes you holy.'

'You are to be holy to me because I, the LORD, am holy, and I have set you apart from the nations to be my own.'

'Sanctify them by the truth; your word is truth.'—May God himself, the God of peace, sanctify you through and through. May your whole spirit, soul and body be kept blameless at the coming of our Lord Jesus Christ.

The sanctifying work of the Spirit
Jesus also suffered outside the city gate to make the people holy through his own blood.—Our great God and Saviour, Jesus Christ, who gave himself for us to redeem us from all wickedness and to purify for himself a people that are his very own, eager to do what is good.—'For I sanctify myself, that they too may be truly sanctified.'—Through the sanctifying work of the Spirit, for obedience to Jesus Christ and sprinkling by his blood.

Leviticus 20:8, 26. John 17:17. 1 Thessalonians 5:23. Hebrews 13:12.
Titus 2:13–14. John 17:19. 1 Peter 1:2.

Evening

Light is shed upon the righteous and joy on the upright in heart.

Those who sow in tears will reap with songs of joy. Those who go out weeping, carrying seed to sow, will return with songs of joy, carrying sheaves with them.

In this you greatly rejoice
Praise be to the God and Father of our Lord Jesus Christ! In his great mercy he has given us new birth into a living hope through the resurrection of Jesus Christ from the dead. . . . In this you greatly rejoice, though now for a little while you may have had to suffer grief in all kinds of trials. These have come so that your faith—of greater worth than gold, which perishes even though refined by fire—may be proved genuine and may result in praise, glory and honour when Jesus Christ is revealed.

Psalms 97:11; 126:5–6. 1 Peter 1:3, 6–7.

Morning

Who, then, are those who fear the LORD? He will instruct them in the way chosen for them.

'The eye is the lamp of the body. If your eyes are good, your whole body will be full of light.'

Whether you turn to the right or to the left, your ears will hear a voice behind you, saying, 'This is the way; walk in it.'

I will counsel you
I will instruct you and teach you in the way you should go; I will counsel you and watch over you. Do not be like the horse or the mule, which have no understanding but must be controlled by bit and bridle or they will not come to you. Many are the woes of the wicked, but the LORD's unfailing love surrounds those who trust in him. Rejoice in the LORD and be glad, you righteous; sing, all you who are upright in heart!

Psalm 25:12. Matthew 6:22. Isaiah 30:21. Psalm 32:8–11.

Evening

When you lie down, you will not be afraid; when you lie down, your sleep will be sweet.

Do not be anxious about anything, but in everything, by prayer and petition, with thanksgiving, present your requests to God. And the peace of God, which transcends all understanding, will guard your hearts and your minds in Christ Jesus.

I will lie down and sleep in peace, for you alone, O LORD, make me dwell in safety. . . . He grants sleep to those he loves.

Stephen prayed
While they were stoning him, Stephen prayed, 'Lord Jesus, receive my spirit.' Then he fell on his knees and cried out, 'Lord, do not hold this sin against them.' When he had said this, he fell asleep.—Away from the body and at home with the Lord.

Proverbs 3:24. Philippians 4:6–7. Psalms 4:8; 127:2. Acts 7:59–60.
2 Corinthians 5:8.

Morning

'Look, the Lamb of God, who takes away the sin of the world!'

The Lamb that was slain from the creation of the world.—It is impossible for the blood of bulls and goats to take away sins. Therefore, when Christ came into the world, he said: 'Sacrifice and offering you did not desire, but a body you prepared for me.'

Just as Christ loved us and gave himself up for us as a fragrant offering and sacrifice to God.

Hearts sprinkled
Let us draw near to God with a sincere heart in full assurance of faith, having our hearts sprinkled to cleanse us from a guilty conscience and having our bodies washed with pure water. . . . We have confidence to enter the Most Holy Place by the blood of Jesus.

> John 1:29. Revelation 13:8. Hebrews 10:4–5, 10. Ephesians 5:2. Hebrews 10:22, 19.

Evening

And the LORD has laid on him the iniquity of us all.

From the sixth hour until the ninth hour darkness came over all the land. About the ninth hour Jesus cried out in a loud voice, *'Eloi, eloi, lama sabachthani?'*—which means, 'My God, my God, why have you forsaken me?'

Therefore, there is now no condemnation for those who are in Christ Jesus . . . Since we have been justified through faith, we have peace with God through our Lord Jesus Christ.—Christ redeemed us from the curse of the law by becoming a curse for us.

An atoning sacrifice for our sins
This is how God showed his love among us: He sent his one and only Son into the world that we might live through him. This is love: not that we loved God, but that he loved us and sent his Son as an atoning sacrifice for our sins.

> Isaiah 53:6. Matthew 27:45–46. Romans 8:1; 5:1. Galatians 3:13. 1 John 4:9–10.

Morning

You do not have, because you do not ask God.

'Ask and it will be given to you; seek and you will find; knock and the door will be opened to you. For everyone who asks receives; everyone who seeks finds; and to everyone who knocks, the door will be opened.'—This is the confidence we have in approaching God: that if we ask anything according to his will, he hears us. And if we know that he hears us—whatever we ask—we know that we have what we asked of him.—Open wide your mouth and I will fill it.— They should always pray and not give up.

'Ask and you will receive'
The eyes of the LORD are on the righteous and his ears are attentive to their cry . . . The righteous cry out, and the LORD hears them; he delivers them from all their troubles. . . . 'You will ask in my name. I am not saying that I will ask the Father on your behalf. No, the Father himself loves you because you have loved me.' . . . 'Ask and you will receive, and your joy will be complete.'

James 4:2. Matthew 7:7–8. 1 John 5:14–15. Psalm 81:10. Luke 18:1.
Psalm 34:15, 17. John 16:26–27, 24.

Evening

I know, O LORD, that your laws are righteous, and in faithfulness you have afflicted me.

Yet, O LORD, you are our Father. We are the clay, you are the potter; we are all the work of your hand.

A refiner and purifier
He will sit as a refiner and purifier of silver.—'Because the Lord disciplines those he loves, and he punishes everyone he accepts as a child.' . . . Although he was a son, he learned obedience from what he suffered.

The great tribulation
But rejoice that you participate in the sufferings of Christ, so that you may be overjoyed when his glory is revealed.—'These are they who have come out of the great tribulation; they have washed their robes and made them white in the blood of the Lamb.'

Psalm 119:75. Isaiah 64:8. Malachi 3:3. Hebrews 12:6; 5:8. 1 Peter 4:13.
Revelation 7:14.

February 25

Morning

Resist the devil, and he will flee from you.

Jesus said to him, 'Away from me, Satan! For it is written: "Worship the Lord your God, and serve him only."' Then the devil left him, and angels came and attended him.

Be strong in the Lord
Finally, be strong in the Lord and in his mighty power. Put on the full armour of God so that you can take your stand against the devil's schemes. . . . Have nothing to do with the fruitless deeds of darkness, but rather expose them.—In order that Satan might not outwit us. For we are not unaware of his schemes.

Be alert
Be self-controlled and alert. Your enemy the devil prowls around like a roaring lion looking for someone to devour. Resist him, standing firm in the faith, because you know that your brothers and sisters throughout the world are undergoing the same kind of sufferings.

> James 4:7. Matthew 4:10–11. Ephesians 6:10–11; 5:11.
> 2 Corinthians 2:11. 1 Peter 5:8–9.

Evening

'You will seek me and find me when you seek me with all your heart.'

'Ask, seek, knock'
'Ask and it will be given to you; seek and you will find; knock and the door will be opened to you. For everyone who asks receives; everyone who seeks finds; and to everyone who knocks, the door will be opened.'

Access to the Father
And our fellowship is with the Father and with his Son, Jesus Christ.—But now in Christ Jesus you who once were far away have been brought near through the blood of Christ . . . For through him we both have access to the Father by one Spirit.

If we claim to have fellowship with him yet walk in the darkness, we lie and do not live by the truth.

'I am with you always.'—'Never will I leave you; never will I forsake you.'—'Counsellor . . . he lives with you and will be in you.'

> Jeremiah 29:13. Luke 11:9–10. 1 John 1:3. Ephesians 2:13, 18.
> 1 John 1:6. Matthew 28:20. Hebrews 13:5. John 14:16–17.

Morning

Let us examine our ways and test them, and let us return to the LORD.

Test me, O LORD, and try me, examine my heart and my mind.—We ought to examine ourselves before we eat of the bread and drink of the cup.

If we confess our sins, he is faithful and just and will forgive us our sins and purify us from all unrighteousness. . . . We have one who speaks to the Father in our defence.

A new and living way
Therefore, brothers and sisters, since we have confidence to enter the Most Holy Place by the blood of Jesus, by a new and living way opened for us through the curtain, that is, his body, and since we have a great priest over the house of God, let us draw near to God with a sincere heart in full assurance of faith, having our hearts sprinkled to cleanse us from a guilty conscience and having our bodies washed with pure water.

Lamentations 3:40. Psalm 26:2. 1 Corinthians 11:28. 1 John 1:9; 2:1.
Hebrews 10:19–22.

Evening

A rainbow, resembling an emerald, encircled the throne.

'The sign of the covenant'
'This is the sign of the covenant I am making between me and you and every living creature with you, a covenant for all generations to come: I have set my rainbow in the clouds, . . . I will see it and remember the everlasting covenant between God and all living creatures of every kind on the earth.'

'Has he not made with me an everlasting covenant, arranged and secured in every part?'

'We tell you the good news: What God promised our ancestors he has fulfilled for us, their children, by raising up Jesus.'

Jesus Christ is the same
Jesus Christ is the same yesterday and today and for ever.

Revelation 4:3. Genesis 9:12–13, 16. 2 Samuel 23:5. Acts 13:32–33.
Hebrews 13:8.

Morning

Count yourselves dead to sin but alive to God in Christ Jesus.

'Those who hear my word and believe him who sent me have eternal life and will not be condemned; they have crossed over from death to life.'—For through the law I died to the law so that I might live for God. I have been crucified with Christ and I no longer live, but Christ lives in me. The life I live in the body, I live by faith in the Son of God, who loved me and gave himself for me.

'Because I live, you also will live.' . . . 'I give them eternal life, and they shall never perish; no-one can snatch them out of my hand. My Father, who has given them to me, is greater than all; no-one can snatch them out of my Father's hand. I and the Father are one.'

Set your hearts on things above
Since, then, you have been raised with Christ, set your hearts on things above, where Christ is seated at the right hand of God. . . . For you died, and your life is now hidden with Christ in God.

Romans 6:11. John 5:24. Galatians 2:19–20. John 14:19; 10:28–30.
Colossians 3:1, 3.

Evening

God . . . gives generously . . . without finding fault.

God's grace and the gift that came by the grace of the one man, Jesus Christ, overflow to the many!

Expressed in his kindness to us
But because of his great love for us, God, who is rich in mercy, made us alive with Christ even when we were dead in transgressions—it is by grace you have been saved. And God raised us up with Christ and seated us with him in the heavenly realms in Christ Jesus, in order that in the coming ages he might show the incomparable riches of his grace, expressed in his kindness to us in Christ Jesus.

He who did not spare his own Son, but gave him up for us all—how will he not also, along with him, graciously give us all things?

James 1:5. Romans 5:15. Ephesians 2:4–7. Romans 8:32.

Morning

'For God so loved the world that he gave his one and only Son, that whoever believes in him shall not perish but have eternal life.'

All this is from God, who reconciled us to himself through Christ and gave us the ministry of reconciliation: that God was reconciling the world to himself in Christ, not counting people's sins against them. And he has committed to us the message of reconciliation. We are therefore Christ's ambassadors, as though God were making his appeal through us. We implore you on Christ's behalf: Be reconciled to God. God made him who had no sin to be sin for us, so that in him we might become the righteousness of God.

This is love
God is love. This is how God showed his love among us: He sent his one and only Son into the world that we might live through him. This is love: not that we loved God, but that he loved us and sent his Son as an atoning sacrifice for our sins. Dear friends, since God so loved us, we also ought to love one another.

John 3:16. 2 Corinthians 5:18–20. 1 John 4:8–11.

Evening

The lamp of the Lord searches the human spirit.

'Let anyone of you who is without sin be the first to throw a stone at her.' . . . Those who heard began to go away one at a time, the older ones first, until only Jesus was left, with the woman still standing there.

God is greater than our hearts
So, then, if you know the good you ought to do and don't do it, you sin.— Whenever our hearts condemn us. For God is greater than our hearts, and he knows everything. Dear friends, if our hearts do not condemn us, we have confidence before God.

All food is clean, but it is wrong for a person to eat anything that causes someone else to stumble. . . . Blessed are those who do not condemn themselves by what they approve.

Search me, O God, and know my heart; test me and know my anxious thoughts. See if there is any offensive way in me, and lead me in the way everlasting.

Proverbs 20:27. John 8:7, 9. James 4:17. 1 John 3:20–21. Romans 14:20, 22.
Psalm 139:23–24.

February 29

Morning

Do not boast about tomorrow, for you do not know what a day may bring forth.

I tell you, now is the time of God's favour, now is the day of salvation.—'Put your trust in the light while you have it, so that you may become children of light.'

Whatever your hand finds to do, do it with all your might, for in the grave, where you are going, there is neither working nor planning nor knowledge nor wisdom.

' "You have plenty of good things laid up for many years. Take life easy; eat, drink and be merry." . . . "You fool! This very night your life will be demanded from you. Then who will get what you have prepared for yourself?" This is how it will be with those who store up things for themselves but are not rich towards God.'

'Eat, drink and be merry'
What is your life? You are a mist that appears for a little while and then vanishes.—The world and its desires pass away, but whoever does the will of God lives for ever.

Proverbs 27:1. 2 Corinthians 6:2. John 12:36. Ecclesiastes 9:10.
Luke 12:19–21. James 4:14. 1 John 2:17.

Evening

But you remain the same, and your years will never end.

Before the mountains were born or you brought forth the earth and the world, from everlasting to everlasting you are God.

'I the LORD do not change. So you, O descendants of Jacob, are not destroyed.'

Every good and perfect gift is from above, coming down from the Father of the heavenly lights, who does not change like shifting shadows.—For God's gifts and his call are irrevocable.

Jesus lives for ever
But because Jesus lives for ever, he has a permanent priesthood. Therefore he is able to save completely those who come to God through him, because he always lives to intercede for them.—'Do not be afraid. I am the First and the Last.'

Psalms 102:27; 90:2; Malachi 3:6. James 1:17. Romans 11:29.
Hebrews 7:24–25. Revelation 1:17.

Morning

The fruit of the Spirit is love.

We love because he first loved us
God is love. Those who live in love live in God, and God in them.—God has poured out his love into our hearts by the Holy Spirit, whom he has given us.—We love because he first loved us. —For Christ's love compels us, because we are convinced that one died for all, and therefore all died. And he died for all, that those who live should no longer live for themselves but for him who died for them and was raised again.

Taught by God to love
You yourselves have been taught by God to love each other.—'My command is this: Love each other as I have loved you.'—Above all, love each other deeply, because love covers over a multitude of sins.

Galatians 5:22. 1 John 4:16. Romans 5:5. 1 John 4:19.
2 Corinthians 5:14–15. 1 Thessalonians 4:9. John 15:12. 1 Peter 4:8.

Evening

If God is for us, who can be against us?

The LORD is my Banner.—The LORD is with me; I will not be afraid. What can human beings do to me?—But for those who fear you, you have raised a banner.

My heart will not fear
The LORD is my light and my salvation—whom shall I fear? . . . Though an army besiege me, my heart will not fear; though war break out against me, even then will I be confident.

'God is with us'
'God is with us; he is our leader.'—The LORD Almighty is with us; the God of Jacob is our fortress.
 Propose your plan, but it will not stand, for God is with us.

Romans 8:31. Exodus 17:15. Psalms 118:6; 60:4; 27:1, 3.
2 Chronicles 13:12. Psalm 46:7. Isaiah 8:10.

March 2

Morning

'God has made me fruitful in the land of my suffering.'

The God of all comfort
Praise be to the God and Father of our Lord Jesus Christ, the Father of compassion and the God of all comfort, who comforts us in all our troubles, so that we can comfort those in any trouble with the comfort we ourselves have received from God. For just as the sufferings of Christ flow over into our lives, so also through Christ our comfort overflows.

In this you greatly rejoice, though now for a little while you may have had to suffer grief in all kinds of trials. These have come so that your faith—of greater worth than gold, which perishes even though refined by fire—may be proved genuine and may result in praise, glory and honour when Jesus Christ is revealed.

So then, those who suffer according to God's will should commit themselves to their faithful Creator and continue to do good.

Genesis 41:52. 2 Corinthians 1:3–5. 1 Peter 1:6–7; 4:19.

Evening

'Blessed are the dead who die in the Lord from now on.' . . . 'They will rest from their labour, for their deeds will follow them.'

'Our friend Lazarus has fallen asleep;' . . . Jesus had been speaking of his death, but his disciples thought he meant natural sleep.

We groan inwardly as we wait
For while we are in this tent, we groan and are burdened.—We ourselves, who have the first-fruits of the Spirit, groan inwardly as we wait eagerly for our adoption, the redemption of our bodies. For in this hope we are saved. But hope that is seen is no hope at all. Who hopes for what one already has? But if we hope for what we do not yet have, we wait for it patiently.

Revelation 14:13. John 11:11, 13:2. 2 Corinthians 5:4. Romans 8:23–25.

Morning

Trust in him at all times, O people; pour out your hearts to him, for God is our refuge.

Trust in the LORD with all your heart and lean not on your own understanding; in all your ways acknowledge him, and he will make your paths straight.

Do not be like the mule
I will instruct you and teach you in the way you should go; I will counsel you and watch over you. Do not be like the horse or the mule, which have no understanding but must be controlled by bit and bridle or they will not come to you. Many are the woes of the wicked, but the LORD's unfailing love surrounds those who trust in him.—Whether you turn to the right or to the left, your ears will hear a voice behind you, saying, 'This is the way; walk in it.'
    'My presence will go with you, and I will give you rest.'

Psalm 62:8. Proverbs 3:5–6. Psalm 32:8–10. Isaiah 30:21. Exodus 33:14.

Evening

The prize for which God has called me heavenwards in Christ Jesus.

'You will have treasure in heaven. Then come, follow me.' 'I am your shield, your very great reward.'
    And they will reign for ever and ever.

A crown that will last for ever
You will receive a crown of glory that will never fade away.—The crown of life.—The crown of righteousness.—A crown that will last for ever.
    'Father, I want those you have given me to be with me where I am, and to see my glory you have given me.'—And so we will be with the Lord for ever.
    I consider that our present sufferings are not worth comparing with the glory that will be revealed to us.

Philippians 3:14. Matthew 19:21. Genesis 15:1. Revelation 22:5.
1 Peter 5:4. James 1:12. 2 Timothy 4:8. 1 Corinthians 9:25. John 17:24.
1 Thessalonians 4:17. Romans 8:18.

March 4

Morning

Set your minds on things above, not on earthly things.

'Do not love the world or anything in the world. If you love the world, the love of the Father is not in you.'

'Treasures in heaven'
'Do not store up for yourselves treasures on earth, where moth and rust destroy, and where thieves break in and steal. But store up for yourselves treasures in heaven, where moth and rust do not destroy, and where thieves do not break in and steal. For where your treasure is, there your heart will be also.'

We live by faith, not by sight. . . . Therefore we do not lose heart. Though outwardly we are wasting away, yet inwardly we are being renewed day by day. For our light and momentary troubles are achieving for us an eternal glory that far outweighs them all. So we fix our eyes not on what is seen, but on what is unseen. For what is seen is temporary, but what is unseen is eternal.

Colossians 3:2. 1 John 2:15. Matthew 6:19–21. 2 Corinthians 5:7; 4:16–18.

Evening

These things happened to them as examples and were written down as warnings for us, on whom the fulfilment of the ages has come.

In all this Job did not sin in what he said. 'He is the LORD; let him do what is good in his eyes.'

Cast your cares on the LORD and he will sustain you; he will never let the righteous fall.—Surely he took up our infirmities and carried our sorrows.

Take my yoke upon you
'Come to me, all you who are weary and burdened, and I will give you rest. Take my yoke upon you and learn from me, for I am gentle and humble in heart, and you will find rest for your souls. For my yoke is easy and my burden is light.'

1 Corinthians 10:11. Job 2:10. 1 Samuel 3:18. Psalm 55:22. Isaiah 53:4.
Matthew 11:28–30.

March 5

Morning

'I am troubled; O Lord, come to my aid!'

Hear my cry, O God; listen to my prayer. From the ends of the earth I call to you. I call as my heart grows faint; lead me to the rock that is higher than I. For you have been my refuge, a strong tower against the foe. I long to dwell in your tent for ever and take refuge in the shelter of your wings.

A refuge for the needy
You have been a refuge for the poor, a refuge for the needy in their distress, a shelter from the storm.

Follow in his steps
Christ suffered for you, leaving you an example, that you should follow in his steps. 'He committed no sin, and no deceit was found in his mouth.' When they hurled their insults at him, he did not retaliate; when he suffered, he made no threats. Instead, he entrusted himself to him who judges justly.

Isaiah 38:14. Psalm 61:1–4. Isaiah 25:4. 1 Peter 2:21–23.

Evening

Fight the good fight of faith.

But we were harassed at every turn—conflicts on the outside, fears within.— 'Don't be afraid, . . . Those who are with us are more than those who are with them.'—Be strong in the Lord and in his mighty power.

'You come against me with sword and spear and javelin, but I come against you in the name of the LORD Almighty, the God of the armies of Israel, whom you have defied.'—'It is God who arms me with strength . . . He trains my hands for battle; my arms can bend a bow of bronze.'—Our competence comes from God.

Weakness was turned to strength
I do not have time to tell about . . . [those] who through faith conquered kingdoms, . . . whose weakness was turned to strength; and who became powerful in battle and routed foreign armies.

1 Timothy 6:12. 2 Corinthians 7:5. 2 Kings 6:16. Ephesians 6:10.
1 Samuel 17:45. 2 Samuel 22:33, 35. 2 Corinthians 3:5.
Hebrews 11:32–34.

March 6

Morning

He . . . protects the way of his faithful ones.

Like an eagle
The LORD your God . . . went ahead of you on your journey, in fire by night and in a cloud by day, . . . Like an eagle that stirs up its nest and hovers over its young, that spreads its wings to catch them and carries them on its pinions. The LORD alone led him.—The LORD makes firm the steps of those who delight in him; though they stumble, they will not fall, for the LORD upholds them with his hand.

And we know that in all things God works for the good of those who love him, who have been called according to his purpose.—'With us is the LORD our God to help us and to fight our battles.'

'The LORD your God is with you, he is mighty to save. He will take great delight in you, he will quiet you with his love, he will rejoice over you with singing.'

Proverbs 2:8. Deuteronomy 1:32–33; 32:11–12. Psalm 37:23–24.
Romans 8:28. 2 Chronicles 32:8. Zephaniah 3:17.

Evening

For the transgression of my people he was stricken.

He was pierced for our transgressions, he was crushed for our iniquities; the punishment that brought us peace was upon him . . . and the LORD has laid on him the iniquity of us all. . . . Yet it was the LORD's will to crush him and cause him to suffer.

The righteous for the unrighteous
Jesus our Lord . . . was delivered over to death for our sins, and was raised to life for our justification.—For Christ died for sins once for all, the righteous for the unrighteous, to bring you to God. . . . He himself bore our sins in his body on the tree, so that we might die to sins and live for righteousness; by his wounds you have been healed.

God made him who had no sin to be sin for us, so that in him we might become the righteousness of God.—Christ redeemed us from the curse of the law by becoming a curse for us.

Isaiah 53:8, 5–6, 10. Romans 4:24–25. 1 Peter 3:18; 2:24.
2 Corinthians 5:21. Galatians 3:13.

Morning

For your Maker is your husband—the LORD Almighty is his name.

No longer will they call you Deserted, or name your land Desolate. But you will be called Hephzibah, and your land Beulah; for the LORD will take great delight in you, . . . As a bridegroom rejoices over his bride, so will your God rejoice over you.

To comfort all who mourn
He has sent me to bind up the broken-hearted, to proclaim freedom for the captives and release from darkness for the prisoners, to proclaim the year of the LORD's favour and the day of vengeance of our God, to comfort all who mourn, and provide for those who grieve in Zion—to bestow on them a crown of beauty instead of ashes, the oil of gladness instead of mourning, and a garment of praise instead of a spirit of despair.

A robe of righteousness
I delight greatly in the LORD; my soul rejoices in my God. For he has clothed me with garments of salvation and arrayed me in a robe of righteousness, as a bridegroom adorns his head like a priest, and as a bride adorns herself with her jewels.

'I will betroth you to me for ever; I will betroth you in righteousness and justice, in love and compassion.'—Who shall separate us from the love of Christ?

Isaiah 54:5; 62:4–5; 61:1–3, 10. Hosea 2:19. Romans 8:35.

Evening

My times are in your hands.

'All the holy ones are in your hand.'—Then the word of the LORD came to Elijah: 'Leave here, turn eastward and hide in the Kerith Ravine, east of the Jordan. You will drink from the brook, and I have ordered the ravens to feed you there.' . . . Then the word of the LORD came to him [Elijah]: 'Go at once to Zarephath of Sidon and stay there. I have commanded a widow in that place to supply you with food.'

'Do not worry'
'Therefore I tell you, do not worry about your life, what you will eat or drink; or about your body, what you will wear. . . . Your heavenly Father knows that you need them.'

Trust in the LORD with all your heart and lean not on your own understanding; in all your ways acknowledge him, and he will make your paths straight.—Cast all your anxiety on him because he cares for you.

Psalm 31:15. Deuteronomy 33:3. 1 Kings 17:2–4, 8–9.
Matthew 6:25, 32. Proverbs 3:5–6. 1 Peter 5:7.

March 8

Morning

You have put all my sins behind your back.

Who is a God like you, who pardons sin and forgives the transgression of the remnant of his inheritance? You do not stay angry for ever but delight to show mercy. You will again have compassion on us; you will tread our sins underfoot and hurl all our iniquities into the depths of the sea.

'I will forgive'
'For I will forgive their wickedness and will remember their sins no more.'

Sins are covered
Blessed are those whose transgressions are forgiven, whose sins are covered. Blessed are those whose sin the LORD does not count against them and in whose spirit is no deceit.—The blood of Jesus, his Son, purifies us from all sin.

Isaiah 38:17. Micah 7:18–19. Jeremiah 31:34. Psalm 32:1–2. 1 John 1:7.

Evening

I know whom I have believed, and am convinced that he is able.

Able to do immeasurably more than all we ask or imagine.—Able to make all grace abound to you, so that in all things at all times, having all that you need, you will abound in every good work.—Able to help those who are being tempted.

Able to keep you from falling
Able to save completely those who come to God through him, because he always lives to intercede for them.—Able to keep you from falling and to present you before his glorious presence without fault and with great joy.—Able to guard what I have entrusted to him for that day.

Who, by the power that enables him to bring everything under his control, will transform our lowly bodies so that they will be like his glorious body.

2 Timothy 1:12. Ephesians 3:20. 2 Corinthians 9:8. Hebrews 2:18; 7:25.
Jude 24. 2 Timothy 1:12. Philippians 3:21.

Morning

God, who richly provides us with everything for our enjoyment.

Be careful that you do not forget the LORD your God, failing to observe his commands, his laws and his decrees that I am giving you this day. Otherwise, when you eat and are satisfied, when you build fine houses and settle down, . . . then your heart will become proud and you will forget the LORD your God . . . But remember the LORD your God, for it is he who gives you the ability to produce wealth.

Unless the LORD builds the house
Unless the LORD builds the house, its builders labour in vain. Unless the LORD watches over the city, the guards stand watch in vain. In vain you rise early and stay up late, toiling for food to eat—for he grants sleep to those he loves.

1 Timothy 6:17. Deuteronomy 8:11–12, 14, 18. Psalm 127:1–2.

Evening

They sang a new song.

By a new and living way opened for us through the curtain, that is, his body.

Renewal by the Holy Spirit
He saved us, not because of his mercy. He saved us through the washing of rebirth and renewal by the Holy Spirit, whom he poured out on us generously through Jesus Christ our Saviour.—For it is by grace that you have been saved, through faith—and this not from yourselves, it is the gift of God—not by works, so that no-one can boast.

Not to us, O LORD, not to us but to your name be the glory.

Priests to serve
To him who loves us and has freed us from our sins by his blood, and has made us to be a kingdom and priests to serve his God and Father—to him be glory and power for ever and ever! Amen.

Revelation 14:3. Hebrews 10:20. Titus 3:5–6. Ephesians 2:8–9.
Psalm 115:1. Revelation 1:5–6.

March 10

Morning

'The Lord will provide.'

'God himself will provide the lamb for the burnt offering, my son.'

Surely the arm of the Lord is not too short to save, nor his ear too dull to hear.

Blessed are those whose help is the God of Jacob, whose hope is in the Lord their God.

God will meet all your needs
My God will meet all your needs according to his glorious riches in Christ Jesus.—'Never will I leave you; never will I forsake you.' So we say with confidence, 'The Lord is my helper; I will not be afraid.'

The Lord is my strength and my shield; my heart trusts in him, and I am helped. My heart leaps for joy and I will give thanks to him in song.

Genesis 22:14, 8. Isaiah 59:1. Psalm 146:5. Philippians 4:19.
Hebrews 13:5–6. Psalm 28:7.

Evening

'For where two or three come together in my name, there am I with them.'

'Those who love me will obey my teaching. My Father will love them, and we will come to them and make our home with them.'

'If you obey my commands, you will remain in my love, just as I have obeyed my Father's commands and remain in his love.'

The fruit of the Spirit
The fruit of the Spirit is love, joy, peace, patience, kindness, goodness, faithfulness, gentleness and self-control.

'Bear much fruit'
'This is to my Father's glory, that you bear much fruit, showing yourselves to be my disciples.' . . . 'Every branch that does bear fruit he prunes so that it will be even more fruitful.'—Filled with the fruit of righteousness that comes through Jesus Christ—to the glory and praise of God.

Matthew 18:20. John 14:23; 15:10. Galatians 5:22–23. John 15:8, 2.
Philippians 1:11.

Morning

'The LORD bless you and keep you.'

The blessing of the LORD brings wealth, and he adds no trouble to it.—For surely, O LORD, you bless the righteous; you surround them with your favour as with a shield.

The LORD watches over you
He will not let your foot slip—he who watches over you will not slumber; indeed, he who watches over Israel will neither slumber nor sleep. The LORD watches over you—the LORD is your shade at your right hand . . . The LORD will keep you from all harm—he will watch over your life; the LORD will watch over your coming and going both now and for evermore.

The Lord will rescue me from every evil attack and will bring me safely to his heavenly kingdom. To him be glory for ever and ever. Amen.

Numbers 6:24. Proverbs 10:22. Psalms 5:12; 121:3–5, 7–8.
2 Timothy 4:18.

Evening

Jesus wept.

A man of sorrows, and familiar with suffering.—For we do not have a high priest who is unable to sympathise with our weaknesses. . . . In bringing many sons and daughters to glory, it was fitting that God, for whom and through whom everything exists, should make the author of their salvation perfect through suffering.

'Mocking and spitting'
Although he was a son, he learned obedience from what he suffered.—'I have not been rebellious; I have not drawn back. I offered my back to those who beat me, my cheeks to those who pulled out my beard; I did not hide my face from mocking and spitting.'

'See how he loved him!'—For this reason he had to be made like his brothers and sisters in every way, in order that he might become a merciful and faithful high priest in service to God, and that he might make atonement for the sins of the people.

John 11:35. Isaiah 53:3. Hebrews 4:15; 2:10; 5:8. Isaiah 50:5–6.
John 11:36. Hebrews 2:17.

March 12

Morning

'The LORD make his face shine upon you and be gracious to you; the LORD turn his face towards you and give you peace.'

No-one has ever seen God, but God the One and Only, who is at the Father's side, has made him known.—The Son is the radiance of God's glory and the exact representation of his being.—The god of this age had blinded the minds of unbelievers, so that they cannot see the light of the gospel of the glory of Christ, who is the image of God.

Unfailing love
Let your face shine on your servant; save me in your unfailing love. Let me not be put to shame, O LORD, for I have cried out to you . . . Blessed are those who have learned to acclaim you, who walk in the light of your presence, O LORD.

The LORD gives strength to his people; the LORD blesses his people with peace.—'Take courage! It is I. Don't be afraid.'

Numbers 6:25–26. John 1:18. Hebrews 1:3. 2 Corinthians 4:4.
Psalms 31:16–17; 89:15; 29:11. Matthew 14:17.

Evening

Do what pleases him.

Without faith it is impossible to please God.—Those controlled by the sinful nature cannot please God.—For the LORD takes delight in his people.

The unfading beauty of a gentle and quiet spirit, . . . which is of great worth in God's sight.

'Those who sacrifice thank-offerings honour me, and they prepare the way so that I may show them the salvation of God.' . . . I will praise God's name in song and glorify him with thanksgiving. This will please the LORD more than an ox, more than a bull with its horn and hoofs.

Offer your bodies as living sacrifices
Therefore, I urge you, brothers and sisters, in view of God's mercy, to offer your bodies as living sacrifices, holy and pleasing to God—this is your spiritual act of worship.

1 John 3:22. Hebrews 11:6. Romans 8:8. Psalm 149:4.
1 Peter 3:4. Psalms 50:23; 69:30–31. Romans 12:1.

Morning

For there is one God and one mediator between God and human beings, Christ Jesus, himself human.

He himself is our peace
We have one who speaks to the Father in our defence—Jesus Christ, the Righteous One.—But now in Christ Jesus you who once were far away have been brought near through the blood of Christ. For he himself is our peace.

The mediator of a new covenant
He entered the Most Holy Place once for all by his own blood, having obtained eternal redemption. . . . For this reason Christ is the mediator of a new covenant, that those who are called may receive the promised eternal inheritance . . . Therefore he is able to save completely those who came to God through him, because he always lives to intercede for them.

1 Timothy 2:5. 1 John 2:1. Ephesians 2:13–14. Hebrews 9:12, 15; 7:25.

Evening

You will keep in perfect peace him whose mind is steadfast, because he trusts in you. Trust in the LORD for ever, for the LORD, the LORD, is the Rock eternal.

Cast your cares on the LORD and he will sustain you . . . For he has not despised or disdained the suffering of the afflicted one; he has not hidden his face from him but has listened to his cry for help.—Is any one of you in trouble? You should pray.

'Look at the birds of the air'
'Do not let your hearts be troubled and do not be afraid.'—'Therefore I tell you, do not worry about your life, what you will eat or drink; or about your body, what you will wear. Is not life more important than food, and the body more important than clothes? Look at the birds of the air; they do not sow or reap or store away in barns, and yet your heavenly Father feeds them. Are you not much more valuable than they?'

Isaiah 26:3–4. Psalms 55:22; 22:24. James 5:13. John 14:27.
Matthew 6:25–26.

March 14

Morning

In every way they will make the teaching about God our Saviour attractive.

Conduct yourselves in a manner worthy of the gospel of Christ.—Avoid every kind of evil.—If you are insulted because of the name of Christ, you are blessed . . . If you suffer, it should not be as a murderer or thief or any other kind of criminal, or even as a meddler.—You may become blameless and pure, children of God without fault in a crooked and depraved generation, in which you shine like stars in the universe.

'Let your light shine'
'Let your light shine before others, that they may see your good deeds and praise your Father in heaven.'
   Finally, brothers and sisters, whatever is true, whatever is noble, whatever is right, whatever is pure, whatever is lovely, whatever is admirable—if anything is excellent or praiseworthy—think about such things.

Titus 2:10. Philippians 1:27. 1 Thessalonians 5:22. 1 Peter 4:14–15.
Philippians 2:15. Matthew 5:16. Philippians 4:8.

Evening

'The words I have spoken to you are spirit and they are life.'

He chose to give us birth through the word of truth.—The letter kills, but the Spirit gives life.
   Christ loved the church and gave himself up for her to make her holy, cleansing her by the washing with water through the word, and to present her to himself as a radiant church, without stain or wrinkle or any other blemish.

Your precepts have renewed my life
How can the young keep their way pure? By living according to your word . . . Your promise preserves my life. . . . I have hidden your word in my heart that I might not sin against you. . . . I will never forget your precepts, for by them you have preserved my life. . . . How sweet are your words to my taste, sweeter than honey to my mouth! I gain understanding from your precepts; therefore I hate every wrong path.

John 6:63. James 1:18. 2 Corinthians 3:6. Ephesians 5:25–27.
Psalm 119:9, 50, 11, 93, 103–104.

Morning

Perfect through suffering.

'My soul is overwhelmed with sorrow to the point of death. Stay here and keep watch with me.' Going a little farther, he fell with his face to the ground and prayed, 'My Father, if it is possible, may this cup be taken from me. Yet not as I will, but as you will.'—And being in anguish, he prayed more earnestly, and his sweat was like drops of blood falling to the ground.

I was overcome
The cords of death entangled me, the anguish of the grave came upon me; I was overcome by trouble and sorrow.

Scorn has broken my heart
Scorn has broken my heart and left me helpless; I looked for sympathy, but there was none, for comforters, but I found none.

> Hebrews 2:10. Matthew 26:38–39. Luke 22:44. Psalms 116:3; 69:20.

Evening

The LORD made the heavens and the earth, the sea, and all that is in them.

The heavens declare the glory of God; the skies proclaim the work of his hands . . . By the word of the LORD were the heavens made, their starry host by the breath of his mouth. . . . For he spoke, and it came to be; he commanded, and it stood firm.

Surely the nations are like a drop in a bucket; they are regarded as dust on the scales; he weighs the islands as though they were fine dust.

By faith we understand that the universe was formed at God's command, so that what is seen was not made out of what was visible.

When I consider your heavens
When I consider your heavens, the work of your fingers, the moon and the stars, which you have set in place, what are mere mortals that you are mindful of them, human beings that you care for them?

> Exodus 20:11. Psalms 19:1; 33:6, 9. Isaiah 40:15. Hebrews 11:3.
> Psalm 8:3–4.

March 16

Morning

What is your life? You are a mist that appears for a little while and then vanishes.

'Like boats of papyrus'
'My days are swifter than a runner; they fly away without a glimpse of joy. They skim past like boats of papyrus, like eagles swooping down on their prey.'—You sweep people away in the sleep of death; they are like the new grass of the morning—though in the morning it springs up new, by evening it is dry and withered.

They will all wear out like a garment
The world and its desires pass away, but whoever does the will of God lives for ever.—'They will perish, but you remain; they will all wear out like a garment. Like clothing you will change them and they will be discarded. But you remain the same, and your years will never end.'—Jesus Christ is the same yesterday and today and for ever.

> James 4:14. Job 9:25–26. Psalm 90:5–6. 1 John 2:17. Psalm 102:26–27.
> Hebrews 13:8.

Evening

I will sing with my spirit, but I will also sing with my mind.

Be filled with the Spirit. Speak to one another with psalms, hymns and spiritual songs. Sing and make music in your heart to the Lord.—Let the word of Christ dwell in you richly as you teach and admonish one another with all wisdom, and as you sing psalms, hymns and spiritual songs with gratitude in your hearts to God.

My mouth will speak in praise to the LORD. Let every creature praise his holy name for ever and ever.

Make music to our God
Praise the LORD. How good it is to sing praises to our God, how pleasant and fitting to praise him! . . . Sing to the LORD with thanksgiving; make music to our God on the harp.

> 1 Corinthians 14:15. Ephesians 5:18–19. Colossians 3:16.
> Psalms 145:21; 147:1, 7.

Morning

He himself bore our sins in his body on the tree, so that we might die to sins.

For you know that it was not with perishable things such as silver or gold that you were redeemed from the empty way of life handed down to you from your ancestors, but with the precious blood of Christ, a lamb without blemish or defect.

He has freely given us in the One he loves.—Therefore, I urge you, brothers and sisters, in view of God's mercy, to offer your bodies as living sacrifices, holy and pleasing to God—this is your spiritual act of worship.

Without fault and with great joy
To him who is able to keep you from falling and to present you before his glorious presence without fault and with great joy—to the only God our Saviour be glory, majesty, power and authority, through Jesus Christ our Lord, before all ages, now and for evermore! Amen.

1 Peter 2:24; 1:18–19. Ephesians 1:6. Romans 12:1. Jude 24–25.

Evening

One who has been tempted in every way, just as we are—yet was without sin.

When the woman saw that the fruit of the tree was good for food and pleasing to the eye, and also desirable for gaining wisdom, she took some and ate it. She also gave some to her husband, who was with her, and he ate it.

'Away from me, Satan!'
The devil . . . showed him [Jesus] all the kingdoms of the world and their splendour. 'All this I will give you,' he said, 'if you will bow down and worship me.' Jesus said to him, 'Away from me, Satan!'

He is able to help
Because he himself suffered when he was tempted, he is able to help those who are being tempted.

Blessed are those who persevere under trial.

Hebrews 4:15. Genesis 3:6. Matthew 4:8–10. Hebrews 2:18. James 1:12.

March 18

Morning

My eyes grew weak as I looked to the heavens.

My heart is in anguish within me; the terrors of death assail me. Fear and trembling have beset me; horror has overwhelmed me. I said, 'Oh, that I had the wings of a dove! I would fly away and be at rest—I would flee far away and stay in the desert.'

You need to persevere.

They were looking intently up into the sky as he was going, when suddenly two men dressed in white stood beside them. 'You Galileans,' they said, 'why do you stand here looking into the sky? This same Jesus, who has been taken from you into the heaven, will come back in the same way you have seen him go into heaven.'

Our citizenship is in heaven

But our citizenship is in heaven. And we eagerly await a Saviour from there, the Lord Jesus Christ.—While we wait for the blessed hope—the glorious appearing of our great God and Saviour, Jesus Christ.

Isaiah 38:14. Psalm 55:4–7. Hebrews 10:36. Acts 1:10–11.
Philippians 3:20. Titus 2:13.

Evening

His name will be on their foreheads.

'I am the good shepherd; I know my sheep.'—God's solid foundation stands firm sealed with this inscription: 'The Lord knows those who are his,' and, 'Everyone who confesses the name of the Lord must turn away from wickedness.'

You were marked in him with a seal

The LORD is good, a refuge in times of trouble. He cares for those who trust in him.—Having believed, you were marked in him with a seal, the promised Holy Spirit, who is a deposit guaranteeing our inheritance.

'I will write on them the name of my God and the name of the city of my God, the new Jerusalem, which is coming down out of heaven from my God; and I will also write on them my new name.'—'This is the name by which it will be called: The LORD Our Righteousness.'

Revelation 22:4. John 10:14. 2 Timothy 2:19. Nahum 1:7.
Ephesians 1:13–14. Revelation 3:12. Jeremiah 33:16.

Morning

'When God raised up his servant, he sent him first to you to bless you by turning each of you from your wicked ways.'

Praise be to the God and Father of our Lord Jesus Christ! In his great mercy he has given us new birth into a living hope through the resurrection of Jesus Christ from the dead.—Saved through his life!

Be holy in all you do
Our great God and Saviour, Jesus Christ, who gave himself for us to redeem us from all wickedness and to purify for himself a people that are his very own, eager to do what is good.—But just as he who called you is holy, so be holy in all you do; for it is written: 'Be holy, because I am holy.'

The God and Father of our Lord Jesus Christ, who has blessed us in the heavenly realms with every spiritual blessing in Christ.

He who did not spare his own Son, but gave him up for us all—how will he not also, along with him, graciously give us all things?

> Acte 3:26. 1 Peter 1:3. Romans 5:10. Titus 2:13–14. 1 Peter 1:15–16.
> Ephesians 1:3. Romans 8:32.

Evening

Strengthen me according to your word.

Remember your word to your servant, for you have given me hope. 'I am troubled; O Lord, come to my aid!'

'Every promise has been fulfilled'
'Heaven and earth will pass away, but my words will never pass away.'—'You know with all your heart and soul that not one of all the good promises the LORD your God gave you has failed. Every promise has been fulfilled; not one has failed.'

'Do not be afraid, O man highly esteemed,' he said. 'Peace! Be strong now; be strong.'

'Not by might nor by power, but by my Spirit,' says the LORD Almighty.— Be strong in the Lord and in his mighty power.

> Psalms 119:28; 49. Isaiah 38:14. Luke 21:33. Joshua 23:14. Daniel 10:19.
> Zechariah 4:6. Ephesians 6:10.

March 20

Morning

The unfolding of your words gives light.

This is the message we have heard from him and declare to you: God is light; in him there is no darkness at all.—For God, who said, 'Let light shine out of darkness,' made his light shine in our hearts to give us the light of the knowledge of the glory of God in the face of Christ.—The Word was God. . . . In him was life, and that life was the light of all people.

I have hidden your word in my heart that I might not sin against you.— 'You are already clean because of the word I have spoken to you.'

Out of darkness
But you are a chosen people, a royal priesthood, a holy nation, a people belonging to God, that you may declare the praises of him who called you out of darkness into this wonderful light.

> Psalm 119:130. 1 John 1:5. 2 Corinthians 4:6. John 1:1, 4.
> Psalm 119:11. John 15:3. 1 Peter 2:9.

Evening

'The righteous will live by faith.'

Then Noah built an altar to the LORD and, taking some of all the clean animals and clean birds, he sacrificed burnt offerings on it. The LORD smelled the pleasing aroma.—The Lamb was slain from the creation of the world.—Since we have been justified through faith, we have peace with God through our Lord Jesus Christ.

Righteousness from God
This righteousness from God comes through faith in Jesus Christ to all who believe. There is no difference.

We also rejoice in God through our Lord Jesus Christ, through whom we have now received reconciliation.

Who will bring any charge against those whom God has chosen? . . . And those he predestined, he also called.

> Galatians 3:11. Genesis 8:20–21. Revelation 13:8.
> Romans 5:1; 3:22; 5:11; 8:33, 30.

Morning

'Wake up! Strengthen what remains and is about to die.'

The end of all things is near. Therefore be clear minded and self-controlled so that you can pray. . . . Be self-controlled and alert. Your enemy the devil prowls around like a roaring lion looking for someone to devour.

Do not forget
Only be careful, and watch yourselves closely so that you do not forget things your eyes have seen or let them slip from your heart as long as you live.

'What I say to you, I say to everyone: "Watch!" '—'So do not fear, for I am with you, do not be dismayed, for I am your God. I will strengthen you and help you; I will uphold you with my righteous right hand. . . . For I am the LORD, your God, who takes hold of your right hand.'

> Revelation 3:2. 1 Peter 4:7; 5:8. Deuteronomy 4:9. Mark 13:37.
> Isaiah 41:10, 13.

Evening

Has his unfailing love vanished for ever?

His love endures for ever—'The LORD is slow to anger, abounding in love.'—Who is a God like you, who pardons sin and forgives the transgression of the remnant of his inheritance? You do not stay angry for ever but delight to show mercy. You will again have compassion on us; you will tread our sins underfoot and hurl all our iniquities into the depths of the sea.

He saved us, not because of righteous things we had done, but because of his mercy.

The Father of compassion
Praise be to the God and Father of our Lord Jesus Christ, the Father of compassion and the God of all comfort, who comforts us in all our troubles, so that we can comfort those in any trouble with the comfort we ourselves have received from God.

> Psalms 77:8. 136:23. Numbers 14:18. Micah 7:18–19. Titus 3:5.
> 2 Corinthians 1:3–4.

March 22

Morning

Lot . . . that righteous man.

'Remember Lot's wife!'
Do not be deceived: God cannot be mocked. A man reaps what he sows.—
'Remember Lot's wife!'

Do not be yoked together with unbelievers. For what do righteousness and
wickedness have in common? Or what fellowship can light have with
darkness?

Live as children of light
'Therefore come out from them and be separate, says the Lord. Touch no
unclean thing.'—Therefore do not be partners with them. For you were once
darkness, but now you are light in the Lord. Live as children of light . . . and
find out what pleases the Lord. Have nothing to do with the fruitless deeds of
darkness, but rather expose them.

> 2 Peter 2:7–8. Galatians 6:7. Luke 17:32. 2 Corinthians 6:14, 17.
> Ephesians 5:7–8, 10–11.

Evening

**Because God has said, 'Never will I leave you; never will I forsake you.'
So we say with confidence, 'The Lord is my helper; I will not be afraid.'**

I will come and proclaim your mighty acts, O Sovereign LORD; I will proclaim
your righteousness, yours alone.

The fruit of righteousness will be peace; the effect of righteousness will be
quietness and confidence for ever.

Put on the full armour of God
Stand firm then, with the belt of truth buckled around your waist, with the
breastplate of righteousness in place. . . . For our struggle is not against flesh
and blood, but against the rulers, against the authorities, against the powers of
this dark world and against the spiritual forces of evil in the heavenly realms.
Therefore put on the full armour of God, so that when the day of evil comes,
you may be able to stand your ground, and after you have done everything, to
stand.

> Hebrews 13:5–6. Psalm 71:16. Isaiah 32:17. Ephesians 6:14, 12–13.

Morning

'Holy, holy, holy is the Lord God Almighty.'

Yet you are enthroned as the Holy One; you are the praise of Israel.—'Do not come any closer,' God said. 'Take off your sandals, for the place where you are standing is holy ground.' . . . 'I am the God of your father, the God of Abraham, the God of Isaac and the God of Jacob.' At this, Moses hid his face, because he was afraid to look at God.

But just as he who called you is holy, so be holy in all you do; for it is written: 'Be holy, because I am holy.'—Do you not know that your body is a temple of the Holy Spirit, who is in you, whom you have received from God?

'I will walk among them'
For we are the temple of the living God. As God has said: 'I will live with them and walk among them, and I will be their God, and they will be my people.'— Do two walk together unless they have agreed to do so?

> Revelation 4:8. Psalm 22:3. Exodus 3:5–6. 1 Peter 1:15–16.
> 1 Corinthians 6:19. 2 Corinthians 6:16. Amos 3:3.

Evening

But they urged him strongly, 'Stay with us.'

'I stand at the door and knock'
'Here I am! I stand at the door and knock. If anyone hears my voice and opens the door, I will come in and eat with them, and they with me.'

'I will be with you always'
'I have not said to Jacob's descendants, "Seek me in vain." '—'I will be with you always, to the very end of the age.'

'You will see me'
'Never will I leave you; never will I forsake you.'—'For where two or three come together in my name, there am I with them.'—'The world will not see me any more, but you will see me.'

> Luke 24:29. Revelation 3:20. Isaiah 45:19. Matthew 28:20.
> Hebrews 13:5. Matthew 18:20. John 14:19.

March 24

Morning

Abraham believed the Lord, and he credited it to him as righteousness.

Yet he did not waver through unbelief regarding the promise of God, but was strengthened in his faith and gave glory to God, being fully persuaded that God had power to do what he had promised.

'The righteous will live by faith'
It was not through law that Abraham and his offspring received the promise that he would be heir of the world, but through the righteousness that comes by faith. . . . 'The righteous will live by faith.'—Let us hold unswervingly to the hope we profess, for he who promised is faithful. Our God is in heaven; he does whatever pleases him.

'Nothing is impossible with God'
'For nothing is impossible with God. . . . Blessed is she who has believed that what the Lord has said to her will be accomplished!'

Genesis 15:6. Romans 4:20–21, 13; 1:17. Hebrews 10:23. Psalm 115:3.
Luke 1:37, 45.

Evening

God . . . calls you into his kingdom and glory.

'My kingdom is not of this world. If it were, my servants would fight to prevent my arrest by the Jews. But now my kingdom is from another place.'— He waits for his enemies to be made his footstool.

I saw thrones on which were seated those who had been given authority to judge. . . . They came to life and reigned with Christ a thousand years.—'Then the righteous will shine like the sun in the kingdom of their Father.'

'I confer on you a kingdom'
'Do not be afraid, little flock, for your Father has been pleased to give you the kingdom.' . . . 'And I confer on you a kingdom, just as my Father conferred one on me, so that you may eat and drink at my table in my kingdom and sit on the thrones, judging the twelve tribes of Israel.'

1 Thessalonians 2:1. John 18:36. Hebrews 10:13. Revelation 20:4.
Matthew 13:43. Luke 12:32; 22:29–30.

Morning

'Never will I leave you, never will I forsake you.'

So we say with confidence, 'The Lord is my helper; I will not be afraid.'

'Be strong and courageous. Do not be afraid or terrified because of them, for the LORD your God goes with you; he will never leave you nor forsake you.'

The Lord stood at my side
Demas, because he loved this world, has deserted me . . . At my first defence, no-one came to my support, but everyone deserted me. May it not be held against them. But the Lord stood at my side and gave me strength.—Though my father and mother forsake me, the LORD will receive me.

'I will come to you'
'I will not leave you as orphans; I will come to you. . . . My peace I give you.'

Hebrews 13:5, 6. Deuteronomy 31:6. 2 Timothy 4:10, 16–17.
Psalm 27:10. John 14:18, 27.

Evening

'The kingdom of heaven is like a net that was let down into the lake.'

'All authority in heaven and on earth has been given to me. Therefore go and make disciples of all nations, baptising them in the name of the Father and of the Son and of the Holy Spirit. . . . And surely I will be with you always, to the very end of the age.'

I am compelled to preach
Yet when I preach the gospel, I cannot boast, for I am compelled to preach. Woe to me if I do not preach the gospel! . . . I have become all things to all people so that by all possible means I might save some.

Let us not become weary in doing good, for at the proper time we will reap a harvest if we do not give up.—My word . . . will not return to me empty, but will accomplish what I desire.

Matthew 13:47. Matthew 28:18–20. 1 Corinthians 9:16, 22.
Galatians 6:9. Isaiah 55:11.

March 26

Morning

I can do everything through him who gives me strength.

Faithfully administering God's grace
All these are the work of one and the same Spirit, and he gives them to each one, just as he determines. . . . Now to each one the manifestation of the Spirit is given for the common good.—Each of you should use whatever gift you have received to serve others, faithfully administering God's grace in its various forms.—Now it is required that those who have been given a trust must prove faithful.

Much will be demanded
'From everyone who has been given much, much will be demanded; and from the one who has been entrusted with much, much more will be asked.'

Philippians 4:13. 1 Corinthians 12:11, 7. 1 Peter 4:10.
1 Corinthians 4:2. Luke 12:48.

Evening

Share with God's people who are in need.

David asked, 'Is there anyone still left of the house of Saul to whom I can show kindness for Jonathan's sake?'

'For I was hungry'
'Come, you who are blessed by my Father, take your inheritance, the kingdom prepared for you since the creation of the world. For I was hungry and you gave me something to eat, I was thirsty and you gave me something to drink, I was a stranger and you invited me in, I needed clothes and you clothed me, I was sick and you looked after me, I was in prison and you came to visit me. . . . Whatever you did for one of these brothers and sisters of mine, you did for me.'

'A cup of cold water'
'And if anyone gives a cup of cold water to one of these little ones who is my disciple, I tell you the truth, that person will certainly be rewarded.'

Romans 12:13. 2 Samuel 9:1. Matthew 25:34–36, 40; 10:42.

Morning

Those who sow righteousness reap a sure reward.

'After a long time the master of those servants returned and settled accounts with them. The man who had received five talents brought the other five. "Master," he said, "you entrusted me with five talents. See, I have gained five more." His master replied, "Well done, good and faithful servant! You have been faithful with a few things; I will put you in charge of many things. Come and share your master's happiness." '

The judgment seat of Christ
For we must all appear before the judgment seat of Christ, that everyone may receive what is due them for the things done while in the body, whether good or bad.

'Hold on to what you have'
'I am coming soon. Hold on to what you have, so that no-one will take your crown.'

> Proverbs 11:18. Matthew 25:19–21. 2 Corinthians 5:10. Revelation 3:11.

Evening

God is faithful.

The Lord has sworn and will not change his mind.—Does he speak and then not act? Does he promise and not fulfil.

Faithful Creator
So then, those who suffer according to God's will should commit themselves to their faithful Creator and continue to do good.

The one who calls you is faithful
I know whom I have believed, and am convinced that he is able to guard what I have entrusted to him for that day.—The one who calls you is faithful and he will do it.—For no matter how many promises God has made, they are 'Yes' in Christ. And so through him the 'Amen' is spoken by us to the glory of God.

> 1 Corinthians 10:13. Hebrews 7:21. Numbers 23:19. 1 Peter 4:19.
> 2 Timothy 1:12. 1 Thessalonians 5:24. 2 Corinthians 1:20.

March 28

Morning

'Be strong and courageous!'

The LORD is my light and my salvation—whom shall I fear? The LORD is my stronghold of my life—of whom shall I be afraid?

Soar on wings like eagles
He gives strength to the weary and increases the power of the weak. Even youths grow tired and weary, and young men stumble and fall; but those who hope in the LORD will renew their strength. They will soar on wings like eagles; they will run and not grow weary, they will walk and not be faint.

My flesh and my heart may fail, but God is the strength of my heart and my portion for ever.—If God is for us, who can be against us?—The LORD is with me; I will not be afraid. What can human beings do to me?

We are more than conquerors through him who loved us.—'Now begin the work, and the LORD be with you.'

> Joshua 1:18. Psalm 27:1. Isaiah 40:29–31. Psalm 73:26. Romans 8:31.
> Psalm 118:6. Romans 8:37. 1 Chronicles 22:16.

Evening

'Our friend . . . has fallen asleep.'

Brothers and sisters, we do not want you to be ignorant about those who fall asleep, or to grieve like the rest, who have no hope. We believe that Jesus died and rose again and so we believe that God will bring with Jesus those who have fallen asleep in him.

Christ has indeed been raised
For if the dead are not raised, then Christ has not been raised either. And if Christ has not been raised, your faith is futile; you are still in your sins. Then those also who have fallen asleep in Christ are lost. . . . But Christ has indeed been raised from the dead, the firstfruits of those who have fallen asleep.

'We are all witnesses of the fact'
'God has raised this Jesus to life, and we are all witnesses of the fact.' . . . 'Witnesses whom God has already chosen—by us who ate and drank with him after he rose from the dead.'

> John 11:11. 1 Thessalonians 4:13–14. 1 Corinthians 15:16–18, 20.
> Acts 2:32; 10:41.

Morning

'Do not be afraid, little flock, for your Father has been pleased to give you the kingdom.'

'Listen, my dear brothers and sisters: Has not God chosen those who are poor in the eyes of the world to be rich in faith and to inherit the kingdom he promised those who love him?'

Co-heirs with Christ
Now if we are children, then we are heirs—heirs of God and co-heirs with Christ.
   'The Father himself loves you because you have loved me.'—Therefore God is not ashamed to be called their God, for he has prepared a city for them.

The crown of righteousness
'Those who overcome will inherit all this, and I will be their God and they will be my children.'—Now there is in store for me the crown of righteousness, which the Lord, the righteous Judge, will award to me on that day—and not only to me, but also to all who have longed for his appearing.

Luke 12:32. James 2:5. Romans 8:17. John 16:27. Hebrews 11:16.
Revelation 21:7. 2 Timothy 4:8.

Evening

Human beings are mere phantoms as they go to and fro: They bustle about, but only in vain; they heap up wealth, not knowing who will get it.

'Treasures in heaven'
'Do not store up for yourselves treasures on earth, where moth and rust destroy, and where thieves break in and steal. But store up for yourselves treasures in heaven, where moth and rust do not destroy, and where thieves do not break in and steal. For where your treasure is, there your heart will be also.'

We fix our eyes on what is unseen
They do it to get a crown that will not last; but we do it to get a crown that will last for ever.—So we fix our eyes not on what is seen, but on what is unseen.— But those who sow righteousness reap a sure reward.
   Now there is in store for me the crown of righteousness, which the Lord, the righteous Judge, will award to me on that day—and not only to me, but also to all who have longed for his appearing.

Psalm 39:6. Matthew 6:19–21. 1 Corinthians 9:25. 2 Corinthians 4:18.
Proverbs 11:18. 2 Timothy 4:8.

March 30

Morning

He went out to the field one evening to meditate.

May the words of my mouth and the meditation of my heart be pleasing in your sight, O LORD, my Rock and my Redeemer.

When I consider your heavens
When I consider your heavens, the work of your fingers, the moon and the stars, which you have set in place, what are mere mortals that you are mindful of them, human beings that you care for them? . . . Great are the works of the LORD; they are pondered by all who delight in them.

Meditate on it day and night
Do not let this Book of the Law depart from your mouth; meditate on it day and night.

My soul will be satisfied as with the richest of foods; with singing lips my mouth will praise you. On my bed I remember you; I think of you through the watches of the night.

Genesis 24:63. Psalms 19:14; 8:3–4; 111:2. Joshua 1:8. Psalm 63:5–6.

Evening

How long, O LORD? Will you forget me for ever? How long will you hide your face from me?

Every good and perfect gift is from above, coming down from the Father of the heavenly lights, who does not change like shifting shadows.

'I will not forget you'
But Zion said, 'The LORD has forsaken me, the Lord has forgotten me.' Can a mother forget the baby at her breast and have no compassion on the child she has borne? Though she may forget, I will not forget you!' . . . 'O Israel, I will not forget you. I have swept away your offences like a cloud, your sins like the morning mist.'

Your faith—of greater worth than gold, which perishes.

Psalm 13:1. James 1:17. Isaiah 49:14–15; 44:21–22. 1 Peter 1:7.

Morning

And my God will meet all your needs according to his glorious riches in Christ Jesus.

'But seek first his kingdom and his righteousness, and all these things will be given to you as well.'—He who did not spare his own Son, but gave him up for us all—how will he not also, along with him, graciously give us all things?—Having nothing, and yet possessing everything.

A sun and a shield
The LORD is my shepherd, I shall not be in want. . . . For the LORD God is a sun and shield; the LORD bestows favour and honour; no good thing does he withhold from those whose walk is blameless.

In all things at all times
God . . . who richly provides us with everything for our enjoyment.—And God is able to make all grace abound to you, so that in all things at all times having all that you need, you will abound in every good thing.

Philippians 4:19. Matthew 6:33. Romans 8:32. 2 Corinthians 6:10.
Psalms 23:1; 84:11. 1 Timothy 6:17. 2 Corinthians 9:8.

Evening

What do righteousness and wickedness have in common?

People loved darkness instead of light because their deeds were evil.—You are all children of the light and children of the day. We do not belong to the night or to the darkness.
    Your word is a lamp to my feet and a light for my path.

The first gleam of dawn
But the way of the wicked is like deep darkness; they do not know what makes them stumble. . . . The path of the righteous is like the first gleam of dawn, shining ever brighter till the full light of day.

You are light in the Lord
'I have come into the world as a light, so that no-one who believes in me should stay in darkness.'—For you were once darkness, but now you are light in the Lord. Live as children of light.

2 Corinthians 6; 14. John 3:19. 1 Thessalonians 5:5. Psalm 119:105.
Proverbs 4:19, 18. John 12:46. Ephesians 5:8.

April 1

Morning

But the fruit of the Spirit is . . . joy.

Joy in the Holy Spirit.—You believe in him and are filled with an inexpressible and glorious joy.

Sorrowful, yet always rejoicing . . . In all our troubles my joy knows no bounds.—We . . . rejoice in our sufferings.

'My joy in you'
Fix our eyes on Jesus, the author and perfecter of our faith, who for the joy set before him endured the cross, scorning its shame.—'I have told you this so that my joy may be in you and that your joy may be complete.'—For just as the sufferings of Christ flow over into our lives, so also through Christ our comfort overflows.

Rejoice in the Lord always. I will say it again: Rejoice!—'The joy of the LORD is your strength.'

You will fill me with joy in your presence, with eternal pleasures at your right hand.

> Galatians 5:22. Romans 14:17. 1 Peter 1.18. 2 Corinthians 6:10; 7:4.
> Romans 5:3. Hebrews 12:2. John 15:11. 2 Corinthians 1:5.
> Philippians 4:4. Nehemiah 8:10. Psalm 16:11.

Evening

'One greater than Solomon is here.'

Prince of Peace
For to us a child is born, to us a son is given, and the government will be on his shoulders. And he will be called Wonderful Counsellor, Mighty God, Everlasting Father, Prince of Peace. . . . My people will live in peaceful dwelling-places, in secure homes, in undisturbed places of rest. Though hail flattens the forest and the city is levelled completely.

For he himself is our peace.—And he will be their peace. When the Assyrian invades our land.—'They will make war against the Lamb, but the Lamb will overcome them because he is Lord of lords and King of kings.'

'Peace I leave with you; my peace I give you.'

> Matthew 12:42. Isaiah 9:6; 32:18–19. Ephesians 2:14. Micah 5:5.
> Revelation 17:14. John 14:27.

Morning

'Commit yourselves to the LORD and serve him only.'

Dear children, keep yourselves from idols.—'Therefore come out from them and be separate says the Lord. Touch no unclean thing, and I will receive you.' 'I will be a Father to you, and you will be my sons and daughters, says the Lord Almighty.'—'You cannot serve both God and Money.'

Do not worship any other god, for the LORD, whose name is Jealous, is a jealous God.—Serve him with wholehearted devotion and with a willing mind, for the LORD searches every heart and understands every motive behind the thoughts.

Teach me wisdom
Surely you desire truth in the inner parts; you teach me wisdom in the inmost place.—Dear friends, if our hearts do not condemn us, we have confidence before God.

1 Samuel 7:3. 1 John 5:21. Exodus 34:14. 1 Chronicles 28:9.
Matthew 6:24. 1 Chronicles 28:9. Psalm 51:6. 1 John 3:21.

Evening

'When the Son of Man comes, will he find faith on the earth?'

The Spirit clearly says that in later times some will abandon the faith.

Preach the Word; be prepared in season and out of season; correct, rebuke and encourage—with great patience and careful instruction. For the time will come when people will not put up with sound doctrine. Instead, to suit their own desires, they will turn their ears away from the truth and turn aside to myths.

Be on guard! Be alert!
'No-one knows about that day or hour, not even the angels in heaven, nor the Son, but only the Father. Be on guard! Be alert! You do not know when that time will come.'—'It will be good for those servants whose master finds them watching when he comes.'—While we wait for the blessed hope—the glorious appearing of our great God and Saviour, Jesus Christ.

Luke 18:8. 1 Timothy 4:1. 2 Timothy 4:2–4. Mark 13:32–33.
Luke 12:37. Titus 2:13.

April 3

Morning

'For my thoughts are not your thoughts, neither are your ways my ways,' declares the LORD.

'The heavens are higher than the earth'
'As the heavens are higher than the earth, so are my ways higher than your ways and my thoughts than your thoughts. As the rain and the snow come down from heaven, . . . so is my word that goes out from my mouth: It will not return to me empty, but will accomplish what I desire and achieve the purpose for which I sent it.'

For God has bound everyone over to disobedience so that he may have mercy on them all. Oh, the depth of the riches of the wisdom and knowledge of God!

A day is like a thousand years
But do not forget this one thing, dear friends: With the Lord a day is like a thousand years, and a thousand years are like a day. The Lord is not slow in keeping his promise, as some understand slowness.

Isaiah 55:8, 9–11. Romans 11:32–33. 2 Peter 3:8–9.

Evening

For the wages of sin is death, but the gift of God is eternal life in Christ Jesus our Lord.

He will deliver us
Indeed, in our hearts we felt the sentence of death. But this happened that we might not rely on ourselves but on God, who raises the dead. He has delivered us from such a deadly peril, and he will deliver us. On him we have set our hope that he will continue to deliver us.

It is a dreadful thing to fall into the hands of the living God.—Since, then, we know what it is to fear the Lord, we try to persuade people.

Be prepared in season and out of season.—Snatch others from the fire and save them.

'Not by might nor by power, but by my Spirit,' says the LORD Almighty.— Who wants all people to be saved and to come to a knowledge of the truth.

Romans 6:23. 2 Corinthians 1:9–10. Hebrews 10:31. 2 Corinthians 5:11.
2 Timothy 4:2. Jude 23. Zechariah 4:6. 1 Timothy 2:4.

Morning

'Do not be afraid. I am the First and the Last.'

The throne of grace
You have come to Mount Zion . . . to God, the judge of all people, to the spirits of the righteous made perfect, to Jesus the mediator of a new covenant. . . . For we do not have a high priest who is unable to sympathise with our weaknesses, but we have one who has been tempted in every way, just as we are—yet was without sin. Let us then approach the throne of grace with confidence, so that we may receive mercy and find grace to help us in our time of need.

'Apart from me there is no God'
'This is what the LORD says—Israel's King and Redeemer, the LORD Almighty: I am the first and I am the last; apart from me there is no God.' . . . Mighty God, Everlasting Father, Prince of Peace.

O LORD, are you not from everlasting? My God, my Holy One.—For who is God besides the LORD? And who is the Rock except God?

Revelation 1:17. Hebrews 12:22–24; 4:15–16. Isaiah 44:6; 9:6.
Habakkuk 1:12. 2 Samuel 22:32.

Evening

Lead me to the rock that is higher than I.

Do not be anxious about anything, but in everything, by prayer and petition, with thanksgiving, present your requests to God. And the peace of God, which transcends all understanding, will guard your hearts and minds in Christ Jesus.

You know my way
When my spirit grows faint within me, it is you who know my way.—But he knows the way that I take; when he has tested me, I shall come forth as gold.

And who is the Rock except our God?—'They shall never perish; no-one can snatch them out of my hand.'—Sustain me according to your promise, and I shall live; do not let my hopes be dashed.—We have this hope as an anchor for the soul, firm and secure. It enters the inner sanctuary behind the curtain.

Psalm 61:2. Philippians 4:6–7. Psalm 142:3. Job 23:10. Psalm 18:31.
John 10:28. Psalm 119:116. Hebrews 6:19.

April 5

Morning

'My Presence will go with you, and I will give you rest.'

Then Jesus answered, 'Woman, you have great faith! Your request is granted.' . . . 'According to your faith will it be done to you.'—But when you ask, you must believe and not doubt, because the one who doubts is like a wave of the sea, blown and tossed by the wind. Those who doubt should not think they will receive anything from the Lord.

'Were not our hearts burning within us?'
As they approached the village to which they were going, Jesus acted as if he were going further. But they urged him strongly, 'Stay with us, for it is nearly evening; the day is almost over.' So he went in to stay with them. . . . Then their eyes were opened and they recognised him, and he disappeared from their sight. They asked each other, 'Were not our hearts burning within us while he talked with us on the road and opened the Scriptures to us?'—If I have found favour in your eyes, teach me your ways so I may know you and continue to find favour with you.

Exodus 33:14. Matthew 15:28; 9:29. James 1:6–7. Luke 24:28–29, 31–32.
Exodus 33:13.

Evening

Jesus, the author and perfecter of our faith.

'I am the Alpha and the Omega,' says the Lord God, 'who is, and who was, and who is to come, the Almighty.'—To those who have been called, who are loved by God the Father and kept by Jesus Christ.

The day of Christ Jesus
May God himself, the God of peace, sanctify you through and through. May your whole spirit, soul and body be kept blameless at the coming of our Lord Jesus Christ.—He who began a good work in you will carry it on to completion until the day of Christ Jesus.—Are you so foolish? After beginning with the Spirit, are you now trying to attain your goal by human effort?—The LORD will fulfil his purpose for me.

For it is God who works in you to will and to act according to his good purpose.

Hebrews 12:2; Revelation 1:8. Jude 1. 1 Thessalonians 5:23–24.
Philippians 1:6. Galatians 3:3. Psalm 138:3. Philippians 2:13.

Morning

He always lives to intercede for them.

Who then can condemn? Christ Jesus, who died—more than that, who was raised to life—is at the right hand of God and is also interceding for us.

But if anybody does sin, we have one who speaks to the Father in our defence—Jesus Christ, the Righteous One.—For there is one God and one mediator between God and human beings, Christ Jesus.

Access to the Father by one Spirit
Therefore, since we have a great high priest who has gone through the heavens, Jesus the Son of God, let us hold firmly to the faith we profess. For we do not have a high priest who is unable to sympathise with our weaknesses, but we have one who has been tempted in every way, just as we are—yet was without sin. Let us then approach the throne of grace with confidence, so that we may receive mercy and find grace to help us in our time of need.—For through him we both have access to the Father by one Spirit.

Hebrews 7:15. Romans 8:34. 1 John 2:1. 1 Timothy 2:5.
Hebrews 4:14–16. Ephesians 2:18.

Evening

Those who know your name will trust in you.

Mighty God, Everlasting Father
And he will be called Wonderful Counsellor, Mighty God, Everlasting Father.—I know whom I have believed, and am convinced that he is able to guard what I have entrusted to him for that day.

Prince of Peace
Prince of Peace.—For he himself is our peace.—Therefore, since we have been justified through faith, we have peace with God through our Lord Jesus Christ.

The name of the LORD is a strong tower; the righteous run to it and are safe.—'Like birds hovering overhead, the LORD Almighty will shield Jerusalem; he will shield it and deliver it, he will "pass over" it and will rescue it.'

Psalm 9:10. Isaiah 9:6. 2 Timothy 1:12. Isaiah 9:6. Ephesians 2:14. 5:1.
Proverbs 18:10. Isaiah 31:5.

April 7

Morning

Sorrowful, yet always rejoicing; poor, yet making many rich; having nothing, and yet possessing everything.

And we rejoice in the hope of the glory of God. Not only so, but we also rejoice in our sufferings.—I am greatly encouraged; in all our troubles my joy knows no bounds.—You believe in him and are filled with an inexpressible and glorious joy.

Overflowing joy
Out of the most severe trial, their overflowing joy and their extreme poverty welled up in rich generosity.

Rich in faith
Has not God chosen those who are poor in the eyes of the world to be rich in faith and to inherit the kingdom he promised those who love him?—And God is able to make all grace abound to you, so that in all things at all times, having all that you need, you will abound in every good work.

2 Corinthians 6:10. Romans 5:2–3. 2 Corinthians 7:4. 1 Peter 1:8.
2 Corinthians 8:2. James 2:5. 2 Corinthians 9:8.

Evening

The LORD will sustain them on their sick-bed and restore them from their bed of illness.

In all their distress he too was distressed, and the angel of his presence saved them. In his love and mercy he redeemed them; he lifted them up and carried them.—'My grace is sufficient for you, for my power is made perfect in weakness.'—Therefore I will boast all the more gladly about my weaknesses, so that Christ's power may rest on me.

Therefore we do not lose heart. Though outwardly we are wasting away, yet inwardly we are being renewed day by day.

The everlasting arms
He gives strength to the weary and increases the power of the weak. Even youths grow tired and weary, and young men stumble and fall; but those who hope in the LORD will renew their strength.—The eternal God is your refuge, and underneath are the everlasting arms.

Psalm 41:3. Isaiah 63:9. 2 Corinthians 12:9; 4:16. Isaiah 40:29–31.
Deuteronomy 33:17.

Morning

For in him you have been enriched in every way.

When we were still powerless, Christ died for the ungodly.—He who did not spare his own Son, but gave him up for us all—how will he not also, along with him, graciously give us all things?

You have been given fulness in Christ, who is the head over every power and authority.

'Remain in the vine'
'Remain in me, and I will remain in you. No branch can bear fruit by itself; it must remain in the vine. Neither can you bear fruit unless you remain in me. I am the vine; you are the branches. If you remain in me and I you, you will bear much fruit; apart from me you can do nothing.'—But to each one of us grace has been given as Christ apportioned it.

'If you remain in me and my words remain in you, ask whatever you wish, and it will be given you.'—Let the word of Christ dwell in you richly.

1 Corinthians 1:5. Romans 5:6. Colossians 2:10. John 15:4–5.
Ephesians 4:7. John 15:7. Colossians 3:16.

Evening

They will see his face.

Then Moses said, 'Now show me your glory.'

Every eye will see him, even those who pierced him; and all the peoples of the earth will mourn because of him.—'I see him, but not now; I behold him, but not near.'

We shall be like him
I know that my Redeemer lives, and that in the end he will stand upon the earth. And after my skin has been destroyed, yet in my flesh I will see God.— We shall be like him, for we shall see him as he is.

For the Lord himself will come down from heaven, with a loud command, with the voice of the archangel and with the trumpet call of God, and the dead in Christ will rise first. After that, we who are still alive and are left will be caught up with them in the clouds to meet the Lord in the air. And so we will be with the Lord for ever.

Revelation 22:4. Exodus 33:18. Revelation 1:7. Numbers 24:17.
Job 19:25–26. 1 John 3:2. 1 Thessalonians 4:16–17.

April 9

Morning

'Fear not, for I have redeemed you.'

'I have swept away your offences like a cloud, your sins like the morning mist. Return to me, for I have redeemed you.'—With the precious blood of Christ, a lamb without blemish or defect.

Their Redeemer is strong

Yet their Redeemer is strong; the LORD Almighty is his name. He will vigorously defend their cause.—'My Father, who has given them to me, is greater than all; no-one can snatch them out of my Father's hand.'

Grace and peace to you

Grace and peace to you from God our Father and the Lord Jesus Christ, who gave himself for our sins to rescue us from the present evil age, according to the will of our God and Father, to whom be glory for ever and ever. Amen.

Isaiah 43:1; 44:22. 1 Peter 1:19. Jeremiah 50:34. John 10:29.
Galatians 1:3–5.

Evening

I will tell of the kindnesses of the LORD.

He lifted me out of the slimy pit, out of the mud and mire; he set my feet on a rock and gave me a firm place to stand.—I live by faith in the Son of God, who loved me and gave himself for me.—He who did not spare his own Son, but gave him up for us all—how will he not also, along with him, graciously give us all things? . . . God demonstrates his own love for us in this: While we were still sinners, Christ died for us.

He anointed us, set his seal of ownership on us, and put his Spirit in our hearts.

God raised us up with Christ

God, who is rich in mercy, made us alive with Christ even when we were dead in transgressions—it is by grace you have been saved. And God raised us up with Christ and seated us with him in the heavenly realms in Christ Jesus.

Isaiah 63:7. Psalm 40:2. Galatians 2:20. Romans 8:32; 5:8.
Ephesians 1:14; 2:5–6.

Morning

'Lord, I am a sinful man!'

Surely I have been a sinner from birth, sinful from the time my mother conceived me.—And your fame spread among the nations on account of your beauty, because the splendour I had given you made your beauty perfect, declares the Sovereign LORD.

'Therefore, I despise myself and repent in dust and ashes.'

When I want to do good, evil is right there with me.—'Take heart, son; your sins are forgiven.'

Washed, sanctified, justified

But you were washed, you were sanctified, you were justified in the name of the Lord Jesus Christ and by the Spirit of our God.—That you may declare the praises of him who called you out of darkness into his wonderful light.

> Luke 5:8. Psalm 51:5. Ezekiel 16:14. Job 42:6. Romans 7:21.
> Matthew 9:2. 1 Corinthians 6:11. 1 Peter 2:9.

Evening

Everyone who wants to live a godly life in Christ Jesus will be persecuted.

Anyone who chooses to be a friend of the world becomes an enemy of God.

Do not love the world

Do not love the world or anything in the world. If anyone loves the world, the love of the Father is not in him. For everything in the world—the cravings of sinful people, the lust of their eyes and the boasting of what they have and do—comes not from the Father but from the world.

'I have chosen you out of the world'

'If the world hates you, keep in mind that it hated me first. If you belonged to the world, it would love you as its own. As it is, you do not belong to the world, but I have chosen you out of the world. That is why the world hates you. Remember the words I spoke to you: "No servant is greater than his master." ' . . . 'I have given them your word and the world has hated them, for they are not of the world any more than I am of the world.'

> 2 Timothy 3:12. James 4:4. 1 John 2:15–16. John 15:18–20; 17:14.

April 11

Morning

Everyone should be quick to listen, slow to speak and slow to become angry.

Better a patient person than a warrior, those who control their temper than those who take a city.—Those who are never at fault in what they say are perfect, able to keep their whole body in check.

Keep watch over the door of my lips
Set a guard over my mouth, O Lord, keep watch over the door of my lips.

Consider him
Christ suffered for you, leaving you an example, that you should follow in his steps. 'He committed no sin, and no deceit was found in his mouth.' When they hurled their insults at him, he did not retaliate; when he suffered, he made no threats. Instead, he entrusted himself to him who judges justly.—Consider him who endured such opposition from sinners, so that you will not grow weary and lose heart.

> James 1:19. Proverbs 16:32. James 3:2. Matthew 12:37. Psalm 141:3.
> 1 Peter 2:21–23. Hebrews 12:3.

Evening

Teach me your way, O Lord.

I will instruct you and teach you in the way you should go; I will counsel you and watch over you. . . . Good and upright is the Lord; therefore he instructs sinners in his ways. He guides the humble in what is right and teaches them his way.

Jesus answered, 'I am the way and the truth and the life. No-one comes to the Father except through me.'

Let us draw near to God
Since we have confidence to enter the Most Holy Place by the blood of Jesus, by a new and living way opened for us through the curtain, that is his body, and since we have a great priest over the house of God, let us draw near to God with a sincere heart in full assurance of faith.

Let us acknowledge the Lord; let us press on to acknowledge him.—All the ways of the Lord are loving and faithful for those who keep the demands of his covenant.

> Psalms 27:11; 32:8; 25:8–9. John 14:6. Hebrews 10:19–22. Hosea 6:3.

Morning

What the law was powerless to do in that it was weakened by the sinful nature, God did by sending his own Son in the likeness of sinful humanity to be a sin offering. And so he condemned sin in our sinful nature.

The law is only a shadow of the good things that are coming—not the realities themselves. For this reason it can never, by the same sacrifices repeated endlessly year after year, make perfect those who draw near to worship. If it could, would they not have stopped being offered?

Justified
Through him everyone who believes is justified from everything you could not be justified from by the law of Moses.

He shared in their humanity
Since the children have flesh and blood, he too shared their humanity so that by his death he might destroy him who holds the power of death—that is, the devil—and free those who all their lives were held in slavery by their fear of death.

Romans 8:3. Hebrews 10:1–2. Acts 13:39. Hebrews 2:14–15.

Evening

For all have sinned and fall short of the glory of God.

'There is no-one righteous, not even one; . . . there is no-one who does good, not even one.'

Called, justified, glorified
'The LORD has taken away your sin. You are not going to die.'—Those he called, he also justified; those he justified, he also glorified.

And we, who with unveiled faces all reflect the Lord's glory, are being transformed into his likeness with ever-increasing glory, which comes from the Lord, who is the Spirit.—If you continue in your faith, established and firm, not moved from the hope held out in the gospel.

Live lives worthy of God, who calls you into his kingdom and glory.

Romans 3:23, 10, 12. 2 Samuel 12:13. Romans 8:30. 2 Corinthians 3:18.
Colossians 1:23. 1 Thessalonians 2:12.

April 13

Morning

Honour the LORD with your wealth, with the firstfruits of all your crops.

Remember this: Whoever sows sparingly will also reap sparingly, and whoever sows generously will also reap generously.—On the first day of every week, each one of you should set aside a sum of money in keeping with your income, saving it up.

God is not unjust; he will not forget your work and the love you have shown him as you have helped his people and continue to help them.

Offer your bodies as living sacrifices
Therefore, I urge you, brothers and sisters, in view of God's mercy, to offer your bodies as living sacrifices, holy and pleasing to God—this is your spiritual act of worship.—For Christ compels us, because we are convinced that one died for all, and therefore all died. And he died for all, that those who live should no longer live for themselves but for him who died for them and was raised again.

Proverbs 3:9. 2 Corinthians 9:6. 1 Corinthians 16:2. Hebrews 6:10.
Romans 12:1. 2 Corinthians 5:14–15.

Evening

There will be no night.

For the LORD will be your everlasting light, and your God will be your glory.
The city does not need the sun or the moon to shine on it, for the glory of God gives it light, and the Lamb is its lamp. . . . They will not need the light of a lamp or the light of the sun, for the Lord God will give them light.

The kingdom of light
Giving thanks to the Father, who has qualified you to share in the inheritance of the saints in the kingdom of light. For he has rescued us from the dominion of darkness and brought us into the kingdom of light.—For you were once darkness, but now you are light in the Lord. Live as children of light.

We do not belong to the night or to the darkness.

The path of the righteous is like the first gleam of dawn, shining ever brighter till the full light of day.

Revelation 21:25. Isaiah 60:19. Revelation 21:23; 22:5. Colossians 1:12.
Ephesians 5:8. 1 Thessalonians 5:5. Proverbs 4:18.

Morning

You are the most excellent of men.

With singing lips my mouth will praise you
My soul will be satisfied with the richest of foods; with singing lips my mouth will praise you. On my bed I remember you; I think of you through the watches of the night.

How sweet are your promises
How precious to me are your thoughts, O God! How vast is the sum of them! Were I to count them, they would outnumber the grains of sand. When I awake, I am still with you. . . . How sweet are your promises to my taste, sweeter than honey to my mouth!—Your love is more delightful than wine.

Whom have I in heaven but you?
Whom have I in heaven but you? And earth has nothing I desire besides you.

Psalms 45:2; 63:5–6; 139:17–18, 73:25.

Evening

Restore to me the joy of your salvation.

I have seen his ways, but I will heal him; I will guide him and restore comfort to him, creating praise on the lips of the mourners in Israel.

'I will cure you of backsliding'
'Return, faithless people; I will cure you of backsliding.' 'Yes, we will come to you, for you are the LORD our God.'—I will listen to what God the LORD will say; he promises peace to his people, his saints—but let them not return to folly.

Praise the LORD, O my soul, and forget not all his benefits—who forgives all your sins and heals all your diseases, . . . He restores my soul.—'I will praise you, O LORD. Although you were angry with me, your anger has turned away and you have comforted me.'

Uphold me, and I shall be delivered.

'I, even I, am he who blots out your transgressions, for my own sake.'

Psalm 51:12. Isaiah 57:18. Jeremiah 3:22. Psalms 85:8; 103:2–3; 23:3.
Isaiah 12:1. Psalm 119:117. Isaiah 43:25.

April 15

Morning

Yet their Redeemer is strong.

'Mighty to save.'—To him who is able to keep you from falling.—But where sin increased, grace increased all the more.

'Those who believe in him are not condemned, but those who do not believe stand condemned already because they have not believed in the name of God's one and only Son.'—Therefore he is able to save completely those who come to God through him.

The love of God that is in Christ
Was my arm too short to ransom you? . . . Who shall separate us from the love of Christ? . . . For I am convinced that neither death nor life, neither angels nor demons, neither the present nor the future, nor any powers, neither height nor depth nor anything else in all creation, will be able to separate us from the love of God that is in Christ Jesus our Lord.

Jeremiah 50:34. Isaiah 63:1. Jude 24. Romans 5:20. John 3:18.
Hebrews 7:25. Isaiah 50:2. Romans 8:35, 38–39.

Evening

Should you then seek great things for yourself? Seek them not.

'Take my yoke upon you and learn from me, for I am gentle and humble in heart, and you will find rest for your souls.'—Your attitude should be the same as that of Christ Jesus: Who, being in very nature God, did not consider equality with God something to be grasped, but made himself nothing, taking the very nature of a servant, being made in human likeness. And being found in appearance as a human being, he humbled himself and became obedient to death—even death on a cross!

Be content
But godliness with contentment is great gain. For we brought nothing into the world, and we can take nothing out of it. But if we have food and clothing, we will be content with that.

I have learned to be content whatever the circumstances.

Jeremiah 45:5. Matthew 11:19. Philippians 2:5–8. 1 Timothy 6:6–8.
Philippians 4:11.

Morning

In my alarm I said, 'I am cut off from your sight!' Yet you heard my cry for mercy when I called to you for help.

The waters closed over my head, and I thought I was about to be cut off, I called on your name, O Lord, from the depths of the pit. You heard my plea: 'Do not close your ears to my cry for relief.' You came near when I called, and you said, 'Do not fear.'

I will see the goodness of the Lord

'Will the Lord reject for ever? Will he never show his favour again? Has his unfailing love vanished for ever? Has his promise failed for all time? Has God forgotten to be merciful? Has he in anger withheld his compassion?' Then I thought, 'To this I will appeal: the years of the right hand of the Most High.' I will remember the deeds of the Lord; yes, I will remember your miracles of long ago. . . . I am still confident of this: I will see the goodness of the Lord in the land of the living.

Psalm 31:22. Lamentations 3:54–57. Psalms 77:7–11; 27:13.

Evening

You will call upon me, and I will answer you; I will be with you in trouble, I will deliver you.

That night God appeared to Solomon and said to him, 'Ask for whatever you want me to give you.' Solomon answered God, . . . 'Give me wisdom and knowledge, that I may lead this people, for who is able to govern this great people of yours?'—God gave Solomon wisdom and very great insight, and a breadth of understanding as measureless as the sand on the seashore.

'We rely on you'

Then Asa called to the Lord his God and said, 'Lord, there is no-one like you to help the powerless against the mighty. Help us, O Lord our God, for we rely on you, and in your name we have come against this vast army. O Lord you are our God; do not let mere mortals prevail against you.' The Lord struck down the Cushites before Asa and Judah.

O you who hear prayer, to you all people come.

Psalm 91:15. 2 Chronicles 1:7–8, 10. 1 Kings 4:29.
2 Chronicles 14:11–12. Psalm 65:2.

April 17

Morning

Those who sacrifice thank-offerings honour me.

You were bought at a price
Let the word of Christ dwell in you richly as you teach and admonish one another with all wisdom, and as you sing psalms, hymns and spiritual songs with gratitude in your hearts to God. And whatever you do, whether in word or deed, do it all in the name of the Lord Jesus, giving thanks to God the Father through him.—You were bought at a price. Therefore honour God with your body.

Sacrifice of praise
You also, like living stones, are being built into a spiritual house to be a holy priesthood, offering spiritual sacrifices acceptable to God through Jesus Christ.—Through Jesus, therefore, let us continually offer to God a sacrifice of praise—the fruit of lips that confess his name.

My soul will boast in the LORD; let the afflicted hear and rejoice. Glorify the LORD with me; let us exalt his name together.

Psalm 50:23. Colossians 3:16–17. 1 Corinthians 6:20. 1 Peter 2:5.
Hebrews 13:15. Psalm 34:2–3.

Evening

'I have loved you with an everlasting love; I have drawn you with loving-kindness.'

'Ties of love'
'I led them with cords of human kindness, with ties of love.'—'But I, when I am lifted up from the earth, will draw all people to myself.'

'The Lamb of God!'
'Look, the Lamb of God!' . . . 'As Moses lifted up the snake in the desert, so the Son of Man must be lifted up, that everyone who believes in him may have eternal life.'

He first loved us
Whom have I in heaven but you? And being with you, I desire nothing on earth.—We love because he first loved us.

Jeremiah 31:3. Hosea 11:4. John 12:32; 1:36; 3:14–15. Psalm 73:25.
1 John 4:19.

Morning

'I will raise up for them a prophet like you from among their brothers.'

For there is one God and one mediator between God and human beings, Christ Jesus, himself human.

'Gentle and humble in heart'
'Take my yoke upon you and learn from me, for I am gentle and humble in heart, and you will find rest for your souls.'—Your attitude should be the same as that of Christ Jesus: Who, being in very nature God, did not consider equality with God something to be grasped, but made himself nothing, taking the very nature of a servant, being made in human likeness.

Moses was faithful as a servant in all God's house, testifying to what would be said in the future. But Christ is faithful as a son over God's house. And we are his house, if we hold on to our courage and the hope of which we boast.

Deuteronomy 18:18. 1 Timothy 2:5. Matthew 11:29. Philippians 2:5–7.
Hebrews 3:5–6.

Evening

Eternal encouragement.

Because by one sacrifice he has made perfect for ever those who are being made holy. . . . Therefore he is able to save completely those who come to God through him, because he always lives to intercede for them.—I know whom I have believed, and am convinced that he is able to guard what I have entrusted to him for that day.

Encourage each other
Who shall separate us from the love of Christ?—'For the Lamb at the centre of the throne will be their shepherd; he will lead them to springs of living water. And God will wipe away every tear from their eyes.'—And so we will be with the Lord for ever. Therefore encourage each other with these words.

For this is not your resting place.—For here we do not have an enduring city, but we are looking for the city that is to come.

2 Thessalonians 2:16. Hebrews 10:14; 7:25. 2 Timothy 1:12.
Romans 8:35. Revelation 7:17. 1 Thessalonians 4:17–18. Micah 2:10.
Hebrews 13:14.

April 19

Morning

The curtain of the temple was torn in two from top to bottom.

For Christ died for sins once for all, the righteous for the unrighteous, to bring you to God.

'I am the gate; whoever enters through me will be saved. He will come in and go out, and find pasture.' . . . 'No-one comes to the Father except through me.'

Members of God's household
For through him we both have access to the Father by one Spirit. Consequently, you are no longer foreigners and aliens, but fellow-citizens with God's people and members of God's household.—Therefore, brothers and sisters, since we have confidence to enter the Most Holy Place by the blood of Jesus, by a new and living way opened for us through the curtain, that is, his body.

> Matthew 27:51. 1 Peter 3:18. John 10:9; 14:6. Ephesians 2:18–19.
> Hebrews 10:19–20.

Evening

His word is in my heart like a burning fire, shut up in my bones. I am weary of holding it in; indeed, I cannot.

I am compelled to preach
Yet when I preach the gospel, I cannot boast, for I am compelled to preach. Woe to me if I do not preach the gospel!

Christ's love compels us
Then they called them in again and commanded them not to speak or teach at all in the name of Jesus. But Peter and John replied, 'Judge for yourselves whether it is right in God's sight to obey you rather than God. For we cannot help speaking about what we have seen and heard.'—For Christ's love compels us.

'Go home to your family'
'Go home to your family and tell them how much the Lord has done for you, and how he has had mercy on you.'

> Jeremiah 20:9. 1 Corinthians 9:16. Acts 4:18–20. 2 Corinthians 5:14.
> Mark 5:19.

Morning

Dear friends, I urge you, as aliens and strangers in the world, to abstain from sinful desires, which war against your soul.

We shall see him as he is
Dear friends, now we are children of God, and what we will be has not yet been made known. But we know that when he appears, we shall be like him, for we shall see him as he is. Everyone who has this hope in him purifies himself, just as he is pure.

Eager to do what is good
For the grace of God that brings salvation has appeared to all people. It teaches us to say 'No' to ungodliness and worldly passions, and to live self-controlled, upright and godly lives in this present age, while we wait for the blessed hope—the glorious appearing of our great God and Saviour, Jesus Christ, who gave himself for us to redeem us from all wickedness and to purify for himself a people that are his very own, eager to do what is good.

1 Peter 2:11. 1 John 3:2–3. Titus 2:11–14.

Evening

'Who are you, Lord?' 'I am Jesus.'

'It is I. Don't be afraid.'—'When you pass through the waters, I will be with you; and when you pass through the rivers, they will not sweep over you. When you walk through the fire, you will not be burned; the flames will not set you ablaze. For I am the LORD, your God, the Holy One of Israel, your Saviour.'

'God with us'
Even though I walk through the valley of the shadow of death, I will fear no evil, for you are with me; your rod and your staff, they comfort me. 'Immanuel'—which means, 'God with us.'
    'You are to give him the name Jesus, because he will save his people from their sins.'—My dear children, I write this to you so that you will not sin. But if anybody does sin, we have one who speaks to the Father in our defence— Jesus Christ, the Righteous One.—Who shall separate us from the love of Christ? Shall trouble or hardship or persecution or famine or nakedness or danger or sword?

Acts 26:15. Matthew 14:17. Isaiah 43:2–3. Psalm 23:4.
Matthew 1:23, 21. 1 John 2:1. Romans 8:35.

April 21

Morning

Stand firm in the Lord.

My feet have closely followed his steps; I have kept to his way without turning aside.

For the LORD loves the just and will not forsake his faithful ones. They will be protected for ever, . . . The LORD will keep you from all harm—he will watch over your life.

'But my righteous one will live by faith. And if he shrinks back, I will not be pleased with him.' But we are not of those who shrink back and are destroyed, but of those who believe and are saved.

Stand firm in the faith
'If you hold to my teaching, you are really my disciples.'—'But whoever stands firm to the end will be saved.'—Be on your guard; stand firm in the faith; be courageous; be strong.—Hold on to what you have, so that no-one will take your crown. . . . 'Those who overcome will, like them, be dressed in white. I will never blot out their names from the book of life.'

> Philippians 4:1. Job 23:11. Psalms 37:28; 121:7. Hebrews 10:38–39. John 8:31. Matthew 24:13. 1 Corinthians 16:13. Revelation 3:11, 5.

Evening

Enoch walked with God.

'Do two walk together unless they have agreed to do so?'

You who once were far away have been brought near through the blood of Christ.

We have now received reconciliation
For if, when we were God's enemies, we were reconciled to him through the death of his Son, how much more, having been reconciled, shall we be saved through his life! Not only is this so, but we also rejoice in God through our Lord Jesus Christ, through whom we have now received reconciliation.

And our fellowship is with the Father and with his Son, Jesus Christ.

May the grace of the Lord Jesus Christ, and the love of God, and the fellowship of the Holy Spirit be with you all.

> Genesis 5:22. Amos 3:3. Ephesians 2:13. Romans 5:10–11. 1 John 1:3.
> 2 Corinthians 13:14.

Morning

'God himself will provide the lamb for the burnt offering, my son.'

'If the offering is a burnt offering from the herd, he is to offer a male without defect. He must present it at the entrance to the Tent of Meeting so that it will be acceptable to the LORD. He is to lay his hand on the head of the burnt offering, and it will be accepted on his behalf to make atonement for him.'

Made holy
'Look, the Lamb of God, who takes away the sin of the world!'—We have been made holy through the sacrifice of the body of Jesus Christ once for all.—'A ransom for many.'

Sin for us
God made him who had no sin to be sin for us, so that in him we might become the righteousness of God.—To the praise of his glorious grace, which he has freely given us in the One he loves.

Genesis 22:8. Leviticus 1:3–4. John 1:29. Hebrews 10:10.
Matthew 20:28. 2 Corinthians 5:21. Ephesians 1:6.

Evening

For great is your love towards me; you have delivered my soul from the depths of the grave.

'Be afraid of the one who can destroy both soul and body in hell.'

I have called you by name
'Fear not, for I have redeemed you; I have called you by name; you are mine.' . . . 'I, even I, am the LORD, and apart from me there is no saviour.' . . . 'I, even I, am he who blots out your transgressions, for my own sake, and remembers your sins no more.'

Alive with Christ
God, who is rich in mercy, made us alive with Christ even when we were dead in transgressions—it is by grace you have been saved.
  'Salvation is found in no-one else, for there is no other name under heaven given to people by which we must be saved.'

Psalm 86:13. Matthew 10:28. Isaiah 43:11, 11, 25. Ephesians 2:4–5.
Acts 4:12.

April 23

Morning

But the LORD was my support.

The LORD is my rock, my fortress and my deliverer; my God is my rock, in whom I take refuge. He is my shield and the horn of my salvation, my stronghold.

The eternal God is your refuge
The angel of the LORD encamps around those who fear him, and he delivers them. . . . The righteous cry out, and the LORD hears them; he delivers them from all their troubles.—The eternal God is your refuge, and underneath are the everlasting arms.—So we say with confidence, 'The Lord is my helper; I will not be afraid. What can human beings do to me?'—For who is God besides the LORD? And who is the Rock except our God? It is God who arms me with strength.

But by the grace of God I am what I am.

> Psalms 18:18, 2; 34:7, 17. Deuteronomy 33:27. Hebrews 13:6.
> Psalm 18:31–32. 1 Corinthians 15:10.

Evening

We all, like sheep, have gone astray.

If we claim to be without sin, we deceive ourselves and the truth is not in us.— 'There is no-one righteous, not even one; there is no-one who understands, no-one who seeks God. All have turned away, they have together become worthless; there is no-one who does good, not even one.'

For you were like sheep going astray, but now you have returned to the Shepherd and Overseer of your souls.—I have strayed like a lost sheep. Seek your servant, for I have not forgotten your commandments.

'No-one can snatch them out of my hand'
He restores my soul. He guides me in paths of righteousness for his name's sake.—'My sheep listen to my voice; I know them, and they follow me. I give them eternal life, and they shall never perish; no-one can snatch them out of my hand.'

> Isaiah 53:6. 1 John 1:8. Romans 3:10–12. 1 Peter 2:25.
> Psalms 119:176; 23:3. John 10:27–28.

Morning

Trust in him at all times, O people; pour out your hearts to him, for God is our refuge.

But David found strength in the LORD his God.—'I have indeed seen the oppression of my people in Egypt. I have heard their groaning and have come down to set them free. Now come, I will send you back to Egypt.' . . . He led them out of Egypt and did wonders and miraculous signs in Egypt, at the Red Sea and for forty years in the desert.—Not one of all the LORD's good promises to the house of Israel failed; every one was fulfilled.

'My words will never pass away'
He who promised is faithful.—Does he speak and then not act? Does he promise and not fulfil?—'Heaven and earth will pass away, but my words will never pass away.'—'The grass withers and the flowers fall, but the word of our God stands for ever.'

Psalm 62:8. 1 Samuel 30:6. Acts 7:34, 36. Joshua 21:45. Hebrews 10:23.
Numbers 23:19. Matthew 24:35. Isaiah 40:8.

Evening

The eyes of all look to you.

He himself gives all life and breath and everything else.—The LORD is good to all; he has compassion on all he has made.—'Look at the birds of the air; they do not sow or reap or store away in barns, and yet your heavenly Father feeds them.'

The same Lord is Lord of all and richly blesses all who call on him.

Our eyes look to the LORD
I lift up my eyes to the hills—where does my help come from? . . . As the eyes of slaves look to the hand of their master, as the eyes of a maid look to the hand of her mistress, so our eyes look to the LORD our God.

But if we hope for what we do not yet have, we wait for it patiently.

Psalm 145:15. Acts 17:25. Psalm 145:9. Matthew 6:26. Romans 10:12.
Psalms 121:1; 123:2. Romans 8:25.

April 25

Morning

'You are to give him the name Jesus, because he will save his people from their sins.'

He appeared so that he might take away our sins.—That we might die to sins and live for righteousness.—He is able to save completely those who come to God through him.

But he was pierced for our transgressions, he was crushed for our iniquities; the punishment that brought us peace was upon him, and by his wounds we are healed. We all, like sheep, have gone astray; . . . The LORD has laid on him the iniquity of us all.

The sacrifice of himself
'The Christ will suffer . . . and repentance and forgiveness of sins will be preached in his name to all nations.'—He has appeared once for all at the end of the ages to do away with sin by the sacrifice of himself.

God exalted him to his own right hand as Prince and Saviour that he might give repentance.—Your sins have been forgiven on account of his name.

Matthew 1:21. 1 John 3:5. 1 Peter 2:24. Hebrews 7:25. Isaiah 53:5–6.
Luke 24:46–47. Hebrews 9:26. Acts 5:31. 1 John 2:12.

Evening

Our Lord Jesus Christ, . . . that though he was rich, yet for your sakes . . . became poor, so that you through his poverty might become rich.

Made himself nothing
The Son is the radiance of God's glory and the exact representation of his being, sustaining all things by his powerful word. After he had provided purification for sins, he sat down at the right hand of the Majesty in heaven. So he became as much superior to the angels as the name he has inherited is superior to theirs.—Who, being in the very nature God, did not consider equality with God something to be grasped, but made himself nothing.

'Foxes have holes and birds of the air have nests, but the Son of Man has no place to lay his head.'

All things are yours, whether Paul or Apollos or Cephas or the world or life or death or the present or the future—all are yours, and you are of Christ, and Christ is of God.

2 Corinthians 8:9. Hebrews 1:3–4; Philippians 2:6–7. Matthew 8:20.
1 Corinthians 3:21–23.

Morning

Underneath are the everlasting arms.

But when he [Peter] saw the wind, he was afraid and, beginning to sink, cried out, 'Lord, save me!' Immediately Jesus reached out his hand and caught him. 'You of little faith,' he said, 'why did you doubt?'

The LORD delights in the way of the man whose steps he has made firm; though he stumble, he will not fall, for the LORD upholds him with his hand.

He cares for you
'Let the beloved of the LORD rest secure in him, for he shields him all day long, and the one the LORD loves rests between his shoulders.'—Cast all your anxiety on him because he cares for you.

'They shall never perish; no-one can snatch them out of my hand. . . . My Father, who has given them to me, is greater than all.'

Deuteronomy 33:27. Matthew 14:30–31. Psalm 37:23–24.
Deuteronomy 33:12. 1 Peter 5:7. John 10:28–29.

Evening

Be shepherds of the church of God, which he bought with his own blood.

A radiant church
Christ loved the church and gave himself up for her to make her holy, cleansing her by the washing with water through the word, and to present her to himself as a radiant church, without stain or wrinkle or any other blemish, but holy and blameless.

Righteousness from God
A great and wondrous sign appeared in heaven; a woman clothed with the sun.—'For the wedding of the Lamb has come, and his bride has made herself ready. Fine linen, bright and clean, was given her to wear.' (Fine linen stands for the righteous acts of the saints.)—This righteousness from God comes through faith in Jesus Christ to all who believe.

'I have given them the glory that you gave me.'

Acts 20:28. Ephesians 5:25–27. Revelation 12:1; 19:7–8. Romans 3:22.
John 17:22.

April 27

Morning

Brothers and sisters . . . the time is short.

For as in Adam all die, so in Christ all will be made alive. . . . 'Death has been swallowed up in victory.'—If we live, we live to the Lord; and if we die, we die to the Lord. So, whether we live or die, we belong to the Lord.—To live is Christ and to die is gain.

The night is nearly over
So do not throw away your confidence; it will be richly rewarded. You need to persevere so that when you have done the will of God, you will receive what he has promised. For in just a very little while, 'He who is coming will come and will not delay.'—The night is nearly over; the day is almost here. So let us put aside the deeds of darkness and put on the armour of light.—The end of all things is near. Therefore be clear minded and self-controlled so that you can pray.

> 1 Corinthians 7:29. 1 Corinthians 15:22, 54. Romans 14:8.
> Philippians 1:21. Hebrews 10:35–37. Romans 13:12. 1 Peter 4:7.

Evening

A new name.

The disciples were first called Christians at Antioch.—'Everyone who confesses the name of the Lord must turn away from wickedness.'

May I never boast except in the cross of our Lord Jesus Christ, through which the world has been crucified to me, and I to the world. Neither circumcision nor uncircumcision means anything; what counts is a new creation.

You are light in the Lord
Be imitators of God, therefore, as dearly loved children and live a life of love, just as Christ loved us and gave himself up for us as a fragrant offering and sacrifice to God. But among you there must not be even a hint of sexual immorality, or of any kind of impurity, or of greed, because these are improper for God's holy people. . . . For you were once darkness, but now you are light in the Lord. Live as children of light.

> Revelation 2:17. Acts 11:26. 2 Timothy 2:19. Galatians 6:14–15.
> Ephesians 5:1–3, 8.

Morning

'Look, the Lamb of God.'

Like a lamb to the slaughter
He was oppressed and afflicted, yet he did not open his mouth, he was led like a lamb to the slaughter, and as a sheep before her shearers is silent, so he did not open his mouth.

A lamb without blemish
For you know that it was not with perishable things such as silver or gold that you were redeemed from the empty way of life handed down to you from your forefathers, but with the precious blood of Christ, a lamb without blemish or defect.

'Worthy is the Lamb'
'Worthy is the Lamb, who was slain, to receive power and wealth and wisdom and strength and honour and glory and praise!'

John 1:29. Isaiah 53:4–7. 1 Peter 1:18–19. Revelation 5:12.

Evening

But as for me, I shall always have hope; I will praise you more and more.

Not that I have already obtained all this, or have already been made perfect.— The path of the righteous is like the first gleam of dawn, shining ever brighter till the full light of day.

I will call on him as long as I live
I love the LORD, for he heard my voice, he heard my cry for mercy. Because he turned his ear to me, I will call on him as long as I live. . . . I will extol the LORD at all times; his praise will always be on my lips.

Praise awaits you, O God, in Zion.—Day and night they never stop saying: 'Holy, holy, holy is the Lord God Almighty.'—Those who sacrifice thank-offerings honour me.—Be joyful always; pray continually; give thanks in all circumstances, for this is God's will for you in Christ Jesus.

Psalm 71:14. Philippians 3:12. Proverbs 4:18.
Psalms 116:1–2; 34:1; 65:1. Revelation 4:8. Psalm 50:23.
1 Thessalonians 5:16–18.

April 29

Morning

Consider what great things he has done for you.

Remember how the LORD your God led you all the way in the desert these forty years, to humble you and to test you in order to know what was in your heart, whether or not you would keep his commands.

In faithfulness you have afflicted me
I know, O LORD, that your laws are righteous, and in faithfulness you have afflicted me. . . . It was good for me to be afflicted so that I might learn your decrees. . . . Before I was afflicted I went astray, but now I obey your word. . . . The LORD has chastened me severely, but he has not given me over to death . . . He does not treat us as our sins deserve or repay us according to our iniquities. For as high as the heavens are above the earth, so great is his love for those who fear him.

1 Samuel 12:24. Deuteronomy 8:2.
Psalms 119:75, 71, 67; 118:18; 103:10–11.

Evening

Blessed hope—the glorious appearing of our great God and Saviour, Jesus Christ.

We have this hope as an anchor for the soul, firm and secure. It enters the inner sanctuary behind the curtain, where Jesus, who went before us, has entered on our behalf.

We know that the whole creation has been groaning as in the pains of childbirth right up to the present time. Not only so, but we ourselves, who have the firstfruits of the Spirit, groan inwardly as we wait eagerly for our adoption as sons, the redemption of our bodies.

We shall see him as he is
Dear friends, now we are children of God, and what we will be has not yet been made known. But we know that when he appears, we shall be like him, for we shall see him as he is.—When Christ, who is your life, appears, then you also will appear with him in glory.

'Yes, I am coming soon.' Amen. Come, Lord Jesus.

Titus 2:13. Hebrews 6:19–20. Romans 8:22–23. 1 John 3:2.
Colossians 3:4. Revelation 22:20.

Morning

But if anyone obeys his word, God's love is truly made complete in him.

May the God of peace, who through the blood of the eternal covenant brought back from the dead our Lord Jesus, that great Shepherd of the sheep, equip you with everything good for doing his will, and may he work in us what is pleasing to him, through Jesus Christ, to whom be glory for ever and ever. Amen.

We know that we have come to know him if we obey his commands.— 'Those who love me will obey my teaching. My Father will love them, and we will come to them and make our home with them.'

Confidence on the day of judgment
Dear children, do not let anyone lead you astray. The one who does what is right is righteous, just as he is righteous. . . . Love is made complete among us so that we will have confidence on the day of judgment, because in this world we are like him.

1 John 2:5. Hebrews 13:20–21. 1 John 2:3. John 14:23. 1 John 3:7; 4:17.

Evening

Those who are patient have great understanding.

'The LORD, the LORD, the compassionate and gracious God, slow to anger, abounding in love and faithfulness.'—The Lord is not slow in keeping his promise, as some understand slowness. He is patient with you, not wanting anyone to perish, but everyone to come to repentance.

You should follow in his steps
Be imitators of God, therefore, as dearly loved children.—But the fruit of the Spirit is love, joy, peace, patience, kindness, goodness, faithfulness, gentleness and self-control. Against such things there is no law.—For it is commendable if you bear up under the pain of unjust suffering because you are conscious of God. But how is it to your credit if you receive a beating for doing wrong and endure it? But if you suffer for doing good and you endure it, this is commendable before God. To this you were called, because Christ suffered for you, leaving you an example, that you should follow in his steps.

'In your anger do not sin.'

Proverbs 14:29. Exodus 34:6. 2 Peter 3:9. Ephesians 5:1.
Galatians 5:22–23. 1 Peter 2:19–21. Ephesians 4:26.

May 1

Morning

The fruit of the Spirit is peace.

The mind controlled by the Spirit is life and peace.

God has called us to live in peace.—'Peace I leave with you; my peace I give you. I do not give to you as the world gives. Do not let your heart be troubled, and do not be afraid.'—May the God of hope fill you with all joy and peace as you trust in him, so that you may overflow with hope by the power of the Holy Spirit.

I know whom I have believed, and am convinced that he is able to guard what I have entrusted to him for that day.

Quietness and confidence
The fruit of righteousness will be peace; the effect of righteousness will be quietness and confidence for ever. My people will live in peaceful dwelling-places, in secure homes, in undisturbed places of rest.

Galatians 5:22. Romans 8:6. 1 Corinthians 7:15. John 14:27.
Romans 15:13. 2 Timothy 1:12. Isaiah 32:17–18.

Evening

'The LORD is there.'

Now the dwelling of God with human beings, and he will live with them. They will be his people, and God himself will be with them and be their God.

The Lord God Almighty and the Lamb are its temple. The city does not need the sun or the moon to shine on it, for the glory of God gives it light, and the Lamb is its lamp.

When I awake, I shall be satisfied with seeing your likeness. . . . Whom have I in heaven but you? And being with you, I desire nothing on earth.

'I will live among you'
'Shout and be glad, O Daughter of Zion. For I am coming, and I will live among you,' declares the LORD.—No longer will there be any curse. The throne of God and of the Lamb will be in the city, and his servants will serve him.

Ezekiel 48:35. Revelation 21:3, 22–23. Psalms 17:15; 73:25.
Zechariah 2:10. Revelation 22:3.

Morning

'Surely the Lᴏʀᴅ is in this place, and I was not aware of it.'

'For where two or three come together in my name, there am I with them.'
. . . 'I will be with you always, to the very end of the age.'

'Do not I fill heaven and earth?'
'My Presence will go with you, and I will give you rest.'—Where can I go from
your Spirit? Where can I flee from your presence? If I go up to the heavens,
you are there; if I make my bed in the depths, you are there.—'Am I only a
God nearby,' declares the Lᴏʀᴅ, 'and not a God far away? Can anyone hide in
secret places so that I cannot see him?' declares the Lᴏʀᴅ. 'Do not I fill heaven
and earth?' declares the Lᴏʀᴅ.

'The heavens, even the highest heaven, cannot contain you. How much less
this temple I have built!'

> Genesis 28:16. Matthew 18:20; 28:20. Exodus 33:14. Psalm 139:7–8.
> Jeremiah 23:23–24. 1 Kings 8:27.

Evening

Keep yourselves from idols.

My son, give me your heart.—Set your minds on things above, not on earthly
things.

The love of money
Put to death, therefore, whatever belongs to your earthly nature: sexual
immorality, impurity, lust, evil desires and greed, which is idolatry.—Those
who want to get rich fall into temptation and a trap and into many foolish and
harmful desires that plunge people into ruin and destruction. For the love of
money is a root of all kinds of evil. Some people, eager for money, have
wandered from the faith and pierced themselves with many griefs.

Though your riches increase, do not set your heart on them.

'For where your treasure is, there your heart will be also.'—'The Lᴏʀᴅ looks
at the heart.'

> 1 John 5:21. Proverbs 23:26. Colossians 3:2, 5. 1 Timothy 6:9–11.
> Psalm 62:10. Matthew 6:21. 1 Samuel 16:7.

May 3

Morning

'Be perfect, therefore, as your heavenly Father is perfect.'

'I am God Almighty; walk before me and be blameless.'—'You are to be holy to me because I, the LORD, am holy, and I have set you apart from the nations to be my own.'

You were bought at a price. Therefore honour God with your body.—Make every effort to be found spotless, blameless and at peace with him.

Blameless
Blessed are they whose ways are blameless, who walk according to the law of the LORD.—But those who look intently into the perfect law that gives freedom, and continue to do this, not forgetting what they have heard, but doing it—they will be blessed in what they do.—Search me, O God, and know my heart; test me and know my anxious thoughts. See if there is any offensive way in me, and lead me in the way everlasting.

> Matthew 5:48. Genesis 17:1. Leviticus 20:26. 1 Corinthians 6:20.
> 2 Peter 3:14. Psalm 119:1. James 1:25. Psalm 139:23–24.

Evening

Perfecting holiness out of reverence for God.

Since we have these promises, dear friends, let us purify ourselves from everything that contaminates body and spirit.—Surely you desire truth in the inner parts; you teach me wisdom in the inmost place.—It teaches us to say 'No' to ungodliness and worldly passions, and to live self-controlled, upright and godly lives in this present age.—'Let your light shine before others, that they may see your good deeds and praise your Father in heaven.'

He is pure
All who have this hope in them purify themselves, just as he is pure.—Now it is God who has made us for this very purpose and has given us the Spirit.—To prepare God's people for works of service, so that the body of Christ may be built up until we all reach unity in the faith and in the knowledge of the Son of God and become mature, attaining to the whole measure of the fulness of Christ.

> 2 Corinthians 7:1c; 7:1a–b. Psalm 51:6. Titus 2:12. Matthew 5:16.
> 1 John 3:3. 2 Corinthians 5:5. Ephesians 4:12–13.

Morning

Surely the arm of the LORD is not too short to save, nor his ear too dull to hear.

When I called, you answered me; you made me bold and stout-hearted. 'Nothing is too hard for you.'

Do not hide your face from me, do not turn your servant away in anger; you have been my helper. Do not reject me or forsake me, O God my Saviour . . . But you, O LORD, be not far off; O my Strength, come quickly to help me.

'Nothing is too hard for you'
'Ah, Sovereign LORD, you have made the heavens and the earth by your great power and outstretched arm. Nothing is too hard for you.'—He has delivered us from such a deadly peril, and he will deliver us.—And will not God bring about justice for his chosen ones, who cry out to him day and night? Will he keep putting them off? I tell you, he will see that they get justice, and quickly.

Isaiah 59:1. Psalms 138:3; 27:9; 22:19. Jeremiah 32:17.
2 Corinthians 1:10. Luke 18:7–8.

Evening

'I have brought you glory on earth.'

'My food,' said Jesus, 'is to do the will of him who sent me and to finish his work.' . . . 'As long as it is day, we must do the work of him who sent me. Night is coming, when no-one can work.'

'Didn't you know I had to be in my Father's house?' But they did not understand what he was saying to them.

All spoke well of him
And Jesus grew in wisdom and stature, and in favour with God and people . . . 'You are my Son, whom I love; with you I am well pleased.' . . . All spoke well of him and were amazed at the gracious words that came from his lips.

'You are worthy to take the scroll and to open its seals, because you were slain, and with your blood you purchased for God members of every tribe and language and people and nation.'

John 17:4; 4:34; 9:4. Luke 2:49–50, 52; 3:22; 4:22. Revelation 5:9–10.

May 5

Morning

'So do not worry, saying, "What shall we eat?" or "What shall we drink?" or "What shall we wear?" . . . Your heavenly Father knows that you need them.'

Fear the LORD, you his saints, for those who fear him lack nothing. The lions may grow weak and hungry, but those who seek the LORD lack no good thing . . . No good thing does he withhold from those whose walk is blameless. O LORD Almighty, blessed are those who trust in you.

I would like you to be free from concern.—Do not be anxious about anything, but in everything, by prayer and petition, with thanksgiving, present your requests to God.

'Two sparrows'
'Are not two sparrows sold for a penny? Yet not one of them will fall to the ground apart from the will of your Father. And even the very hairs of your head are all numbered. So don't be afraid; you are worth more than many sparrows.'

> Matthew 6:31–32. Psalms 34:9–10; 84:11–12; 1 Corinthians 7:32.
> Philippians 4:6. Matthew 10:29–31.

Evening

He spread out a cloud as a covering, and a fire to give light at night.

A refuge and hiding place
The sun will not harm you by day, nor the moon by night.—It will be a shelter and shade from the heat of the day, and a refuge and hiding-place from the storm and rain.

By day . . . by night
The LORD watches over you.—The LORD is your shade at your right hand; . . . The LORD will watch over your coming and going both now and for evermore.—By day the LORD went ahead of them in a pillar of cloud to guide them on their way and by night in a pillar of fire to give them light, so that they could travel by day or night. Neither the pillar of cloud by day nor the pillar of fire by night left its place in front of the people.

Jesus Christ is the same yesterday and today and for ever.

> Psalms 105:39; 121:6. Isaiah 4:6. Psalm 121:5, 8. Exodus 13:21–22.
> Hebrews 13:8.

Morning

Love and faithfulness meet together; righteousness and peace kiss each other.

A righteous God and a Saviour.

It pleased the LORD for the sake of his righteousness to make his law great and glorious.—God was reconciling the world to himself in Christ, not counting people's sins against them.

To demonstrate his justice

God presented him as a sacrifice of atonement, through faith in his blood. He did this to demonstrate his justice, because in his forbearance he had left the sins committed beforehand unpunished—he did it to demonstrate his justice at the present time, so as to be just and the one who justifies those who have faith in Jesus.

Who will bring any charge against those whom God has chosen? It is God who justifies. Who then can condemn? Christ Jesus . . . However, to the one who does not work but trusts God who justifies the wicked, that person's faith is credited as righteousness.

Psalm 85:10. Isaiah 45:21; 42:21. 2 Corinthians 5:19.
Romans 3:25–26; 8:33–34; 4:5.

Evening

'How are the dead raised? With what kind of body will they come?'

Dear friends, now we are children of God, and what we will be has not yet been made known. But we know that when he appears, we shall be like him, for we shall see him as he is.—And just as we have borne the likeness of the earthly, so shall we bear the likeness of the heavenly.

Like his glorious body

The Lord Jesus Christ, who, by the power that enables him to bring everything under his control, will transform our lowly bodies so that they will be like his glorious body.

Life to your mortal bodies

And if the Spirit of him who raised Jesus from the dead is living in you, he who raised Christ from the dead will also give life to your mortal bodies through his Spirit, who lives in you.

1 Corinthians 15:35. 1 John 3:2. 1 Corinthians 15:49.
Philippians 3:20–21. Romans 8:11.

May 7

Morning

'You will hear of wars and rumours of wars, but see to it that you are not alarmed.'

God is our refuge and strength, an ever present help in trouble. Therefore, we will not fear, though the earth give way and the mountains fall into the heart of the sea, though its waters roar and foam and the mountains quake with their surging.—I will take refuge in the shadows of your wings until the disaster has passed.

Their hearts are steadfast
Your life is now hidden with Christ in God.—They will have no fear of bad news; their hearts are steadfast, trusting in the LORD.

'In me you may have peace'
'I have told you these things, so that in me you may have peace. In this world you will have trouble. But take heart! I have overcome the world.'

> Matthew 24:6. Psalm 46:1–3. Psalm 57:1. Colossians 3:3.
> Psalm 112:7. John 16:33.

Evening

Surely he took up our infirmities and carried our sorrows, yet we considered him stricken by God, smitten by him, and afflicted.

'This man was handed over to you by God's set purpose and foreknowledge; and you, with the help of wicked people, put him to death by nailing him to the cross.'—Then they spat in his face and struck him with their fists. Others slapped him and said, 'Prophesy to us, Christ. Who hit you?'

Decided beforehand
In the same way the chief priests, the teachers of the law and the elders mocked him. 'He saved others,' they said, 'but he can't save himself! He's the king of Israel! Let him come down now from the cross, and we will believe in him.'— 'Indeed Herod and Pontius Pilate met together with the Gentiles and the people of Israel in this city to conspire against your holy servant Jesus, whom you anointed. They did what your power and will had decided beforehand should happen.'

> Isaiah 53:4. Acts 2:23. Matthew 26:67–68; 27:41–42. Acts 4:27–28.

Morning

Yet it was the Lord's will to crush him and cause him to suffer.

'Now my heart is troubled, and what shall I say? "Father, save me from this hour"? No, it was for this very reason I came to this hour. Father, glorify your name!' Then a voice came from heaven. 'I have glorified it, and will glorify it again.'

'I lay down my life'
And being found in appearance as a human being, he humbled himself and became obedient to death—even death on a cross!—'The reason my Father loves me is that I lay down my life—only to take it up again.' . . . 'For I have come down from heaven not to do my will but to do the will of him who sent me.' . . . 'Shall I not drink the cup the Father has given me?'

'The one who sent me is with me; he has not left me alone, for I always do what pleases him.'—'This is my Son, whom I love; with him I am well pleased.'—'My chosen one in whom I delight.'

Isaiah 53:10. John 12:27–28. Philippians 2:8. John 10:17; 6:38; 18:11;
8:29. Matthew 3:17. Isaiah 42:1.

Evening

You who call on the Lord, give yourselves no rest.

'The sons of Aaron, the priests, are to blow the trumpets. This is to be a lasting ordinance for you and the generations to come. When you go into battle in your own land against an enemy who is oppressing you, sound a blast on the trumpets. Then you will be remembered by the Lord and rescued from your enemies.'

Their prayer reached heaven
God heard them, for their prayer reached heaven, his holy dwelling-place.—The eyes of the Lord are on the righteous and his ears are attentive to their cry.—Pray for each other so that you may be healed. The prayer of a righteous person is powerful and effective.

Come, Lord Jesus.—O my God, do not delay.—We are looking forward to a new heaven and a new earth, the home of righteousness.

Isaiah 62:6. Numbers 10:8–9. 2 Chronicles 30:27. Psalm 34:15.
James 5:16. Revelation 22:20. Psalm 40:17. 2 Peter 3:13.

May 9

Morning

Now faith is being sure of what we hope for and certain of what we do not see.

If only for this life we have hope in Christ, we are to be pitied more than all people.

God's possession
'No eye has seen, no ear has heard, no mind has conceived what God has prepared for those who love him.'—but God has revealed it to us by his Spirit.—Having believed, you were marked in him with a seal, the promised Holy Spirit, who is a deposit guaranteeing our inheritance until the redemption of those who are God's possession.

Then Jesus told him, 'Because you have seen me, you have believed; blessed are those who have not seen and yet have believed.'

We live by faith, not by sight.—So do not throw away your confidence; it will be richly rewarded.

Hebrews 11:1. 1 Corinthians 15:19; 2:9–10. Ephesians 1:13–14.
John 20:29. 2 Corinthians 5:7; Hebrews 10:35.

Evening

'It is I; don't be afraid.'

When I saw him, I fell at his feet as though dead. Then he placed his right hand on me and said: 'Do not be afraid. I am the First and the Last. I am the Living One; I was dead, and behold I am alive for ever and ever! And I hold the keys of death and Hades.'—'I, even I, am he who blots out your transgressions, for my own sake, and remembers your sins no more.'

'Your guilt is taken away'
'Woe to me!' I cried. 'I am ruined! For I am a man of unclean lips, and I live among a people of unclean lips, and my eyes have seen the King, the LORD Almighty.' Then one of the seraphs flew to me with a live coal in his hand, which he had taken with tongs from the altar. With it he touched my mouth and said, 'See, this has touched your lips; your guilt is taken away and your sin is atoned for.'

But if anybody does sin, we have one who speaks to the Father in our defence—Jesus Christ, the Righteous One.

John 6:20. Revelation 1:17–18. Isaiah 43:25; 6:5–7. I John 2:1.

Morning

The reason the Son of God appeared was to destroy the devil's work.

For our struggle is not against flesh and blood, but against the rulers, against the authorities, against the powers of this dark world and against the spiritual forces of evil in the heavenly realms.—And having disarmed the powers and authorities, he made a public spectacle of them, triumphing over them by the cross.

They overcame
Then I heard a loud voice in heaven say: 'Now have come the salvation and the power and the kingdom of our God, and the authority of his Christ. For the accuser of our brothers, who accuses them before our God day and night, has been hurled down. They overcame him by the blood of the Lamb and by the word of their testimony; they did not love their lives so much as to shrink from death.'

But thanks be to God! He gives us the victory through our Lord Jesus Christ.

1 John 3:8. Ephesians 6:12. Colossians 2:15. Revelation 12:10–11.
1 Corinthians 15:57.

Evening

If only for this life we have hope in Christ, we are to be pitied more than all people.

We eagerly await a Saviour
For here we do not have an enduring city, but we are looking for the city that is to come.—I the LORD do not change.—But our citizenship is in heaven. And we eagerly await a Saviour from there, the Lord Jesus Christ, who, by the power that enables him to bring everything under his control, will transform our lowly bodies so that they will be like his glorious body.—For the creation was subjected to frustration, not by its own choice, but by the will of the one who subjected it, in hope.

'Holy, holy, holy'
Jesus Christ is the same yesterday and today and for ever.—'Holy, holy, holy is the Lord God Almighty, who was, and is, and is to come.'

1 Corinthians 15:19. Hebrews 13:14. Malachi 3:6. Philippians 3:20–21.
Romans 8:20. Hebrews 13:8. Revelation 4:8.

May 11

Morning

Come back to your senses as you ought, and stop sinning.

You are all children of the light and children of the day. We do not belong to the night or to the darkness. So then, let us not be like others, who are asleep, but let us be alert and self-controlled.

Put aside the deeds of darkness
The hour has come for you to wake up from your slumber, because our salvation is nearer now than when we first believed. The night is nearly over; the day is almost here. So let us put aside the deeds of darkness and put on the armour of light.—Therefore put on the full armour of God, so that when the day of evil comes, you may be able to stand your ground, and after you have done everything, to stand.

And now, dear children, continue in him, so that when he appears we may be confident and unashamed before him at his coming. If you know that he is righteous, you know that everyone who does what is right has been born of him.

1 Corinthians 15:34. 1 Thessalonians 5:5–6. Romans 13:11–12.
Ephesians 6:13. 1 John 2:28–29.

Evening

'My sheep listen to my voice.'

'I stand at the door and knock'
'Here I am! I stand at the door and knock. If anyone hears my voice and opens the door, I will eat with them, and they with me.'

Zacchaeus welcomed him gladly
'Speak, for your servant is listening.'—When Jesus reached the spot, he looked up and said to him, 'Zacchaeus, come down immediately. I must stay at your house today.' So he came down at once and welcomed him gladly.

He promises peace
I will listen to what God the LORD will say; he promises peace to his people, his saints—but let them not return to folly.

John 10:27. Revelation 3:20. 1 Samuel 3:10. Luke 19:5–6. Psalm 85:8.

Morning

Dear friends, let us love one another, for love comes from God. Everyone who loves has been born of God and knows God.

God has poured out his love into our hearts by the Holy Spirit, whom he has given us. . . . For you did not receive a spirit that makes you a slave again to fear, but you received the Spirit of adoption. And by him we cry, *'Abba, Father.'* The Spirit himself testifies with our spirit that we are God's children.

Incomparable riches
This is how God showed his love among us. He sent his one and only Son into the world that we might live through him.—In him we have redemption through his blood, the forgiveness of sins, in accordance with the riches of God's grace. . . . In order that in the coming ages he might show the incomparable riches of his grace, expressed in his kindness to us in Christ Jesus.

1 John 3:7. Romans 5:5; 8:15–16. 1 John 4:9. Ephesians 1:7; 2:7.

Evening

Scorn has broken my heart.

'Isn't this the carpenter's son?'—'Nazareth! Can anything good come from there?' . . . 'Aren't we right in saying that you are a Samaritan and demon-possessed?'—'It is by the prince of demons that he drives out demons.'—'We know this man is a sinner.' . . . 'No, he deceives the people.'—'This fellow is blaspheming!' . . . 'Here is a glutton and a drunkard, a friend of tax collectors and "sinners".'

Insulted because of the name of Christ
'It is enough for the student to be like his teacher, and the servant like his master.'—'He committed no sin, and no deceit was found in his mouth.' When they hurled their insults at him, he did not retaliate; when he suffered, he made no threats. Instead, he entrusted himself to him who judges justly.—If you are insulted because of the name of Christ, you are blessed, for the Spirit of glory and of God rests on you.

Psalm 69:20. Matthew 13:55. John 1:46; 8:48. Matthew 9:34.
John 9:24; 7:12. Matthew 9:3; 11:19; 10:25. 1 Peter 2:22–23; 4:14.

May 13

Morning

I want men everywhere to lift up holy hands in prayer, without anger or disputing.

'God is spirit, and his worshippers must worship in spirit and in truth.'—Then you will call, and the LORD will answer; you will cry for help, and he will say: Here am I.—'And when you stand praying, if you hold anything against anyone, forgive.'

He must believe and not doubt
Without faith it is impossible to please God, because anyone who comes to him must believe that he exists and that he rewards those who earnestly seek him.—But when you ask, you must believe and not doubt, because the one who doubts is like a wave of the sea, blown and tossed by the wind. Those who doubt should not think they will receive anything from the LORD.

If I had cherished sin in my heart, the Lord would not have listened.

1 Timothy 2:8. John 4:24. Isaiah 58:9. Mark 11:25. Hebrews 11:6.
James 1:6–7. Psalm 66:18.

Evening

Hear my cry, O God; listen to my prayer. From the ends of the earth I call to you.

But he said to me, 'My grace is sufficient for you, for my power is made perfect in weakness.' Therefore I will boast all the more gladly about my weaknesses, so that Christ's power may rest on me. That is why, for Christ's sake, I delight in weaknesses, in insults, in hardships, in persecutions, in difficulties. For when I am weak, then I am strong.

According to his glorious might
But when he saw the wind, he was afraid and, beginning to sink, cried out, 'Lord save me!' Immediately Jesus reached out his hand and caught him. 'You of little faith,' he said, 'why did you doubt?'—If you falter in times of trouble, how small is your strength!—He gives strength to the weary and increases the power of the weak.—Being strengthened with all power according to his glorious might.

Psalm 61:1–2. 2 Corinthians 12:9–10. Matthew 14:30–31.
Proverbs 24:10. Isaiah 40:29. Colossians 1:11.

Morning

The fellowship of sharing in his sufferings.

It is enough for the students to be like their teachers, and the servants like their masters.

'In this world you will have trouble . . . As it is, you do not belong to the world, but I have chosen you out of the world. That is why the world hates you.'

I looked for sympathy, but there was none.—At my first defence, no-one came to my support, but everyone deserted me.

Let us fix our eyes on Jesus
'Foxes have holes and birds of the air have nests, but the Son of Man has no place to lay his head.'—For here we do not have an enduring city, but we are looking for the city that is to come. . . . Let us run with perseverance the race marked out for us. Let us fix our eyes on Jesus, the author and perfecter of our faith, who for the joy set before him endured the cross, scorning its shame, and sat down at the right hand of the throne of God.

Philippians 3:10. Matthew 10:25. John 16:33; 15:19. Psalm 69:20.
2 Timothy 4:16. Matthew 8:20. Hebrews 13:14; 12:1–2.

Evening

They overcame him by the blood of the Lamb.

It is the blood that makes atonement for one's life.—'I am the LORD. The blood will be a sign for you on the houses where you are; and when I see the blood, I will pass over you.'

White robes
Therefore, there is now no condemnation for those who are in Christ Jesus.—'These in white robes—who are they, and where did they come from?' I answered, 'Sir, you know.' And he said, 'These are they who have come out of the great tribulation; they have washed their robes and made them white in the blood of the Lamb.'

To him who loves us and has freed us from our sins by his blood, and has made us to be a kingdom and priests to serve his God and Father—to him be glory and power for ever and ever! Amen.

Revelation 12:11. Leviticus 17:11. Exodus 12:12–13.
Romans 8:1. Revelation 7:13–14; 1:5–6.

Morning

'He will wipe every tear from their eyes. There will be no more death or mourning or crying or pain, for the old order of things has passed away.'

He will swallow up death for ever. The Sovereign LORD will wipe away the tears from all faces; he will remove the disgrace of his people from all the earth. The LORD has spoken—Your sun will never set again, and your moon will wane no more; the LORD will be your everlasting light, and your days of sorrow will end.

'Death has been swallowed up in victory'
'I will ransom them from the power of the grave; I will redeem them from death. Where, O death, are your plagues? Where, O grave, is your destruction?'—The last enemy to be destroyed is death. . . . Then the saying that is written will come true: 'Death has been swallowed up in victory.'
    What is unseen is eternal.

> Revelation 21:4. Isaiah 25:8; 60:20. Hosea 13:14. 1 Corinthians 15:26, 54. 2 Corinthians 4:18.

Evening

God raised us up with Christ.

'Do not be afraid . . . I am the Living One.'—'Father, I want those you have given me to be with me where I am.'
    Since the children have flesh and blood, he too shared in their humanity so that by his death he might destroy him who holds the power of death—that is, the devil—and free those who all their lives were held in slavery by their fear of death.

The perishable clothed with the imperishable
For the perishable must clothe itself with the imperishable, and the mortal with immortality. When the perishable has been clothed with the imperishable, and the mortal with immortality, then the saying that is written will come true: 'Death has been swallowed up in victory.'

> Ephesians 2:6. Revelation 1:17–18. John 17:24. Hebrews 2:14–15. 1 Corinthians 15:53–54.

Morning

A servant of Christ Jesus.

'You call me, "Teacher" and "Lord", and rightly so, for that is what I am.' . . .
'Whoever serves me must follow me; and where I am, my servant also will be.
My Father will honour the one who serves me.'—'Take my yoke upon you and
learn from me, for I am gentle and humble in heart, and you will find rest for
your souls. For my yoke is easy and my burden is light.'

No longer slaves, but God's children
'I no longer call you servants, because a servant does not know his master's
business. Instead, I have called you friends, for everything that I learned from
my Father I have made known to you.'—So you are no longer slaves, but
God's children.

Called to be free
Stand firm, then, and do not let yourselves be burdened again by a yoke of
slavery. . . . You, my brothers and sisters, were called to be free. But do not use
your freedom to indulge the sinful nature.

Romans 1:1. John 13:13; 12:26. Matthew 11:29–30. John 15:15.
Galatians 4:7; 5:1, 13.

Evening

I will praise the LORD, who counsels me.

And he will be called Wonderful Counsellor, Mighty God.—'Counsel and
sound judgment are mine; I have understanding and power.'—Your word is a
lamp to my feet and a light for my path.

Commit to the LORD whatever you do
Whether you turn to the right or to the left, your ears will hear a voice behind
you, saying, 'This is the way; walk in it.'—Commit to the LORD whatever you
do, and your plans will succeed.—But he knows the way that I take.—A
person's steps are directed by the LORD. How then can any understand their
own way?

You guide me with your counsel, and afterwards you will take me into
glory.

Psalm 16:7; Isaiah 9:6. Proverbs 8:14. Psalm 119:105. Isaiah 30:21.
Proverbs 16:3. Job 23:10. Proverbs 20:24. Psalm 73:24.

May 17

Morning

I am the LORD your God; follow my decrees and be careful to keep my laws.

But just as he who called you is holy, so be holy in all you do.—Whoever claims to live in him must walk as Jesus did. . . . If you know that he is righteous, you know that everyone who does what is right has been born of him.

Not that we are competent to claim anything for ourselves, but our competence comes from God.—Teach me, O LORD, to follow your decrees.

Work out your salvation
Continue to work out your salvation with fear and trembling, for it is God who works in you to will and to act according to his good purpose.—May the God of peace, who through the blood of the eternal covenant brought back from the dead our Lord Jesus, that great Shepherd of the sheep, equip you with everything good for doing his will, and may he work in us what is pleasing to him, through Jesus Christ.

> Ezekiel 20:19. 1 Peter 1:15. 1 John 2:6, 29. 2 Corinthians 3:5.
> Psalm 119:33. Philippians 2:12–13. Hebrews 13:20–21.

Evening

'I have exalted a young man from among the people.'

High above on the throne was a figure like that of a man.—'The one who came from heaven—the Son of Man.'—'Look at my hands and my feet. It is I myself! Touch me and see; a ghost does not have flesh and bones, as you see I have.'

God exalted him
But made himself nothing, taking the very nature of a servant, being made in human likeness. And being found in appearance as a human being, he humbled himself and became obedient to death—even death on a cross! Therefore God exalted him to the highest place and gave him the name that is above every name, that at the name of Jesus every knee should bow.—'Wake up! Strengthen what remains and is about to die, for I have not found your deeds complete in the sight of my God.'

> Psalm 89:19. Ezekiel 1:26. John 3:13. Luke 24:39. Philippians 2:7–10.
> Revelation 3:2.

Morning

'For as the Father has life in himself, so he has granted the Son to have life in himself.'

Our Saviour, Christ Jesus, who has destroyed death and has brought life and immortality to light through the gospel.—'I am the resurrection and the life.'—Listen, I tell you a mystery: We will not all sleep, but we will all be changed—in a flash, in the twinkling of an eye, at the last trumpet. For the trumpet will sound, the dead will be raised imperishable, and we will be changed.

Whom no-one has ever seen
'Holy, holy, holy is the Lord God Almighty, who was, and is, and is to come.' . . . Who lives for ever and ever.—The blessed and only Ruler, the King of kings and Lord of lords, who alone is immortal and who lives in unapproachable light, whom no-one has seen or can see. To him be honour and might for ever. Amen. . . . Now to the king eternal, immortal, invisible, the only God, be honour and glory for ever and ever. Amen.

John 5:26. 2 Timothy 1:10. John 11:25; 14:19. 1 Corinthians 15:51–52.
Revelation 4:8–9. 1 Timothy 6:15–16; 1:17.

Evening

Let us not become conceited, provoking and envying each other.

And he [Gideon] said, 'I do have one request, that each of you give me an ear-ring from your share of the plunder.' (It was the custom of the Ishmaelites to wear gold ear-rings.) They answered, 'we'll be glad to give them.' So they spread out a garment, and each one threw a ring from his plunder onto it. . . . Gideon made the gold into an ephod, which he placed in Ophrah, his town. All Israel prostituted themselves by worshipping it there, and it became a snare to Gideon and his family.

Do nothing out of vain conceit
Do nothing out of selfish ambition or vain conceit, but in humility consider others better than yourselves.—Love is patient, love is kind. It does not envy, it does not boast, it is not proud. It is not rude, it is not self-seeking.

Galatians 5:26. Judges 8:24–25, 27. Philippians 2:3. 1 Corinthians 13:4–5.

May 19

Morning

Wash away all my iniquity and cleanse me from my sin.

'I will cleanse them from all the sin they have committed against me and will forgive all their sins of rebellion against me.'

'Born of water and the Spirit'
'No-one can enter the kingdom of God without being born of water and the Spirit.'—The blood of goats and bulls and the ashes of a heifer sprinkled on those who are ceremonially unclean sanctify them so that they are outwardly clean. How much more, then, will the blood of Christ, who through the eternal Spirit offered himself unblemished to God, cleanse our consciences from acts that lead to death, so that we may serve the living God!

Yet he saved them for his name's sake, to make his mighty power known. . . . Not to us, O LORD, not to us but to your name be the glory, because of your love and faithfulness.

Psalm 51:2. Jeremiah 33:8. John 3:5. Hebrews 9:13–14.
Psalms 106:8; 115:1.

Evening

Partnership in the gospel.

The body is a unit, though it is made up of many parts; and though all its parts are many, they form one body. So it is with Christ. For we were all baptised by one Spirit into one body—whether Jews or Greeks, slave or free—and we were all given the one Spirit to drink.

God, who has called you into fellowship with his Son Jesus Christ our Lord, is faithful.

'My prayer is that all of them may be one'
But if we walk in the light, as he is in the light, we have fellowship with one another, and the blood of Jesus, his Son, purifies us from all sin.—'My prayer is not for them alone. I pray also for those who will believe in me through their message, that all of them may be one, Father, just as you are in me and I am in you. May they also be in us so that the world may believe that you have sent me.'

Philippians 1:5. 1 Corinthians 12:12–13; 1:9. 1 John 1:7. John 17:20–21.

Morning

You too should be on your guard.

I beat my body and make it my slave so that after I have preached to others, I myself will not be disqualified for the prize.

Put on the full armour of God so that you can take your stand against the devil's schemes. For our struggle is not against flesh and blood, but against the rulers, against the authorities, against the powers of this dark world and against the spiritual forces of evil in the heavenly realms.

Keep in step with the Spirit
Those who belong to Christ Jesus have crucified the sinful nature with its passions and desires. Since we live by the Spirit, let us keep in step with the Spirit.—Because those who are led by the Spirit of God are children of God.—Be diligent in these matters; give yourself wholly to them, so that everyone may see your progress.

> 2 Timothy 4:15. 1 Corinthians 9:27. Ephesians 6:11–12.
> Galatians 5:24–25. Romans 8:14. 1 Timothy 4:15.

Evening

Jesus said to her, 'Mary.'

'Fear not, for I have redeemed you; I have called you by name; you are mine.'—'The sheep listen to his voice. He calls his own sheep by name and leads them out. And his sheep follow him because they know his voice.'

'See, I have engraved you on the palms of my hands; your walls are ever before me.'

'The Lord knows those who are his'
God's solid foundation stands firm, sealed with this inscription: 'The Lord knows those who are his.'—We have a great high priest who has gone through the heavens, Jesus the Son of God.

'Take two onyx stones and engrave on them the names of the sons of Israel. . . . And fasten them on the shoulder pieces of the ephod as memorial stones for the sons of Israel. Aaron is to bear the names on his shoulders as a memorial before the LORD.

> John 20:16. Isaiah 43:1. John 10:3–4. Isaiah 49:16. 2 Timothy 2:19.
> Hebrews 4:14. Exodus 28:9, 12.

May 21

Morning

Finally, be strong in the Lord and in his mighty power.

'My grace is sufficient for you, for my power is made perfect in weakness.' Therefore I will boast all the more gladly about my weaknesses, so that Christ's power may rest on me. That is why, for Christ's sake, I delight in weaknesses, in insults, in hardships, in persecutions, in difficulties. For when I am weak, then I am strong.

Treasure in jars of clay
I can do everything through him who gives me strength.—I labour, struggling with all his energy, which so powerfully works in me.—But we have this treasure in jars of clay to show that this all-surpassing power is from God and not from us.
 'The joy of the LORD is your strength.'

> Ephesians 6:10. 2 Corinthians 12:9–10. Philippians 4:13.
> Colossians 1:29. 2 Corinthians 4:7. Nehemiah 8:10.

Evening

Jesus Christ our Lord.

'Jesus, because he will save his people from their sins.'—He humbled himself and became obedient to death—even death on a cross! Therefore God exalted him to the highest place and gave him the name that is above every name, that at the name of Jesus every knee should bow, in heaven and on earth and under the earth.

'I have set you an example'
'Because the LORD has anointed me to preach good news to the poor. He has sent me to bind up the broken-hearted, to proclaim freedom for the captives.' —'You call me "Teacher" and "Lord", and rightly so, for that is what I am. Now that I, your Lord and Teacher, have washed your feet, you also should wash one another's feet. I have set you an example that you should do as I have done for you.'

> 1 Corinthians 1:9. Matthew 1:21. Philippians 2:8–10. Isaiah 61:1.
> John 13:13–15.

Morning

'Peace I leave with you; my peace I give you. I do not give to you as the world gives.'

The world and its desires pass away.—Human beings are mere phantoms as they go to and fro: They bustle about, but only in vain; they heap up wealth, not knowing who will get it.—What benefit did you reap at that time from the things you are now ashamed of? Those things result in death!—'Martha, Martha,' the Lord answered, 'you are worried and upset about many things, but only one thing is needed. Mary has chosen what is better, and it will not be taken from her.'

'The Lord make his face shine upon you'
'I have told you these things, so that in me you may have peace. In this world you will have trouble. But take heart! I have overcome the world.'—'The Lord bless you and keep you; the Lord make his face shine upon you and be gracious to you; the Lord turn his face towards you and give you peace.'

John 14:27. 1 John 2:17. Psalm 39:6. Romans 6:21. Luke 10:41–42.
John 16:33. Numbers 6:24–26.

Evening

The Spirit helps us in our weakness.

'The Counsellor, the Holy Spirit.'—Do you not know that your body is a temple of the Holy Spirit, who is in you, whom you have received from God? You are not your own.—For it is God who works in you to will and to act according to his good purpose.

Groans that words cannot express
We do not know what we ought to pray for, but the Spirit himself intercedes for us with groans that words cannot express. And he who searches our hearts knows the mind of the Spirit, because the Spirit intercedes for the saints in accordance with God's will.
'The spirit is willing, but the body is weak.'

Romans 8:26. John 14:26. 1 Corinthians 6:19. Philippians 2:13.
Romans 8:26–27. Matthew 26:41.

May 23

Morning

But because Jesus lives for ever, he has a permanent priesthood.

Therefore he is able to save completely those who come to God through him, because he always lives to intercede for them.

To him who is able to keep you from falling and to present you before his glorious presence without fault and with great joy.

Hold firmly to the faith
Therefore, since we have a great high priest who has gone through the heavens, Jesus the Son of God, let us hold firmly to the faith we profess. For we do not have a high priest who is unable to sympathise with our weaknesses, but we have one who has been tempted in every way, just as we are—yet was without sin. Let us approach the throne of grace with confidence.

Hebrews 7:24, 24–25. Jude 24. Hebrews 4:14–16.

Evening

That night the king could not sleep.

You kept my eyes from closing . . . Who is like the LORD our God, the One who sits enthroned on high, who stoops down to look on the heavens and the earth?

God works for the good of those who love him
For the eyes of the LORD range throughout the earth to strengthen those whose hearts are fully committed to him.—We know that in all things God works for the good of those who love him.

'The very hairs of your head are all numbered'
'Are not two sparrows sold for a penny? Yet not one of them will fall to the ground apart from the will of your Father. And even the very hairs of your head are all numbered.'

Esther 6:1. Psalms 77:4; 113:5–6. 2 Chronicles 16:9.
Romans 8:28. Matthew 10:29–30.

Morning

Do not grieve the Holy Spirit of God, with whom you were sealed for the day of redemption.

The love of the Spirit.—The Counsellor, the Holy Spirit.

They rebelled
In all their distress he too was distressed, and the angel of his presence saved them. In his love and mercy he redeemed them; he lifted them up and carried them all the days of old. Yet they rebelled and grieved his Holy Spirit. So he turned and became their enemy and he himself fought against them.

You were marked in him with a seal
We know that we live in him and he in us, because he has given us of his Spirit.—Having believed, you were marked in him with a seal, the promised Holy Spirit, who is a deposit guaranteeing our inheritance until the redemption of those who are God's possession.
  The Spirit helps us in our weakness.

> Ephesians 4:30. Romans 15:30. John 14:26. Isaiah 63:9–10. 1 John 4:13.
> Ephesians 1:13–14. Romans 8:26.

Evening

But your iniquities have separated you from your God; your sins have hidden his face from you.

'I punished him, and hid my face in anger, yet he kept on in his wilful ways. I have seen his ways, but I will heal him.'—Have you not brought this on yourselves by forsaking the LORD your God when he led you in the way?

'I will heal their waywardness'
'So he got up and went to his father. But while he was still a long way off, his father saw him and was filled with compassion for him; he ran to his son, threw his arms around him and kissed him.'—'I will heal their waywardness and love them freely, for my anger has turned away from them.'
  If we confess our sins, he is faithful and just and will forgive us our sins and purify us from all unrighteousness.

> Isaiah 59:2; 57:17–18. Jeremiah 2:17. Luke 15:20. Hosea 14:4.
> 1 John 1:9.

May 25

Morning

How great is your goodness, which you have stored up for those who fear you.

Since ancient times no-one has heard, no ear has perceived, no eye has seen any God besides you, who acts on behalf of those who wait for him.—'No eye has seen, no ear has heard, no mind has conceived what God has prepared for those who love him'—but God has revealed it to us by his Spirit.—You have made known to me the path of life; you will fill me with joy in your presence, with eternal pleasures at your right hand.

River of delights
How priceless is your unfailing love! Both high and low find refuge in the shadow of your wings. They feast in the abundance of your house; and give them drink from your river of delights. For with you is the fountain of life; in your light we see light.

Godliness has value for all things, holding promise for both the present life and the life to come.

Psalm 31:19. Isaiah 64:4. 1 Corinthians 2:9–10. Psalms 16:11; 36:7–9.

Evening

'The Son of God, whose eyes are like blazing fire.'

The heart is deceitful above all things and beyond cure. Who can understand it?—You have set our iniquities before you, our secret sins in the light of your presence.—The Lord turned and looked straight at Peter. . . . And he went outside and wept bitterly.

'The Lord knows those who are his.'

'I give them eternal life'
'I am the good shepherd; I know my sheep and my sheep know me.' . . . 'My sheep listen to my voice; I know them, and they follow me. I give them eternal life, and they shall never perish; no-one can snatch them out of my hand.'

Revelation 2:18, Jeremiah 17:9. Psalm 90:8. Luke 22:61–62.
2 Timothy 2:19. John 10:14, 27–28.

Morning

Our Lord Jesus, that great Shepherd of the sheep.

The Chief Shepherd.—'I am the good shepherd; I know my sheep and my sheep know me.' . . . 'My sheep listen to my voice; I know them, and they follow me. I give them eternal life, and they shall never perish; no-one can snatch them out of my hand.'

'I will search for the lost'

The LORD is my shepherd, I shall lack nothing. He makes me lie down in green pastures, he leads me beside quiet waters, he restores my soul. He guides me in paths of righteousness for his name's sake.—'I am the good shepherd. The good shepherd lays down his life for the sheep.'—'I will search for the lost and bring back the strays. I will bind up the injured and strengthen the weak.'—For you were like sheep going astray, but now you have returned to the Shepherd and Overseer of your souls.

Hebrews 13:20. 1 Peter 5:4. John 10:14, 27–28. Psalm 23:1–3.
John 10:11. Ezekiel 34:16. 1 Peter 2:25.

Evening

The city does not need the sun or the moon to shine on it, for the glory of God gives it light, and the Lamb is its lamp.

'I saw a light from heaven, brighter than the sun, blazing around me and my companions. . . . Then I asked, "Who are you, Lord?" "I am Jesus, whom you are persecuting," the Lord replied.'

He was transfigured

Jesus took with him Peter, James and John the brother of James, and led them up a high mountain by themselves. There he was transfigured before them. His face shone like the sun, and his clothes became as white as the light.

Your everlasting light

The sun will no more be your light by day, nor will the brightness of the moon shine on you, for the LORD will be your everlasting light, and your God will be your glory.

Revelation 21:23. Acts 26:13, 15. Matthew 17:1–2. Isaiah 60:19.

May 27

Morning

The LORD is good, a refuge in times of trouble. He cares for those who trust in him.

'Give thanks to the LORD Almighty, for the LORD is good; his love endures for ever.'

God is our refuge and strength, an ever present help in trouble. . . . I will say of the LORD, 'He is my refuge and my fortress, my God, in whom I trust.'— Who is like you, a people saved by the LORD? He is your shield and helper and your glorious sword.

'His way is perfect'
'As for God, his way is perfect; the word of the LORD is flawless. He is a shield for all who take refuge in him. For who is God besides the LORD? And who is the Rock except our God?'

For the LORD watches over the way of the righteous, but the way of the wicked will perish.—'I am pleased with you and I know you by name.'

Nahum 1:7. Jeremiah 33:11. Psalms 46:1; 91:2. Deuteronomy 33:29.
2 Samuel 22:31–32. Psalm 1:6. Exodus 33:17.

Evening

He cares for you.

Taste and see that the LORD is good; blessed are those who take refuge in him. . . . The lions may grow weak and hungry, but those who seek the LORD lack no good thing.

'Look at the birds of the air'
'Therefore I tell you, do not worry about your life, what you will eat or drink; or about your body, what you will wear. Is not life more important than food, and the body more important than clothes? Look at the birds of the air; they do not sow or reap or store away in barns, and yet your heavenly Father feeds them. Are you not much more valuable than they?'

Present your requests to God
Do not be anxious about anything, but in everything, by prayer and petition, with thanksgiving, present your requests to God.

1 Peter 5:7. Psalm 34:8, 10. Matthew 6:25–26. Philippians 4:6–7.

Morning

We eagerly await a Saviour.

For the grace of God that brings salvation has appeared to all people. It teaches us to say 'No' to ungodliness and worldly passions, and to live self-controlled, upright and godly lives in this present age, while we wait for the blessed hope—the glorious appearing of our great God and Saviour, Jesus Christ, who gave himself for us to redeem us from all wickedness and to purify for himself a people that are his very own, eager to do what is good.

He will appear a second time
So Christ was sacrificed once to take away the sins of many people; and he will appear a second time, not to bear sin, but to bring salvation to those who are waiting for him.

'This is our God'
In that day they will say, 'Surely this is our God; we trusted in him, and he saved us. This is the LORD, we trusted in him, and he saved us. This is the LORD, we trusted in him; let us rejoice and be glad in his salvation.'

Philippians 3:20. Titus 2:11–14. Hebrews 9:28. Isaiah 25:9.

Evening

Run in such a way as to get the prize.

The sluggard says, 'There is a lion outside!'—Let us throw off everything that hinders and the sin that so easily entangles, and let us run with perseverance the race marked out for us. Let us fix our eyes on Jesus, the author and perfecter of our faith.—Let us purify ourselves from everything that contaminates body and spirit, perfecting holiness out of reverence for God.

I do not run aimlessly
I press on towards the goal.—Therefore I do not run like someone running aimlessly; I do not fight like someone beating the air. No, I beat my body and make it my slave so that after I have preached to others, I myself will not be disqualified for the prize.

For this world in its present form is passing away.

Make every effort to be found spotless, blameless and at peace with him.

1 Corinthians 9:24. Proverbs 22:13. Hebrews 12:1–2. 2 Corinthians 7:1.
Philippians 3:14. 1 Corinthians 9:26–27; 7:31. 2 Peter 3:14.

May 29

Morning

'Look, the Lamb of God, who takes away the sin of the world!'

The blood of the Lamb.—The precious blood of Christ, a lamb without blemish or defect.—Without the shedding of blood there is no forgiveness.—The blood of Jesus, his Son, purifies us from every sin.

The blood of Jesus
He entered the Most Holy Place once for all by his own blood, having obtained eternal redemption. . . . Therefore, brothers, since we have confidence to enter the Most Holy Place by the blood of Jesus, by a new and living way opened for us through the curtain, that is, his body, and since we have a great priest over the house of God, let us draw near to God with a sincere heart in full assurance of faith.

You were bought at a price. Therefore honour God with your body.

John 1:29. Revelation 7:14. 1 Peter 1:19. Hebrews 9:22. 1 John 1:7. Hebrews 9:12; 10:19–22. 1 Corinthians 6:20.

Evening

'Oh that I had the wings of a dove! I would fly away and be at rest.'

Jonah
When the sun rose, God provided a scorching east wind, and the sun blazed on Jonah's head so that he grew faint. He wanted to die, and said, 'It would be better for me to die than to live.'

Job
Job opened his mouth and . . . said: 'May the day of my birth perish, and the night it was said, "A boy is born!" ' —The righteous may have many troubles, but the LORD delivers them from them all.

He is able to help
'Now my heart is troubled, and what shall I say? "Father, save me from this hour"?'—Because he himself suffered when he was tempted, he is able to help those who are being tempted.

Psalm 5:6. Jonah 4:8. Job 3:1–3. Psalm 34:19. John 12:27. Hebrews 2:18.

Morning

Let us, therefore, make every effort to enter that rest.

'Enter through the narrow gate. For wide is the gate and broad is the road that leads to destruction, and many enter through it. But small is the gate and narrow the road that leads to life, and only a few find it.'

'Do not work for food that spoils, but for food that endures to eternal life, which the Son of Man will give you.'

Make your calling and election sure
Therefore, my brothers and sisters, be all the more eager to make your calling and election sure. For if you do these things, you will never fall, and you will receive a rich welcome into the eternal kingdom of our Lord and Saviour Jesus Christ.

Your everlasting light
For those who enter God's rest also rest from their own work, just as God did from his.—For the LORD will be your everlasting light, and your God will be your glory.

Hebrews 4:11. Matthew 7:13–14. John 6:27. 2 Peter 1:10–11.
Hebrews 4:10. Isaiah 60:19.

Evening

'You always hear me.'

Then Jesus looked up and said, 'Father, I thank you that you have heard me.' . . . 'Father, glorify your name!' Then a voice came from heaven, 'I have glorified it, and will glorify it again.'—'I have come to do your will, O God.'—'Yet not my will, but yours be done.'

He hears us
In this world we are like him. . . . This is the confidence we have in approaching God: that if we ask anything according to his will, he hears us. . . . And receive from him anything we ask, because we obey his commands and do what pleases him.

He always lives to intercede
He always lives to intercede for them.—We have one who speaks to the Father in our defence—Jesus Christ, the Righteous One.

John 11:42, 41; 12:28. Hebrews 10:7. Luke 22:42.
1 John 4:17; 5:14; 3:22. Hebrews 7:25. 1 John 2:1.

May 31

Morning

'Your name will no longer be Jacob, but Israel, because you have struggled with God and with men and have overcome.'

Yet he [Abraham] did not waver through unbelief regarding the promise of God, but was strengthened in his faith and gave glory to God.

'Whatever you ask in prayer'
'Have faith in God,' Jesus answered. 'I tell you the truth, if you say to this mountain, "Go, throw yourself into the sea," and do not doubt in your heart but believe that what you say will happen, it will be done for you. Therefore I tell you, whatever you ask in prayer, believe that you have received it, and it will be yours.'

' "If you can"?' said Jesus. 'Everything is possible for one who believes.'— 'Blessed is she who has believed that what the Lord has said to her will be accomplished!'

'Increase our faith.'

> Genesis 32:28. Romans 4:20. Mark 11:22–24; 9:23. Luke 1:45; 17:5.

Evening

Dear children, continue in him.

The one who doubts is like a wave of the sea, blown and tossed by the wind. Those who doubt should not think they will receive anything from the Lord; they are double-minded and unstable in all they do.

You have fallen away from grace
You who are trying to be justified by law have been alienated from Christ; you have fallen away from grace. . . . You were running a good race. Who cut in on you and kept you from obeying the truth?

'Remain in the vine'
'No branch can bear fruit by itself; it must remain in the vine. . . . If you remain in me and my words remain in you, ask whatever you wish, and it will be given you.'—For no matter how many promises God has made, they are 'Yes' in Christ. And so through him the 'Amen' is spoken by us to the glory of God.

> 1 John 2:28. James 1:6–8. Galatians 5:4, 7. John 15:4, 7.
> 2 Corinthians 1:20.

Morning

The fruit of the Spirit is faithfulness, gentleness.

The LORD, the LORD, the compassionate and gracious God, slow to anger, abounding in love and faithfulness.

Be kind
Live a life worthy of the calling you have received. Be completely humble and gentle; be patient, bearing with one another in love. . . . Be kind and compassionate to one another, forgiving each other, just as in Christ God forgave you.

The wisdom that comes from heaven
The wisdom that comes from heaven is first of all pure; then peace loving, considerate, submissive, full of mercy and good fruit, impartial and sincere.—Love is patient, love is kind.
   Be patient, then, brothers and sisters, until the Lord's coming.

Galatians 5:22. Exodus 34:6. Ephesians 4:1–2, 32. James 3:17.
1 Corinthians 13:4. James 5:7.

Evening

'Immanuel' . . . 'God with us.'

The Word became flesh and made his dwelling among us. We have seen his glory, the glory of the One and Only, who came from the Father, full of grace and truth.

He has spoken to us by his Son
But in these last days he has spoken to us by his Son, whom he appointed heir of all things, and through whom he made the universe.

Stop doubting
Then he [Jesus] said to Thomas, 'Put your finger here; see my hands. Reach out your hand and put it into my side. Stop doubting and believe.' Thomas said to him, 'My Lord and my God!'—To us a son is given . . . Mighty God.

Matthew 1:23. John 1:14. Hebrews 1:2. John 20:26–28. Isaiah 9:6.

June 2

Morning

For here we do not have an enduring city, but we are looking for the city that is to come.

Watching
'Be dressed ready for service and keep your lamps burning, like those waiting for their master to return from a wedding banquet, so that when he comes and knocks they can immediately open the door for him. It will be good for those servants whose master finds them watching when he comes.'

Be self-controlled
Therefore, prepare your minds for action; be self-controlled; set your hope fully on the grace to be given you when Jesus Christ is revealed.

I press on
But one thing I do: Forgetting what is behind, . . . I press on towards the goal to win the prize for which God has called me heavenwards in Christ Jesus.

> Hebrews 13:14. Luke 12:35–37. 1 Peter 1:13. Philippians 3:13–15.

Evening

Lord, you have assigned me my portion and my cup.

Heirs of God and co-heirs with Christ.—All things are yours.—The Son of God . . . loved me and gave himself for me.

'I am your inheritance'
The LORD said to Aaron, 'You will have no inheritance in their land, nor will you have any share among them; I am your share and your inheritance among the Israelites.'

Whom have I in heaven but you? And being with you, I desire nothing on earth. My flesh and my heart may fail, but God is the strength of my heart and my portion for ever.

Earnestly I seek you
O God, you are my God, earnestly I seek you; my soul thirsts for you, my body longs for you, in a dry and weary land where there is no water.

> Psalm 16:5. Romans 8:17. 1 Corinthians 3:21. Galatians 2:20.
> Numbers 18:20. Psalms 73:25–26; 63:1.

Morning

'Therefore keep watch, because you do not know the day or the hour.'

'Be careful or your hearts will be weighed down with dissipation, drunkenness and the anxieties of life, and that day will close on you unexpectedly like a trap. For it will come upon all those who live on the face of the whole earth. Be always on the watch, and pray that you may be able to escape all that is about to happen, and that you may be able to stand before the Son of Man.'

Alert and self-controlled
The day of the Lord will come like a thief in the night. While people are saying, 'Peace and safety', destruction will come on them suddenly, as labour pains on a pregnant woman, and they will not escape. But you, brothers and sisters, are not in darkness so that this day should surprise you like a thief. You are all children of the light and children of the day. We do not belong to the night or to the darkness. So then, let us not be like others, who are asleep, but let us be alert and self-controlled.

Matthew 25:13. Luke 21:34–36. 1 Thessalonians 5:2–6.

Evening

'I am God Almighty; walk before me and be blameless.'

Not that I have obtained all this, or have already been made perfect, but I press on to take hold of that for which Christ Jesus took hold of me. Brothers and sisters, I do not consider myself yet to have taken hold of it. But one thing I do: Forgetting what is behind and straining towards what is ahead, I press on towards the goal to win the prize for which God has called me heavenwards in Christ Jesus.

Enoch
Enoch walked with God; then he was no more, because God took him away.

Transformed into his likeness
Grow in the grace and knowledge of our Lord and Saviour Jesus Christ.—We, who with unveiled faces all reflect the Lord's glory, are being transformed into his likeness with ever-increasing glory, which comes from the Lord, who is the Spirit.

Genesis 17:1. Philippians 3:12–14. Genesis 5:24. 2 Peter 3:18.
2 Corinthians 3:18.

June 4

Morning

'The glory of this present house will be greater than the glory of the former house, . . . And in this place I will grant peace.'

'The house to be built for the LORD should be of great magnificence and fame and splendour in the sight of all the nations.'

We have seen his glory
The Word became flesh and lived for a while among us. We have seen his glory, the glory of the One and Only, who came from the Father, full of grace and truth.—God . . . in these last days has spoken to us by his Son, whom he appointed heir of all things and through whom he made the universe.

For he himself is our peace.—The peace of God, which transcends all understanding, will guard your hearts and your minds in Christ Jesus.

Haggai 2:9. 1 Chronicles 22:5. John 1:14. Hebrews 1:1–2.
Ephesians 2:14. Philippians 4:7.

Evening

Put on the armour of light.

Rather, clothe yourselves with the Lord Jesus Christ.—That I may gain Christ and be found in him, not having a righteousness of my own that comes from the law, but that which is through faith in Christ—the righteousness that comes from God and is by faith.—This righteousness from God comes through faith in Christ Jesus to all who believe.

A robe of righteousness
For he . . . arrayed me in a robe of righteousness.—I will come and proclaim your mighty acts, O Sovereign LORD; I will proclaim your righteousness, yours alone.

Children of light
For you were once darkness, but now you are light in the Lord. Live as children of light.

Romans 13:12, 14. Philippians 3:8–9. Romans 3:22. Isaiah 61:10.
Psalm 71:16. Ephesians 5:8.

Morning

'So you also, when you have done everything you were told to do, should say, "We are unworthy servants."'

Where, then, is boasting? It is excluded. On what principle? On that of observing the law? No, but on that of faith.—What do you have that you did not receive? And if you did receive it, why do you boast as though you did not?—For it is by grace you have been saved, through faith—and this not from yourselves, it is the gift of God—not by works, so that no-one can boast. For we are God's handiwork, created in Christ Jesus to do good works, which God prepared in advance for us to do.

The grace of God
But by the grace of God I am what I am, and his grace to me was not without effect.—Everything comes from you, and we have given you only what comes from your hand.

Luke 17:10. Romans 3:27. 1 Corinthians 4:7. Ephesians 2:8–10.
1 Corinthians 15:10. 1 Chronicles 29:14.

Evening

For he knows how we are formed, he remembers that we are dust.

I praise you because I am fearfully and wonderfully made; your works are wonderful, I know that full well. My frame was not hidden from you when I was made in the secret place. When I was woven together in the depths of the earth, your eyes saw my unformed body. All the days ordained for me were written in your book before one of them came to be.

For in him we live and move and have our being.

A passing breeze
Yet he was merciful; he atoned for their iniquities and did not destroy them. Time after time he restrained his anger and did not stir up his full wrath. He remembered that they were but flesh, a passing breeze that does not return.

Psalm 103:14. Psalm 139:14–16. Acts 17:28. Psalm 78:38–39.

June 6

Morning

He will quiet you with his love.

He first loved us
The LORD did not set his affection on you and choose you because you were more numerous than other people, for you were the fewest of all peoples. But it was because the LORD loved you.—We love because he first loved us.

While we were still sinners
He has reconciled you by Christ's body through death to present you holy in his sight.—This is love: not that we loved God, but that he loved us and sent his Son as an atoning sacrifice for our sins.—But God demonstrates his own love for us in this: While we were still sinners, Christ died for us.

And a voice from heaven said, 'This is my Son whom I love; with him I am well pleased.'—'The reason my Father loves me is that I lay down my life—only to take it up again.'

> Zephaniah 3:17. Deuteronomy 7:7–8. 1 John 4:19. Colossians 1:22.
> 1 John 4:10. Romans 5:8. Matthew 3:17. John 10:17.

Evening

A new and living way.

So Cain went out from the LORD's presence.—But your iniquities have separated you from your God; your sins have hidden his face from you.—Without holiness no-one will see the Lord.

'I am the way and the truth and the life. No-one comes to the Father except through me.'—Our Saviour, Christ Jesus, who has destroyed death and has brought life and immortality to light through the gospel.

He himself is our peace
For he himself is our peace, who has made the two one and has destroyed the barrier, the dividing wall of hostility.—The curtain of the temple was torn in two from top to bottom.

'Small is the gate and narrow the road that leads to life, and only a few find it.'

> Hebrews 10:20. Genesis 4:16. Isaiah 59:2. Hebrews 12:14. John 14:6.
> 2 Timothy 1:10. Ephesians 2:14. Matthew 27:51; 7:14.

Morning

They should always pray and not give up.

'Suppose one of you has a friend, and he goes to him at midnight and says, "Friend, lend me three loaves of bread, because a friend of mine on a journey has come to me, and I have nothing to set before him." Then the one inside answers, "Don't bother me. The door is already locked, and my children are with me in bed. I can't get up and give you anything." I tell you that he will not get up and give him the bread because he is his friend, yet because of the man's boldness he will get up and give him as much as he needs.'

Keep on praying
Pray in the Spirit on all occasions with all kinds of prayers and requests. With this in mind, be alert and always keep on praying for all the saints.

Jesus spent the night praying
Jesus went out into the hills to pray, and spent the night praying to God.

Luke 18:1; 11:5–8. Ephesians 6:18. Luke 6:12.

Evening

Take away all my sins.

'Come now, let us reason together,' says the LORD. 'Though your sins are like scarlet, they shall be as white as snow, though they are red as crimson, they shall be like wool.'
   'Take heart, son; your sins are forgiven.'—'I, even I, am he who blots out your transgressions, for my own sake, and remembers your sins no more.'
   'The Son of Man has authority on earth to forgive sins.'—In him we have redemption through his blood, the forgiveness of sins, in accordance with the riches of God's grace.

Nailing it to the cross
Having cancelled the written code, with its regulations, that was against us and that stood opposed to us; he took it away, nailing it to the cross.
   Praise the LORD, O my soul . . . He forgives all my sins.

Psalm 25:18. Isaiah 1:18. Matthew 9:2. Isaiah 43:25. Matthew 9:6.
Ephesians 1:7. Colossians 2:14. Psalm 103:2–3.

June 8

Morning

The LORD gave him success in everything he did.

Blessed are all who fear the LORD, who walk in his ways. You will eat the fruit of your labour; blessings and prosperity will be yours. . . . Trust in the LORD and do good; dwell in the land and enjoy safe pasture. Delight yourself in the LORD and he will give you the desires of your heart.—'Do not be terrified; do not be discouraged, for the LORD your God will be with you wherever you go.'

'Seek first his kingdom'
'But seek first his kingdom and his righteousness, and all these things will be given to you as well.'

Do not forget the LORD
As long as he sought the LORD, God gave him success.—Be careful that you do not forget the LORD your God, failing to observe his commands, his laws and his decrees that I am giving you this day.

Genesis 39:3. Psalms 128:1–2; 37:3–4. Joshua 1:9. Matthew 6:33.
2 Chronicles 26:5. Deuteronomy 8:11.

Evening

And my God will meet all your needs according to his glorious riches in Christ Jesus.

'Which is easier: to say to the paralytic, "Your sins are forgiven," or to say, "Get up, take your mat and walk"?' . . . ' "If you can"?' . . . 'Everything is possible for one who believes.'

'All authority'
'All authority in heaven and on earth has been given to me.'—'Why are you so afraid? Do you still have no faith?'

'Your heavenly Father feeds them'
'Look at the birds of the air . . . your heavenly Father feeds them. Are you not much more valuable than they?' . . . 'Why are you talking among yourselves about having no bread? . . . Don't you remember the five loaves for the five thousand?'

Philippians 4:19. Mark 2:9; 9:23. Matthew 28:18. Mark 4:40.
Matthew 6:26; 16:8–9.

Morning

'No-one ever spoke the way this man does.'

An instructed tongue
You are the most excellent of men and your lips have been anointed with grace,
since God has blessed you for ever.—The Sovereign LORD has given me an
instructed tongue, to know the word that sustains the weary.

All spoke well of him and were amazed at the gracious words that came from
his lips.—He taught as one who had authority, and not as their teachers of the
law.

The sword of the Spirit
Let the word of Christ dwell in you richly.—The sword of the Spirit . . . is the
word of God.—The word of God is living and active. Sharper than any double-
edged sword.—The weapons we fight with are not the weapons of the world.
On the contrary, they have divine power to demolish strongholds.

John 7:46. Psalm 45:2. Isaiah 50:4. Luke 4:22. Matthew 7:29.
Colossians 3:16. Ephesians 6:17. Hebrews 4:12. 2 Corinthians 10:4.

Evening

'But this is your hour—when darkness reigns.'

Since the children have flesh and blood, he too shared in their humanity so that
by his death he might destroy him who holds the power of death—that is, the
devil.—Having disarmed the powers and authorities, he made a public
spectacle of them, triumphing over them by the cross.

Like a roaring lion
Be self-controlled and alert. Your enemy the devil prowls around like a roaring
lion looking for someone to devour. Resist him, standing firm in the faith.—
Resist the devil and he will flee from you.

The God of peace
The wicked plot against the righteous and gnash their teeth at them; but the
Lord laughs at the wicked, for he knows their day is coming.—The God of
peace will soon crush Satan under your feet.

Luke 22:53. Hebrews 2:14. Colossians 2:15. 1 Peter 5:8–9. James 4:7.
Psalm 37:12–13. Romans 16:20.

June 10

Morning

'The younger son got together all he had, set off for a distant country and there squandered his wealth in wild living.'

That is what some of you were. But you were washed, you were sanctified, you were justified in the name of the Lord Jesus Christ and by the Spirit of our God.

By grace you have been saved
We were by nature objects of wrath. But because of his great love for us, God, who is rich in mercy, made us alive with Christ even when we were dead in transgressions—it is by grace you have been saved. And God raised us up with Christ and seated us with him in the heavenly realms in Christ Jesus.

This is love: not that we loved God, but that he loved us and sent his Son as an atoning sacrifice for our sins.

God demonstrates his own love for us
But God demonstrates his own love for us in this: While we were still sinners, Christ died for us.

Luke 15:13. 1 Corinthians 6:11. Ephesians 2:3–6. 1 John 4:10. Romans 5:8.

Evening

Forgive as the Lord forgave you.

'Two people owed money to a certain money-lender. One owed him five hundred denarii, and the other fifty. Neither of them had the money to pay him back, so he cancelled the debts of both.'—' "I cancelled all that debt of yours because you begged me to. Shouldn't you have had mercy on your fellow-servant just as I had on you?" '

Bear with each other
God's chosen people, holy and dearly loved, clothe yourselves with compassion, kindness, humility, gentleness and patience. Bear with each other and forgive whatever grievances you may have against one another.

Seventy-seven times
'Lord, how many times shall I forgive someone who sins against me? Up to seven times?' Jesus answered, 'I tell you, not seven times, but seventy-seven times.'

Love . . . binds them all together in perfect unity.

Colossians 3:13. Luke 7:41–42. Matthew 18:32–33. Colossians 3:12–13.
Matthew 18:21–22. Colossians 3:14.

Morning

'So he got up and went to his father. But while he was still a long way off, his father saw him and was filled with compassion for him; he ran to his son, threw his arms around him and kissed him.'

Great is his love
The LORD is compassionate and gracious, slow to anger, abounding in love. He will not always accuse, nor will he harbour his anger for ever; he does not treat us as our sins deserve or repay us according to our iniquities. For as high as the heavens are above the earth, so great is his love for those who fear him; as far as the east is from the west, so far has he removed our transgressions from us. As a father has compassion on his children, so the LORD has compassion on those who fear him.

You have been brought near
You received the Spirit of adoption. And by him we cry, '*Abba,* Father.' The Spirit himself testifies with our spirit that we are God's children.—You who once were far away have been brought near through the blood of Christ.

Luke 15:20. Psalm 103:8–13. Romans 8:15–16. Ephesians 2:13.

Evening

'I am making everything new!'

'No-one can see the kingdom of God without being born again.'—If anyone is in Christ, he is a new creation; the old has gone, the new has come!

A new heart
'I will give you a new heart and put a new spirit in you; I will remove from you your heart of stone and give you a heart of flesh.'—Get rid of the old yeast that you may be a new batch.—The new self, created to be like God in true righteousness and holiness.

A new name
You will be called a new name that the mouth of the LORD will bestow.

New heavens
'Behold, I will create new heavens and a new earth. The former things will not be remembered, nor will they come to mind.'

Revelation 21:5. John 3:3. 2 Corinthians 5:17. Ezekiel 36:26.
1 Corinthians 5:7. Ephesians 4:24. Isaiah 62:2; 65:17.

June 12

Morning

The LORD your God is testing you to find out whether you love him with all your heart and with all your soul.

He will sit as a refiner and purifier of silver; he will purify the Levites and refine them like gold and silver. Then the LORD will have men who will bring offerings in righteousness.

I will refine them
I will turn my hand against you; I will thoroughly purge away your dross and remove your impurities.—I will refine and test them.

For you, O God, tested us; you refined us like silver. . . . We went through fire and water, but you brought us to a place of abundance.

When you walk through the fire, you will not be burned; the flames will not set you ablaze.

> Deuteronomy 13:3. Malachi 3:3. Isaiah 1:25. Jeremiah 9:7.
> Psalm 66:10, 12. Isaiah 43:2.

Evening

We might die to sins and live for righteousness.

Put off . . . put on
Put off your old self, which is being corrupted by its deceitful desires; to be made new in the attitude of your minds; and to put on the new self, created to be like God in true righteousness and holiness.

For you died and your life is now hidden with Christ in God.

Instruments of righteousness
Count yourselves dead to sin but alive to God in Christ Jesus. Therefore do not let sin reign in your mortal body so that you obey its evil desires. Do not offer the parts of your body to sin, as instruments of wickedness, but rather offer yourselves to God, as those who have been brought from death to life; and offer the parts of your body to him as instruments of righteousness.

> 1 Peter 2:24. Ephesians 4:22–24. Colossians 3:3. Romans 6:11–13.

Morning

'Remain in me, and I will remain in you.'

I live by faith
I have been crucified with Christ and I no longer live, but Christ lives in me. The life I live in the body, I live by faith in the Son of God, who loved me and gave himself for me.

Your spirit is alive
I know that nothing good lives in me, that is, in my sinful nature. For I have the desire to do what is good, but I cannot carry it out. . . . What a wretched man I am! Who will rescue me from this body of death? Thanks be to God— through Jesus Christ our Lord! . . . But if Christ is in you, your body is dead because of sin, yet your spirit is alive because of righteousness.—If you continue in your faith, established and firm, not moved from the hope held out in the gospel. This is the gospel that you heard.

John 15:4. Galatians 2:20. Romans 7:18, 24–25; 8:10. Colossians 1:23.

Evening

'Do you believe in the Son of Man?'

'Who is he, sir?' the man asked. 'Tell me so that I may believe in him.'

'The Alpha and the Omega'
The Son is the radiance of God's glory and the exact representation of his being.—God, the blessed and only Ruler, the King of kings and Lord of lords, who alone is immortal and who lives in unapproachable light, whom no-one has seen or can see. To him be honour and might for ever. Amen.—'I am the Alpha and the Omega,' says the Lord God, 'who is, and who was, and who is to come, the Almighty.'

Lord, I believe'
'Lord, I believe.'—I know whom I have believed and am convinced that he is able to guard what I have entrusted to him for that day.

John 9:35, 36. Hebrews 3:1. 1 Timothy 6:15–16. Revelation 1:8.
John 9:38. 2 Timothy 1:12.

June 14

Morning

For just as the sufferings of Christ flow over into our lives, so also through Christ our comfort overflows.

Sharing his sufferings.—Rejoice that you participate in the sufferings of Christ, so that you may be overjoyed when his glory is revealed.

If we died with him, we will also live with him.

We are heirs
Now if we are children, then we are heirs—heirs of God and co-heirs with Christ, if indeed we share in his sufferings in order that we may also share in his glory.

Good hope
Our Lord Jesus Christ himself and God our Father, who loved us and by his grace gave us eternal encouragement and good hope, encourage your hearts and strengthen you in every good deed and word.

2 Corinthians 1:5. Philippians 3:10. 1 Peter 4:13. 2 Timothy 2:11.
Romans 8:17. 2 Thessalonians 2:16–17.

Evening

'Consider the ravens. They do not sow or reap.'

'Consider how the lilies grow. They do not labour or spin. . . . And do not set your heart on what you will eat or drink; do not worry about it. For the pagan world runs after all such things, and your Father knows that you need them.'

But if we have food and clothing, we will be content with that. Those who want to get rich fall into temptation and a trap and into many foolish and harmful desires that plunge people into ruin and destruction. For the love of money is a root of all kinds of evil. Some people, eager for money, have wandered from the faith and pierced themselves with many griefs.

'The deceitfulness of wealth'
'The worries of this life, the deceitfulness of wealth and the desires for other things come in and choke the word, making it unfruitful.'

Luke 12:24, 27, 29–30. 1 Timothy 6:8–10. Mark 4:19.

Morning

The secret things belong to the LORD our God, but the things revealed belong to us.

My heart is not proud, O LORD, my eyes are not haughty; I do not concern myself with great matters or things too wonderful for me. But I have stilled and quietened my soul; like a weaned child with its mother, like a weaned child is my soul within me.

God reveals mysteries
The LORD confides in those who fear him; he makes his covenant known to them.—'But there is a God in heaven who reveals mysteries.'

'The Spirit of truth'
'If you love me, you will obey what I command. And I will ask the Father, and he will give you another Counsellor to be with you for ever—the Spirit of truth.'

Deuteronomy 29:29. Psalms 131:1–2; 25:14. Daniel 2:28. John 14:15–17.

Evening

The Spirit intercedes for the saints in accordance with God's will.

'I tell you the truth, my Father will give you whatever you ask in my name. Until now you have not asked for anything in my name. Ask and you will receive, and your joy will be complete.'—And pray in the Spirit on all occasions with all kinds of prayers and requests.

Ask according to his will
This is the confidence we have in approaching God: that if we ask anything according to his will, he hears us. And if we know that he hears us—whatever we ask—we know that we have what we asked of him.

Give thanks in all circumstances
Be joyful always; pray continually; give thanks in all circumstances, for this is God's will for you in Christ Jesus. Do not put out the Spirit's fire.

Romans 8:27. John 16:23–24. Ephesians 6:18. 1 John 5:14–15.
1 Thessalonians 5:16–19.

June 16

Morning

Be very careful, then, how you live—not as unwise but as wise, making the most of every opportunity, because the days are evil.

Make the most of every opportunity
'But be very careful to keep the commandment and the law . . . to love the LORD your God, to walk in all his ways, to obey his commands, to hold fast to him and to serve him with all your heart and all your soul.'—Be wise in the way you act towards outsiders; make the most of every opportunity. Let your conversation be always full of grace, seasoned with salt, so that you may know how to answer anyone.—Avoid every kind of evil.

Make your calling sure
My brothers and sisters, be all the more eager to make your calling and election sure. For if you do these things, you will never fall.—It will be good for those servants whose master finds them watching when he comes.

> Ephesians 5:15–16. Joshua 22:5. Colossians 4:5–6. 1 Thessalonians 5:22.
> 2 Peter 1:10. Luke 12:37.

Evening

'Hold on to what you have, so that no-one will take your crown.'

'Lord, if you are willing, you can make me clean.' 'I am willing, be clean!' . . . 'Faith as small as a mustard seed.'

God works in you
Work out your salvation with fear and trembling, for it is God who works in you to will and to act according to his good purpose.

'First the stalk, then the ear, then the full kernel in the ear.'—Let us acknowledge the LORD; let us press on to acknowledge him.—'The kingdom of heaven has been forcefully advancing, and forceful people lay hold of it.'

I have kept the faith
I have fought the good fight, I have finished the race, I have kept the faith. Now there is in store for me the crown of righteousness, which the Lord, the righteous Judge, will award to me on that day.

> Revelation 3:11. Matthew 8:2–3; 17:20. Hebrews 10:35.
> Philippians 2:12–13. Hosea 6:3. 2 Timothy 4:7–8.

Morning

In everything, by prayer and petition, with thanksgiving, present your requests to God.

I love the LORD, for he heard my voice; he heard my cry for mercy. Because he turned his ear to me, I will call on him as long as I live.

The Spirit himself intercedes for us
'And when you pray, do not keep on babbling like pagans, for they think they will be heard because of their many words.'—The Spirit himself intercedes for us with groans that words cannot express.

I want men everywhere to lift up holy hands in prayer, without anger or disputing.—Pray in the Spirit on all occasions with all kinds of prayers and requests. With this in mind, be alert and always keep on praying for all the saints.

'If two of you on earth agree about anything you ask for, it will be done for you by my Father in heaven.'

Philippians 4:6. Psalm 116:1–2. Matthew 6:7. Romans 8:26.
1 Timothy 2:8. Ephesians 6:18. Matthew 18:19.

Evening

All you have made will praise you, O LORD; your saints will extol you.

Praise the LORD, O my soul; all my inmost being, praise his holy name. Praise the LORD, O my soul, and forget not all his benefits . . . I will extol the LORD at all times; his praise will always be on my lips.

Your love is better than life
Because your love is better than life, my lips will glorify you. I will praise you as long as I live, and in your name I will lift up my hands. My soul will be satisfied as with the richest of foods; with singing lips my mouth will praise you.

'My soul praises the Lord and my spirit rejoices in God my Saviour.'

'You are worthy, our Lord and God, to receive glory and honour and power, for you created all things, and by your will they were created and have their being.'

Psalms 145:10; 103:1–2; 31:1; 63:3–5. Luke 1:46–47. Revelation 4:11.

June 18

Morning

'Place the cover on top of the ark and put in the ark.' . . . 'There . . . I will meet with you.'

The way into the Most Holy Place had not yet been disclosed.—When Jesus had cried out again in a loud voice, he gave up his spirit. At that moment the curtain of the temple was torn in two from top to bottom.

Let us draw near to God
Therefore, brothers and sisters, since we have confidence to enter the Most Holy Place by the blood of Jesus, by a new and living way opened for us through the curtain, that is, his body, . . . let us draw near to God with a sincere heart in full assurance of faith, having our hearts sprinkled to cleanse us from a guilty conscience and having our bodies washed with pure water.
   Christ Jesus. God presented him as a sacrifice of atonement, through faith in his blood. He did this to demonstrate his justice, because in his forbearance he had left the sins committed beforehand unpunished.—Through him we both have access to the Father by one Spirit.

Exodus 25:21–22. Hebrews 9:8. Matthew 27:50–51.
Hebrews 10:19–20, 22. Romans 3:24–25. Ephesians 2:18.

Evening

'Faith as small as a mustard seed.'

Little strength
'You have little strength, yet you have kept my word and have not denied my name.'—Who despises the day of small things?

'Lord increase our faith'
We ought always to thank God for you, brothers and sisters, and rightly so, because your faith is growing more and more.—'Lord, increase our faith.'

Like a cedar of Lebanon
I will be like the dew to Israel; he will blossom like a lily. Like a cedar of Lebanon he will send down his roots; his young shoots will grow. His splendour will be like an olive tree, his fragrance like a cedar of Lebanon.

Matthew 17:20. Revelation 3:8. Zechariah 4:10. 2 Thessalonians 1:3.
Luke 17:5. Hosea 14:5–6.

Morning

Without holiness no-one will see the Lord.

'No-one can see the kingdom of God without being born again.'—Nothing impure will ever enter it.

As obedient children, do not conform to the evil desires you had when you lived in ignorance. But just as he who called you is holy, so be holy in all you do; for it is written: 'Be holy, because I am holy.' Since you call on a Father who judges each person's work impartially, live your lives as strangers here in reverent fear.

Put on the new self
Put off your old self, which is being corrupted by its deceitful desires; to be made new in the attitude of your minds; and to put on the new self, created to be like God in true righteousness and holiness. . . . For he chose us in him before the creation of the world to be holy and blameless in his sight.

Hebrews 12:14. John 3:3. Revelation 21:17. 1 Peter 1:14–17.
Ephesians 4:22–24; 1:4.

Evening

'Gold refined in the fire.'

'No-one who has left home or brothers or sisters or mother or father or children or fields for me and the gospel will fail to receive a hundred times as much in this present age (home, brothers, sisters, mothers, children and fields—and with them, persecutions) and in the age to come, eternal life.'

'Do not be surprised'
Dear friends, do not be surprised at the painful trial you are suffering, as though something strange were happening to you. . . . In this you greatly rejoice, though now for a little while you may have had to suffer grief in all kinds of trials.

Take heart!
And the God of all grace, who called you to his eternal glory in Christ, after you have suffered a little while, will himself restore you and make you strong, firm and steadfast.—'In this world you will have trouble. But take heart! I have overcome the world.'

Revelation 3:18. Mark 10:29–30. 1 Peter 4:12; 1:6; 5:10. John 16:33.

June 20

Morning

A generous person will prosper; the one who refreshes others will be refreshed.

God is not unjust; he will not forget your work and the love you have shown him as you have helped his people and continue to help them.

Each will be rewarded according to their own labour.

'You did it for me'
'Lord, when did we see you hungry and feed you, or thirsty and give you something to drink? When did we see you a stranger and invite you in, or needing clothes and clothe you?' . . . 'The King will reply, "I tell you the truth, whatever you did for one of the least of these brothers of mine, you did for me."' . . . 'Come, you who are blessed by my Father; take your inheritance, the kingdom prepared for you since the creation of the world.'

Proverbs 11:25. Hebrews 6:10. 1 Corinthians 3:8.
Matthew 25:37–38, 40, 34.

Evening

You discern my going out and my lying down.

When Jacob awoke from his sleep, he thought, 'Surely the LORD is in this place, and I was not aware of it.' . . . 'How awesome is this place! This is none other than the house of God; this is the gate of heaven.'

The eyes of the LORD
The eyes of the LORD range throughout the earth to strengthen those whose hearts are fully committed to him.—I will lie down and sleep in peace, for you alone, O LORD, make me dwell in safety.

Your sleep will be sweet
If you make the Most High your dwelling—even the LORD, who is my refuge—then no harm will befall you, no disaster will come near your tent. For he will command his angels concerning you to guard you in all your ways.— When you lie down, you will not be afraid; when you lie down, your sleep will be sweet.

Psalm 139:3. Genesis 28:16–17. 2 Chronicles 16:9. Psalms 4:8; 91:9–11.
Proverbs 3:24.

Morning

Christ suffered for you, leaving you an example, that you should follow in his steps.

'Even the Son of Man did not come to be served, but to serve.' . . . 'Whoever wants to be first must be slave of all.'

Jesus of Nazareth . . . went around doing good.—Carry each other's burdens, and in this way you will fulfil the law of Christ.

Consider others better than yourselves
The meekness and gentleness of Christ.—But in humility consider others better than yourselves.

Be compassionate
'Father, forgive them, for they do not know what they are doing.'—Be kind and compassionate to one another, forgiving each other just as in Christ God forgave you.

Whoever claims to live in him must walk as Jesus did.

1 Peter 2:21. Mark 10:45, 44. Acts 10:38. Galatians 6:2.
2 Corinthians 10:2. Philippians 2:3. Luke 23:34. Ephesians 4:32.
1 John 2:6.

Evening

If I had cherished sin in my heart, the Lord would not have listened.

'O LORD, what can I say, now that Israel has been routed by its enemies?' . . . The LORD said to Joshua, 'Stand up! What are you doing down on your face? Israel has sinned; . . . They have taken some of the devoted things; . . . they have put them with their own possessions.'

Separated
Surely the arm of the LORD is not too short to save, nor his ear too dull to hear. But your iniquities have separated you from your God; your sins have hidden his face from you, so that he will not hear.

We do what pleases him
Dear friends, if our hearts do not condemn us, we have confidence before God and receive from him anything we ask, because we obey his commands and do what pleases him.

Psalm 66:18. Joshua 7:8, 10–11. Isaiah 59:1–2. 1 John 3:21–22.

June 22

Morning

For you died, and your life is now hidden with Christ in God.

We died to sin; how can we live in it any longer?—I have been crucified with Christ and I no longer live, but Christ lives in me. The life I live in the body, I live by faith in the Son of God, who loved me and gave himself for me.—He died for all that those who live should no longer live for themselves but for him who died for them and was raised again. . . . Therefore, if anyone is in Christ, there is a new creation; the old has gone, the new has come!

We are in him who is true—even in his Son Jesus Christ.

'A new name'
'To those who overcome, I will give some of the hidden manna. I will also give each of them a white stone with a new name written on it, known only to the one who receives it.'

Colossians 3:3. Romans 6:2. Galatians 2:20. 2 Corinthians 5:15, 17.
1 John 5:20. Revelation 2:17.

Evening

'See how he loved him!'

He died for all.—'Greater love has no-one than this, to lay down one's life for one's friends.'

'Father, I want those you have given to me to be with me where I am.'—Having loved his own who were in the world, he now showed them the full extent of his love.

Christ's love compels us
We loved because he first loved us.—Christ's love compels us, because we are convinced that one died for all, and therefore all died. And he died for all, that those who live should no longer live for themselves but for him who died for them and was raised again.

'If you obey my commands, you will remain in my love, just as I have obeyed my Father's commands and remain in his love.'

John 11:36. 2 Corinthians 5:15. John 15:13; 17:24; 13:1. 1 John 4:19.
2 Corinthians 5:14–15. John 15:10.

Morning

'I will ask the Father, and he will give you another Counsellor to be with you for ever—the Spirit of truth.'

'It is for your good that I am going away. Unless I go away, the Counsellor will not come to you; but if I go, I will send him to you.'—The Spirit himself testifies with our spirit that we are God's children.

The Spirit helps us in our weaknesses
For you did not receive a spirit that makes you a slave . . . The Spirit helps us in our weaknesses. We do not know what we ought to pray, but the Spirit himself intercedes for us with groans that words cannot express.

May the God of hope fill you with all joy and peace as you trust in him, so that you may overflow with hope by the power of the Holy Spirit. . . . Hope does not disappoint us, because God has poured out his love into our hearts by the Holy Spirit, whom he has given us.

John 14:16–17; 16:7. Romans 8:16, 15, 26; 15:13; 5:5.

Evening

'They will rest from their labour.'

Where Jesus, who went before us, has entered on our behalf. He has become a high priest for ever, in the order of Melchizedek.

'I will give you rest'
'Come to me, all you who are weary and burdened, and I will give you rest. Take my yoke upon you and learn from me, for I am gentle and humble in heart, and you will find rest for your souls. For my yoke is easy and my burden is light.'—'In repentance and rest is your salvation, in quietness and trust is your strength.'

Quiet waters
The LORD is my shepherd, I shall lack nothing. He makes me lie down in green pastures, he leads me beside quiet waters.

Revelation 14:13. Hebrews 6:20. Matthew 11:28–30. Isaiah 30:15.
Psalm 23:1–2.

June 24

Morning

My times are in your hands.

In all your ways acknowledge him, and he will make your paths straight.—Whether you turn to the right or to the left, your ears will hear a voice behind you, saying, 'This is the way; walk in it.'

He cares for you
The LORD is my shepherd, I shall lack nothing. He makes me lie down in green pastures, he leads me beside quiet water. . . . 'As a father has compassion on his children, so the LORD has compassion on those who fear him; for he knows how we are formed, he remembers that we are dust.'—Your heavenly Father knows that you need them.'—Cast all your anxiety on him because he cares for you.

Psalms 31:15. Proverbs 3:6. Psalms 23:1–2; 103:13–14. Matthew 6:32.
1 Peter 5:7.

Evening

'To those who overcome, I will give the right to sit with me on my throne.'

'In my Father's house are many rooms; if it were not so, I would have told you. I am going there to prepare a place for you. And if I go and prepare a place for you, I will come back and take you to be with me that you also may be where I am.'

'Here I am! I stand at the door and knock. If anyone hears my voice and opens the door, I will come in and eat with them, and they with me.'

Unfailing love!
'I will be with you always, to the very end of the age.'—How priceless is your unfailing love! Both highborn and low find refuge in the shadow of your wings.

Revelation 3:21. John 14:2–3. Revelation 3:20. Matthew 28:20.
Psalm 36:7.

Morning

But we know that when he appears we shall be like him, for we shall see him as he is.

Through these he has given us his very great and precious promises, so that through them you may participate in the divine nature and escape the corruption in the world caused by evil desires.

Since ancient times no-one has heard, no ear has perceived, no eye has seen any God besides you, who acts on behalf of those who wait for him.

Face to face
Now we see but a poor reflection; then we shall see face to face. Now I know in part; then I shall know fully, even as I am fully known.

The Lord Jesus Christ, who, by the power that enables him to bring everything under his control, will transform our lowly bodies so that they will be like his glorious body.

1 John 3:2. 2 Peter 1:4. Isaiah 64:4. 1 Corinthians 13:12.
Philippians 3:20–21.

Evening

KING OF KINGS AND LORD OF LORDS.

Beyond all question, the mystery of godliness is great.

For to us a child is born, to us a son is given, and the government will be on his shoulders. And he will be called Wonderful Counsellor, Mighty God, Everlasting Father, Prince of Peace.

The radiance of God's glory
The Son is the radiance of God's glory and the exact representation of his being, sustaining all purification for sins, he sat down at the right hand of the Majesty in heaven. . . . But about the Son he says, 'Your throne, O God, will last for ever and ever.'

'Let all God's angels worship him.'

Revelation 19:16. 1 Timothy 3:16. Isaiah 9:6. Hebrews 1:3, 8, 6.

June 26

Morning

'Oh that you would bless me and enlarge my territory! Let your hand be with me, and keep me from harm so that I will be free from pain.' And God granted his request.

From the LORD comes deliverance. May your blessing be on your people. . . . How great is your goodness, which you have stored up for those who fear you, which you bestow in the sight of all on those who take refuge in you.—'My prayer is not that you take them out of the world but that you protect them from the evil one.'

'Ask, seek, knock'
'Ask and it will be given to you; seek and you will find; knock and the door will be opened to you. For everyone who asks receives; everyone who seeks finds; and to everyone who knocks, the door will be opened.'

1 Chronicles 4:10. Psalms 3:8; 31:19. John 17:15. Matthew 7:7–8.

Evening

Because the LORD kept vigil that night to bring them out of Egypt.

The Lord Jesus, on the night he was betrayed, took bread, and when he had given thanks, he broke it and said, 'This is my body, which is for you; do this in remembrance of me.' In the same way, after supper he took the cup, saying, 'This cup is the new covenant in my blood; do this, whenever you drink it, in remembrance of me.'

It was the day of Preparation of Passover Week, about the sixth hour. . . . So the soldiers took charge of Jesus. Carrying his own cross, he went out to The Place of the Skull (which in Aramaic is called Golgotha). Here they crucified him.

Our Passover lamb
For Christ, our Passover lamb, has been sacrificed. Therefore let us keep the festival.

Exodus 12:42. 1 Corinthians 11:23–25. John 19:14, 16–18.
1 Corinthians 5:7–8.

Morning

'Who can stand?'

After this I looked and there before me was a great multitude that no-one could count, from every nation, tribe, people and language, standing before the throne and in front of the Lamb. They were wearing white robes and were holding palm branches in their hands.

'Springs of living water'

'These are they who have come out of the great tribulation, they have washed their robes and made them white in the blood of the Lamb. Therefore, they are before the throne of God and serve him day and night in his temple; and he who sits on the throne will spread his tent over them. Never again will they hunger; never again will they thirst. The sun will not beat upon them, nor any scorching heat. For the Lamb at the centre of the throne will be their shepherd; he will lead them to springs of living water. And God will wipe away every tear from their eyes.'

Revelation 6:17; 7:9, 14–17.

Evening

Do not bring your servant into judgment, for no-one living is righteous before you.

'Come now, let us reason together,' says the LORD. 'Though your sins are like scarlet, they shall be as white as snow; though they are red as crimson, they shall be like wool.'

'Submit to God'

Or else let them come to me for refuge; let them make peace with me, yes, let them make peace with me.—'Submit to God and be at peace with him.'

Since we have been justified through faith, we have peace with God through our Lord Jesus Christ.

Victory

Through him everyone who believes is justified from everything you could not be justified from by the law of Moses.—But thanks be to God. He gives us the victory through our Lord Jesus Christ.

Psalm 143:2. Isaiah 1:18; 27:5. Job 22:21. Romans 5:1. Acts 13:39.
1 Corinthians 15:57.

June 28

Morning

'I know that my Redeemer lives.'

For if, when we were God's enemies, we were reconciled to him through the death of his Son, how much more, having been reconciled, shall we be saved through his life!

To save completely
But because Jesus lives for ever, he has a permanent priesthood. Therefore he is able to save completely those who come to God through him, because he always lives to intercede for them.

Christ has indeed been raised
'Because I live, you also will live.'—If only for this life we have hope in Christ, we are to be pitied more than all people. But Christ has indeed been raised from the dead, the firstfruits of those who have fallen asleep.

For you know that it was not with perishable things such as silver or gold that you were redeemed from the empty way of life handed down to you from your forefathers, but with the precious blood of Christ, a lamb without blemish or defect.

Job 19:25. Romans 5:10. Hebrews 7:24–25. John 14:19.
1 Corinthians 15:19–20. 1 Peter 1:18–19.

Evening

The Spirit clearly says that in later times some will abandon the faith and follow deceiving spirits and things taught by demons.

Consider carefully how you listen.—Let the word of Christ dwell in you richly as you teach and admonish one another with all wisdom.—In addition to all this, take up the shield of faith, with which you can extinguish all the flaming arrows of the evil one.

A light for my path
Your word is a lamp to my feet and a light for my path. . . . I have more insight than all my teachers, for I meditate on your statutes.

For Satan himself masquerades as an angel of light.—Even if we or an angel from heaven should preach a gospel other than the one we preached to you, let him be eternally condemned!

1 Timothy 4:1. Luke 8:18. Colossians 3:16. Ephesians 6:16.
Psalm 119:105, 99. 2 Corinthians 11:14. Galatians 1:8.

Morning

His commands are not burdensome.

'For my yoke is easy and my burden is light.'

'Loved by my Father'
'If you love me, you will obey what I command. . . . Those who have my commands and obey them, are the ones who love me. Those who love me will be loved by my Father, and I too will love them and show myself to them.'

Great peace
Blessed are those who find wisdom, those who gain understanding.—Her ways are pleasant ways, and all her paths are peace.—Great peace have they who love your law, and nothing can make them stumble.—For in my inner being I delight in God's law.

Love does no harm to its neighbour. Therefore love is the fulfilment of the law.

> 1 John 5:3. Matthew 11:30. John 14:15, 21. Proverbs 3:13, 17.
> Psalm 119:165. Romans 7:22; 13:10.

Evening

Remember not the sins of my youth and my rebellious ways.

'I have swept away your offences like a cloud, your sins like the morning mist.'

'White as snow'
'Come now, let us reason together,' says the LORD. 'Though your sins are like scarlet, they shall be as white as snow; though they are red as crimson, they shall be like wool.'—'For I will forgive their wickedness and will remember their sins no more.'—You will hurl all our iniquities into the depths of the sea.

In your love
In your love you kept me from the pit of destruction; you have put all my sins behind your back.

> Psalm 25:7. Isaiah 44:22; 1:18. Jeremiah 31:34. Micah 7:19. Isaiah 38:17.

June 30

Morning

'Those whom I love I rebuke and discipline.'

'My child, do not make light of the Lord's discipline, and do not lose heart when he rebukes you, because the Lord disciplines those he loves, and he punishes everyone he accepts as a child.'—Because the LORD disciplines those he loves, as parents the children they delight in.

His hands also heal
For he wounds, but he also binds up, he injures, but his hands also heal.

The LORD has compassion
He does not treat us as our sins deserve or repay us according to our iniquities. For as high as the heavens are above the earth, so great is his love for those who fear him; as far as the east is from the west, so far has he removed our transgressions from us. As parents have compassion on their children, so the LORD has compassion on those who fear him; for he knows how we are formed, he remembers that we are dust.

Revelation 3:19. Hebrews 12:5–6. Proverbs 3:12. Job 5:18.
Psalm 103:10–14.

Evening

Do not be quick with your mouth, do not be hasty in your heart to utter anything before God.

'When you pray, do not keep on babbling like pagans, for they think they will be heard because of their many words. Do not be like them, for your Father knows what you need before you ask him.'

'God, have mercy on me, a sinner'
'Two men went up to the temple to pray, one a Pharisee and the other a tax collector. The Pharisee stood up and prayed about himself: "God, I thank you that I am not like other people—robbers, evildoers, adulterers—or even like this tax collector." . . . But the tax collector stood at a distance. He would not even look up to heaven, but beat his breast and said, "God, have mercy on me, a sinner." I tell you that this man, rather than the other, went home justified before God.'

Ecclesiastes 5:2. Matthew 6:7–8. Luke 18:10–11, 13–14.

Morning

The fruit of the Spirit is goodness.

Be imitators of God, therefore, as dearly loved children.—'Love your enemies and pray for those who persecute you, that you may be children of your Father in heaven. He causes his sun to rise on the evil and the good, and sends rain on the righteous and the unrighteous.'—'Be merciful, just as your Father is merciful.'

The fruit of the light
For the fruit of the light consists in all goodness, righteousness and truth.—But when the kindness and love of God our Saviour appeared, he saved us, not because of righteous things we had done, but because of his mercy. He saved us through the washing of rebirth and renewal by the Holy Spirit, whom he poured out on us generously through Jesus Christ our Saviour.

Galatians 5:22. Ephesians 5:1. Matthew 5:44–45. Luke 6:36.
Ephesians 5:9. Titus 3:4–6.

Evening

Ebenezer . . . 'Thus far has the Lord helped us.'

When I was in great need, he saved me. . . . Praise be to the Lord, for he has heard my cry for mercy. The Lord is my strength and my shield; my heart trusts in him, and I am helped. My heart leaps for joy and I will give thanks to him in song.

Refuge in the Lord
It is better to take refuge in the Lord than to trust in human beings. It is better to take refuge in the Lord than to trust in princes. . . . Blessed are those whose help is the God of Jacob, whose hope is in the Lord his God. . . . He led them by a straight way to a city where they could settle.—Not one of all the Lord's good promises to the house of Israel failed; every one was fulfilled.

1 Samuel 7:12; Psalms 116:6; 28:6–7; 118:8–9; 146:5; 107:7.
Joshua 21:45.

Morning

'These are the regulations for the Passover: No foreigner is to eat of it.'

We have an altar from which those who minister at the tabernacle have no right to eat.—'No-one can see the kingdom of God without being born again.'—At that time you were separate from Christ, excluded from citizenship in Israel and foreigners to the covenants of the promise. . . . But now in Christ Jesus you who once were far away have been brought near through the blood of Christ.

He himself is our peace
For he himself is our peace, who has made the two one . . . by abolishing in his flesh the law with its commandments and regulations. His purpose was to create in himself one new humanity out of the two, thus making peace.

Exodus 12:43. Hebrews 13:10. John 3:3. Ephesians 2:12–13, 14–15.

Evening

[Jesus] prayed the third time, saying the same thing.

During the days of Jesus' life on earth, he offered up prayers and petitions with loud cries and tears to the one who could save him from death.

Be faithful in prayer
Let us acknowledge the LORD.—Be . . . faithful in prayer.—Pray in the Spirit on all occasions with all kinds of prayers and requests. With this in mind, be alert and always keep on praying.—But in everything, by prayer and petition, with thanksgiving, present your requests to God. And the peace of God, which transcends all understanding, will guard your hearts and your minds in Christ Jesus.

This is the assurance we have in approaching God: that if we ask anything according to his will, he hears us.

Matthew 26:44. Hebrews 5:7. Hosea 6:3. Romans 12:12. Ephesians 6:18.
Philippians 4:6–7. 1 John 5:14.

Morning

If we are children, then we are heirs—heirs of God and co-heirs with Christ.

If you belong to Christ, then you are Abraham's seed, and heirs according to the promise.

An heir

How great is the love the Father has lavished on us, that we should be called children of God.—So you are no longer slaves, but God's children; and since you are his children, God has made you also heirs.—He predestined us to be adopted as his children through Jesus Christ, in accordance with his pleasure and will.

'Father, I want those you have given me to be with me where I am, and to see my glory, the glory you have given me.'

Romans 8:17. Galatians 3:29. 1 John 3:1. Galatians 4:7. Ephesians 1:5.
John 17:24.

Evening

[God] chose the lowly things of this world and the despised things.

Ordinary men

When they saw the courage of Peter and John and realised that they were unschooled, ordinary men, they were astonished and they took note that these men had been with Jesus.

My message and my preaching were not with wise and persuasive words, but with a demonstration of the Spirit's power, so that your faith might not rest on human wisdom, but on God's power.

'Apart from me you can do nothing'

'You did not choose me, but I chose you to go and bear fruit.' . . . 'If you remain in me and I you, you will bear much fruit; apart from me you can do nothing.'

We have this treasure in jars of clay to show that this all-surpassing power is from God.

1 Corinthians 1:28. Acts 4:13. 1 Corinthians 2:4–5. John 15:16, 5.
2 Corinthians 4:7.

July 4

Morning

Reclining next to him.

'As a mother comforts her child, so will I comfort you.'—People were bringing little children to Jesus to have him touch them. . . . And he took the children in his arms, put his hands on them and blessed them.—Jesus called his disciples to him and said, 'I have compassion for these people; they have already been with me three days and have nothing to eat. I do not want to send them away hungry, or they may collapse on the way.'

'I will not forget you!'
'I will not leave you as orphans; I will come to you.'—'Can a mother forget the baby at her breast and have no compassion on the child she has borne? Though she may forget, I will not forget you!'
'For the Lamb at the centre of the throne will be their shepherd; he will lead them to springs of living water. And God will wipe away every tear from their eyes.'

John 13:23. Isaiah 66:13. Mark 10:13, 16. Matthew 15:32. John 14:18.
Isaiah 49:15. Revelation 7:17.

Evening

[Jesus] is the atoning sacrifice for our sins.

Surely his salvation is near those who fear him. Love and faithfulness meet together; righteousness and peace kiss each other.

O Israel, put your hope in the LORD, for with the LORD is unfailing love and with him is full redemption. He himself will redeem Israel from all their sins.

The one who justifies
All have sinned and fall short of the glory of God, and are justified freely by his grace through the redemption that came by Christ Jesus. God presented him as a sacrifice of atonement, through faith in his blood. He did this to demonstrate his justice, because in his forbearance he had left the sins committed beforehand unpunished—he did it to demonstrate his justice at the present time, so as to be just and the one who justifies those who have faith in Jesus.

John 2:1–2. Psalms 85:9–10; 130:7–8. Romans 3:23–25.

Morning

So we know and rely on the love God has for us.

And God raised us up with Christ and seated us with him in the heavenly realms in Christ Jesus, in order that in the coming ages he might show the incomparable riches of his grace, expressed in his kindness to us in Christ Jesus.

'God so loved the world'
'God so loved the world that he gave his one and only Son, that whoever believes in him shall not perish but have eternal life.'—He who did not spare his own Son, but gave him up for us all—how will he not also, along with him, graciously give us all things?—The LORD is good to all; he has compassion on all he has made.

We love him because he first loved us.

1 John 4:16. John 3:16. Romans 8:32. Psalm 145:9. 1 John 4:19.

Evening

Do not be proud, but be willing to associate with people of low position. Do not be conceited.

My brothers and sisters, as believers in our glorious Lord Jesus Christ, don't show favouritism. . . . Has not God chosen those who are poor in the eyes of the world to be rich in faith and to inherit the kingdom he promised those who love him?

But if we have food and clothing, we will be content with that. People who want to get rich fall into temptation and a trap and into many foolish and harmful desires that plunge people into ruin and destruction.

No-one may boast before him
But God chose the foolish things of the world to shame the wise; God chose the weak things of the world to shame the strong. He chose the lowly things of this world and the despised things—and the things that are not—to nullify the things that are, so that no-one may boast before him.

My heart is not proud, O LORD, my eyes are not haughty.

Romans 12:16. James 2:1, 5. 1 Timothy 6:8–9. 1 Corinthians 1:27–29.
Psalm 131:1.

July 6

Morning

Let your conversation be always full of grace.

A word aptly spoken is like apples of gold in settings of silver. Like an ear-ring of gold or an ornament of fine gold is a wise rebuke to a listening ear.

The tongue of the wise brings healing
'Do not let any unwholesome talk come out of your mouths, . . . but only what is helpful for building others up according to their needs.'—The tongue of the wise brings healing.

Then those who feared the LORD talked with each other, and the LORD listened and heard. A scroll of remembrance was written in his presence concerning those who feared the LORD and honoured his name.

But just as you excel in everything—in faith, in speech, in knowledge, in complete earnestness, . . . see that you also excel in this grace of giving.

Colossians 4:6. Proverbs 25:11–12. Ephesians 4:29. Proverbs 12:18.
Malachi 3:16. 2 Corinthians 8:7.

Evening

For your love is ever before me.

The LORD is gracious and compassionate, slow to anger and rich in love.

Christ's love compels us
Be imitators of God, therefore, as dearly loved children and live a life of love, just as Christ loved us and gave himself up for us as a fragrant offering and sacrifice to God. . . . Be kind and compassionate to one another, forgiving each other, just as in Christ God forgave you.—For Christ's love compels us.

'But love your enemies, do good to them, and lend to them without expecting to get anything back. Then your reward will be great, and you will be sons of the Most High, because he is kind to the ungrateful and wicked. Be merciful, just as your Father is merciful.'

Psalms 26:3; 145:8. Ephesians 5:1–2; 4:32. 2 Corinthians 5:14.
Luke 6:35–36.

Morning

Then Jesus was led by the Spirit into the desert to be tempted by the devil.

During the days of Jesus' life on earth, he offered up prayers and petitions with loud cries and tears to the one who could save him from death, and he was heard because of his reverent submission. Although he was a son, he learned obedience from what he suffered and, once made perfect, he became the source of eternal salvation for all who obey him.

God is faithful
No temptation has seized you except what is common to all people. And God is faithful; he will not let you be tempted beyond what you can bear. But when you are tempted, he will also provide a way out so that you can stand up under it.

Matthew 4:1. Hebrews 5:7–9. 1 Corinthians 10:13.

Evening

'The Son of Man . . . [came] to give his life as a ransom for many.'

The blood of goats and bulls and the ashes of a heifer sprinkled on those who are ceremonially unclean sanctify them so that they are outwardly clean. How much more, then, will the blood of Christ, who through the eternal Spirit offered himself unblemished to God, cleanse our consciences from acts that lead to death, so that we may serve the living God!

A lamb to the slaughter
He was led like a lamb to the slaughter.—'I lay down my life for the sheep. . . . No-one takes it from me, but I lay it down of my own accord. I have authority to lay it down and authority to take it up again.'
  Without the shedding of blood there is no forgiveness.

Matthew 20:28. Hebrews 9:13–14. Isaiah 53:7. John 10:15, 18.
Hebrews 9:22.

July 8

Morning

If we confess our sins, he is faithful and just and will forgive us our sins and purify us from all unrighteousness.

For I know my transgressions, and my sin is always before me. Against you, you only, have I sinned and done what is evil in your sight.—'So he got up and went to his father. But while he was still a long way off, his father saw him and was filled with compassion for him; he ran to his son, threw his arms around him and kissed him.'

'I have redeemed you'
'I have swept away your offences like a cloud, your sins like the morning mist. Return to me, for I have redeemed you.'

'I will sprinkle clean water on you, and you will be clean.'—'They will walk with me, dressed in white, for they are worthy.'

> 1 John 1:9. Psalm 51:3–4. Luke 15:20. Isaiah 44:22. Ezekiel 36:25.
> Revelation 3:4.

Evening

Can a corrupt throne be allied with you?

We shall be like him
Our fellowship is with the Father and with his Son, Jesus Christ. . . . Dear friends, now we are children of God, and what we will be has not yet been made known. But we know that when he appears, we shall be like him, for we shall see him as he is. All who have this hope in them purify themselves, just as he is pure.

Spiritual forces of evil
For our struggle is not against flesh and blood, but against the rulers, against the authorities, against the powers of this dark world and against the spiritual forces of evil in the heavenly realms. . . . The ruler of the kingdom of the air, the spirit who is now at work in those who are disobedient.

> Psalm 94:20. 1 John 1:3; 3:2–3. Ephesians 6:12; 2:2.

Morning

'I have taken away your sin, and I will put rich garments on you.'

Blessed are those whose transgressions are forgiven, whose sins are covered.—All of us have become like one who is unclean.—I know that nothing good lives in me, that is, in my sinful nature. For I have the desire to do what is good, but I cannot carry it out.

For all of you who were baptised into Christ have clothed yourselves with Christ.—You have taken off your old self with its practices and have put on the new self, which is being renewed in knowledge in the image of its Creator.

Garments of salvation
I delight greatly in the LORD; my soul rejoices in my God. For he has clothed me with garments of salvation and arrayed me in a robe of righteousness.

Zechariah 3:4. Psalm 32:1. Isaiah 64:6. Romans 7:18. Galatians 3:27.
Colossians 3:9–10. Isaiah 61:10.

Evening

Day will bring it to light.

You, then, why do you judge your brother or sister? Or why do you look down on your brother or sister? For we will all stand before God's judgment seat. . . . So then, each of us will give an account of ourselves to God. Therefore let us stop passing judgment on one another.

God will judge everyone's secrets
Therefore judge nothing before the appointed time; wait till the Lord comes. He will bring to light what is hidden in darkness and will expose the motives of people's hearts. At that time each will receive praise from God.—God will judge everyone's secrets through Jesus Christ.—'The Father judges no-one, but has entrusted all judgment to the Son. . . . And he has given him authority to judge because he is the Son of Man.'

1 Corinthians 3:13. Romans 14:10, 12–13. 1 Corinthians 4:5.
Romans 2:16. John 5:22, 27.

July 10

Morning

'A servant [is not] above his master.'

'You call me, "Teacher" and "Lord", and rightly so, for that is what I am.'
'It is enough for the student to be like his teacher, and the servant like his master.'—'If they persecuted me, they will persecute you also. If they obeyed my teaching, they will obey yours also.' . . . 'I have given them your word and the world has hated them, for they are not of the world any more than I am of the world.'

Christ suffered in his body
Let us run with perseverance the race marked out for us. Let us fix our eyes on Jesus, the author and perfecter of our faith, who for the joy set before him endured the cross, scorning its shame, and sat down at the right hand of the throne of God.—Since Christ suffered in his body, arm yourselves also with the same attitude.

> Matthew 10:24. John 13:13. Matthew 10:25. John 15:20; 17:14.
> Hebrews 12:1–2. 1 Peter 4:1.

Evening

My son, give me your heart.

'Oh, that their hearts would be inclined to fear me and keep all my commands always, so that it might go well with them and their children for ever!'
Your heart is not right before God.—The sinful mind is hostile to God. It does not submit to God's law, nor can it do so. Those controlled by the sinful nature cannot please God.
But they gave themselves first to the Lord.—In everything that he [Hezekiah] undertook . . . he sought his God and worked wholeheartedly. And so he prospered.

Guard your heart
Guard your heart, for it is the wellspring of life.
I run in the path of your commands, for you have set my heart free.

> Proverbs 23:26. Deuteronomy 5:29. Acts 8:21. Romans 8:7–8.
> 2 Corinthians 8:5. 2 Chronicles 31:21. Proverbs 4:23. Psalm 119:32.

Morning

'I am with you to rescue and save you.'

'So do not fear, for I am with you; do not be dismayed, for I am your God. I will strengthen you and help you; I will uphold you with my righteous right hand.'

He himself was tempted
We do not have a high priest who is unable to sympathise with our weaknesses, but we have one who has been tempted in every way, just as we are—yet was without sin. . . . Because he himself suffered when he was tempted, he is able to help those who are being tempted.

The LORD upholds with his hand
The LORD makes firm the steps of those who delight in him; though they stumble, they will not fall, for the LORD upholds them with his hand.

Jeremiah 15:20. Isaiah 41:10. Hebrews 4:15; 2:18. Psalm 37:23–24.

Evening

For he satisfies the thirsty and fills the hungry with good things.

You have tasted that the Lord is good.—O God, you are my God, earnestly I seek you; my soul thirsts for you, my body longs for you, in a dry and weary land where there is no water. I have seen you in the sanctuary and behold your power and your glory.

My soul yearns, even faints for the courts of the LORD; my heart and my flesh cry out for the living God—I desire to depart and be with Christ, which is far better.

'The Lamb will be their shepherd'
'Never again will they hunger; never again will they thirst. The sun will not beat upon them, for the Lamb at the centre of the throne will be their shepherd; he will lead them to springs of living water. And God will wipe away every tear from their eyes.'

Psalm 107:9. 1 Peter 2:3. Psalms 63:1–2; 84:2. Philippians 1:23.
Revelation 7:16–17.

July 12

Morning

'My Presence will go with you, and I will give you rest.'

'Have I not commanded you? Be strong and courageous. Do not be terrified; do not be discouraged, for the LORD your God will be with you wherever you go.'—In all your ways acknowledge him, and he will make your paths straight.

'Never will I leave you'
God has said, 'Never will I leave you; never will I forsake you.' So we say with confidence, 'The Lord is my helper; I will not be afraid. What can human beings do to me?'—Our competence comes from God.

My times are in your hands
'Lead us not into temptation.'—My times are in your hands.

Exodus 33:14. Joshua 1:9. Proverbs 3:6. Hebrews 13:5–6.
2 Corinthians 3:5. Matthew 6:13. Psalm 31:15.

Evening

Let us consider how we may spur one another on towards love and good deeds.

A scroll of remembrance
Then those who feared the LORD talked with each other, and the LORD listened and heard. A scroll of remembrance was written in his presence concerning those who feared the LORD and honoured his name.—'If two of you on earth agree about anything you ask for, it will be done for you by my Father in heaven.'

'It is not good for the man to be alone'
The Lord God said, 'It is not good for the man to be alone.'
Make up your mind not to put any stumbling-block or obstacle in another believer's way.—Carry each other's burdens, and in this way you will fulfil the law of Christ. . . . But watch yourself, or you also may be tempted.

Hebrews 10:24. Malachi 3:16. Matthews 18:19. Genesis 2:18.
Romans 14:13. Galatians 6:1.

Morning

I know whom I have believed, and am convinced that he is able to guard what I have entrusted to him for that day.

For I am convinced that neither death nor life, neither angels nor demons, neither the present nor the future, nor any powers, neither height nor depth, nor anything else in all creation, will be able to separate us from the love of God that is in Christ Jesus our Lord.—'I protected them and kept them safe by that name you gave me. None has been lost.'

For the LORD takes delight in his people.—'Greater love has no-one than this, to lay down one's life for one's friends.'

We belong to the Lord
You were bought with a price. Therefore honour God with your body.—If we live, we live to the Lord; and if we die, we die to the Lord. So, whether we live or die, we belong to the Lord.

> 2 Timothy 1:12. Romans 8:38–39. John 17:12. Psalm 149:4. John 15:13.
> 1 Corinthians 6:20. Romans 14:8.

Evening

Look in the scroll of the LORD and read.

'Fix these words of mine in your hearts and minds; tie them as symbols on your hands and bind them on your foreheads.'—'Do not let this Book of the Law depart from your mouth; meditate on it day and night, so that you may be careful to do everything written in it. Then you will be prosperous and successful.'

The law of their God is in their hearts; their feet do not slip.

Encouragement of the Scriptures
We have the word of the prophets made more certain, and you will do well to pay attention to it, as to a light shining in a dark place, until the day dawns and the morning star rises in your hearts.—That through endurance and the encouragement of the Scriptures we might have hope.

> Isaiah 34:16. Deuteronomy 11:18. Joshua 1:8. Psalm 37:31. 2 Peter 1:19.
> Romans 15:4.

July 14

Morning

Let the word of Christ dwell in you richly as you teach and admonish one another with all wisdom.

Guard your heart, for it is the wellspring of life. . . . The tongue has power of life and death.—Do not let any unwholesome talk come out of your mouths, but only what is helpful for building others up according to their needs, that it may benefit those who listen.

'For we cannot help speaking about what we have seen and heard.'

It is with your heart that you believe
'Those who acknowledge me before others, I will also acknowledge before my Father in heaven.'—For it is with your heart that you believe and are justified, and it is with your mouth that you confess and are saved.

Colossians 3:16. Proverbs 4:23; 18:21. Ephesians 4:29. Acts 4:20.
Matthew 10:32. Romans 10:10.

Evening

I hope to see you soon, and we will talk face to face.

Oh, that you would rend the heavens and come down.—As the deer pants for streams of water, so my soul pants for you, O God. My soul thirsts for God, for the living God. When can I go and meet with God?'

We eagerly await a Saviour
Our citizenship is in heaven. And we eagerly await a Saviour from there, the Lord Jesus Christ.—We wait for the blessed hope—the glorious appearing of our great God and Saviour, Jesus Christ.—God our Saviour and . . . Christ Jesus our hope.

In that day they will say, 'Surely this is our God; we trusted in him, and he saved us. This is the LORD, we trusted in him; let us rejoice and be glad in his salvation.'

3 John 14. Isaiah 64:1. Psalm 42:1–2. Philippians 3:20. Titus 2:13.
1 Timothy 1:1. Isaiah 25:9.

Morning

'Your will be done on earth as it is in heaven.'

Praise the LORD, you his angels, you mighty ones who do his bidding, who obey his word. Praise the LORD, all his heavenly hosts, you his servants who do his will.

'I desire to do your will'
'For I have come down from heaven not to do my will but to do the will of him who sent me.'—'I desire to do your will, O my God; your law is within my heart.'—'My Father, if it is not possible for this cup to be taken away unless I drink it, may your will be done.'

'Now that you know these things, you will be blessed if you do them.'—If you know the good you ought to do and don't do it, you sin.

Matthew 6:10. Psalm 103:20–21. John 6:38. Psalm 40:8. Matthew 26:42.
John 13:17. James 4:17.

Evening

'Stop judging by mere appearances, and make a right judgment.'

Let the word of Christ dwell in you richly as you teach and admonish one another with all wisdom.

'Those who have ears, let them hear what the Spirit says.'—The person with the Spirit makes judgments about all things. 'Consider carefully what you hear.'

'I know your deeds, your hard work . . . that you have tested those who claim to be apostles but are not, and have found them false.'—Test everything. Hold on to the good.

'They know his voice'
'He calls his own sheep by name and leads them out. When he has brought out all his own, he goes on ahead of them, and his sheep follow him because they know his voice. But they will never follow a stranger; in fact, they will run away from him because they do not recognise a stranger's voice.'

John 7:24. Colossians 3:16. Revelation 2:29. 1 Corinthians 2:15.
Mark 4:24. Revelation 2:2. 1 Thessalonians 5:21. John 10:3–5.

July 16

Morning

'You will be for me a kingdom of priests and a holy nation.'

'You were slain, and with your blood you purchased for God members of every tribe and language and people and nation. You have made them to be a kingdom and priests to serve our God.'—You are a chosen people, a royal priesthood, a holy nation, a people belonging to God, that you may declare the praises of him who called you out of darkness into his wonderful light.

And you will be called the priests of the LORD, you will be named ministers of our God.

We are God's handiwork
For we are God's handiwork, created in Christ Jesus to do good works, which God prepared in advance for us to do.—God's temple is sacred, and you are that temple.

> Exodus 19:6. Revelation 5:9–10. 1 Peter 2:9. Isaiah 61:6. Ephesians 2:10.
> 1 Corinthians 3:17.

Evening

But we prayed to our God and posted a guard day and night to meet this threat.

'Watch and pray so that you will not fall into temptation.'—Devote yourselves to prayer, being watchful and thankful.—Cast all your anxiety on him because he cares for you. Be self-controlled and alert. Your enemy the devil prowls around like a roaring lion looking for someone to devour. Resist him, standing firm in the faith.

'Why do you call me, "Lord, Lord," and do not do what I say?'

By prayer and petition
Do not be anxious about anything, but in everything, by prayer and petition, with thanksgiving, present your requests to God. And the peace of God, which transcends all understanding, will guard your hearts and your minds in Christ Jesus.

> Nehemiah 4:9. Matthew 26:41. Colossians 4:2. 1 Peter 5:7–9. Luke 6:46.
> Philippians 4:6–7.

Morning

'You are a gracious and compassionate God, slow to anger and abounding in love, a God who relents from sending calamity.'

Do not hold against us the sins of past generations; may your mercy come quickly to meet us, for we are in desperate need. Help us, O God our Saviour, for the glory of your name; deliver us and forgive our sins for your name's sake.—Although our sins testify against us, O LORD, do something for the sake of your name. For our backsliding is great; we have sinned against you.

Forgiveness
If you, O LORD, kept a record of sins, O Lord, who could stand? But with you there is forgiveness; therefore you are feared.

> Jonah 4:2. Psalm 79:8–9. Jeremiah 14:7. Psalm 130:3–4.

Evening

Sanctifying work of the Spirit.

See what this godly sorrow has produced in you: what earnestness, what eagerness to clear yourselves, what indignation, what alarm, what longing, what concern, what readiness to see justice done.—(For the fruit of the light consists in all goodness, righteousness and truth) and find out what pleases the Lord.

Out of the most severe trial, their overflowing joy and their extreme poverty welled up in rich generosity.

The work of the one and the same Spirit
All these are the work of one and the same Spirit, and he gives them to each one, just as he determines.

> 2 Thessalonians 2:13. 2 Corinthians 7:11. Ephesians 5:9–10.
> 2 Corinthians 8:2. 1 Corinthians 12:11.

July 18

Morning

'He calls his own sheep by name and leads them out.'

God's solid foundation stands firm, sealed with this inscription: 'The Lord knows those who are his,' and, 'Everyone who confesses the name of the Lord must turn away from wickedness.'—'Many will say to me on that day, "Lord, Lord, did we not prophesy in your name, and in your name drive out demons and perform many miracles?" Then I will tell them plainly, "I never knew you. Away from me, you evildoers!"'—The LORD watches over the way of the righteous, but the way of the wicked will perish.

A refuge in times of trouble
See, I have engraved you on the palms of my hands; your walls are ever before me.—The LORD is good, a refuge in times of trouble. He cares for those who trust in him.

> John 10:3. 2 Timothy 2:19. Matthew 7:22–23. Psalm 1:6. Isaiah 49:16.
> Nahum 1:7.

Evening

'This poor widow has put in more than all the others.'

'Anyone who gives you a cup of water in my name because you belong to Christ will certainly be rewarded.'

Suppose a brother or sister is without clothes and daily food. If one of you says to them, 'Go, I wish you well; keep warm and well fed,' but does nothing about their physical needs, what good is it?

God loves a cheerful giver
Whoever sows generously will also reap generously. Each of you should give what you have decided in your heart to give, not reluctantly or under compulsion, for God loves a cheerful giver.

'So you also, when you have done everything you were told to do, should say, "We are unworthy servants; we have only done our duty."'

> Luke 21:3. Mark 9:41. James 2:15–16. 2 Corinthians 9:6–7. Luke 17:10.

Morning

For the Mighty One has done great things for me—holy is his name.

'Who among the gods is like you, O LORD? Who is like you—majestic in holiness, awesome in glory, working wonders?'

'You alone are holy'
Among the gods there is none like you, O Lord; no deeds can compare with yours.—'Who will not fear you, O Lord, and bring glory to your name? For you alone are holy.'—'Hallowed be your name.'

   'Praise be to the Lord, the God of Israel, because he has come and has redeemed his people.'

   Now to him who is able to do immeasurably more than all we ask or imagine, according to his power that is at work within us, to him be glory.

Luke 1:49. Exodus 15:11. Psalm 86:8. Revelation 15:4. Matthew 6:9.
Luke 1:68. Ephesians 3:20–21.

Evening

Let my teaching fall like rain and my words descend like dew, like showers on new grass.

'My word will accomplish what I desire'
'As the rain and the snow come down from heaven, and do not return to it without watering the earth and making it bud and flourish, so that it yields seed for the sower and bread for the eater, so is my word that goes out from my mouth: It will not return to me empty, but will accomplish what I desire and achieve the purpose for which I sent it.'

   'For God gives the Spirit without limit.' . . . From the fulness of his grace we have all received one blessing after another.—It is like precious oil poured on the head, running down on the beard, running down on Aaron's beard, down upon the collar of his robes.

Deuteronomy 32:2. Isaiah 55:10–11. John 3:34; 1:16. Psalm 133:2.

July 20

Morning

'They are not of the world, even as I am not of it.'

'In this world you will have trouble. But take heart! I have overcome the world.'

Become blameless and pure
Such a high priest meets our need—one who is holy, blameless, pure, set apart from sinners.—So that you may become blameless and pure, children of God without fault in a crooked and depraved generation.

Jesus of Nazareth . . . went around doing good and healing all who were under the power of the devil, because God was with him.—As we have opportunity, let us do good to all people, especially to those who belong to the family of believers.

> John 17:16. John 16:33. Hebrews 7:26. Philippians 2:15. Acts 10:38.
> Galatians 6:10.

Evening

But the cheerful heart has a continual feast.

The joy of the LORD is your strength.—For the kingdom of God is not a matter of eating and drinking, but of righteousness, peace and joy in the Holy Spirit.—Instead, be filled with the Spirit. Speak to one another with psalms, hymns and spiritual songs. Sing and make music in your heart to the Lord, always giving thanks to God the Father for everything, in the name of our Lord Jesus Christ.

Yet I will rejoice in the LORD
Though the fig tree does not bud and there are no grapes on the vines, though the olive crop fails and the fields produce no food, though there are no sheep in the pen and no cattle in the stalls, yet I will rejoice in the LORD, I will be joyful in God my Saviour.—Sorrowful, yet always rejoicing.

> Proverbs 15:15. Nehemiah 8:10. Romans 14:17. Ephesians 5:18–20.
> Habakkuk 3:17–18. 2 Corinthians 6:10.

Morning

Circumcise yourselves to the LORD, circumcise your hearts.

Then when their uncircumcised hearts are humbled and they pay for their sin, I will remember my covenant with Jacob and my covenant with Isaac and my covenant with Abraham, and I will remember the land.—Christ has become a servant of the Jews on behalf of God's truth, to confirm the promises made to the patriarchs.

God made you alive
In him you were also circumcised, in the putting off of sinful nature, not with a circumcision done by human hands but with the circumcision done by Christ, . . . When you were dead in your sins and in the uncircumcision of your sinful nature, God made you alive with Christ. He forgave us all our sins.

Jeremiah 4:4. Leviticus 26:41–42. Romans 15:8. Colossians 2:11, 13.

Evening

The curtain of the temple was torn in two from top to bottom.

The Lord Jesus, on the night he was betrayed, took bread, and when he had given thanks, he broke it and said, 'This is my body, which is for you; do this in remembrance of me.'—'This bread is my flesh, which I will give for the life of the world.'

'Eat . . . drink'
'Unless you eat the flesh of the Son of Man and drink his blood, you have no life in you. Whoever eats my flesh and drinks my blood has eternal life.'

Through the curtain
A new and living way opened for us through the curtain, that is, his body, . . . Let us draw near to God.

Matthew 27:51. 1 Corinthians 11:23–24. John 6:51, 53–54.
Hebrews 10:20, 22.

July 22

Morning

The death he died, he died to sin once for all; but the life he lives, he lives to God.

He was numbered with the transgressors.—Christ was sacrificed once to take away the sins of many people.—He himself bore our sins in his body on the tree, so that we might die to sins and live for righteousness; by his wounds you have been healed.

Christ died for us
While we were still sinners, Christ died for us. Since we have now been justified by his blood, how much more shall we be saved from God's wrath through him!

Christ suffered in his body
Therefore, since Christ suffered in his body, arm yourselves also with the same attitude, because he who has suffered in his body is done with sin. As a result, he does not live the rest of his earthly life for evil human desires but rather for the will of God.

> Romans 6:10. Isaiah 53:12. Hebrews 9:28. 1 Peter 2:24. Romans 5:8–9.
> 1 Peter 4:1–2.

Evening

Keep yourselves in God's love.

'Remain in me, and I will remain in you. No branch can bear fruit by itself, it must remain in the vine. Neither can you bear fruit unless you remain in me. I am the vine; you are the branches. If you remain in me and I in you, you will bear much fruit; apart from me you can do nothing.'

Love made complete
But if anyone obeys his word, God's love is truly made complete in that person.

'Love each other'
'My command is this: Love each other as I have loved you.'—But God demonstrates his own love for us in this: While we were still sinners, Christ died for us.—God is love. Those who live in love live in God, and God in them.

> Jude 21. John 15:4–5. 1 John 2:5. John 15:12. Romans 5:8. 1 John 4:16.

Morning

The end will come.

'No-one knows about the day or hour, not even the angels in heaven, nor the Son, but only the Father. Be on guard! Be alert! You do not know when that time will come. . . . What I say to you, I say to everyone: "Watch!"'

Everything will be destroyed
Since everything will be destroyed in this way, what kind of people ought you to be? You ought to live holy and godly lives.

'Keep your lamps burning'
The end of all things is near. Therefore be clear minded and self-controlled so that you can pray.—'Be dressed ready for service and keep your lamps burning, like those waiting for their master to return from a wedding banquet, so that when he comes and knocks they can immediately open the door for him.'

1 Corinthians 15:24. Mark 13:32–33, 37. 2 Peter 3:11. 1 Peter 4:7.
Luke 12:35–36.

Evening

Brothers and sisters, pray for us.

Is any one of you sick? Call the elders of the church to pray over you and anoint you with oil in the name of the Lord. And the prayer offered in faith will make you well; the Lord will raise you up. If you have sinned, you will be forgiven. Therefore confess your sins to each other and pray for each other so that you may be healed. The prayer of a righteous person is powerful and effective.

Elijah prayed earnestly
Elijah was human just as we are. He prayed earnestly that it would not rain, and it did not rain on the land for three and a half years. Again he prayed, and the heavens gave rain, and the earth produced crops.

Praying for all the saints
Pray in the Spirit on all occasions with all kinds of prayers and requests. With this in mind, be alert and always keep on praying for all the saints.

1 Thessalonians 5:25. James 5:14–16, 17–18. Ephesians 6:18.

July 24

Morning

Patient in affliction.

A man of sorrows
Jesus wept.—A man of sorrows, and familiar with suffering. . . . Surely he took up our infirmities and carried our sorrows.

'The Lord disciplines those he loves, and he punishes everyone he accepts as a child.' . . . No discipline seems pleasant at the time, but painful. Later on, however, it produces a harvest of righteousness and peace for those who have been trained by it.

'Take heart!'
Strengthened with all power according to his glorious might so that you may have great endurance and patience.—'In this world you will have trouble. But take heart! I have overcome the world.'

Romans 12:12. John 11:35. Isaiah 53:3–4. Hebrews 12:6, 11.
Colossians 1:11. John 16:33.

Evening

He did not waver through unbelief regarding the promise of God.

'Have faith in God'
'Have faith in God,' Jesus answered. 'I tell you the truth, if you say to this mountain, "Go, throw yourself into the sea," and do not doubt in your heart but believe that what you say will happen, it will be done for you. Therefore I tell you, whatever you ask for in prayer, believe that you have received it, and it will be yours.'

Without faith
Without faith it is impossible to please God, because anyone who comes to him must believe that he exists and that he rewards those who earnestly seek him.

'Increase our faith!'
'Increase our faith!'

Romans 4:20. Mark 11:22–24. Hebrews 11:6. Luke 17:5.

Morning

We know that we have passed from death to life.

'Those who hear my word and believe him who sent me have eternal life and will not be condemned; they have crossed over from death to life.'

Anointed
Now it is God who makes both us and you stand firm in Christ. He anointed us, set his seal of ownership on us, and put his Spirit in our hearts.

At rest in his presence
This is how we know that we belong to the truth, and how we set our hearts at rest in his presence. . . . Dear friends, if our hearts do not condemn us, we have confidence before God. . . . We know that we are children of God, and that the whole world is under the control of the evil one.

1 John 3:14. John 5:24. 2 Corinthians 1:21–22. 1 John 3:19, 21; 5:19.

Evening

You have made known to me the path of life.

'This is what the LORD says: See, I am setting before you the way of life and the way of death.'—'I am the way and the truth and the life. No-one comes to the Father except through me.'
    There is a way that seems right to a person, but in the end it leads to death.—'Wide is the gate and broad is the road that leads to destruction, and many enter through it. But small is the gate and narrow the road that leads to life, and only a few find it.'

Let us acknowledge the LORD
Let us acknowledge the LORD; let us press on to acknowledge him.

Psalm 16:11. Jeremiah 21:8. John 14:6. Proverbs 14:12.
Matthew 7:13–14. Hosea 6:3.

July 26

Morning

By faith Abraham, when called to go to a place he would later receive as his inheritance, obeyed.

He guarded him as the apple of his eye, like an eagle that stirs up its nest and hovers over its young, that spreads its wings to catch them and carries them on its pinions. The LORD alone led him; no foreign god was with him.

We live by faith
We live by faith, not by sight.—Here we do not have an enduring city, but we are looking for the city that is to come.

As aliens and strangers
Dear friends, I urge you, as aliens and strangers in the world, to abstain from sinful desires, which war against your soul.

> Hebrews 11:8. Deuteronomy 32:10–12. 2 Corinthians 5:7. Hebrews
> 13:14. 1 Peter 2:11.

Evening

Rejoice in the LORD, you who are righteous, and praise his holy name.

'Who among the gods is like you, O LORD? Who is like you—majestic in holiness?'—'Holy, holy, holy is the LORD Almighty.'

Spotless, blameless
God's temple is sacred, and you are that temple.—What kind of people ought you to be? You ought to live holy and godly lives, . . . spotless, blameless.

Sealed for the day of redemption
Do not let any unwholesome talk come out of your mouths, but only what is helpful for building others up according to their needs. . . . And do not grieve the Holy Spirit of God, with whom you were sealed for the day of redemption.

> Psalm 97:12. Exodus 15:11. Isaiah 6:3. 1 Corinthians 3:17.
> 2 Peter 3:11, 14. Ephesians 4:29–30.

Morning

Christ, who is the image of God.

No-one has ever seen God, but God the One and Only, who is at the Father's side, has made him known. . . . The Word became flesh and made his dwelling among us. We have seen his glory, the glory of the One and Only, who came from the Father, full of grace and truth.—'Anyone who has seen me has seen the Father.'

The image of the invisible God
In whom we have redemption, the forgiveness of sins. He is the image of the invisible God, the firstborn over all creation.—For those God foreknew he also predestined to be conformed to the likeness of his Son, that he might be the firstborn among many brothers and sisters.

2 Corinthians 4:4. John 1:18, 14; 14:9. Colossians 1:14–15.
Romans 8:29.

Evening

You armed me with strength for battle.

When I am weak, then I am strong.

Asa
Then Asa called to the Lord his God and said, 'Lord, there is no-one like you to help the powerless against the mighty. Help us, O Lord our God, for we rely on you, and in your name we have come against this vast army.' . . . Jehosaphat cried out, and the Lord helped him.

The powers of this darkness
For our struggle is not against flesh and blood, but against the rulers, against the authorities, against the powers of this dark world and against the spiritual forces of evil in the heavenly realms. Therefore put on the full armour of God.

Psalm 18:39. 2 Corinthians 12:10. 2 Chronicles 14:11; 18:31.
Ephesians 6:12–13.

July 28

Morning

Live a life of love.

'A new command I give you: Love one another. As I have loved you, so you must love one another.'—Above all, love each other deeply, because love covers over a multitude of sins.—Love covers over all wrongs.

'Forgive'
'And when you stand praying, if you hold anything against anyone, forgive them, so that your Father in heaven may forgive you your sins.'—'But love your enemies, do good to them, and lend to them without expecting to get anything back.'—Do not gloat when your enemy falls; when he stumbles, do not let your heart rejoice.

Do not repay insult with insult
Do not repay evil with evil or insult with insult, but with blessing, because to this you were called so that you may inherit a blessing.

Ephesians 5:2. John 13:34. 1 Peter 4:8. Proverbs 10:12. Mark 11:25.
Luke 6:35. Proverbs 24:17. 1 Peter 3:9.

Evening

Present your requests to God.

'*Abba*, Father,' he said, 'everything is possible for you. Take this cup from me. Yet not what I will, but what you will.'

Three times I pleaded with the Lord
There was given me a thorn in my flesh, a messenger of Satan, to torment me. Three times I pleaded with the Lord to take it away from me. But he said to me, 'My grace is sufficient for you, for my power is made perfect in weakness.' Therefore I will boast all the more gladly about my weaknesses.

Before him I tell my trouble
I pour out my complaint before him; before him I tell my trouble.
We do not know what we ought to pray.—He chose our inheritance for us.

Philippians 4:6. Mark 14:36. 2 Corinthians 12:7–9. Psalm 142:2.
Romans 8:26. Psalm 47:4.

Morning

Oh, that you would rend the heavens and come down.

We ourselves, who have the firstfruits of the Spirit, groan inwardly as we wait eagerly for our adoption, the redemption of our bodies.

He will appear a second time
'This same Jesus, who has been taken from you into heaven, will come back in the same way you have seen him go into heaven.'—He will appear a second time, not to bear sin, but to bring salvation to those who are waiting for him.

Our citizenship is in heaven
He who testifies of these things says, 'Yes, I am coming soon.' Amen. Come, Lord Jesus.—The blessed hope—the glorious appearing of our great God and Saviour, Jesus Christ.—Our citizenship is in heaven.

> Isaiah 64:1. Romans 8:23. Acts 1:11. Hebrews 9:28. Revelation 22:20.
> Titus 2:13. Philippians 3:20.

Evening

You have given me the heritage of those who fear your name.

The angel of the LORD encamps around those who fear him, and he delivers them.

Taste and see
Taste and see that the LORD is good; blessed are those who take refuge in him. Fear the LORD, you his saints, for those who fear him lack nothing. The lions may grow weak and hungry, but those who seek the LORD lack no good thing.

Healing in its wings
But for you who revere my name, the sun of righteousness will rise with healing in its wings. And you will go out and leap like calves released from the stall.

> Psalms 61:5; 34:7, 8–10. Malachi 4:2.

July 30

Morning

Set your hearts on things above, where Christ is seated at the right hand of God.

We were therefore buried with him through baptism into death in order that, just as Christ was raised from the dead through the glory of the Father, we too may live a new life. If we have been united with him in his death, we will certainly also be united with him in his resurrection.

Seated in the heavenly realms
Let us throw off everything that hinders and the sin that so easily entangles, and let us run with perseverance the race marked out for us.—God . . . made us alive with Christ . . . God raised us up with Christ and seated us with him in the heavenly realms in Christ Jesus.

Seek righteousness, seek humility, perhaps you will be sheltered on the day of the LORD's anger.

> Colossians 3:1. Romans 6:4–5. Hebrews 12:1. Ephesians 2:4–6.
> Zephaniah 2:3.

Evening

Peter followed him at a distance.

Many even among the leaders believed in him. But because of the Pharisees they would not confess their faith for fear they would be put out of the synagogue; for they loved human praise more than praise from God.—To fear anyone will prove to be a snare, but whoever trusts in the LORD is kept safe.

Confident and unashamed
God did not give us a spirit of timidity, but a spirit of power, of love and of self-discipline. So do not be ashamed to testify about our Lord.—Dear children, continue in him, so that when he appears we may be confident and unashamed before him at his coming.—'Those who acknowledge me before others, I will also acknowledge before my Father in heaven.'

> Matthew 26:58. John 12:42–43. Proverbs 29:25. 2 Timothy 1:7–8.
> 1 John 2:28. Matthew 10:32.

Morning

Endure hardship with us like a good soldier of Christ Jesus.

'We must go through many hardships to enter the kingdom of God.'

For our struggle is not against flesh and blood, but against the rulers, against the authorities, against the powers of this dark world and against the spiritual forces of evil in the heavenly realms. Therefore put on the full armour of God.

We do not wage war as the world does. The weapons we fight with are not the weapons of the world. On the contrary, they have divine power to demolish strongholds.

After you have suffered
The God of all grace, who called you to his eternal glory in Christ, after you have suffered a little while, will himself restore you and make you strong, firm and steadfast.

2 Timothy 2:3. Acts 14:22. Ephesians 6:12–13. 2 Corinthians 10:3–4.
1 Peter 5:10.

Evening

The unity of the Spirit.

Built together
There is one body and one Spirit . . . For through him we both have access to the Father by one Spirit. Consequently, you are no longer foreigners and aliens, but fellow-citizens with God's people and members of God's household, built on the foundations of the apostles and prophets, with Christ Jesus himself as the chief cornerstone. In him the whole building is joined together and rises to become a holy temple in the Lord. And in him you too are being built together to become a dwelling in which God lives by his Spirit.

Now that you have purified yourselves by obeying the truth so that you have sincere mutual affection, love one another deeply, from the heart.

Ephesians 4:3, 4; 2:18–22. 1 Peter 1:22.

August 1

Morning

The fruit of the Spirit is . . . faithfulness.

By grace you have been saved, through faith—and this is not from yourselves, it is a gift of God.—Without faith it is impossible to please God.

We live by faith
We live by faith, not by sight.—I have been crucified with Christ and no longer live, but Christ lives in me. The life I live in the body, I live by faith in the Son of God, who loved me and gave himself for me.

Though you have not seen him, you love him; and even though you do not see him now, you believe in him and are filled with an inexpressible and glorious joy, for you are receiving the goal of your faith, the salvation of your souls.

Galatians 5:22. Ephesians 2:8. Hebrews 11:6. 2 Corinthians 5:7.
Galatians 2:20. 1 Peter 1:8–9.

Evening

The Lord is full of compassion and mercy.

Like an eagle
Like an eagle that stirs up its nest and hovers over its young, that spreads its wings to catch them and carries them on its pinions. The LORD alone led him; no foreign god was with him.

New every morning
His compassions never fail. They are new every morning; great is your faithfulness.

'The very hairs of your head are all numbered.' . . . 'Are not two sparrows sold for a penny? Yet not one of them will fall to the ground apart from the will of your Father.' . . . 'So don't be afraid; you are worth more than many sparrows.'

James 5:11. Deuteronomy 32:11–12. Lamentations 3:22–23.
Matthew 10:30, 29, 31.

Morning

In him we have redemption through his blood, the forgiveness of sins.

'The animals you choose must be year-old males without defect, . . . And the people of the community of Israel must slaughter them at twilight. Then they are to take some of the blood and put it on the sides and tops of the door-frames of the houses where they eat the lambs . . . when I see the blood, I will pass over you.'

The sprinkled blood
The sprinkled blood.—For Christ, our Passover lamb, has been sacrificed.

Therefore, since Christ suffered in his body, arm yourselves also with the same attitude, because all who have suffered in their bodies are done with sin. As a result, they do not live the rest of their earthly lives for evil human desires, but rather for the will of God.

Ephesians 1:7. Exodus 12:5–7, 13. Hebrews 12:24. 1 Corinthians 5:7.
1 Peter 4:1–2.

Evening

They overcame him by the blood of the Lamb and by the word of their testimony.

He himself bore our sins in his body on the tree.—Becoming a curse for us.

Marvellous things
Sing to the LORD a new song, for he has done marvellous things; his right hand and his holy arm have worked salvation for him.

He will bear their iniquities
After the suffering of his soul, he will see the light of life and be satisfied; by his knowledge my righteous servant will justify many, and he will bear their iniquities.

Revelation 12:11. 1 Peter 2:24. Galatians 3:13. Psalm 98:1. Isaiah 53:11.

August 3

Morning

His mercy extends to those who fear him.

Reverent fear
Since you call on a Father who judges each person's work impartially, live your lives as strangers here in reverent fear.—The LORD is near to all who call on him, to all who call on him in truth. He fulfils the desires of those who fear him; he hears their cry and saves them.

'Because your heart was responsive and you humbled yourself before the LORD, . . . and because you tore your robes and wept in my presence, I have heard you, declares the LORD.'

The broken-hearted
The LORD is close to the broken-hearted and saves those who are crushed in spirit.

> Luke 1:50. 1 Peter 1:17. Psalm 145:18–19. 2 Kings 22:19. Psalm 34:18.

Evening

'Those who honour me I will honour.'

'Those who acknowledge me before others, I will also acknowledge before my Father in heaven.'

'Anyone who loves father or mother more than me is not worthy of me; anyone who loves son or daughter more than me is not worthy of me; those who do not take up their cross and follow me are not worthy of me. Those who find their lives will lose them, and those who lose their lives for my sake will find them.'

The crown of life
Blessed are those who persevere under trial, because when they have stood the test, they will receive the crown of life that God has promised to those who love him.

'Do not be afraid of what you are about to suffer. . . . Be faithful, even to the point of death, and I will give you the crown of life.'

> 1 Samuel 2:30. Matthew 10:32, 37–39. James 1:12. Revelation 2:10.

Morning

'It is finished.' With that, he bowed his head and gave up his spirit.

The sacrifice of the body of Jesus
We have been made holy through the sacrifice of the body of Jesus Christ once for all. Day after day every priest stands and performs his religious duties; again and again he offers the same sacrifices, which can never take away sins. But when this priest had offered for all time one sacrifice for sins, he sat down at the right hand of God. Since that time he waits for his enemies to be made his footstool, because by one sacrifice he has made perfect for ever those who are being made holy.

Nailing it to the cross
Having cancelled the written code, with its regulations, that was against us and that stood opposed to us; he took it away, nailing it to the cross.

John 19:30. Hebrews 10:10–14. Colossians 2:14.

Evening

He reached down from on high and took hold of me; he drew me out of deep waters.

He lifted me out of the slimy pit, out of the mud and mire; he set my feet on a rock and gave me a firm place to stand.

Hear my cry, O God; listen to my prayer. From the ends of the earth I call to you, I call as my heart grows faint.

Jonah
'From the depths of the grave I called for help, and you listened to my cry. You hurled me into the deep, into the very heart of the seas, and the currents swirled about me; all your waves and breakers swept over me.'

'When you pass through the rivers'
'When you pass through the waters, I will be with you; and when you pass through the rivers, they will not sweep over you.'

Psalms 18:16; 40:2; 61:1–2. Jonah 2:2–3. Isaiah 43:2.

August 5

Morning

Live a new life.

Therefore, I urge you, brothers and sisters, in view of God's mercy, to offer your bodies as living sacrifices, holy and pleasing to God—this is your spiritual act of worship. Do not conform any longer to the pattern of this world, but be transformed by the renewing of your mind.

A new creation
If anyone is in Christ, there is a new creation: the old has gone, the new has come!—So I tell you this, and insist on it in the Lord, that you must no longer live as the Gentiles do, in the futility of their thinking. . . . You, however, did not come to know Christ that way. Surely you heard of him and were taught in him in accordance with the truth that is in Jesus.

A new self
Put on a new self, created to be like God in true righteousness and holiness.

Romans 6:4; 12:1–2. 2 Corinthians 5:17. Ephesians 4:17, 20–21, 24.

Evening

'May your will be done.'

'Not as I will, but as you will.'—But I have stilled and quieted my soul; like a weaned child with its mother, like a weaned child is my soul within me.

The Spirit himself intercedes for us
We do not know what we ought to pray, but the Spirit himself intercedes for us with groans that words cannot express. And he who searches our hearts knows the mind of the Spirit, because the Spirit intercedes for the saints, in accordance with God's will.

Examples
'You don't know what you are asking.'—He gave them what they asked for, but sent a wasting disease upon them.—These things occurred as examples, to keep us from setting our hearts on evil things as they did.

Matthew 26:42. Matthew 26:39. Psalm 131:2. Romans 8:26–27.
Matthew 20:22. Psalm 106:15. 1 Corinthians 10:6.

Morning

The LORD disciplines those he loves.

'I know the plans I have for you,' declares the LORD, 'plans to prosper you and not to harm you, plans to give you hope and a future.'—'For my thoughts are not your thoughts, neither are your ways my ways,' declares the LORD.

No discipline seems pleasant at the time but painful. Later on, however, it produces a harvest of righteousness and peace for those who have been trained by it.—Humble yourselves, therefore, under God's mighty hand, that he may lift you in due time.

Your laws are righteous
I know, O LORD, that your laws are righteous, and in faithfulness you have afflicted me.

Proverbs 3:12. Jeremiah 29:11. Isaiah 55:8. Hebrews 12:11. 1 Peter 5:6.
Psalm 119:75.

Evening

The earth is the LORD's, and everything in it.

'Everything comes from you'
'Everything comes from you, and we have given you only what comes from your hand. We are aliens and strangers in your sight, as were all our forefathers. Our days on earth are like a shadow, without hope. O LORD our God, as for all this abundance, . . . it comes from your hand, and all of it belongs to you.'—From him and through him and to him are all things. To him be the glory for ever! Amen.

Everything God created is good
God . . . richly provides us with everything for our enjoyment. . . . For everything God created is good, and nothing is to be rejected if it is received with thanksgiving, because it is consecrated by the word of God and power.

Psalm 24:1. 1 Chronicles 29:14–16. Romans 11:36.
1 Timothy 6:17; 4:4–5.

August 7

Morning

'The Counsellor, the Holy Spirit, whom the Father will send in my name.'

'If you then, though you are evil, know how to give good gifts to your children, how much more will your Father in heaven give the Holy Spirit to those who ask him!'—'I tell you the truth, my Father will give you whatever you ask in my name. Until now you have not asked for anything in my name. Ask and you will receive, and your joy will be complete.'

'He will guide you into all truth'
'But when he, the Spirit of truth, comes, he will guide you into all truth. He will not speak on his own; he will speak only what he hears, and he will tell you what is yet to come. He will bring glory to me by taking from what is mine and making it known to you.'

John 14:26. Luke 11:13. John 16:23–24, 13–14.

Evening

'What do you think about the Christ?'

On his robes and on his thigh he has this name written: KING OF KINGS AND LORD OF LORDS.

Now to you who believe, this stone is precious. But to those who do not believe, 'The stone the builders rejected has become the capstone.'

Christ the power of God
Christ crucified: a stumbling-block to Jews and foolishness to Gentiles, but to those whom God has called, both Jew and Greeks, Christ the power of God and the wisdom of God.

I consider everything a loss compared to the surpassing greatness of knowing Christ Jesus my Lord, for whose sake I have lost all things. I consider them rubbish, that I may gain Christ.—'Lord, you know all things; you know that I love you.'

Matthew 22:42. Revelation 19:16. 1 Peter 2:7. 1 Corinthians 1:23–24.
Philippians 3:8. John 21:17.

Morning

The path of the righteous is like the first gleam of dawn, shining ever brighter till the full light of day.

Not that I have already obtained all this, or have already been made perfect, but I press on to take hold of that for which Christ Jesus took hold of me.—Let us acknowledge the LORD; let us press on to acknowledge him.

Reflect the Lord's glory
Then the righteous will shine like the sun in the kingdom of their Father.— We, who with unveiled faces all reflect the Lord's glory, are being transformed into his likeness with ever-increasing glory, which comes from the Lord, who is the Spirit.

Then I shall know fully
But when perfection comes, the imperfect disappears. . . . Now we see but a poor reflection; then we shall see face to face. Now I know in part; then I shall know fully, even as I am fully known.

> Proverbs 4:18. Philippians 3:12. Hosea 6:3. Matthew 13:43.
> 2 Corinthians 3:18. 1 Corinthians 13:10, 12.

Evening

'Everyone who calls on the name of the Lord will be saved.'

'Whoever comes to me I will never drive away.'

'Today you will be with me in paradise'
'Jesus, remember me when you come into your kingdom.' Jesus answered him, 'I tell you the truth, today you will be with me in paradise.'—'If you then, though you are evil, know how to give good gifts to your children, how much more will your Father in heaven give the Holy Spirit to those who ask him!'

According to his will
This is the assurance we have in approaching God: that if we ask anything according to his will, he hears us. And if we know that he hears us—whatever we ask—we know that we have what we asked of him.

> Romans 10:13. John 6:37. Luke 23:42–43. Luke 11:13. 1 John 5:14–15.

August 9

Morning

I know that nothing good lives in me, that is, in my sinful nature.

All of us have become like one who is unclean, and all our righteous acts are like filthy rags.

You were washed
You were washed, you were sanctified, you were justified in the name of the Lord Jesus Christ and by the Spirit of our God.—'The splendour I had given you made your beauty perfect, declares the Sovereign LORD.'
   May the favour of the Lord our God rest upon us.

A radiant church
'These are they who have . . . washed their robes and made them white in the blood of the Lamb.'—To present her to himself as a radiant church, without stain or wrinkle or any other blemish, but holy and blameless.

Romans 7:18. Isaiah 64:6. 1 Corinthians 6:11. Ezekiel 16:14.
Psalm 90:17. Revelation 7:14. Ephesians 5:27.

Evening

Broken cisterns that cannot hold water.

'Come, let us build ourselves a city, with a tower that reaches to the heavens.' . . . The LORD scattered them.

Everything was meaningless
Then I applied myself to the understanding of wisdom, and also of madness and folly, but I learned that this, too, is a chasing after the wind. For with much wisdom comes much sorrow; the more knowledge, the more grief . . . I undertook great projects: I built houses for myself and planted vineyards . . . I amassed silver and gold for myself, . . . Yet when I surveyed all that my hands had done and what I had toiled to achieve, everything was meaningless.
   'Let anyone who is thirsty come to me and drink.'

Jeremiah 2:13. Genesis 11:4, 8. Ecclesiastes 1:17–18; 2:4, 8, 11.
John 7:37.

Morning

'My prayer is not that you take them out of the world but that you protect them from the evil one.'

Blameless and pure, children of God without fault in a crooked and depraved generation, in which you shine like stars in the universe.

He will protect you
The Lord is faithful, and he will strengthen and protect you from the evil one.—But out of reverence for God I did not act like that.—Who gave himself for our sins to rescue us from the present evil age, according to the will of our God and Father.

Before his glorious presence
To him who is able to keep you from falling and to present you before his glorious presence without fault and with great joy—to the only God our Saviour be glory, majesty, power and authority, through Jesus Christ our Lord, before all ages, now and for evermore! Amen.

John 17:15. Philippians 2:15. 2 Thessalonians 3:3. Nehemiah 5:15.
Galatians 1:4. Jude 24–25.

Evening

Whoever trusts in the LORD is kept safe.

The LORD is exalted, for he dwells on high.

By grace you have been saved
God, who is rich in mercy, made us alive with Christ even when we were dead in transgressions—it is by grace you have been saved. And God raised us up with Christ and seated us with him in the heavenly realms in Christ Jesus.

He did not spare his own Son
He who did not spare his own Son, but gave him up for us all—how will he not also, along with him, graciously give us all things?

Proverbs 29:25. Isaiah 33:5. Ephesians 2:4–6. Romans 8:32.

August 11

Morning

By his death he might destroy him who holds the power of death.

Our Saviour, Christ Jesus, . . . has destroyed death and has brought life and immortality to light through the gospel.

He will swallow up death for ever
He will swallow up death for ever. The Sovereign LORD will wipe away the tears from all faces; he will remove the disgrace of his people from all the earth. The LORD has spoken.

The valley of the shadow of death
For God did not give us a spirit of timidity, but a spirit of power, of love and of self-discipline.—Even though I walk through the valley of the shadow of death, I will fear no evil, for you are with me; your rod and your staff, they comfort me.

Hebrews 2:14. 2 Timothy 1:10. Isaiah 25:8. 2 Timothy 1:7. Psalm 23:4.

Evening

God is light; in him there is no darkness at all.

'While I am in the world, I am the light of the world.'

Fellowship
If we claim to have fellowship with him yet walk in the darkness, we lie and do not live by the truth. But if we walk in the light, as he is in the light, we have fellowship with one another, and the blood of Jesus, his Son, purifies us from every sin.

The inheritance of the saints
The Father . . . has qualified you to share in the inheritance of the saints in the kingdom of light. For he has rescued us from the dominion of darkness and brought us into the kingdom of the Son he loves, in whom we have redemption, the forgiveness of sins.

You are all children of the light and children of the day. We do not belong to the night or to the darkness.

1 John 1:5. John 9:5. 1 John 1:6–7. Colossians 1:12–14.
1 Thessalonians 5:5.

Morning

'Do not fear, . . . for I am with you,' declares the LORD.

'I will bring you back'
'For a brief moment I abandoned you, but with deep compassion I will bring you back. In a surge of anger I hid my face from you for a moment, but with everlasting kindness I will have compassion on you,' says the LORD your Redeemer.

Unfailing love
'Though the mountains be shaken and the hills be removed, yet my unfailing love for you will not be shaken nor my covenant of peace be removed,' says the LORD, who has compassion on you. 'O afflicted city, lashed by storms and not comforted, I will build you with stones of turquoise, your foundations with sapphires.'

Jeremiah 46:28. Isaiah 54:7–8, 10–11.

Evening

God chose the weak things of the world to shame the strong.

Gideon
The LORD turned to him and said, 'Go in the strength you have . . . Am I not sending you?' 'But Lord,' Gideon asked, 'how can I save Israel? My clan is the weakest in Manasseh, and I am the least in my family.'—The LORD said to Gideon, 'You have too many men for me to deliver Midian into their hands. In order that Israel may not boast against me that her own strength has saved her.'

'Not by might nor by power'
'Not by might nor by power, but by my Spirit,' says the LORD Almighty.—Be strong in the Lord and in his mighty power.

1 Corinthians 1:27. Judges 6; 14–15; 7:2. Zechariah 4:6. Ephesians 6:10.

August 13

Morning

He has prepared a city for them.

An inheritance that can never perish, spoil or fade—kept in heaven for you.—
Here we do not have an enduring city, but we are looking for the city that is to
come.

Be patient
Be patient, then, brothers and sisters, until the Lord's coming. See how the
farmer waits for the land to yield its valuable crop, patiently waiting for the
autumn and spring rains.

To meet the Lord in the air
We who are still alive and are left will be caught up with them in the clouds to
meet the Lord in the air. And so we will be with the Lord for ever. Therefore
encourage each other with these words.

Hebrews 11:16. 1 Peter 1:4. Hebrews 13:14. James 5:7–8.
1 Thessalonians 4:17–18.

Evening

He chose the lowly things of this world.

You were dead
You were dead in your transgressions and sins, in which you used to live when
you followed the ways of this world and of the ruler of the kingdom of the air,
the spirit who is now at work in those who are disobedient. All of us who lived
among them at one time, gratifying the cravings of our sinful nature and
following its desires and thoughts.

Because of his mercy
He saved us . . . because of his mercy. He saved us through the washing of
rebirth and renewal by the Holy Spirit, whom he poured out on us generously
through Jesus Christ our Saviour.

'For my thoughts are not your thoughts, neither are your ways my ways,'
declares the LORD.

1 Corinthians 1:28. Ephesians 2:1–3. Titus 3:5–6. Isaiah 55:8.

Morning

'The joy of the LORD is your strength.'

Shout for joy, O heavens; rejoice, O earth; burst into song, O mountains! For the LORD comforts his people and will have compassion on his afflicted ones. . . . 'Surely God is my salvation; I will trust and not be afraid. The LORD, the LORD, is my strength and my song; he has become my salvation.'

My heart leaps for joy
The LORD is my strength and my shield; my heart trusts in him, and I am helped. My heart leaps for joy and I will give thanks to him in song.

My soul rejoices in my God. For he has clothed me with garments of salvation and arrayed me in a robe of righteousness, as a bridegroom adorns his head like a priest, and as a bride adorns herself with her jewels.

I will be joyful in God my Saviour.

Nehemiah 8:10. Isaiah 49:13; 12:2. Psalm 28:7. Isaiah 61:10.
Habakkuk 3:18.

Evening

I know whom I have believed, and am convinced that he is able to guard what I have entrusted to him for that day.

He chose us
Praise be to the God and Father of our Lord Jesus Christ, who has blessed us in the heavenly realms with every spiritual blessing in Christ. For he chose us in him before the creation of the world to be holy and blameless in his sight. In love he predestined us to be adopted as his children through Jesus Christ, in accordance with his pleasure and will.

Called according to his purpose
We know that in all things God works for the good of those who love him, who have been called according to his purpose.

2 Timothy 1:12. Ephesians 1:3–5. Romans 8: 28.

August 15

Morning

May the God of peace . . . equip you with everything good for doing his will.

Aim for perfection, listen to my appeal, be of one mind, live in peace. And the God of love and peace will be with you.

Work out your salvation with fear and trembling, for it is God who works in you to will and to act according to his good purpose.

The renewing of your mind
Be transformed by the renewing of your mind. Then you will be able to test and approve what God's will is—his good, pleasing and perfect will.—Filled with the fruit of righteousness that comes through Jesus Christ—to the glory and praise of God.

Not that we are competent to claim anything for ourselves, but our competence comes from God.

> Hebrews 13:20–21. 2 Corinthians 13:11. Philippians 2:12–13.
> Romans 12:2. Philippians 1:11. 2 Corinthians 3:5.

Evening

Since we have these promises, dear friends, let us purify ourselves from everything that contaminates body and spirit, perfecting holiness out of reverence for God.

Outside the city
Jesus also suffered outside the city gates to make the people holy through his own blood. Let us, then, go to him outside the camp, bearing the disgrace he bore.

[Jesus] said, . . . 'Come with me by yourselves to a quiet place and get some rest.'

Quiet waters
The LORD is my shepherd, I shall lack nothing. He makes me lie down in green pastures, he leads me beside quiet waters, he restores my soul. He guides me in paths of righteousness for his name's sake.

> 2 Corinthians 7:1. Hebrews 13:12–13. Mark 6:31. Psalm 23:1–3.

Morning

'The house to be built for the LORD should be of great magnificence.'

You also, like living stones, are being built into a spiritual house.—Don't you know that you yourselves are God's temple and that God's Spirit lives in you? If anyone destroys God's temple, God will destroy that person; for God's temple is sacred, and you are that temple. . . . Do you not know that your body is a temple of the Holy Spirit, who is in you, whom you have received from God? You are not your own; you were bought with a price. Therefore honour God with your body.

A holy temple in the Lord
You are . . . built on the foundation of the apostles and prophets, with Christ Jesus himself as the chief cornerstone. In him the whole building is joined together and rises to become a holy temple in the Lord. And in him you too are being built together to become a dwelling in which God lives.

> 1 Chronicles 22:5. 1 Peter 2:5. 1 Corinthians 3:16–17; 6:19–20.
> Ephesians 2:19–22.

Evening

He is before all things.

'The Amen, the faithful and true witness, the ruler of God's creation.'—The beginning and the firstborn from among the dead, so that in everything he might have the supremacy.

The foundations of the earth
I was there when he set the heavens in place, when he marked out the horizon on the face of the deep, when he established the clouds above and fixed securely the foundations of the deep, when he gave the sea its boundary so that the waters would not overstep his command, and when he marked out the foundations of the earth.

The Lamb that was slain from the creation of the world.—The author and perfecter of our faith, who for the joy set before him endured the cross, scorning its shame, and sat down at the right hand of the throne of God.

> Colossians 1:17. Revelation 3:14. Colossians 1:18. Proverbs 8:27–29.
> Revelation 13:8. Hebrews 12:2.

August 17

Morning

Pray for each other so that you may be healed.

'Father, forgive them, for they do not know what they are doing.'—'Pray for those who persecute you.'

'I pray for them. I am not praying for the world, but for those you have given me, for they are yours. . . . My prayer is not for them alone. I pray also for those who will believe in me through their message.'—Carry each other's burdens, and in this way you will fulfil the law of Christ.

Elijah
The prayer of a righteous person is powerful and effective. Elijah was human just as we are. He prayed earnestly that it would not rain, and it did not rain on the land for three and a half years.

James 5:16. Luke 23:34. Matthew 5:44. John 17:9, 20. Galatians 6:2.
James 5:16–17.

Evening

Teach us to number our days aright, that we may gain a heart of wisdom.

'What good is it for you if you gain the whole world, yet forfeit your soul?'

The word of our God stands for ever
'The grass withers and the flowers fall, because the breath of the LORD blows on them. Surely the people are grass. The grass withers and the flowers fall, but the word of our God stands for ever.'

The world and its desires pass away, but whoever does the will of God lives for ever.

Now is the day of salvation
I tell you, now is the time of God's favour, now is the day of salvation.—Use the things of the world, as if not engrossed in them. For this world in its present form is passing away.

Psalm 90:12. Mark 8:36. Isaiah 40:7–8. 1 John 2:17. 2 Corinthians 6:2.
1 Corinthians 7:31.

Morning

For what god is there in heaven or on earth who can do the deeds and mighty works you do?

'There is no-one like you'
'For the sake of your word and according to your will, you have done this great thing and made it known to your servant. How great you are, O Sovereign LORD! There is no-one like you, and there is no God but you, as we have heard with our own ears.'

God has revealed it
'No eye has seen, no ear has heard, no mind has conceived what God has prepared for those who love him'—but God has revealed it to us by his Spirit.—The secret things belong to the LORD our God, but the things revealed belong to us and to our children.

> Deuteronomy 3:24. 2 Samuel 7:21–22. 1 Corinthians 2:9–10.
> Deuteronomy 29:29.

Evening

'Let those who boast boast in the Lord.'

Everything a loss
I consider everything a loss compared to the surpassing greatness of knowing Christ Jesus my Lord, for whose sake I have lost all things. I consider them rubbish, that I may gain Christ.

The power of God
I am not ashamed of the gospel, because it is the power of God for the salvation of everyone who believes. . . . Therefore I glory in Christ Jesus in my service to God.

Not to us, O LORD, not to us but to your name be the glory, because of your love and faithfulness.

> 1 Corinthians 1:31. Philippians 3:8. Romans 1:16; 15:17. Psalm 115:1.

August 19

Morning

But just as he who called you is holy, so be holy in all you do.

We dealt with each of you . . . urging you to live lives worthy of God, who calls you into his kingdom and glory.

The fruit of righteousness
For you were once darkness, but now you are light in the LORD. Live as children of light (for the fruit of the light consists in all goodness, righteousness and truth) and find out what pleases the Lord. Have nothing to do with the fruitless deeds of darkness, but rather expose them.—Filled with the fruit of righteousness that comes through Jesus Christ—to the glory and praise of God.

So whether you eat or drink or whatever you do, do it all for the glory of God.

> 1 Peter 1:15. 1 Thessalonians 2:11–12. Ephesians 5:8–11.
> Philippians 1:11. 1 Corinthians 10:31.

Evening

'I will give you a new heart and put a new spirit in you; I will remove from you your heart of stone and give you a heart of flesh.'

'And I will put my Spirit in you and move you to follow my decrees and be careful to keep my laws.' This is what the Sovereign LORD says . . . 'I will yield to the plea of the house of Israel and do this for them.'

'If two of you agree'
'If two of you on earth agree about anything you ask for, it will be done for you by my Father in heaven. For where two or three come together in my name, there am I with them.'

'Have faith in God'
'Have faith in God,' Jesus answered. 'I tell you the truth, if you say to this mountain, "Go, throw yourself into the sea," and do not doubt in your heart but believes that what you say will happen, it will be done for you.'

> Ezekiel 36:26, 27, 37. Matthew 18:19–20. Mark 11:22–23.

Morning

Faithful for ever.

The Father of the heavenly lights, who does not change like shifting shadows. His faithfulness will be your shield and rampart.

Two unchangeable things
Because God wanted to make the unchanging nature of his purpose very clear to the heirs of what was promised, he confirmed it with an oath. God did this so that, by two unchangeable things in which it is impossible for God to lie, we who have fled to take hold of the hope offered to us may be greatly encouraged.

Faithful for ever
All the ways of the LORD are loving and faithful for those who keep the demands of his covenant. . . . Blessed are those whose help is the God of Jacob, whose hope is in the LORD their God, . . . who remains faithful for ever.

James 1:17. Psalm 91:4. Hebrews 6:17–18. Psalms 25:10; 146:5–6.

Evening

He gives strength to the weary and increases the power of the weak.

'He will call upon me, and I will answer him; I will be with him in trouble, I will deliver him.'

Everlasting arms
The eternal God is your refuge, and underneath are the everlasting arms. He will drive out your enemy before you.

The source of eternal salvation
Every high priest is selected from among human beings and is appointed to represent them in matters related to God. . . . He is able to deal gently with those who are ignorant and are going astray, since he himself is subject to weakness. . . . So Christ also, . . . although he was a son, he learned obedience from what he suffered and, once made perfect, he became the source of eternal salvation for all who obey him.

Isaiah 40:29. Psalm 91:15. Deuteronomy 33:27. Hebrews 5:1–2, 5, 8–9.

August 21

Morning

You are my portion, O LORD.

All things are yours, . . . and you are of Christ and Christ is of God.—God placed all things under his feet and appointed him to be head over everything for the church . . . Christ loved the church and gave himself up for her . . . to present her to himself as a radiant church, without stain or wrinkle or any other blemish, but holy and blameless.

'You are my Lord'
Whom have I in heaven but you? And being with you, I desire nothing on earth. My flesh and my heart may fail, but God is the strength of my heart and my portion for ever . . . I said to the LORD, 'You are my lord.' . . . LORD, you have assigned me my portion and my cup; you have made my lot secure. The boundary lines have fallen for me in pleasant places; surely I have a delightful inheritance.

> Psalm 119:57. 1 Corinthians 3:21, 23. Ephesians 1:22; 5:25, 27.
> Psalms 73:25–26; 16:2, 5–6.

Evening

There is a way that seems right to a person, but in the end it leads to death.

Those who trust in themselves are fools.

Hold fast to him
If a prophet, or one who foretells by dreams, appears among you and announces to you a miraculous sign or wonder, and if the sign or wonder of which he has spoken takes place, and he says, 'Let us follow other gods' (gods you have not known) 'and let us worship them,' you must not listen to the words of that prophet or dreamer. The LORD your God is testing you to find out whether you love him with all your heart and with all your soul.

It is the LORD your God you must follow, and him you must revere. Keep his commands and obey him; serve him and hold fast to him.

I will instruct you and teach you in the way you should go; I will counsel you and watch over you.

> Proverbs 14:12; 28:26. Deuteronomy 13:1–4. Psalm 32:8.

Morning

For we do not live to ourselves alone and we do not die to ourselves alone.

If we live, we live to the Lord; and if we die, we die to the Lord. So, whether we live or die, we belong to the Lord.

Honour God with your bodies
None of us should seek our own good, but the good of others. . . . You were bought at a price. Therefore honour God with your bodies.

To live is Christ and to die is gain
Christ will be exalted in my body, whether by life or by death. For to me, to live is Christ and to die is gain. If I am to go on living in the body, this will mean fruitful labour for me. Yet what shall I choose? I do not know! I am torn between the two: I desire to depart and be with Christ, which is better by far.

Romans 14:7, 8. 1 Corinthians 10:24; 6:20. Philippians 1:20–23.

Evening

God gave Solomon wisdom and very great insight, and a breadth of understanding as measureless as the sand on the seashore.

'One greater than Solomon is here.'—Prince of Peace.

Obedient to death
Who, being in very nature God, did not consider equality with God something to be grasped, but made himself nothing, taking the very nature of a servant, being made in human likeness. And being found in appearance as a man, he humbled himself and became obedient to death—even death on a cross!

Christ the wisdom of God
Christ the power of God and the wisdom of God—In whom are hidden all the treasures of wisdom and knowledge.

1 Kings 4:29. Matthew 12:42. Isaiah 9:6. Philippians 2:6–8.
1 Corinthians 1:24. Colossians 2:3.

August 23

Morning

'I have loved you with an everlasting love; I have drawn you with loving-kindness.'

Belief in the truth
But we ought always to thank God for you, brothers and sisters loved by the Lord, because from the beginning God chose you to be saved through the sanctifying work of the Spirit and through belief in the truth. He called you to this through our gospel, that you might share in the glory of our Lord Jesus Christ.

'Eternal life'
'For God so loved the world that he gave his one and only Son, that whoever believes in him shall not perish but have eternal life.'

This is love: not that we loved God, but that he loved us and sent his Son as an atoning sacrifice for our sins.

Jeremiah 31:3. 2 Thessalonians 2:13–14. John 3:16. 1 John 4:10.

Evening

'I will sustain you and I will rescue you.'

But now, this is what the LORD says—he who created you, O Jacob, he who formed you, O Israel: 'Fear not, for I have redeemed you; I have called you by name; you are mine. When you pass through the waters, I will be with you; and when you pass through the rivers, they will not sweep over you.'

'To your old age'
'Even to your old age and grey hairs I am he, I am he who will sustain you.'

For I am convinced that neither . . . height nor depth, nor anything else in all creation, will be able to separate us from the love of God that is in Christ Jesus our Lord.

'I will not forget you!'
'Can a mother forget the baby at her breast and have no compassion on the child she has borne? Though she may forget, I will not forget you!'

Isaiah 46:4; 43:1–2; 46:4. Romans 8:38–39. Isaiah 49:15.

Morning

A man of sorrows, and familiar with suffering.

'He took up our infirmities and carried our diseases.'

He was deeply moved
When Jesus saw her weeping, and the Jews who had come along with her also weeping, he was deeply moved in spirit and troubled . . . Jesus wept.

   'The LORD looked down from his sanctuary on high, from heaven he viewed the earth, to hear the groans of the prisoners and release those condemned to death.'

The angel of his presence
For whoever touches you touches the apple of his eye.—In all their distress he too was distressed, and the angel of his presence saved them.

> Isaiah 53:3. Matthew 8:17. John 11:33, 35. Psalm 102:19–20.
> Zechariah 2:8. Isaiah 63:9.

Evening

'As long as it is day, we must do the work of him who sent me.'

'Look at the fields!'
'My food,' said Jesus, 'is to do the will of him who sent me and to finish his work. Do you not say, "Four months more and then the harvest"? I tell you, open your eyes and look at the fields! They are ripe for harvest. Even now the reaper draws his wages, even now he harvests the crop for eternal life, so that the sower and the reaper may be glad together.'

Be prepared
Preach the Word; be prepared in season and out of season.

   No, I worked harder than all of them—yet not I, but the grace of God that was with me.

> John 9:4; 4:34–36. 2 Timothy 4:2. 1 Corinthians 15:10.

August 25

Morning

'Look to the rock from which you were cut and to the quarry from which you were hewn.'

'No-one looked on you with pity . . . You were thrown out into the open field, for on the day you were born you were despised. Then I passed by and saw you kicking about in your blood, and as you lay there in your blood I said to you, "Live!" '

He lifted me out of the slimy pit
He lifted me out of the slimy pit, out of the mud and mire; he set my feet on a rock and gave me a firm place to stand. He put a new song in my mouth, a hymn of praise to our God.

While we were still sinners
You see, at just the right time, when we were still powerless, Christ died for the ungodly. Very rarely will anyone die for a righteous person, though for a good person someone might possibly dare to die. But God demonstrates his own love for us in this: While we were still sinners, Christ died for us.

Isaiah 51:1. Ezekiel 16:5–6. Psalm 40:2–3. Romans 5:6–8.

Evening

I delight greatly in the LORD; my soul rejoices in my God.

I will extol the LORD at all times; his praise will always be on my lips. My soul will boast in the LORD; let the afflicted hear and rejoice. Glorify the LORD with me; let us exalt his name together . . . Praise the LORD, O my soul; all my inmost being, praise his holy name.

Make music in your heart to the Lord
Is anyone happy? Sing songs of praise.—Be filled with the Spirit. Speak to one another with psalms, hymns and spiritual songs. Sing and make music in your heart to the Lord, always giving thanks to God the Father for everything.—Sing psalms, hymns and spiritual songs with gratitude in your hearts to God.

Isaiah 61:10. Psalms 34:1–3; 103:1. James 5:13. Ephesians 5:18–20.
Colossians 3:16.

Morning

'Make a plate of pure gold and engrave on it as on a seal: HOLY TO THE LORD.'

Without holiness no-one will see the Lord.—'God is spirit, and his worshippers must worship in spirit and in truth.'

Holiness adorns your house
'This is the law of the temple: All the surrounding area on top of the mountain will be most holy.'—Holiness adorns your house for endless days, O LORD.

Grace to help
'For them I sanctify myself, that they too may be truly sanctified.'—Therefore, since we have a great high priest who has gone through the heavens, Jesus the Son of God, let us . . . then approach the throne of grace with confidence, so that we may receive mercy and find grace to help us in our time of need.

Exodus 28:36. Hebrews 12:14. John 4:24. Ezekiel 43:12. Psalm 93:5.
John 17:19. Hebrews 4:14, 16.

Evening

My cup overflows.

Taste and see
Taste and see that the LORD is good; blessed are those who take refuge in him. Fear the LORD, you his saints, for those who fear him lack nothing. The lions may grow weak and hungry, but those who seek the LORD lack no good thing.—His compassions never fail. They are new every morning; great is your faithfulness.

Whether Paul or Apollos or Cephas or the world or life or death or the present or the future—all are yours.—Praise be to the God and Father of our Lord Jesus Christ, who has blessed us in the heavenly realms with every spiritual blessing in Christ.

Godliness with contentment
I have learned to be content whatever the circumstances.—Godliness with contentment is great gain.

Psalms 23:5; 34:8–10. Lamentations 3:22–23. 1 Corinthians 3:22.
Ephesians 1:3. Philippians 4:11. 1 Timothy 6:6.

August 27

Morning

Your word is a lamp to my feet and a light for my path.

When you walk, they will guide you; when you sleep, they will watch over you; when you awake, they will speak to you. For these commands are a lamp, this teaching is a light.

'This is the way; walk in it'
Whether you turn to the right or to the left, your ears will hear a voice behind you, saying, 'This is the way; walk in it.'

A light shining
We have the word of the prophets made more certain, and you will do well to pay attention to it, as to a light shining in a dark place.—Now we see but a poor reflection; then we shall see face to face. Now I know in part; then I shall know fully; even as I am fully known.

Psalm 119:105. Proverbs 6:22–23. Isaiah 30:21. 2 Peter 1:19.
1 Corinthians 13:12.

Evening

Set your minds on things above, not on earthly things.

Though your riches increase, do not set your heart on them.—Now devote your heart and soul to seeking the LORD your God.
  'Why are you sleeping?' he asked them. 'Get up and pray so that you will not fall into temptation.' . . . 'Be careful, or your hearts will be weighed down with dissipation, drunkenness and the anxieties of life, and that day will close on you unexpectedly.'
  'He who is coming will come and will not delay.'

'Watch'
'Watch because you do not know when the owner of the house will come back—whether in the evening or at midnight, or when the cock crows, or at dawn. If he comes suddenly, do not let him find you sleeping.'

Colossians 3:2. Psalm 62:10. 1 Chronicles 22:19. Luke 22:46; 21:34.
Hebrews 10:37. Mark 13:35–36.

Morning

Thanks be to God! He gives us the victory through our Lord Jesus Christ.

Who will bring any charge against those whom God has chosen? It is God who justifies. Who then can condemn? Christ Jesus, who died—more than that, who was raised to life—is at the right hand of God and is also interceding for us.

So that by his death he might destroy him who holds the power of death—that is, the devil—and free those who all their lives were held in slavery by their fear of death.

Take the helmet of salvation
In all these things we are more than conquerors through him who loved us.—Put on the full armour of God so that you can take your stand against the devil's schemes. . . . Take the helmet of salvation and the sword of the Spirit, which is the word of God.

> 1 Corinthians 15:57. Romans 8:33–34. Hebrews 2:14–15. Romans 8:37.
> Ephesians 6:11, 17.

Evening

The tree of life.

'He gave his one and only Son, that whoever believes in him shall not perish but have eternal life.'

The healing of the nations
'To those who overcome, I will give the right to eat from the tree of life, which is in the paradise of God.' . . . On each side of the river stood the tree of life, bearing twelve crops of fruit, yielding its fruit every month. And the leaves of the tree are for the healing of the nations.

She is a tree of life
Blessed are those who find wisdom, those who gain understanding, . . . Long life is in her right hand; . . . She is a tree of life to those who embrace her; those who lay hold of her will be blessed.—Christ Jesus . . . has become for us wisdom.

> Genesis 2:9. John 3:16. Revelation 2:7; 22:2. Proverbs 3:13, 16, 18.
> 1 Corinthians 1:30.

August 29

Morning

Blessed are those who trust in the LORD.

[Abraham] did not waver through unbelief regarding the promise of God, but was strengthened in his faith and gave glory to God, being fully persuaded that God had power to do what he had promised.

Take refuge in the LORD
God is our refuge and strength, an ever present help in trouble. Therefore we will not fear, though the earth give way and the mountains fall into the heart of the sea. . . . It is better to take refuge in the LORD than to trust in human beings. It is better to take refuge in the LORD than to trust in princes.

Fear the LORD
Taste and see that the LORD is good; blessed are those who take refuge in him. Fear the LORD, you his saints, for those who fear him lack nothing.

> Proverbs 16:20. Romans 4:20–21. Psalms 46:1–2; 118:8–9; 34:8–9.

Evening

I will lie down and sleep in peace, for you alone, O LORD, make me dwell in safety.

You will not fear the terror of night, nor the arrow that flies by day. . . . He will cover you with his feathers, and under his wings you will find refuge.—He will not let your foot slip—he who watches over you will not slumber; indeed, he who watches over Israel will neither slumber nor sleep. The LORD watches over you—the LORD is your shade at your right hand.

The shelter of your wings
I long to dwell in your tent for ever and take refuge in the shelter of your wings. . . . The darkness will not be dark to you; the night will shine like the day, for darkness is as light to you.
  I will trust and not be afraid.

> Psalms 4:8; 91:5, 4; 121:3–5; 61:4; 139:12. Isaiah 12:2.

Morning

When he cries out to me, I will hear, for I am compassionate.

We know and rely on the love God has for us. God is love. Those who live in love live in God, and God in them. In this way, love is made complete among us so that we will have confidence on the day of judgment, because in this world we are like him. There is no fear in love. But perfect love drives out fear, because fear has to do with punishment. The one who fears is not made perfect in love. We love because he first loved us.

We may approach God
Let us draw near to God with a sincere heart in full assurance of faith, having our hearts sprinkled to cleanse us from a guilty conscience and having our bodies washed with pure water.—For through him we both have access to the Father by one Spirit. . . . In him and through faith in him we may approach God with freedom and confidence.

Exodus 22:27. 1 John 4:16–19. Hebrews 10:22. Ephesians 2:18; 3:12.

Evening

Beyond all question, the mystery of godliness is great: He appeared in a body.

'For the bread of God is he who comes down from heaven and gives life to the world.'

'My flesh is real food'
'Your forefathers ate the manna in the desert, yet they died . . . Whoever eats of this bread will live for ever. . . . This bread is my flesh, which I will give for the life of the world.' . . . My flesh is real food and my blood is real drink.'

'Your heavenly Father knows'
'So do not worry, saying, "What shall we eat?" or "What shall we drink?" or "What shall we wear?" For the pagans run after all these things, and your heavenly Father knows that you need them. But seek first his kingdom and his righteousness, and all these things will be given to you as well.'

1 Timothy 3:16. John 6:33, 49, 51, 55. Matthew 6:31–33.

August 31

Morning

'Though your sins are like scarlet, they shall be as white as snow; though they are red as crimson, they shall be like wool.'

'I, even I, am he who blots out your transgressions, for my own sake, and remembers your sins no more. Review the past for me, let us argue the matter together, state the case for your innocence.' . . . 'Return to me, for I have redeemed you.'

The gift came by the one man
But the gift is not like the trespass. For if the many died by the trespass of the one man, how much more did God's grace and the gift that came by the grace of the one man, Jesus Christ, overflow to the many!—And that is what some of you were. But you were washed, you were sanctified, you were justified in the name of the Lord Jesus Christ and by the Spirit of our God.

Isaiah 1:18; 43:25–26; 44:22. Romans 5:15. 1 Corinthians 6:11.

Evening

'Put this money to work . . . until I come back.'

'It's like a man going away: He leaves his house in charge of his servants, each with his assigned task, and tells the one at the door to keep watch.'—'To one he gave five talents of money, to another two talents, and to another one talent, each according to his ability. Then he went on his journey.'

'Didn't you know I had to be in my Father's house?'—Leaving you an example, that you should follow in his steps.

The work of the Lord
That person's work will be shown for what it is, because the Day will bring it to light. . . . Therefore, my dear brothers and sisters, stand firm. Let nothing move you. Always give yourselves fully to the work of the Lord, because you know that your labour in the Lord is not in vain.

Luke 19:13. Mark 13:34. Matthew 25:15. Luke 2:49. 1 Peter 2:21.
1 Corinthians 3:13; 15:58.

September 1

Morning

The fruit of the Spirit is . . . gentleness.

The humble will rejoice in the LORD; the needy will rejoice in the Holy One of
Israel.—The unfading beauty of a gentle and quiet spirit . . . is of great worth
in God's sight.

He did not retaliate
Pursue gentleness.—'Take my yoke upon you and learn from me, for I am
gentle and humble in heart.'—Christ suffered for you, leaving you an
example, that you should follow in his steps. 'He committed no sin, and
no deceit was found in his mouth.' When they hurled their insults at him, he
did not retaliate . . . Instead, he entrusted himself to him who judges justly.

Galatians 5:22. Isaiah 29:19. Matthew 18:3–4. 1 Peter 3:4.
1 Timothy 6:11. Matthew 11:29. 1 Peter 2:21–23.

Evening

**Everyone who wants to live a godly life in Christ Jesus will be
persecuted.**

The offence of the cross.
   If you are insulted because of the name of Christ, you are blessed, for the
Spirit of glory and of God rests on you. If you suffer, it should not be as a
murderer or thief or any other kind of criminal, or even as a meddler.
However, if you suffer as a Christian, do not be ashamed, but praise God
that you bear that name.

Suffer for him
For it has been granted to you on behalf of Christ not only to believe in him,
but also to suffer for him.—That one died for all, and therefore all died. And he
died for all, that those who live should no longer live for themselves but for
him who died for them and was raised again.

2 Timothy 3:12. Galatians 5:11; 1 Peter 4:14–16. Philippians 1:29.
2 Corinthians 5:14–15.

September 2

Morning

Wait for the LORD, be strong and take heart and wait for the LORD.

Do you not know? Have you not heard? The LORD is the everlasting God, the Creator of the ends of the earth. He will not grow tired or weary. He gives strength to the weary and increases the power of the weak . . . 'So do not fear, for I am with you; do not be dismayed, for I am your God. I will strengthen you and help you; I will uphold you with my righteous right hand.' . . . You have been a refuge for the poor, a refuge for the needy in his distress, a shelter from the storm and a shade from the heat. For the breath of the ruthless is like a storm driving against a wall.

Faith develops perseverance
The testing of your faith develops perseverance. Perseverance must finish its work so that you may be mature and complete, not lacking anything.

Psalm 27:14. Isaiah 40:28–29; 41:10; 25:4. James 1:3–4.

Evening

He makes me lie down in green pastures.

Be still
'Come to me, all you who are weary and burdened, and I will give you rest.'—Be still before the LORD.

So do not be carried away by all kinds of strange teachings. It is good for our hearts to be strengthened by grace.

No longer tossed by the waves
Then we will no longer be infants, tossed back and forth by the waves, and blown here and there by every wind of teaching and by the cunning and craftiness of people in their deceitful scheming. Instead, speaking the truth in love, we will in all things grow up into him who is the Head, that is, Christ.

Psalm 23:2. Matthew 11:28. Psalm 37:7. Hebrews 13:9.
Ephesians 4:14–15.

Morning

To fear the LORD is to hate evil.

Hate what is evil.—Avoid every kind of evil. See to it that no-one misses the grace of God and that no bitter root grows up to cause trouble and defile many.
  If I had cherished sin in my heart, the Lord would not have listened.

The bread of sincerity and truth
Don't you know that a little yeast works through the whole batch of dough? Get rid of the old yeast that you may be a new batch without yeast—as you really are. For Christ, our Passover lamb, has been sacrificed. Therefore let us keep the Festival, not with the old yeast, the yeast of malice and wickedness, but with bread without yeast, the bread of sincerity and truth . . . We ought to examine ourselves before we eat of the bread and drink of the cup.

Proverbs 8:13. Romans 12:9. 1 Thessalonians 5:22. Hebrews 12:15.
Psalm 66:18. 1 Corinthians 5:6–8; 11:28.

Evening

I am afraid that just as Eve was deceived by the serpent's cunning, your minds may somehow be led astray from your sincere and pure devotion to Christ.

Finally, be strong in the Lord and in his mighty power. Put on the full armour of God so that you can take your stand against the devil's schemes.

Stand firm
Therefore put on the full armour of God, so that when the day of evil comes, you may be able to stand your ground, and after you have done everything, to stand. Stand firm then, with the belt of truth buckled round your waist, with the breastplate of righteousness that comes from the gospel of peace. In addition to all this, take up the shield of faith, with which you can extinguish all the flaming arrows of the evil one. Take the helmet of salvation and the sword of the Spirit, which is the word of God.

2 Corinthians 11:3. Ephesians 6:10–11, 13–17.

September 4

Morning

'Be careful, keep calm and don't be afraid. Do not lose heart.'

'Be still, and know that I am God.'—'Did I not tell you that if you believed, you would see the glory of God?'

In quietness and trust
Mary . . . sat at the Lord's feet listening to what he said . . . 'Mary has chosen what is better, and it will not be taken away from her.'—'In repentance and rest is your salvation, in quietness and trust is your strength.'—When you are on your beds, search your hearts and be silent.

Be still before the LORD and wait patiently for him; do not fret when people succeed in their ways, when they carry out their wicked schemes.

Isaiah 7:4. Romans 46:10. John 11:40. Luke 10:39, 42. Isaiah 30:15.
Psalms 4:4; 37:7.

Evening

'You do not realise now what I am doing, but later you will understand.'

Remember how the LORD your God led you all the way in the desert these forty years, to humble you and to test you in order to know what was in your heart, whether or not you would keep his commands.

Do not be surprised
Dear friends, do not be surprised at the painful trial you are suffering, as though something strange were happening to you. But rejoice that you participate in the sufferings of Christ, so that you may be overjoyed when his glory is revealed.

Momentary troubles
For our light and momentary troubles are achieving for us an eternal glory that far outweighs them all. So we fix our eyes not on what is seen, but on what is unseen. For what is seen is temporary, but what is unseen is eternal.

John 13:7. Deuteronomy 8:2. 1 Peter 4:12–13. 2 Corinthians 4:17–18.

Morning

He is the head of the body, the church.

Head over everything for the church, which is his body, the fulness of him who fills everything in every way. . . . For we are members of his body.

A body you prepared for me.—Your eyes saw my unformed body. All the days ordained for me were written in your book before one of them came to be.

Before the creation of the world
'They were yours; you gave them to me.'—He chose us in him before the creation of the world.—For those God foreknew he also predestined to be conformed to the likeness of his Son.

Grow up into him who is the Head, that is, Christ. From him the whole body, joined and held together by every supporting ligament, grows and builds itself up in love.

> Colossians 1:18. Ephesians 1:22–23; 5:30. Hebrews 10:5. Psalm 139:16.
> John 17:6. Ephesians 1:4. Romans 8:29. Ephesians 4:15–16.

Evening

The spring of living water.

How priceless is your unfailing love! Both highborn and low find refuge in the shadow of your wings. They feast in the abundance of your house; you give them drink from your river of delights. For with you is the fountain of life.

'Welling up to eternal life'
Therefore this is what the Sovereign LORD says: 'My servants will eat, but you will go hungry; my servants will drink, but you will go thirsty.'—'But those who drink the water I give them will never thirst. Indeed, the water I give them will become in them a spring of water welling up to eternal life.' . . . By this he meant the Spirit, whom those who believed in him were later to receive.

'Come, all you who are thirsty, come to the waters.'

> Jeremiah 2:13. Psalm 36:7–9. Isaiah 65:13. John 4:14; 7:39. Isaiah 55:1.

September 6

Morning

Let us lift up our hearts and our hands to God in heaven.

Who is like the LORD our God, the One who sits enthroned on high, who stoops down to look on the heavens and the earth? . . . To you, O LORD, I lift up my soul.

Your unfailing love
I spread out my hands to you; my soul thirsts for you like a parched land. Answer me quickly, O LORD; my spirit faints with longing. Do not hide your face from me or I will be like those who go down to the pit. Let the morning bring me word of your unfailing love, for I have put my trust in you. Show me the way I should go, for to you I lift up my soul.

I will praise you as long as I live
Because your love is better than life, my lips will glorify you. I will praise you as long as I live, and in your name I will lift up my hands.

Lamentations 3:41. Psalms 113:5–6; 25:1; 143:6–8; 63:3–4.

Evening

'Heaven and earth will pass away, but my words will never pass away.'

Put aside the deeds of darkness
The hour has come for you to wake up from your slumber, because our salvation is nearer now than when we first believed. The night is nearly over; the day is almost here. So let us put aside the deeds of darkness and put on the armour of light.

'Now learn this lesson from the fig-tree: As soon as its twigs get tender and its leaves come out, you know that summer is near. Even so, when you see all these things, you know that it is near, right at the door.'

I wait for the LORD, my soul waits, and in his word I put my hope. My soul waits for the Lord more than those on watch wait for the morning, more than those on watch wait for the morning.

'Therefore keep watch, because you do not know the day or the hour.'

Matthew 24:35. Romans 13:11–12. Matthew 24:32–33. Psalm 130.5–6.
Matthew 25:13.

Morning

Be joyful in hope.

The hope that is stored up for you in heaven.—If only for this life we have hope in Christ, we are to be pitied more than all people.—'Those who do not carry their cross and follow me cannot be my disciples.'

Overflow with hope
Rejoice in the Lord always, I will say it again: Rejoice!—The God of hope fill you with all joy and peace as you trust in him, so that you may overflow with hope by the power of the Holy Spirit.

Praise be to the God and Father of our Lord Jesus Christ! In his great mercy he has given us new birth into a living hope through the resurrection of Jesus Christ from the dead. . . . Though you have not seen him, you love him; and even though you do not see him now, you believe in him and are filled with an inexpressible and glorious joy.

> Romans 12:12. Colossians 1:5. 1 Corinthians 15:19. Luke 14:27.
> Philippians 4:4. Romans 15:13. 1 Peter 1:3, 8.

Evening

Yet I am poor and needy; may the Lord think of me.

'For I know the plans I have for you,' declares the LORD, 'plans to prosper you and not to harm you.'—'For my thoughts are not your thoughts, neither are your ways my ways,' declares the LORD. 'As the heavens are higher than the earth, so are my ways higher than your ways and my thoughts than your thoughts.'

How precious to me are your thoughts, O God! How vast is the sum of them! Were I to count them, they would outnumber the grains of sand. When I awake, I am still with you.

Poor in the eyes of the world
Not many were influential; not many were of noble birth.—Has not God chosen those who are poor in the eyes of the world to be rich in faith and to inherit the kingdom?—Having nothing, and yet possessing everything.

> Psalm 40:17. Jeremiah 29:11. Isaiah 55:8–9. Psalm 139:17–18.
> 1 Corinthians 1:26. James 2:5. 2 Corinthians 6:10.

September 8

Morning

'You have been weighed on the scales and found wanting.'

The LORD is a God who knows, and by him deeds are weighed.—'You are the ones who justify yourselves in the eyes of others, but God knows your hearts.'

God cannot be mocked
Do not be deceived: God cannot be mocked. People reap what they sow. Those who sow to please their sinful nature, from that nature will reap destruction; those who sow to please the Spirit, from the Spirit will reap eternal life.

'What good will it be for you to gain the whole world, yet forfeit your soul? Or what can you give in exchange for your soul?'—Whatever was to my profit I now consider loss for the sake of Christ.

Daniel 5:27. 1 Samuel 2:3. Luke 16:15. Galatians 6:7–8. Matthew 16:26.
Philippians 3:7.

Evening

Christ, the firstfruits.

'Unless an ear of wheat falls to the ground and dies, it remains only a single seed. But if it dies, it produces many seeds.'—If the part of the dough offered as firstfruits is holy, then the whole batch is holy; if the root is holy, so are the branches.—But Christ has indeed been raised from the dead, the firstfruits of those who have fallen asleep.—If we have been united with him in his death, we will certainly also be united with him in his resurrection.

Like his glorious body
The Lord Jesus Christ, who, by the power that enables him to bring everything under his control, will transform our lowly bodies so that they will be like his glorious body.

'I am the resurrection and the life. He who believes in me will live, even though he dies.'

1 Corinthians 15:23. John 12:24. Romans 11:16. 1 Corinthians 15:20.
Romans 6:5. Philippians 3:20–21. John 11:25.

Morning

'He has filled the hungry with good things but has sent the rich away empty.'

'You say, "I am rich; I have acquired wealth and do not need a thing." But you do not realise that you are wretched, pitiful, poor, blind and naked. I counsel you to buy from me gold refined in the fire, so that you can become rich; and white clothes to wear, so that you can cover your shameful nakedness; and salve to put on your eyes, so that you can see. Those whom I love I rebuke and discipline. So be earnest, and repent.'

'Blessed are those who hunger and thirst for righteousness, for they will be filled.'

'I am the bread of life'
'Why spend money on what is not bread, and your labour on what does not satisfy? Listen, listen to me, and eat what is good, and your soul will delight in the richest of fare.'—'I am the bread of life. He who comes to me will never go hungry, and he who believes in me will never be thirsty.'

Luke 1:53. Revelation 3:17–19. Matthew 5:6. Isaiah 55:2. John 6:35.

Evening

My feet had almost slipped; I had nearly lost my foothold.

When I said, 'My foot is slipping,' your love, O LORD, supported me.

'Simon, Simon, Satan has asked to sift you as wheat. But I have prayed for you, Simon, that your faith may not fail.'—For though the righteous fall seven times, they rise again.

From six calamities he will rescue you; in seven no harm will befall you.

He always lives to intercede
But if anybody does sin, we have one who speaks to the Father in our defence.—Jesus Christ, the Righteous One.—Therefore he is able to save completely those who come to God through him, because he always lives to intercede for them.

Psalms 73:2; 94:18. Luke 22:31–32. Proverbs 24:16. Job 5:19.
1 John 2:1. Hebrews 7:25.

September 10

Morning

' "I will give you a new heart and put a new spirit in you." '

Good and upright is the LORD; therefore he instructs sinners in his ways. He guides the humble in what is right and teaches them his way. All the ways of the LORD are loving and faithful for those who keep the demands of his covenant.

Keep the unity of the Spirit
I urge you to live a life worthy of the calling you have received. Be completely humble and gentle; be patient, bearing with one another in love. Make every effort to keep the unity of the Spirit through the bond of peace. There is one body and one Spirit—just as you were called to one hope when you were called—one Lord, one faith, one baptism; one God and Father of all, who is over all and through all and in all.

Ezekiel 36:26. Psalm 25:8–10. Ephesians 4:1–6.

Evening

Those who hope in the LORD will renew their strength.

My God has been my strength.—He said to me, 'My grace is sufficient for you, for my power is made perfect in weakness.' Therefore I will boast all the more gladly about my weaknesses, so that Christ's power may rest on me.—'Let them come to me for refuge.'

In the name of the LORD Almighty'
'You come against me with sword and spear and javelin, but I come against you in the name of the LORD Almighty, the God of the armies of Israel, whom you have defied.'—Contend, O LORD, with those who contend with me; fight against those who fight against me. Take up shield and buckler, arise and come to my aid.

Isaiah 40:31; 49:5. 2 Corinthians 12:9. Isaiah 27:5. 1 Samuel 17:45.
Psalm 35:1–2.

Morning

'Do not follow the crowd in doing wrong.'

Don't you know that friendship with the world is hatred towards God? Anyone who chooses to be a friend of the world becomes an enemy of God.

Christ and Belial
For what do righteousness and wickedness have in common? Or what fellowship can light have with darkness? What harmony is there between Christ and Belial? What does a believer have in common with an unbeliever? What agreement is there between the temple of God and idols?

In which you used to live when you followed the ways of this world and of the ruler of the kingdom of the air, the spirit who is now at work in those who are disobedient. . . . You, however, did not come to know Christ that way. Surely you heard of him and were taught in him in accordance with the truth that is in Jesus.

Exodus 23:2. James 4:4. 2 Corinthians 6:14–16. Ephesians 2:2; 4:20–21.

Evening

Then people go out to their work, to their labour until evening.

By the sweat of your brow you will eat your food until you return to the ground.

Lead a quiet life
Make it your ambition to lead a quiet life, to mind your own business and to work with your hands.

We will reap a harvest
Whatever your hand finds to do, do it with all your might, for in the grave, where you are going, there is neither working nor planning nor knowledge nor wisdom.—Let us not become weary in doing good; for at the proper time we will reap a harvest if we do not give up.—Always give yourselves fully to the work of the Lord, because you know that your labour in the Lord is not in vain.

Psalm 104:23. Genesis 3:19. 1 Thessalonians 4:11. Ecclesiastes 9:10.
Galatians 6:9. 1 Corinthians 15:58.

September 12

Morning

'I am the LORD who heals you.'

O LORD, you have searched me and you know me. You know when I sit and when I rise; you perceive my thoughts from afar. You discern my going out and my lying down; you are familiar with all my ways. . . . You have set our iniquities before you, our secret sins in the light of your presence.

'Let us reason together'
'Come now, let us reason together,' says the LORD. 'Though your sins are like scarlet, they shall be as white as snow; though they are red as crimson, they shall be like wool.'

To bind up the broken-hearted
But he was pierced for our transgressions, he was crushed for our iniquities; the punishment that brought us peace was upon him, and by his wounds we are healed. . . . He has sent me to bind up the broken-hearted.

Exodus 15:26. Psalms 139:1–3; 90:8. Isaiah 1:18; 53:5; 61:1.

Evening

The LORD is with me; he is my helper.

May the LORD answer you when you are in distress; may the name of the God of Jacob protect you. May he send you help from the sanctuary and grant you support from Zion. . . . We will shout for joy when you are victorious and will lift up our banners in the name of our God.

Some trust in chariots and some in horses, but we trust in the name of the LORD our God. They are brought to their knees and fall, but we rise up and stand firm.

He will provide a way out
No temptation has seized you except what is common to all people. And God is faithful; he will not let you be tempted beyond what you can bear. But when you are tempted, he will also provide a way out so that you can stand up under it.

The God we serve is able to save us from it, he will rescue us.

Psalms 118:7; 20:1–2, 5, 7–8. 1 Corinthians 10:13. Daniel 3:17.

Morning

'Let anyone who is thirsty come to me and drink.'

My soul yearns, even faints for the courts of the LORD; my heart and my flesh cry out for the living God.

'Come, all you who are thirsty, come to the waters; and you who have no money, come, buy and eat! Come, buy wine and milk without money and without cost.'

The water of life
The Spirit and the bride say, 'Come!' Let those who are thirsty come; and let all who wish to take the free gift of the water of life.

'Those who drink the water I give them will never thirst. Indeed, the water I give them will become in them a spring of water welling up to eternal life.'

John 7:37. Psalm 84:2. Isaiah 55:1. Revelation 22:17. John 4:14.

Evening

'You are the salt of the earth.'

Unfading beauty . . . For you have been born again, not of perishable seed, but of imperishable, through the living and enduring word of God.

Alive because of righteousness
If anyone does not have the Spirit of Christ, that person does not belong to Christ. But if Christ is in you, your body is dead because of sin, yet your spirit is alive because of righteousness. And if the Spirit of him who raised Jesus from the dead is living in you, he who raised Christ from the dead will also give life to your mortal bodies through his Spirit, who lives in you.

'Have salt in yourselves'
'Have salt in yourselves, and be at peace with each other.'—Do not let any unwholesome talk come out of your mouths, but only what is helpful for building others up according to their needs, that it may benefit those who listen.

Matthew 5:13. 1 Peter 3:4; 1:23. Romans 8:9–11. Mark 9:50.
Ephesians 4:19.

September 14

Morning

'I, even I, am he who comforts you.'

Praise to the God and Father of our Lord Jesus Christ, the Father of compassion and the God of all comfort, who comforts us in all our troubles, so that we can comfort those in any trouble with the comfort we ourselves have received from God.

'As a mother comforts her child'
As a father has compassion on his children, so the LORD has compassion on those who fear him; for he knows how we are formed, he remembers that we are dust.—'As a mother comforts her child, so will I comfort you.'

You, O Lord, are a compassionate and gracious God, slow to anger, abounding in love and faithfulness.

'He will wipe every tear from their eyes. There will be no more death or mourning or crying or pain, for the old order of things has passed away.'

Isaiah 51:12. 2 Corinthians 1:3–4. Psalm 103:13–14. Isaiah 66:13.
Psalm 86:15. Revelation 21:4.

Evening

God . . . has called you into fellowship with his Son.

For he received honour and glory from God the Father when the voice came to him from the Majestic Glory, saying, 'This is my Son, whom I love; with him I am well pleased.'—How great is the love the Father has lavished on us, that we should be called children of God!

'Let your light shine before others, that they may see your good deeds and praise your Father in heaven.'

Through Christ our comfort overflows
Jesus, the author and perfecter of our faith, who for the joy set before him endured the cross, scorning its shame.—'I say these things while I am still in the world, so that they may have the full message of my joy within them.'—For just as the sufferings of Christ flow over into our souls, so also through Christ our comfort overflows.

1 Corinthians 1:9. 2 Peter 1:17. 1 John 3:1. Matthew 5:16.
Hebrews 12:2. John 17:13. 2 Corinthians 1:5.

Morning

For sin shall not be your master, because you are not under law, but under grace.

What then? Shall we sin because we are not under law but under grace? By no means! . . . My brothers and sisters, you also died to the law through the body of Christ, that you might belong to another, to him who was raised from the dead, in order that we might bear fruit.—(I am not free from God's law but am under Christ's law.) . . . The sting of death is sin, and the power of sin is the law. But thanks be to God! He gives us the victory through our Lord Jesus Christ.

'You will be free indeed'
The law of the Spirit of life set me free from the law of sin and death.—'Everyone who sins is a slave to sin. . . . So if the Son sets you free, you will be free indeed.'

Romans 6:14, 15; 7:4. 1 Corinthians 9:21; 15:56–57. Romans 8:2.
John 8:34, 36.

Evening

Anyone who comes to him must believe that he exists and that he rewards those who earnestly seek him.

But when you ask, you must believe and not doubt, because the one who doubts is like a wave of the sea, blown and tossed by the wind. Those who doubt should not think they will receive anything from the Lord; they are double-minded and unstable in all they do.—'Whatever you ask for in prayer, believe that you have received it, and it will be yours.'

Grow up into him
We will no longer be infants, tossed back and forth by the waves, and blown here and there by every wind of teaching and by the cunning and craftiness of people in their deceitful scheming. Instead, speaking the truth in love, we will in all things grow up into him who is the Head, that is, Christ.
    'Remain in him.'

Hebrews 11:6. James 1:6–7. Mark 11:24. Ephesians 4:14–15. John 15:4.

September 16

Morning

The LORD weighs the heart.

For the LORD watches over the way of the righteous, but the way of the wicked will perish.—The LORD will show who belongs to him and who is holy.—'Then your Father, who sees what is done in secret, will reward you.'

Search me, O God, and know my heart; test me and know my anxious thoughts. See if there is any offensive way in me, and lead me in the way everlasting.

He who searches our hearts knows the mind of the Spirit, because the Spirit intercedes for the saints in accordance with God's will.

'The Lord knows those who are his'
God's solid foundation stands firm, sealed with this inscription: 'The Lord knows those who are his,' and, 'Everyone who confesses the name of the Lord must turn away from wickedness.'

> Proverbs 21:2. Psalm 1:6. Numbers 16:5. Matthew 6:4.
> Psalm 139:23–24. Romans 8:27. 2 Timothy 2:19.

Evening

Weeping may remain for a night, but rejoicing comes in the morning.

So that no-one would be unsettled by these trials. You know quite well that we are destined for them. In fact, when we were with you, we kept telling you that we would be persecuted.—'In me you may have peace. In this world you will have trouble. But take heart! I have overcome the world.'

Like a cloudless morning
He is like the light of morning at sunrise on a cloudless morning, like the brightness after rain.

No more crying
He will swallow up death for ever. The Sovereign LORD will wipe away the tears from all faces.—'There will be no more death or mourning or crying or pain, for the old order of things has passed away.'

> Psalm 30:5. 1 Thessalonians 3:3–4. John 16:33. 2 Samuel 23:4.
> Isaiah 25:8. Revelation 21:4.

Morning

A bruised reed he will not break.

The sacrifices of God are a broken spirit; a broken and contrite heart, O God, you will not despise.

He heals the broken-hearted
He heals the broken-hearted and binds up their wounds.

'I will bind up the injured'
'I will search for the lost and bring back the strays. I will bind up the injured and strengthen the weak.'—Therefore, strengthen your feeble arms and weak knees! 'Make level paths for your feet,' so that the lame may not be disabled, but rather healed.—'Your God will come, . . . He will come to save you.'

> Matthew 12:20. Psalms 51:17; 147:3. Ezekiel 34:16. Hebrews 12:12–13.
> Isaiah 35:4.

Evening

Taste and see that the LORD is good; blessed are those who take refuge in him.

For the ear tests words as the tongue tastes food.—'I believed; therefore I have spoken.'—I know whom I have believed.
   God's kindness . . . He who did not spare his own Son, but gave him up for us all—how will he not also, along with him, graciously give us all things?

Crave pure spiritual milk
Like newborn babies, crave pure spiritual milk, so that by it you may grow up in your salvation, now that you have tasted that the Lord is good.
   Let all who take refuge in you be glad; let them ever sing for joy.

> Psalm 34:8. Job 34:3. 2 Corinthians 4:13. 2 Timothy 1:12.
> Romans 2:4; 8:32. 1 Peter 2:2–3. Psalm 5:11.

September 18

Morning

Open my eyes that I may see wonderful things in your law.

Then he opened their minds so they could understand the Scriptures.—'I praise you, Father, Lord of heaven and earth, because you have hidden these things from the wise and learned, and revealed them to little children. Yes, Father, for this was your good pleasure.'—We have not received the spirit of the world but the Spirit who is from God, that we may understand what God has freely given us.

The wisdom and knowledge of God
Oh, the depth of the riches of the wisdom and knowledge of God! How unsearchable his judgments, and his paths beyond tracing out! 'Who has known the mind of the Lord? Or who has been his counsellor?'

> Psalm 119:18. Luke 24:45. Matthew 11:25–26. 1 Corinthians 2:12.
> Romans 11:33–34.

Evening

Because you are sons, God sent the Spirit of his Son into our hearts, the Spirit who calls out, 'Abba, Father.'

'If you knew the gift of God and who it is that asks you for a drink, you would have asked him and he would have given you living water.' . . . 'Let anyone who is thirsty come to me and drink.' . . . By this he meant the Spirit, whom those who believed in him were later to receive.

The floodgates of heaven
'Test me in this,' says the LORD Almighty, 'and see if I will not throw open the floodgates of heaven and pour out so much blessing that you will not have room enough for it.'
  'If you then, though you are evil, know how to give good gifts to your children, how much more will your Father in heaven give the Holy Spirit to those who ask him!' . . . 'Ask and it will be given to you; seek and you will find.'

> Galatians 4:6. John 4:10; 7:37, 39. Malachi 3:10. Luke 11:13, 9.

Morning

The God of all grace.

Justified freely by his grace through the redemption that came by Christ Jesus. God presented him as a sacrifice of atonement, through faith in his blood. He did this to demonstrate his justice, because in his forbearance he had left the sins committed beforehand unpunished.—Grace and truth came through Jesus Christ.

God's grace in its various forms
For it is by grace you have been saved, through faith—and this not from yourselves.—Grace mercy and peace from God the Father and Christ Jesus our Lord.—But to each one of us grace has been given as Christ appointed it.— Each one should use whatever gift he has received to serve others, faithfully administering God's grace in its various forms.—He gives us more grace.

1 Peter 5:10. Romans 3:24–25. John 1:17. Ephesians 2:8. 1 Timothy 1:2.
Ephesians 4:7. 1 Peter 4:10. James 4:6.

Evening

I lift up my eyes to the hills—where does my help come from? My help comes from the LORD.

As the mountains surround Jerusalem, so the LORD surrounds his people both now and for evermore.

I lift up my eyes to you, to you whose throne is in heaven. As the eyes of slaves look to the hand of their master, as the eyes of a maid look to the hand of their mistress, so our eyes look to the LORD our God, till he shows us his mercy. . . . Because you are my help, I sing in the shadow of your wings.

'O our God, will not you judge them? For we have no power to face this vast army that is attacking us. We do not know what to do, but our eyes are upon you.'—My eyes are ever on the LORD, for only he will release my feet from the snare . . . Our help is in the name of the LORD, the Maker of heaven and earth.

Psalms 121:1–2; 125:2; 123:1–2; 63:7. 2 Chronicles 20:12.
Psalms 25:15; 124:8.

September 20

Morning

Blessed are those who find wisdom, those who gain understanding.

Whoever finds me finds life and receives favour from the LORD.—'The fear of the LORD is the beginning of wisdom.'

The treasures of wisdom

Whatever was to my profit I now consider loss for the sake of Christ. What is more, I consider everything a loss compared to the surpassing greatness of knowing Christ Jesus my Lord, for whose sake I have lost all things. I consider them rubbish, that I may gain Christ.—In whom are hidden all the treasures of wisdom and knowledge.—Counsel and sound judgment are mine; I have understanding and power.

Christ Jesus . . . has become for us our righteousness, holiness and redemption.—He who wins souls is wise.

Proverbs 3:13; 8:35; 9:10. Philippians 3:7–8. Colossians 2:3.
Proverbs 8:14. 1 Corinthians 1:30. Proverbs 11:30.

Evening

Poor, yet making many rich.

You know the grace of our Lord Jesus Christ, that though he was rich, yet for your sakes he became poor, so that you through his poverty might become rich.—From the fulness of his grace we have all received one blessing after another.

God chose the weak

Has not God chosen those who are poor in the eyes of the world to be rich in faith and to inherit the kingdom he promised those who love him?—Not many of you were wise by human standards; not many were influential; not many were of noble birth. But God chose the foolish things of the world to shame the wise; God chose the weak things of the world to shame the strong.

We have this treasure in jars of clay to show that this all-surpassing power is from God and not from us.

2 Corinthians 6:10; 8:9. John 1:16. James 2:5. 1 Corinthians 1:26–27.
2 Corinthians 4:7.

Morning

We know that in all things God works for the good of those who love him.

Joseph
'You intended to harm me, but God intended it for good.'

All this is for your benefit, so that the grace that is reaching more and more people may cause thanksgiving to overflow to the glory of God.

Therefore we do not lose heart. Though outwardly we are wasting away, yet inwardly we are being renewed day by day. For our light and momentary troubles are achieving for us an eternal glory that far outweighs them all.

The testing of your faith
Consider it pure joy, my brothers and sisters, whenever you face trials of many kinds, because you know that the testing of your faith develops perseverance. Perseverance must finish its work so that you may be mature and complete, not lacking anything.

Romans 8:28. Genesis 50:20. 2 Corinthians 4:15, 16–17. James 1:2–4.

Evening

The fellowship of the Holy Spirit be with you all.

'I will ask the Father, and he will give you another Counsellor to be with you for ever—the Spirit of truth. The world cannot accept him, because it neither sees him nor knows him. But you know him, for he lives with you and will be in you.' . . . 'He will not speak on his own; he will speak only what he hears, and he will tell you what is yet to come. He will bring glory to me by taking from what is mine and making it known to you.'

The Spirit helps us
Do not grieve the Holy Spirit of God, with whom you were sealed for the day of redemption.—The Spirit helps us in our weakness. We do not know what we ought to pray, but the Spirit himself intercedes for us with groans that words cannot express.

2 Corinthians 13:14. John 14:16–17; 16:13–14. Ephesians 4:30.
Romans 8:26.

September 22

Morning

May my meditation be pleasing to him, as I rejoice in the LORD.

For who in the skies above can compare with the LORD? Who is like the LORD among the heavenly beings?

The ruler of the kings of the earth
'One [pearl] of great value.'—The ruler of the kings of the earth.

He is the head of the church
Head over everything.—He is the head of the body, the church.

Let your face shine on your servant
'No-one ever spoke the way this man does.'—Let your face shine on your servant . . . Let the light of your face shine upon us, O LORD.

Psalms 104:34; 89:6. Matthew 13:46. Revelation 1:5. Ephesians 1:22.
Colossians 1:18. John 7:46. Psalms 31:16; 4:6.

Evening

He . . . became obedient to death—even death on a cross!

'Now my heart is troubled, and what shall I say? "Father, save me from this hour"? No, it was for this very reason I came to this hour.' . . . 'I have come down from heaven not to do my will but to do the will of him who sent me.'

Reverent submission
During the days of Jesus' life on earth, he offered up prayers and petitions with loud cries and tears to the one who could save him from death, and he was heard because of his reverent submission. Although he was a son, he learned obedience from what he suffered.

'This is what is written: The Christ will suffer and rise from the dead on the third day, and repentance and forgiveness of sins will be preached in his name to all nations, beginning at Jerusalem.'

Philippians 2:8. John 12:27; 6:38. Hebrews 5:7–8. Luke 24:46–47.

Morning

God has not deserted us.

Dear friends, do not be surprised at the painful trial you are suffering, as though something strange were happening to you.—Endure hardship as discipline; God is treating you as children. For what children are not disciplined by their parents? If you are not disciplined (and everyone undergoes discipline), then you are illegitimate and not true children.—The LORD your God is testing you to find out whether you love him with all your heart and with all your soul.

'I will not forget you!'
For the sake of his great name the LORD will not reject his people, because the LORD was pleased to make you his own.—'Can a mother forget the baby at her breast and have no compassion on the child she has borne? Though she may forget, I will not forget you!'

Ezra 9:9. 1 Peter 4:12. Hebrews 12:7–8. Deuteronomy 13:3.
1 Samuel 12:22. Isaiah 49:15.

Evening

'He who overcomes will inherit all this.'

If only for this life we have hope in Christ, we are to be pitied more than all people.

A better country
They were longing for a better country—a heavenly one. Therefore God is not ashamed to be called their God, for he has prepared a city for them.—An inheritance that can never perish, spoil or fade—kept in heaven for you.

All things are yours, . . . the world or life or death or the present or the future—all are yours . . . 'No eye has seen, no ear has heard, no mind has conceived what God has prepared for those who love him'—but God has revealed it to us by his Spirit.

Rewarded fully
Watch out that you do not lose what you have worked for, but that you may be rewarded fully.

Revelation 21:7. 1 Corinthians 15:19. Hebrews 11:16. 1 Peter 1:4.
1 Corinthians 3:21–22; 2:9–10. 2 John 8.

September 24

Morning

I love the house where you live, O LORD, the place where your glory dwells.

Better is one day in your courts than a thousand elsewhere; I would rather be a doorkeeper in the house of my God than dwell in the tents of the wicked. . . . Blessed are those you choose and bring near to live in your courts! We are filled with the good things of your house, of your holy temple.

The LORD is good to those whose hope is in him, to the one who seeks him.

Draw near to God
Therefore, brothers and sisters, since we have confidence to enter the Most Holy Place by the blood of Jesus, by a new and living way opened for us through the curtain, that is his body, . . . let us draw near to God with a sincere heart in full assurance of faith, having our hearts sprinkled to cleanse us from a guilty conscience.

Psalms 26:8; 84:10; 65:4. Lamentations 3:25. Hebrews 10:19–20, 22.

Evening

You know the grace of our Lord Jesus Christ.

The Word became flesh and lived for a while among us. We have seen his glory, the glory of the One and Only, who came from the Father, full of grace and truth.—You are the most excellent of men and your lips have been anointed with grace.—All spoke well of him and were amazed at the gracious words that came from his lips.

You have tasted that the Lord is good.—Those who believe in the Son of God have this testimony in their hearts.

Taste and see that the LORD is good
Taste and see that the LORD is good; blessed are those who take refuge in him.

He said to me, 'My grace is sufficient for you, for my power is made perfect in weakness.'—Each of you should use whatever gift you have received to serve others, faithfully administering God's grace in its various forms.

2 Corinthians 8:9. John 1:14. Psalm 45:2. Luke 4:22. 1 Peter 2:3.
1 John 5:10. Psalm 34:8. 2 Corinthians 12:9. 1 Peter 4:10.

Morning

Perseverance must finish its work so that you may be mature and complete, not lacking anything.

Though now for a little while you may have had to suffer grief in all kinds of trials. These have come so that your faith—of greater worth than gold, which perishes even though refined by fire—may be proved genuine and may result in praise, glory and honour when Jesus Christ is revealed.

We also rejoice in our sufferings, because we know that suffering produces perseverance; perseverance, character; and character, hope.

Wait quietly for salvation
It is good to wait quietly for the salvation of the LORD.—May our Lord Jesus Christ himself and God our Father, who loved us and by his grace gave us eternal encouragement and good hope, encourage your hearts.

James 1:4. 1 Peter 1:6–7. Romans 5:3–4. Lamentations 3:26.
2 Thessalonians 2:16–17.

Evening

God will judge everyone's secrets through Jesus Christ.

'Eyes like blazing fire'
'The Father judges no-one, but has entrusted all judgment to the Son. . . . Because he is the Son of man.'—'The Son of God, whose eyes are like blazing fire.'

They say, 'How can God know? Does the Most High have knowledge?' . . . 'These things you have done and I kept silent; you thought I was altogether like you. But I will rebuke you and accuse you to your face.'—'There is nothing concealed that will not be disclosed, or hidden that will not be made known.'

My sighing is not hidden from you
All my longings lie open before you, O Lord: my sighing is not hidden from you . . . Test me, O LORD, and try me, examine my heart and my mind.

Romans 2:16. John 5:22, 27. Revelation 2:18. Psalms 73:11; 50:21.
Luke 12:2. Psalms 38:9; 26:2.

Morning

A faithful God who does no wrong, upright and just is he.

Him who judges justly.—For we must all appear before the judgment seat of Christ, that everyone may receive what is due to them for the things done while in the body, whether good or bad.—So then, we will all give an account of ourselves to God.—The soul who sins is the one who will die.

Righteousness and peace kiss each other
The LORD has laid on him the iniquity of us all.—Love and faithfulness meet together; righteousness and peace kiss each other.—Mercy triumphs over judgment!—For the wages of sin is death, but the gift of God is eternal life in Christ Jesus our Lord.
    'A righteous God and a Saviour; there is none but me.'

> Deuteronomy 32:4. 1 Peter 2:23. 2 Corinthians 5:10. Romans 14:12.
> Ezekiel 18:4. Isaiah 53:6. Psalm 85:10. James 2:13. Romans 6:23.
> Isaiah 45:21.

Evening

But thanks be to God! He gives us the victory through our Lord Jesus Christ.

Since the children have flesh and blood, he too shared in their humanity so that by his death he might destroy him who holds the power of death—that is, the devil—and free those who all their lives were held in slavery by their fear of death.

If we died with Christ, we believe that we will also live with him. For we know that since Christ was raised from the dead, he cannot die again; death no longer has mastery over him. The death he died, he died to sin once for all; but the life he lives, he lives to God.

Count yourselves dead to sin
In the same way, count yourselves dead to sin but alive to God in Christ Jesus.

> 1 Corinthians 15:54, 57. Hebrews 2:14–15. Romans 6:8–11.

Morning

Humble yourselves, therefore, under God's mighty hand, that he may lift you up in due time.

The LORD detests all the proud of heart. Be sure of this: They will not go unpunished.

You are the potter

O LORD, you are our Father. We are the clay, you are the potter; we are all the work of your hand. Do not be angry beyond measure, O LORD; do not remember our sins for ever. Oh, look upon us, we pray, for we are all your people.

'After I strayed, I repented'

'You disciplined me like an unruly calf, and I have been disciplined. Restore me, and I will return, because you are the Lord my God. After I strayed, I repented; after I came to understand, I beat my breast. I was ashamed and humiliated because I bore the disgrace of my youth.'

1 Peter 5:6. Proverbs 16:5. Isaiah 64:8–9. Jeremiah 31:18–19.

Evening

'Did God really say . . .?'

The tempter came to him and said, 'If you are the Son of God.' . . . Jesus answered, 'It is written.'

'The word of the LORD warned him'

'I cannot turn back and go with you, nor can I eat bread or drink water with you in this place. I have been told by the word of the LORD: "You must not eat bread or drink water there or return by the way you came."' The old prophet answered, 'I too am a prophet, as you are. And an angel said to me by the word of the LORD: "Bring him back with you to your house so that he may eat bread and drink water."' (But he was lying to him.) So the man of God . . . 'defied the word of the LORD. The LORD has given him over to the lion, which has mauled him and killed him, as the word of the LORD had warned him.'

I have hidden your word in my heart that I might not sin against you.

Genesis 3:1. Matthew 4:3–4. 1 Kings 13:1–19, 26. Psalm 119:11.

September 28

Morning

'So they will put my name on the Israelites, and I will bless them.'

O LORD, our God, other Lords besides you have ruled over us, but your name alone do we honour. . . . We are yours from of old; but you have not ruled over them, they have not been called by your name.

All the peoples on earth will see that you are called by the name of the LORD, and they will fear you.—The LORD will not reject his people, because the LORD was pleased to make you his own.

'Your people bear your Name'
'O Lord, listen! O Lord, forgive! O Lord, hear and act! For your sake, O my God, do not delay, because your city and your people bear your Name.'—The name of the LORD is a strong tower; the righteous run to it and are safe.

Numbers 6:27. Isaiah 26:13; 63:19. Deuteronomy 28:10.
1 Samuel 12:22. Daniel 9:19. Proverbs 18:10.

Evening

The heavens declare the glory of God; the skies proclaim the work of his hands.

For since the creation of the world God's invisible qualities—his eternal power and divine nature—have been clearly seen, being understood from what has been made.—'He has not left himself without testimony.'

The moon and the stars
When I considered your heavens, the work of your fingers, the moon and the stars, which you have set in place, what are mere mortals that you are mindful of them, human beings that you care for them?

Lead many to righteousness
Those who are wise will shine like the brightness of the heavens, and those who lead many to righteousness, like the stars for ever and ever.

Psalm 19:1. Romans 1:20. Acts 14:17. Psalm 8:3–4. Daniel 12:3.

Morning

This is how we know what love is: Jesus Christ laid down his life for us.

This love that surpasses knowledge.—'Greater love has no-one than this, to lay down one's life for one's friends.'—You know the grace of our Lord Jesus Christ, that though he was rich, yet for your sakes he became poor, so that you through his poverty might become rich.—Dear friends, since God so loved us, we also ought to love one another.

Forgive as the Lord forgave you
Be kind and compassionate to one another, forgiving each other, just as in Christ God forgave you.—Bear with each other and forgive whatever grievances you may have against one another. Forgive as the Lord forgave you.
   'You also should wash one another's feet. I have set you an example that you should do as I have done for you.'

1 John 3:16. Ephesians 3:19. John 15:13. 2 Corinthians 8:9. 1 John 4:11.
Ephesians 4:32. Colossians 3:13. John 13:14–15.

Evening

'Whatever the Father does the Son also does.'

For the LORD gives wisdom, and from his mouth come knowledge and understanding.—'For I will give you words and wisdom that none of your adversaries will be able to resist or contradict.'
   Wait for the LORD; be strong and take heart and wait for the LORD.
   Who are loved by God the Father.—Both the one who makes people holy and those who are holy are of the same family. So Jesus is not ashamed to call them brothers and sisters.

'Apart from me there is no saviour'
'I, even I, am the LORD, and apart from me there is no saviour.'—'This man really is the Saviour of the world.'—Grace and peace from God the Father and Christ Jesus our Saviour.

John 5:19. Proverbs 2:6. Luke 21:15. Psalm 27:14. Jude 1.
Hebrews 2:11. Isaiah 43:11. John 4:42. Titus 1:4.

September 30

Morning

He knows the way that I take; when he has tested me, I shall come forth as gold.

He knows how we are formed.

God's solid foundation stands firm, sealed with this inscription: 'The Lord knows those who are his,' and, 'Everyone who confesses the name of the Lord must turn away from wickedness.' In a large house there are articles not only of gold and silver, but also of wood and clay; some are for noble purposes and some for ignoble. Any who cleanse themselves from the latter will be instruments for noble purposes, made holy, useful to the Master and prepared to do any good work.

'I will refine them like silver'
'I will refine them like silver and test them like gold. They will call on my name and I will answer them; I will say, "They are my people," and they will say, "The LORD is our God."'

> Job 23:10. Psalm 103:14. 2 Timothy 2:19–21. Zechariah 13:9.

Evening

Show me your ways, O LORD, teach me your paths.

Moses said to the LORD, . . . 'If I have found favour in your eyes, teach me your ways so I may know you.' . . . The LORD replied, 'My Presence will go with you, and I will give you rest.'—He made known his ways to Moses, his deeds to the people of Israel.

In all your ways acknowledge him
He guides the humble in what is right and teaches them his way. . . . Who, then, are those who fear the LORD? He will instruct them in the way chosen for them.—Trust in the LORD with all your heart and lean not on your own understanding; in all your ways acknowledge him, and he will make your paths straight.

You have made known to me the path of life; you will fill me with joy in your presence. . . . I will instruct and teach you in the way you should do; I will counsel you and watch over you.

> Psalm 25:4. Exodus 33:12–14. Psalms 103:7; 25:9, 12. Proverbs 3:5–6.
> Psalms 16:11; 32:8.

Morning

The fruit of the Spirit is . . . self-control.

Everyone who competes in the games goes into strict training. They do it to get a crown that will not last; but we do it to get a crown that will last for ever. Therefore I do not run like someone running aimlessly; I do not fight like someone beating the air. No, I beat my body and make it my slave so that after I have preached to others, I myself will not be disqualified for the prize.

Do not get drunk on wine, which leads to debauchery. Instead, be filled with the Spirit.—'Those who would come after me must deny themselves and take up their cross and follow me.'

Be self-controlled
Let us not be like others, who are asleep, but let us be alert and self-controlled. For those who sleep, sleep at night, and those who get drunk, get drunk at night. But since we belong to the day, let us be self-controlled.

Galatians 5:22. 1 Corinthians 9:25–27. Ephesians 5:18. Matthew 16:24.
1 Thessalonians 6:6–8.

Evening

Grow up into him who is the Head, that is, Christ.

Until we all reach unity in the faith and in the knowledge of the Son of God and become mature, attaining to the whole measure of the fulness of Christ.

'Let those who boast boast in the Lord.' For it is not those who commend themselves who are approved, but those whom the Lord commends.

Found in Christ. Do not let anyone who delights in false humility and the worship of angels disqualify you for the prize. Such people go into great detail about what they have seen, and their unspiritual minds puff them up with idle notions. They have lost connection with the Head, from whom the whole body, supported and held together by its ligaments and sinews, grows as God causes it to grow.

Grow in grace and knowledge
Grow in the grace and knowledge of our Lord and Saviour Jesus Christ.

Ephesians 4:15, 13. 2 Corinthians 10:17–18. Colossians 2:17–19.
2 Peter 3:18.

October 2

Morning

'The goat will carry on itself all their sins to a solitary place; and the man shall release it in the desert.'

As far as the east is from the west, so far has he removed our transgressions from us.

You will tread our sins underfoot
You will tread our sins underfoot and hurl our iniquities into the depths of the sea. . . . Who is a God like you, who pardons sins?

He will bear their iniquities
After the suffering of his soul, he will see the light of life and be satisfied; by his knowledge my righteous servant will justify many, and he will bear their iniquities. Therefore I will give him a portion among the great, and he will divide the spoils with the strong, because he poured out his life unto death, and was numbered with the transgressors.

'Look, the Lamb of God, who takes away the sin of the world!'

Leviticus 16:22. Psalm 103:12. Micah 7:19, 18. Isaiah 53:11–12.
John 1:29.

Evening

For who makes you different from anyone else? What do you have that you did not receive?

By the grace of God I am what I am.—He chose to give us birth through the word of truth.—It does not, therefore, depend on human desire or effort, but on God's mercy.

You were dead in your trespasses and sins, in which you used to live when you followed the ways of this world and of the ruler of the kingdom of the air, the spirit who is now at work in those who are disobedient. All of us also lived among them at one time, gratifying the cravings of our sinful nature and following its desires and thoughts. Like the rest, we were by nature objects of wrath.

Washed, sanctified, justified
You were washed, you were sanctified, you were justified in the name of the Lord Jesus Christ and by the Spirit of our God.

1 Corinthians 4:7; 15:10. James 1:18. Romans 9:16. Ephesians 2:1–3.
1 Corinthians 6:11.

Morning

To him who loves us and has freed us from our sins by his blood.

'Greater love has no-one than this, to lay down one's life for one's friends.'
   He himself bore our sins in his body on the tree, so that we might die to sins and live for righteousness, by his wounds you have been healed.

A people belonging to God
You are a chosen people, a royal priesthood, a holy nation, a people belonging to God, that you may declare the praises of him who called you out of darkness into his wonderful light.

   Therefore, I urge you, brothers and sisters, in view of God's mercy, to offer your bodies as living sacrifices, holy and pleasing to God—which is your spiritual worship.

Revelation 1:5. John 15:13. 1 Peter 2:24, 9. Romans 12:1.

Evening

There are different kinds of service, but the same Lord.

Azmaveth son of Adiel was in charge of the royal storehouses. Jonathan son of Uzziah was in charge of the storehouses in the outlying districts, in the towns, the villages and the watchtowers. Ezri son of Kelub was in charge of the field workers who farmed the land. Shimei the Ramathite was in charge of the vineyards. . . . All these were the officials in charge of King David's property.

The work of the same Spirit
And in the church God has appointed first of all apostles, second prophets, third teachers, then workers of miracles, also those having gifts of healing, those able to help others, those with gifts of administration, and those speaking in different kinds of tongues. . . . All these are the work of one and the same Spirit, and he gives them to each one, just as he determines.

   Each of you should use whatever gift you have received to serve others, faithfully administering God's grace in its various forms.

1 Corinthians 12:5. 1 Chronicles 27:25–27, 31. 1 Corinthians 12:28, 11.
1 Peter 4:10.

October 4

Morning

He was not aware that his face was radiant because he had spoken with the LORD.

'Lord, when did we see you hungry and feed you, or thirsty and give you something to drink?'—But in humility consider others better than yourselves.—Clothe yourselves with humility.

Transformed into his likeness
There he [Jesus] was transfigured before them. His face shone like the sun, and his clothes became as white as the light.—All who were sitting in the Sanhedrin looked intently at Stephen, and they saw that his face was like the face of an angel.—'I have given them the glory that you gave me.'—We, who with unveiled faces all reflect the Lord's glory, are being transformed into his likeness with ever-increasing glory, which comes from the Lord.

Exodus 34:29. Matthew 25:37. Philippians 2:3. 1 Peter 5:5.
Matthew 17:2. Acts 6:15. John 17:22. 2 Corinthians 3:18.

Evening

There are different kinds of working, but the same God works all of them in everyone.

Now to each one the manifestation of the Spirit is given for the common good.

The message of wisdom
To one there is given through the Spirit the message of wisdom, to another the message of knowledge by means of the same Spirit.

Men of Zebulun, experienced soldiers prepared for battle with every type of weapon, to help David with undivided loyalty—50,000.—They are double-minded and unstable in all they do.

One Lord, one faith, one baptism
There should be no division in the body, but . . . its parts should have equal concern for each other. If one part suffers, every part suffers with it; if one part is honoured, every part rejoices with it.—One Lord, one faith, one baptism.

1 Corinthians 12:6, 7, 8. 1 Chronicles 12:33. James 1:8.
1 Corinthians 12:25–26. Ephesians 4:5.

Morning

'Call upon me in the day of trouble; I will deliver you, and you will honour me.'

Why are you downcast, O my soul? Why so disturbed within me? Put your hope in God, for I will yet praise him, my Saviour and my God.

You are kind and forgiving
You hear, O LORD, the desire of the afflicted; you encourage them, and you listen to their cry. . . . You are kind and forgiving, O Lord, abounding in love to all who call to you.

Praise the LORD, O my soul, and forget not all his benefits.

I will call on him
I love the LORD, for he heard my voice; he heard my cry for mercy. Because he turned his ear to me, I will call on him as long as I live. The cords of death entangled me, the anguish of the grave came upon me; I was overcome by trouble and sorrow. Then I called on the name of the LORD.

Psalm 50:15; 42:11; 10:17; 86:5; 103:2; 116:1–4.

Evening

For in just a very little while, 'He who is coming will come and will not delay.'

'Write down the revelation and make it plain on tablets so that a herald may run with it. For the revelation awaits an appointed time; it speaks of the end and will not prove false. Though it linger, wait for it; it will certainly come and will not delay.'

The Lord is not slow
But do not forget this one thing, dear friends: With the Lord a day is like a thousand years, and a thousand years are like a day. The Lord is not slow in keeping his promise, as some understand slowness. He is patient with you, not wanting anyone to perish, but everyone to come to repentance.

Since ancient times no-one has heard, no ear has perceived, no eye has seen any God besides you, who acts on behalf of those who wait for him.

Hebrews 10:37. Habakkuk 2:2–3. 2 Peter 3:8–9. Isaiah 64:4.

October 6

Morning

For our Lord God Almighty reigns.

'I know that you can do all things.'

'What is humanly impossible is possible with God.'—'No-one can deliver out of my hand. When I act, who can reverse it?'—'*Abba*, Father,' he said, 'everything is possible for you.'

Mighty God
'Do you believe that I am able to do this?' 'Yes, Lord,' they replied. Then he touched their eyes and said, 'According to your faith will it be done to you.' . . . 'Lord, if you are willing, you can make me clean.' Jesus reached out his hand and touched the man. 'I am willing,' he said. 'Be clean!'—Mighty God.—'All authority in heaven and on earth has been given to me.'

'Be strong and courageous. Do not be afraid or discouraged, . . . there is a greater power with us than with him.'

> Revelation 19:6. Job 42:2. Luke 18:27. Isaiah 43:13. Mark 14:36.
> Matthew 9:28–29. Isaiah 9:6. Matthew 28:18. 2 Chronicles 32:7.

Evening

'What was it he said to you?'

He has showed you, O man, what is good. And what does the LORD require of you? To act justly and to love mercy and to walk humbly with your God.

'The righteous will live by faith'
All who rely on observing the law are under a curse, for it is written: 'Cursed is everyone who does not continue to do everything written in the Book of the Law.' Clearly no-one is justified before God by the law, because, 'The righteous will live by faith.' . . . What, then, was the purpose of the law? It was added because of transgressions until the Seed to whom the promise referred had come.

In the past God spoke to our ancestors through the prophets at many times and in various ways, but in these last days he has spoken to us by his Son.— 'Speak, LORD, for your servant is listening.'

> 1 Samuel 3:17. Micah 6:8. Galatians 3:10–11, 19. Hebrews 1:1–2.
> 1 Samuel 3:9.

Morning

He guides the humble in what is right and teaches them his way.

'Blessed are the meek.'—In your heart you may plan your course, but the LORD determines your steps.

Show me the way I should go
I lift up my eyes to you, to you whose throne is in heaven. As the eyes of slaves look to the hand of their master, as the eyes of a female servant look to the hand of her mistress, so our eyes look to the LORD our God. . . . Show me the way I should go, for to you I lift up my soul.

'The Spirit of truth will guide you'
'O our God, will you not judge them? For we have no power to face this vast army that is attacking us. We do not know what to do, but our eyes are upon you.'—'But when he, the Spirit of truth, comes, he will guide you into all truth.'

Psalm 25:9. Matthew 5:5. Proverbs 16:9. Psalms 123:1–2; 143:8.
2 Chronicles 20:12. John 16:13.

Evening

'O Sovereign LORD, . . . with your blessings the house of your servant will be blessed for ever.'

The blessing of the LORD brings wealth, and he adds no trouble to it.
   'Remembering the words the Lord Jesus himself said: "It is more blessed to give than to receive." '—'But when you give a banquet, invite the poor, the crippled, the lame, the blind, and you will be blessed. Although they cannot repay you, you will be repaid at the resurrection of the righteous.'

'Blessed by my Father'
'Come, you who are blessed by my Father; take your inheritance, the kingdom prepared for you since the creation of the world. For I was hungry and you gave me something to eat, I was thirsty and you gave me something to drink, I was a stranger and you invited me in, I needed clothes and you clothed me, I was sick and you looked after me, I was in prison and you came to visit me.'

2 Samuel 7:29. Proverbs 10:22. Acts 20:35. Luke 14:13–14.
Matthew 25:34–36.

October 8

Morning

'I will not be afraid. What can human beings do to me?'

Who shall separate us from the love of Christ? Shall trouble or hardship or persecution or famine or nakedness or danger or sword? . . . No, in all these things we are more than conquerors through him who loved us.

'Do not be afraid of those who kill the body and after that can do no more. But I will show you whom you should fear: Fear him who, after the killing of the body, has power to throw you into hell. Yes, I tell you, fear him.'

'Blessed are those who are persecuted'

'Blessed are those who are presecuted because of righteousness, for theirs is the kingdom of heaven. Blessed are you when people insult you, persecute you and falsely say all kinds of evil against you because of me. Rejoice and be glad, because great is your reward in heaven.'

Hebrews 13:6. Romans 8:35, 37. Luke 12:4–5. Matthew 5:10–12.

Evening

He set my feet on a rock.

That rock was Christ.—Simon Peter answered, 'You are the Christ, the Son of the living God.' . . . 'On this rock I will build my church, and the gates of Hades will not overcome it.'—'Salvation is found in no-one else, for there is no other name under heaven given to people by which we must be saved.'

You must believe and not doubt

You must believe and not doubt, because the one who doubts is like a wave of the sea, blown and tossed by the wind.

Who shall separate us from the love of Christ? Shall trouble or hardship or persecution or famine or nakedness or danger or sword? . . . No in all these things we are more than conquerors through him who loved us . . . Neither height nor depth, nor anything else in all creation, will be able to separate us from the love of God that is in Christ Jesus our Lord.

Psalm 40:2. 1 Corinthians 10:4. Matthew 16:16, 18. Acts 4:12.
James 1:6. Romans 8:35, 37, 39.

Morning

But you are a forgiving God, gracious and compassionate, slow to anger and abounding in love.

The LORD is not slow in keeping his promise, as some understand slowness. He is patient with you, not wanting anyone to perish, but everyone to come to repentance. . . . Bear in mind that our Lord's patience means salvation.

The encouragement of the Scriptures

For that very reason I was shown mercy so that in me, the worst of sinners, Christ Jesus might display his unlimited patience as an example of those who would believe in him and receive eternal life.—For everything that was written in the past was written to teach us, so that through endurance and the encouragement of the Scriptures we might have hope.

Rend your heart and not your garments. Return to the LORD your God, for he is gracious and compassionate, slow to anger and abounding in love, and he relents from sending calamity.

Nehemiah 9:17. 2 Peter 3:9. 1 Timothy 1:16. Romans 15:4. Joel 2:13.

Evening

And the words of the LORD are flawless.

Your promises have been thoroughly tested, and your servant loves them . . . The precepts of the LORD are right, giving joy to the heart. The commands of the LORD are radiant, giving light to the eyes.

I meditate on your precepts

I have hidden your word in my heart that I might not sin against you . . . I meditate on your precepts and consider your ways.

Like newborn babies

Finally, brothers and sisters, whatever is noble, whatever is right, whatever is pure, whatever is lovely, whatever is admirable—if anything is excellent or praiseworthy—think about such things.—Like newborn babies, crave pure spiritual milk, so that by it you may grow up in your salvation.

Psalms 12:6; 119:140; 19:8; 119:11, 15. Philippians 4:8. 1 Peter 2:2.

October 10

Morning

His whole family in heaven and on earth.

One God and Father of all, who is over all and through all and in all.—You are all children of God through faith in Christ Jesus.

'My brother and sister and mother'
Jesus is not ashamed to call them brothers and sisters.—'Here are my mother and my brothers. For whoever does the will of my Father in heaven is my brother and sister and mother.'

Slain because of the word of God
I saw under the altar the souls of those who had been slain because of the word of God and the testimony they had maintained. They called out in a loud voice, 'How long, Sovereign Lord, holy and true, until you judge the inhabitants of the earth and avenge our blood?' Then each of them was given a white robe, and they were told to wait a little longer, until the number of their fellow-servants and brothers and sisters who were to be killed as they had been was completed.—That only together with us would they be made perfect.

Ephesians 3:15; 4:6. Galatians 3:26. Hebrews 2:11. Matthew 12:49–50.
Revelation 6:9–11. Hebrews 11:40.

Evening

'This is how you should pray: "Our Father in heaven."'

After Jesus said this, he looked towards heaven and prayed: 'Father.' . . . 'My Father and your Father.'

The Spirit of adoption
You are all children of God through faith in Christ Jesus.—For you did not receive a spirit that makes you a slave again to fear, but you received the Spirit of adoption. And by him we cry, *'Abba,* Father.' The Spirit himself testifies with our spirit that we are God's children.

'Abba, Father'
Because you are sons, God sent the Spirit of his Son into our hearts, the Spirit who calls out, *'Abba,* Father.'
'I will receive you. I will be a Father to you, and you will be my sons and daughters, says the Lord Almighty.'

Matthew 6:9. John 17:1; 20:17. Galatians 3:26. Romans 8:15–16.
Galatians 4:6–7. 2 Corinthians 6:17–18.

Morning

Do not be far from me, for trouble is near.

How long, O LORD? Will you forget me for ever? How long will you hide your face from me? How long must I wrestle with my thoughts and every day have sorrow in my heart?

The LORD is near
'He will call upon me, and I will answer him; I will be with him in trouble, I will deliver him and honour him.' . . . The LORD is near to all who call on him, to all who call on him in truth. He fulfils the desires of those who fear him; he hears their cry and saves them.

'I will not leave you as orphans; I will come to you.'—'And surely I will be with you always, to the very end of the age.'

God is our refuge and strength, an ever present help in trouble . . . My soul finds rest in God alone; my salvation comes from him.

Psalms 22:11; 13:1–2; 91:15; 145:18–19. John 14:18. Matthew 28:20.
Psalms 46:1; 62:1.

Evening

'Hallowed be your name.'

'Do not worship any other god, for the LORD, whose name is Jealous, is a jealous God.' . . . 'Who among the gods is like you, O LORD? Who is like you—majestic in holiness, awesome in glory, working wonders?'—'Holy, holy, holy is the Lord God Almighty.'

The splendour of his holiness
Worship the LORD in the splendour of his holiness.

'Woe to me!'
I saw the Lord seated on a throne, high and exalted, and the train of his robe filled the temple. Above him were seraphs, each with six wings: With two wings they covered their faces, with two they covered their feet, and with two they were flying. And they were calling to one another: 'Holy, holy, holy is the LORD Almighty; the whole earth is full of his glory.' . . . 'Woe to me!' I cried. 'I am ruined!'

The blood of Jesus, his son, purifies us from every sin.

Matthew 6:9. Exodus 34:14; 15:11. Revelation 4:8. 1 Chronicles 16:29.
Isaiah 6:1–3, 5. 1 John 1:7.

October 12

Morning

God was reconciling the world to himself in Christ, not counting people's sins against them.

For God was pleased to have all his fulness dwell in him, and through him to reconcile to himself all things, whether things on earth or things in heaven, by making peace through his blood, shed on the cross.—Love and faithfulness meet together; righteousness and peace kiss each other.

'As white as snow'
'I know the plans I have for you,' declares the LORD, 'plans to prosper you and not to harm you, plans to give you hope and a future.'—'Come now, let us reason together,' says the LORD. 'Though your sins are scarlet, they shall be as white as snow; though they are red as crimson, they shall be like wool.'

Who is a God like you, who pardons sin?—LORD, you establish peace for us; all that we have accomplished you have done for us.

2 Corinthians 5:19. Colossians 1:19–20. Psalm 85:10. 1 John 29:11.
Isaiah 1:18. Micah 7:18. Isaiah 26:12.

Evening

'Your kingdom come.'

'Not by might nor by power, but by my Spirit,' says the LORD Almighty.—'The kingdom of God does not come with your careful observation, nor will people say, "Here it is," or "There it is," because the kingdom of God is within you.'

'The secret of the kingdom of God has been given to you.' . . . He also said, 'This is what the kingdom of God is like. A man scatters seed on the ground. Night and day, whether he sleeps or gets up, the seed sprouts and grows, though he does not know how. . . . As soon as the grain is ripe, he puts the sickle to it, because the harvest has come.'

'Be ready'
'So you also must be ready, because the Son of Man will come at an hour when you do not expect him.'—The Spirit and the bride say, 'Come!' And let those who hear say, 'Come!'

Matthew 6:10. Zechariah 4:6. Luke 17:20–21. Mark 4:11, 26–27, 29.
Matthew 24:44. Revelation 22:17.

Morning

'Since the first day that you set your mind to gain understanding and to humble yourself before your God, your words were heard.'

For this is what the high and lofty One says—he who lives for ever, whose name is holy: 'I live in a high and holy place, but also with him who is contrite and lowly in spirit, to revive the spirit of the lowly and to revive the heart of the contrite.'

He looks upon the lowly
The sacrifices of God are a broken spirit; a broken and contrite heart, O God, you will not despise. . . . Though the LORD is on high, he looks upon the lowly, but the proud he knows from afar.

Humble yourselves, therefore, under God's mighty hand, that he may lift you up in due time.—'God opposes the proud but gives grace to the humble.'

Daniel 10:12. Isaiah 57:15. Psalms 51:17; 138:6. 1 Peter 5:6.
James 4:6–7.

Evening

'Your will be done on earth as it is in heaven.'

It is God's will that you should be sanctified.—He chose to give birth through the word of truth. . . . Therefore, get rid of all moral filth.

'Be holy'
'Be holy, because I am holy.'—Jesus said, 'Here are my mother and my brothers! Whoever does God's will is my brother and sister and mother.'

'Therefore everyone who hears these words of mine and puts them into practice is like a wise man who built his house on the rock. The rain came down, the streams rose, and the winds blew and beat against that house; yet it did not fall, because it had its foundation on the rock.'

The will of God lives for ever
The world and its desires pass away, but whoever does the will of God lives for ever.

Matthew 6:10. 1 Thessalonians 4:3. James 1:18, 21. 1 Peter 1:16.
Mark 3:34–35. Matthew 7:24–25. 1 John 2:17.

October 14

Morning

Christ died and returned to life so that he might be the Lord of both the dead and the living.

It was the LORD's will to crush him and cause him to suffer, and though the LORD makes his life a guilt offering, he will see his offspring and prolong his days, and the will of the LORD will prosper in his hand. After the suffering of his soul, he will see the light of life and be satisfied; by his knowledge my righteous servant will justify many, and he will bear their iniquities.

One died for all
'Did not the Christ have to suffer these things and then enter his glory?'—We are convinced that one died for all, and therefore all died. And he died for all, that those who live should no longer live for themselves but for him who died for them and was raised again.

'Let all Israel be assured of this: God has made this Jesus, whom you crucified, both Lord and Christ.'

Romans 14:9. Isaiah 53:10–11. Luke 24:26. 2 Corinthians 5:14–15.
Acts 2:36.

Evening

'Give us today our daily bread.'

His bread will be supplied, and water will not fail him.—The ravens brought him bread and meat in the morning and bread and meat in the evening, and he drank from the brook.

My God will meet all your needs according to his glorious riches in Christ Jesus.—Be content with what you have, because God has said, 'Never will I leave you; never will I forsake you.'

'The bread of God'
'I tell you the truth, it is not Moses who has given you the bread from heaven, but it is my Father who gives you the true bread from heaven. For the bread of God is he who comes down from heaven and gives life to the world.' 'Sir,' they said, 'from now on give us this bread.'

Matthew 6:11. Isaiah 33:16. 1 Kings 17:6. Philippians 4:19.
Hebrews 13:5. John 6:32–34.

Morning

O God, . . . my fortress.

'The LORD is my rock, my fortress and my deliverer; my God is my rock, in whom I take refuge, my shield and the horn of my salvation. He is my stronghold, my refuge and my saviour.'—The LORD is my strength and my shield; my heart trusts in him, and I am helped. My heart leaps for joy and I will give thanks to him in song.

For he will come like a pent-up flood that the breath of the LORD drives along.—'The LORD is my helper; I will not be afraid. What can human beings do to me?'

The LORD surrounds his people
The LORD is my light and my salvation—whom shall I fear? . . . As the mountains surround Jerusalem so the LORD surrounds his people both now and for evermore. . . . Because you are my help, I sing in the shadow of your wings. . . . For the sake of your name lead and guide me.

Psalm 59:9. 2 Samuel 22:2–3. Psalm 28:7. Isaiah 59:19. Hebrews 13:6.
Psalms 27:1; 125:2; 63:7; 31:3.

Evening

'Forgive us our debts, as we also have forgiven our debtors.'

'LORD, how many times shall I forgive someone who sins against me? Up to seven times?' Jesus answered, 'I tell you, not seven times, but seventy-seven times.' . . . ' "You wicked servant," he said, "I cancelled all that debt of yours because you begged me to. Shouldn't you have had mercy on your fellow-servant just as I had on you?" In anger his master turned him over to the jailers until he should pay back all he owed. This is how my heavenly Father will treat each of you unless you forgive one another from your heart.'

Forgiving each other
Be kind and compassionate to one another, forgiving each other, just as in Christ God forgave you.

Forgive as the Lord forgave you.

Matthew 6:12; 18:21–22, 32–35. Ephesians 4:32. Colossians 3:13.

October 16

Morning

Never be lacking in zeal, but keep your spiritual fervour, serving the Lord.

Whatever your hand finds to do, do it with all your might, for in the grave, where you are going, there is neither working nor planning nor knowledge nor wisdom.—Whatever you do, work at it with all your heart, as working for the Lord, not for human masters, since you know that you will receive an inheritance from the Lord as a reward. It is the Lord Christ you are serving.—Because you know that the Lord will reward each one of you for whatever good you do.

Make your hope sure
My brothers and sisters, be all the more eager to make your calling and election sure. For if you do these things, you will never fall.—We want each of you to show this same diligence to the very end, in order to make your hope sure. We do not want to become lazy, but to imitate those who through faith and patience inherit what has been promised.

Romans 12:11. Ecclesiastes 9:10. Colossians 3:23–24. Ephesians 6:8.
2 Peter 1:10. Hebrews 6:11–12.

Evening

'And lead us not into temptation, but deliver us from the evil one.'

Those who trust in themselves are fools, but those who walk in wisdom are kept safe.

When tempted, no-one should say, 'God is tempting me.' For God cannot be tempted by evil, nor does he tempt anyone; but each of you is tempted when, by your own evil desire, you are dragged away and enticed.

'Come out from among them'
'Therefore come out from them and be separate. Touch no unclean thing, and I will receive you.'

Lot
[The Lord] rescued Lot, a righteous man, who was distressed by the filthy lives of the lawless. . . . The Lord knows how to rescue the godly from trials.—And they will stand, for the Lord is able to make them stand.

Matthew 6:13. Proverbs 28:26. James 1:13–14. 2 Corinthians 6:17.
2 Peter 2:7, 9. Romans 14:4.

Morning

They rejoice in your name all day long; they exult in your righteousness.

'In the LORD are righteousness and strength.' All who have raged against him will come to him and be put to shame. But in the LORD all the descendants of Israel will be found righteous and will exult.—Rejoice in the LORD and be glad, you righteous; sing, all you who are upright in heart!

But now a righteousness from God, apart from law, has been made known, to which the Law and Prophets testify. This righteousness from God comes through faith in Jesus Christ to all who believe.

Rejoice
Rejoice in the Lord always. I will say it again: Rejoice!—Though you have not seen him, you love him; and even though you do not see him now, you believe in him and are filled with an inexpressible and glorious joy.

Psalm 89:16. Isaiah 45:24–25. Psalm 32:11. Romans 3:21–22.
Philippians 4:4. 1 Peter 1:8.

Evening

'He will reign over the house of Jacob for ever; his kingdom will never end.'

The LORD reigns, he is robed in majesty; the LORD is robed in majesty . . .
Your throne was established long ago; you are from all eternity.

The LORD is . . . great in power.—'The God we serve is able to save us.'—
'My Father, who has given them to me, is greater than all; no-one can snatch them out of my Father's hand.'—'The one who is in you is greater than the one who is in the world.'

Majesty and splendour
Yours, O LORD, is the greatness and the power and the glory and the majesty and the splendour, for everything in heaven and earth is yours. Yours, O LORD, is the kingdom. . . . Now, our God, we give you thanks and praise your glorious name. 'But who am I, and who are my people, that we should be able to give as generously as this? Everything comes from you, and we have given you only what comes from your hand.'

Luke 1:33. Psalm 93:1–2. Nahum 1:3. Daniel 3:17. John 10:29.
1 John 4:4. 1 Chronicles 29:11, 13–14.

October 18

Morning

One of the soldiers pierced Jesus' side with a spear, bringing a sudden flow of blood and water.

'This is the blood of the covenant that the LORD has made with you.'—'For the life of a creature is in the blood, and I have given it to you to make atonement for yourselves on the altar; it is the blood that makes atonement for one's life.'

'This is my blood of the covenant, which is poured out for many,' he [Jesus] said to them.—He entered the Most Holy Place once for all by his own blood, having obtained eternal redemption.—Peace through his blood, shed on the cross.

For you know that it was not with perishable things such as silver or gold, that you were redeemed, . . . but with the precious blood of Christ, a lamb without blemish or defect, . . . revealed in these last times for your sake.

Hearts sprinkled to cleanse us
Let us draw near to God with a sincere heart in full assurance of faith, having our hearts sprinkled to cleanse us from a guilty conscience.

> John 19:34. Exodus 24:8. Leviticus 17:11. Mark 14:24. Hebrews 9:12.
> Colossians 1:20. 1 Peter 1:18–20. Hebrews 10:22.

Evening

'Amen.'

'Amen! May the LORD, the God of my lord the king, so declare it.'

When God made his promise to Abraham, since there was no-one greater for him to swear by, he swore by himself. . . . People swear by someone greater than themselves, and the oath confirms what is said and puts an end to all argument. Because God wanted to make the unchanging nature of his purpose very clear to the heirs of what was promised, he confirmed it with an oath. God did this so that, by two unchangeable things in which it is impossible for God to lie, we who have fled to take hold of the hope offered to us may be greatly encouraged.

'The words of the Amen'
'These are the words of the Amen, the faithful and true witness.'—Praise be to the Lord God, the God of Israel, who alone does marvellous deeds. Praise be to his glorious name for ever; may the whole earth be filled with his glory. Amen and Amen.

> 1 Corinthians 14:16. 1 Kings 1:36. Hebrews 6:13, 16–18.
> Revelation 3:14. Psalm 72:18–19.

Morning

For the LORD will be your confidence and will keep your foot from being snared.

Surely your wrath against human beings brings you praise, and the survivors of your wrath are restrained.—The king's heart is in the hand of the LORD; he directs it like a watercourse wherever he pleases . . . When people's ways are pleasing to the LORD, he makes even their enemies live at peace with them.

My soul waits for the Lord
I wait for the LORD, my soul waits, and in his word I put my hope. My soul waits for the Lord more than those on watch wait for the morning, more than those on watch wait for the morning. . . . I sought the LORD; and he answered me; he delivered me from all my fears.

What, then, shall we say in response to this? If God is for us, who can be against us?

> Proverbs 3:26. Psalm 76:10. Proverbs 21:1; 16:7. Psalms 130:5–6; 34:4.
> Romans 8:31.

Evening

If you have any encouragement from being united with Christ, if any comfort from his love, if any fellowship with the Spirit.

'The Father . . . will give you another Counsellor to be with you for ever . . . The Counsellor, the Holy Spirit, whom the Father will send in my name.'

The God of all comfort
Praise be to the God and Father of our Lord Jesus Christ, the Father of compassion and the God of all comfort, who comforts us in all our troubles, so that we can comfort those in any trouble with the comfort we ourselves have received from God.

We believe that Jesus died and rose again and so we believe that God will bring with Jesus those who have fallen asleep in him. . . . And so we will be with the Lord for ever. Therefore encourage each other with these words.

> Philippians 2:1. John 14:16, 26. 2 Corinthians 1:3–4.
> 1 Thessalonians 4:14, 17–18.

October 20

Morning

For in my inner being I delight in God's law.

Oh, how I love your law! I meditate on it all day long.—When your words came, I ate them; they were my joy and my heart's delight.

'I desire to do your will, O my God; your law is within my heart.'—'My food,' said Jesus, 'is to do the will of him who sent me and to finish his work.'

More precious than gold
The precepts of the LORD are right, giving joy to the heart. The commands of the LORD are radiant. . . . They are more precious than gold, than much pure gold; they are sweeter than honey, than honey from the comb.—Do not merely listen to the word, and so deceive yourselves. Do what it says. Those who listen to the word but do not do what it says are like people who look at their faces in a mirror and . . . go away and immediately forget what they look like.

> Romans 7:22. Psalm 119:97. Jeremiah 15:16. Psalm 40:8. John 4:34.
> Psalm 19:8, 10. James 1:22–24.

Evening

'May the LORD your God accept you.'

Like filthy rags
All of us become like one who is unclean, and all our righteous acts are like filthy rags.

'There is no-one righteous'
'There is no-one righteous, not even one.'

Faith in Jesus
For all have sinned and fall short of the glory of God, and are justified freely by his grace through the redemption that came by Christ Jesus. God presented him as a sacrifice of atonement, through faith in his blood. He did this to demonstrate his justice, because in his forbearance he had left the sins committed beforehand unpunished—he did it to demonstrate his justice at the present time, so as to be just and the one who justifies those who have faith in Jesus.

> 2 Samuel 24:23. Isaiah 64:6. Romans 3:10, 23–26.

Morning

From the fulness of his grace we have all received one blessing after another.

'This is my Son, whom I love; with him I am well pleased.'—How great is the love the Father has lavished on us, that we should be called children of God!—His Son, whom he appointed heir of all things.

Heirs of God
Now if we are children, then we are heirs—heirs of God and co-heirs with Christ, if indeed we share in his sufferings in order that we may also share in his glory.

Let us purify ourselves
The church, which is his body, the fulness of him who fills everything in every way.—Since we have these promises, dear friends, let us purify ourselves from everything that contaminates body and spirit, perfecting holiness out of reverence for God.

> John 1:16. Matthew 17:5. 1 John 3:1. Hebrews 1:2. Romans 8:17.
> Ephesians 1:22–23. 2 Corinthians 7:1.

Evening

'Servants are not greater than their masters.'

'Servants are not greater than their masters, nor are messengers greater than those who sent them. Now that you know these things, you will be blessed if you do them.'

A dispute arose among them as to which of them was considered to be greatest. Jesus said to them, 'The kings of the Gentiles lord it over them; and those who exercise authority over them call themselves Benefactors. But you are not to be like that. Instead, the greatest among you should be like the youngest, and the one who rules like the one who serves. For who is the greater, the one who is at the table or the one who serves? Is it not the one who is at the table? But I am among you as one who serves.'

He began to wash his disciples' feet
[Jesus] got up from the meal, took off his outer clothing, and wrapped a towel around his waist. After that, he poured water into a basin and began to wash his disciples' feet, drying them with the towel that was wrapped around him.

> John 13:16–17. Luke 22:24–27. John 13:3–5.

October 22

Morning

My heart is steadfast, O God.

The LORD is my light and my salvation—whom shall I fear? The LORD is the stronghold of my life—of whom shall I be afraid?

They have no fear of bad news; their hearts are steadfast, trusting in the LORD. Their hearts are secure, they will have no fear; in the end they will look in triumph on their foes.

The day of trouble
For in the day of trouble he will keep me safe in his dwelling; he will hide me in the shelter of his tabernacle and set me high upon a rock. Then my head will be exalted above the enemies who surround me; at his tabernacle will I sacrifice with shouts of joy; I will sing and make music to the LORD.

Firm and steadfast
The God of all grace, who called you to eternal glory in Christ, after you have suffered a little while, will himself restore you and make you strong, firm and steadfast. To him be the power for ever and ever.

Psalms 108:1; 27:1; 112:7–8; 27:5–6. 1 Peter 5:10–11.

Evening

The LORD has established his throne in heaven, and his kingdom rules over all.

The lot is cast into the lap, but its every decision is from the LORD.—When disaster comes to a city, has not the LORD caused it?

If God is for us
He does as he pleases with the powers of heaven and the peoples of the earth. No-one can hold back his hand or say to him: 'What have you done?'—If God is for us, who can be against us?

'Do not be afraid'
For he must reign until he has put all his enemies under his feet.—'Do not be afraid, little flock, for your Father has been pleased to give you the kingdom.'

Psalm 103:19. Proverbs 16:33. Amos 3:6. Daniel 4:35. Romans 8:31.
1 Corinthians 15:25. Luke 12:32.

Morning

'Life does not consist in the abundance of possessions.'

Better a little with the fear of the LORD than wealth with turmoil.—Godliness with contentment is great gain. . . . If we have food and clothing, we will be content with that.

'Daily bread'
'Give us today our daily bread.' . . . 'Do not worry about your life, what you eat or drink; or about your body, what you will wear. Is not life more important than food, and the body more important than clothes?'—'When I sent you without purse, bag or sandals, did you lack anything?'—Keep your lives free from the love of money and be content with what you have, because God has said, 'Never will I leave you; never will I forsake you.'

Luke 12:15. Proverbs 15:16. 1 Timothy 6:6, 8. Matthew 6:11, 25.
Luke 22:35. Hebrews 13:5.

Evening

'The Spirit gives life.'

'The first Adam became a living being'; the last Adam, a life-giving spirit.—'Flesh gives birth to flesh, but the Spirit gives birth to spirit.'

Rebirth and renewal
He saved us, not because of righteous things we had done, but because of his mercy. He saved us through the washing of rebirth and renewal by the Holy Spirit.

The Spirit of Christ
If anyone does not have the Spirit of Christ, that person does not belong to Christ. But if Christ is in you, your body is dead because of sin, yet your spirit is alive because of righteousness. And if the Spirit of him who raised Jesus from the dead is living in you, he who raised Christ from the dead will also give life to your mortal bodies through his Spirit, who lives in you.

John 6:63. 1 Corinthians 15:45. John 3:6. Titus 3:5. Romans 8:9–11.

October 24

Morning

'I have been banished from your sight; yet I will look again towards your holy temple.'

But Zion said, 'The LORD has forsaken me, the Lord has forgotten me. Can a mother forget the baby at her breast and have no compassion on the child she has borne? Though she may forget, I will not forget you!'

I have forgotten what prosperity is. So I say, 'My splendour is gone and all that I had hoped from the LORD.'—Awake, O Lord! Why do you sleep? Rouse yourself! Do not reject us for ever.

Struck down, but not destroyed
Why are you downcast, O my soul? Why so disturbed within me? Put your hope in God, for I will yet praise him, my Saviour and my God.—We are hard pressed on every side, but not crushed; perplexed, but not in despair; persecuted, but not abandoned; struck down, but not destroyed.

> Jonah 2:4. Isaiah 49:14–15. Lamentations 3:17–18. Psalms 44:23; 43:5.
> 2 Corinthians 4:8–9.

Evening

'The poor and needy search for water, but there is none; their tongues are parched with thirst. But I the LORD will answer them.'

Many are asking, 'Who can show us any good?'

'They have forsaken me'
'They have forsaken me, the spring of living water, and have dug their own cisterns, broken cisterns that cannot hold water.'

'Hunger and thirst for righteousness'
'Whoever comes to me I will never drive away.'—'For I will pour water on the thirsty land.'—'Blessed are those who hunger and thirst for righteousness, for they will be filled.'

O God, you are my God, earnestly I seek you; my soul thirsts for you, my body longs for you, in a dry and weary land where there is no water.

> Isaiah 41:17. Psalm 4:6. Jeremiah 2:13. John 6:37. Isaiah 44:3.
> Matthew 5:6. Psalm 63:1.

Morning

'Surely I will be with you always, to the very end of the age.'

'If two of you on earth agree about anything you ask for, it will be done for you by my Father in heaven. For where two or three come together in my name, there am I with them.'

'Loved by my Father'
'Those who have my commands and obey them are the ones who love me. Those who love me will be loved by my Father, and I too will love them and show myself to them.'

To keep you from falling
To him who is able to keep you from falling and to present you before his glorious presence without fault and with great joy—to the only God our Saviour be glory, majesty, power and authority, through Jesus Christ our Lord, before all ages, now and for evermore! Amen.

Matthew 28:20; 18:19–20. John 14:21. Jude 24–25.

Evening

The end of all things is near.

I saw a great white throne and him who was seated on it. Earth and sky fled from his presence.—The present heavens and earth are reserved for fire, being kept for the day of judgment.

God is our refuge and strength, an ever present help in trouble. Therefore we will not fear, though the earth give way and the mountains fall into the heart of the sea, though its waters roar and foam and the mountains quake with surging.

The home of righteousness
We have a building from God, an eternal house in heaven, not built by human hands.—We are looking forward to a new heaven and a new earth, the home of righteousness. So then, dear friends, since you are looking forward to this, make every effort to be found spotless, blameless and at peace with him.

1 Peter 4:7. Revelation 20:11. 2 Peter 3:7. Psalm 46:1–3.
2 Corinthians 5:1. 2 Peter 3:13–14.

October 26

Morning

The LORD reigns.

'Should you not fear me?' declares the LORD. 'Should you not tremble in my presence? I made the sand a boundary for the sea, an everlasting barrier it cannot cross. The waves may roll, but they cannot prevail; they may roar, but they cannot cross it.'

No-one from the east or the west or from the desert can exalt a human being. But it is God who judges: He brings one down, he exults another.

'You are worth more than many sparrows'
If God is for us, who can be against us?—'Are not two sparrows sold for a penny? Yet not one of them will fall to the ground apart from the will of your Father. And even the very hairs of your head are all numbered. So don't be afraid; you are worth more than many sparrows.'

Psalm 99:1. Jeremiah 5:22. Psalm 75:6–7. Romans 8:31.
Matthew 10:29–31.

Evening

So guard yourself in your spirit.

'Master,' said John, 'we saw someone driving out demons in your name and we tried to stop him, because he is not one of us.' 'Do not stop him,' Jesus said, 'for whoever is not against you is for you.'

Prophets
'Eldad and Medad are prophesying in the camp.' Joshua . . . spoke up and said, 'Moses, my lord, stop them!' But Moses replied, 'Are you jealous for my sake? I wish that all the LORD's people were prophets and that the LORD would put his Spirit on them!'

The fruit of the Spirit
But the fruit of the Spirit is love, joy, peace, patience, kindness, goodness, faithfulness, gentleness and self-control. . . . Those who belong to Christ Jesus have crucified the sinful nature with its passions and desires. Since we live by the Spirit, let us keep in step with the Spirit. Let us not become conceited, provoking and envying each other.

Malachi 2:15. Luke 9:49–50. Numbers 11:27–29. Galatians 5:22–26.

Morning

'He took up our infirmities and carried our diseases.'

'The priest shall order that two live clean birds and some cedar wood, scarlet yarn and hyssop be brought for the one to be cleansed. Then the priest shall order that one of the birds be killed over fresh water in a clay pot. He is then to take the live bird and dip it, together with the cedar wood, the scarlet yarn and the hyssop, into the blood of the bird that was killed over the fresh water. Seven times he shall sprinkle the one to be cleansed of the infectious disease and pronounce him clean. Then he is to release the live bird in the open fields.'

'Be clean!'
A man came along who was covered with leprosy. When he saw Jesus, he fell with his face to the ground and begged him. 'Lord, if you are willing, you can make me clean.'—Filled with compassion, Jesus reached out his hand and touched the man. 'I am willing,' he said. 'Be clean!' Immediately the leprosy left him and he was cured.

Matthew 8:17. Leviticus 14:4–7. Luke 5:12. Mark 1:41–42.

Evening

Those you bless are blessed.

'Blessed are the poor in spirit, for theirs is the kingdom of heaven. Blessed are those who mourn, for they will be comforted. Blessed are the meek, for they will inherit the earth. Blessed are those who hunger and thirst for right-eousness, for they will be filled. Blessed are the merciful, for they will be shown mercy. Blessed are the pure in heart, for they will see God. Blessed are the peacemakers, for they will be called children of God. Blessed are those who are persecuted because of righteousness, for theirs is the kingdom of heaven.'

'Hear and obey'
'Blessed rather are those who hear the word of God and obey it.'

'Blessed are those who wash their robes, that they may have the right to the tree of life and may go through the gates into the city.'

Numbers 22:6. Matthew 5:3–10. Luke 11:28. Revelation 22:14.

October 28

Morning

He saw that there was no-one, and he was appalled that there was no-one to intercede; so his own arm worked salvation for him.

Sacrifice and offering you did not desire, but my ears you have pierced; burnt offerings and sin offerings you did not require. Then I said, 'Here I am, I have come—it is written about me in the scroll. I desire to do your will, O my God; your law is within my heart.'

'No God apart from me'
'And there is no God apart from me, a righteous God and a Saviour; there is none but me. Turn to me and be saved, all you ends of the earth; for I am God, and there is no other.'

'There is no other name under heaven given to people by which we must be saved.'

Isaiah 59:16. Psalm 40:6–8. Isaiah 45:21–22. Acts 4:12.

Evening

'The enemy.'

Resist the devil, and he will flee from you.

The full armour of God
Put on the full armour of God so that you can take your stand against the devil's schemes. For our struggle is not against flesh and blood, but against rulers, against the authorities, against the powers of this dark world and against the spiritual forces of evil in the heavenly realms. Therefore put on the full armour of God, so that when the day of evil comes, you may be able to stand your ground, and after you have done everything, to stand. Stand firm then, with the belt of truth buckled around your waist, with the breastplate of righteousness in place, and with your feet fitted with the readiness that comes from the gospel of peace. In addition to all this, take up the shield of faith, with which you can extinguish all the flaming arrows of the evil one.

Luke 10:19. James 4:7. Ephesians 6:11–16.

Morning

May my meditation be pleasing to him.

'A chosen and precious cornerstone, and the one who trusts in him will never be put to shame.'—You are the most excellent of men and your lips have been anointed with grace.—Therefore God exalted him to the highest place and gave him the name that is above every name.

Though you have not seen him, you love him and even though you do not see him now, you believe in him and are filled with an inexpressible and glorious joy.

Knowing Christ
I consider everything a loss compared to the surpassing greatness of knowing Christ Jesus my Lord, for whose sake I have lost all things. I consider them rubbish, that I may gain Christ and be found in him, not having a righteousness of my own that comes from the law, but that which is through faith in Christ—the righteousness that comes from God and is by faith.

Psalm 104:34. 1 Peter 2:6. Psalm 45:2. Philippians 2:9. 1 Peter 1:8.
Philippians 3:8–9.

Evening

David found strength in the LORD his God.

I know whom I have believed, and am convinced that he is able to guard what I have entrusted to him for that day.

The LORD was my support
They confronted me in the day of my disaster, but the LORD was my support. He brought me out into a spacious place; he rescued me because he delighted in me.

I will extol the LORD at all times; his praise will always be on my lips. My soul will boast in the LORD; let the afflicted hear and rejoice. Glorify the LORD with me; let us exalt his name together. I sought the LORD, and he answered me; he delivered me from all my fears.

Taste and see
Taste and see that the LORD is good; blessed are those who take refuge in him.

1 Samuel 30:6. 2 Timothy 1:12. Psalms 18:18–19; 34:1–4, 8.

October 30

Morning

It is good to wait quietly for the salvation of the LORD.

'Will not God bring about justice for his chosen ones, who cry out to him day and night? Will he keep putting them off? I tell you, he will see that they get justice, and quickly.'

Be still before the LORD
Wait for the LORD, and he will deliver you.—Wait for the LORD and wait patiently for him; do not fret when people succeed in their ways, when they carry out their wicked schemes.

Stand firm
You will not have to fight this battle. Take up your position; stand firm and see the deliverance the LORD will give you.—Let us not become weary in doing good, for at the proper time we will reap a harvest if we do not give up.

Lamentations 3:26. Luke 18:7–8. Proverbs 20:22. Psalm 37:7.
2 Chronicles 20:17. Galatians 6:9.

Evening

Who can discern his errors? Forgive my hidden faults.

See to it that no-one misses the grace of God and that no bitter root grows up to cause trouble and defile many.—You were running a good race. Who cut in on you and kept you from obeying the truth?
  Conduct yourselves in a manner worthy of the gospel of Christ.

The tongue
The tongue is a small part of the body, but it makes great boasts. Consider what a great forest is set on fire by a small spark. The tongue also is a fire, a world of evil among the parts of the body. It corrupts the whole person, sets the whole course of one's life on fire, and is itself set on fire by hell. . . . But no-one can tame the tongue. It is a restless evil, full of deadly poison.

Psalm 19:12. Hebrews 12:15. Galatians 5:7. Philippians 1:27.
James 3:5–6, 8.

Morning

'Not by might nor by power, but by my Spirit,' says the LORD Almighty.

But God chose the foolish things of the world to shame the wise; God chose the weak things of the world to shame the strong. He chose the lowly things of this world and the despised things—and the things that are not—to nullify the things that are, so that no-one may boast before him.

'Born of the Spirit'
'The wind blows wherever it pleases. You hear its sound, but you cannot tell where it comes from or where it is going. So it is with everyone born of the Spirit.'

The battle is God's
'And my Spirit remains among you. Do not fear.'—For the battle is God's.

> Zechariah 4:6. 1 Corinthians 1:27–29. John 3:8. Haggai 2:5.
> 2 Chronicles 20:15.

Evening

Your decrees are the theme of my song wherever I lodge.

The law from your mouth is more precious to me than thousands of pieces of silver and gold. . . . Your word, O LORD, is eternal; it stands firm in the heavens. Your faithfulness continues through all generations.

An anchor for the soul
Because God wanted to make the unchanging nature of his purpose very clear to the heirs of what was promised, he confirmed it with an oath. God did this so that, by two unchangeable things in which it is impossible for God to lie, we who have fled to take hold of the hope offered to us may be greatly encouraged. We have this hope as an anchor for the soul, firm and secure. It enters the inner sanctuary behind the curtain, where Jesus, who went before us, has entered on our behalf.

> Psalm 119:54, 72, 89–90. Hebrews 6:17–20.

November 1

Morning

Blessed are those who listen to me; watching daily at my doors, waiting at my doorway.

'For the generations to come this burnt offering is to be made regularly at the entrance to the Tent of Meeting before the LORD. There I will meet you and speak to you.' . . . 'Wherever I cause my name to be honoured, I will come to you and bless you.'

'Worship the Father in spirit and truth'
'For where two or three come together in my name, there am I with them.' 'Yet a time is coming and has now come when the true worshippers will worship the Father in spirit and truth, for they are the kind of worshippers the Father seeks. God is spirit, and his worshippers must worship in spirit and in truth.'
Pray in the Spirit on all occasions with all kinds of prayers and requests.

Proverbs 8:34. Exodus 29:42; 20:24. Matthew 18:20. John 4:23–24.
Ephesians 6:18.

Evening

He will be called Wonderful Counsellor.

The Spirit of the LORD will rest on him—the Spirit of wisdom and of understanding, the Spirit of counsel and of power, the Spirit of knowledge and of the fear of the LORD—and he will delight in the fear of the LORD.

Counsel and sound judgment
Does not wisdom call out? Does not understanding raise her voice? . . . Counsel and sound judgment are mine; I have understanding and power.

Magnificent in wisdom
The LORD Almighty, wonderful in counsel and magnificent in wisdom.—If any of you lacks wisdom, you should ask God, who gives generously to all without finding fault, and it will be given to you.

Isaiah 9:6; 11:2–3. Proverbs 8:1, 14. Isaiah 28:29. James 1:5.

Morning

Always try to be kind.

To this you were called, because Christ suffered for you, leaving you an example, that you should follow in his steps. 'He committed no sin, and no deceit was found in his mouth.' When they hurled their insults at him, he did not retaliate; when he suffered he made no threats. Instead, he entrusted himself to him who judges justly.

Consider him who endured such opposition from sinners, so that you will not grow weary and lose heart.

Run with perseverance
Let us throw off everything that hinders and the sin that so easily entangles, and let us run with perseverance the race marked out for us. Let us fix our eyes on Jesus, the author and perfecter of our faith, who for the joy set before him endured the cross, scorning its shame, and sat down at the right hand of the throne of God.

1 Thessalonians 5:15. 1 Peter 2:21–23. Hebrews 12:3; 1–2.

Evening

Mighty God.

Your throne, O God, will last for ever and ever; a sceptre of justice will be the sceptre of your kingdom. . . . Once you spoke in a vision, to your faithful people you said: 'I have bestowed strength on a warrior.'

'The LORD, is my strength'
'Surely God is my salvation; I will trust and not be afraid. The LORD, the LORD, is my strength and my song; he has become my salvation.'—Thanks be to God, who always leads us in triumphal procession in Christ.

To him who is able to keep you from falling and to present you before his glorious presence without fault and with great joy—to the only God our Saviour be glory, majesty, power and authority, through Jesus Christ our Lord, before all ages, now and for evermore!

Isaiah 9:6. Psalms 45:6; 89:19. Isaiah 12:2. 2 Corinthians 2:14.
Jude 24–25.

November 3

Morning

The ways of the LORD are right; the righteous walk in them, but the rebellious stumble in them.

Now to you who believe, this stone is precious. But to those who do not believe, 'The stone the builders rejected has become the capstone.'—The way of the LORD is a refuge for the righteous, but it is the ruin of those who do evil.

Consider the great love of the LORD
Let those who are wise heed these things and consider the great love of the LORD.—'Anyone who chooses to do the will of God will find out whether my teaching comes from God.'—'Those who have will be given more, and they will have an abundance.'

'Whoever belongs to God hears what God says. The reason you do not hear is that you do not belong to God.' . . . 'My sheep listen to my voice; I know them, and they follow me.'

Hosea 14:9. 1 Peter 2:7–8. Proverbs 10:29. Psalm 107:43. John 7:17.
Matthew 13:12. John 8:47; 10:27.

Evening

Everlasting Father.

'I and the Father are one . . . The Father is in me, and I in the Father.' . . . 'If you knew me, you would know my Father also.' . . . Philip said, 'Lord, show us the Father and that will be enough for us.' Jesus answered: 'Don't you know me, Philip, even after I have been among you such a long time? Anyone who has seen me has seen the Father.'—'Here am I, and the children God has given me.'

The Alpha and the Omega
'I am the Alpha and the Omega,' says the Lord God, 'who is, and who was, and who is to come, the Almighty.'—'Before Abraham was born, I am!'—God said to Moses, 'I am who I am. This is what you are to say to the Israelites: "I AM has sent me to you."'

About the Son he says, 'Your throne, O God, will last for ever and ever.'

Isaiah 9:6. John 10:30, 38; 8:19; 14:8–9. Hebrews 2:13. Revelation 1:8.
John 8:58. Exodus 3:14. Hebrews 1:8.

Morning

In this you greatly rejoice, though now for a little while you may have had to suffer grief in all kinds of trials.

Dear friends, do not be surprised at the painful trial you are suffering, as though something strange were happening to you. But rejoice that you participate in the sufferings of Christ, so that you may be overjoyed when his glory is revealed.

Word of encouragement

That word of encouragement that addresses you as children: 'My child, do not make light of the Lord's discipline, and do not lose heart when he rebukes you.' . . . No discipline seems pleasant at the time, but painful. Later on, however, it produces a harvest of righteousness and peace for those who have been trained by it.

For we do not have a high priest who is unable to sympathise with our weaknesses, but we have one who has been tempted in every way, just as we are—yet without sin.

1 Peter 1:6; 4:12–13. Hebrews 12:5, 11; 4:15.

Evening

Prince of Peace.

He will judge your people in righteousness, your afflicted ones with justice. The mountains will bring prosperity to the people, the hills the fruit of righteousness. He will defend the afflicted among the people and save the children of the needy; he will crush the oppressor. He will endure as long as the sun, as long as the moon, through all generations. He will be like rain falling on a mown field, like showers watering the earth. In his days the righteous will flourish, prosperity will abound till the moon is no more.

'The path of peace'

'Because of the tender mercy of our God, by which the rising sun will come to us from heaven to shine on those living in darkness and in the shadow of death, to guide our feet into the path of peace.'

'I have told you these things, so that in me you may have peace. In this world you will have trouble. But take heart! I have overcome the world.'

Isaiah 9:6. Psalm 72:2–7. Luke 1:78–79. John 16:33.

November 5

Morning

One Spirit.

There are different kinds of gifts, but the same Spirit.

Therefore God, your God has set you above your companions by anointing you with the oil of joy.—'God anointed Jesus of Nazareth with the Holy Spirit and power.'—'God gives the Spirit without limit.'

His anointing teaches you
From the fulness of his grace we have all received.—The anointing you received from him remains in you, and you do not need anyone to teach you. But as his anointing teaches you about all things and as that anointing is real, not counterfeit—just as it has taught you, remain in him.

God who . . . anointed us, set his seal of ownership on us, and put his Spirit in our hearts.

Ephesians 4:4. 1 Corinthians 12:4. Psalm 45:7. Acts 10:38.
John 3:34; 1:16. 1 John 2:27. 2 Corinthians 1:21–22.

Evening

For this world in its present form is passing away.

Believers in humble circumstances ought to take pride in their high position. But those who are rich should take pride in their low position, because they will pass away like a wild flower. For the sun rises with scorching heat and withers the plant; its blossom falls and its beauty is destroyed. In the same way, the rich will fade away even while they go about their business.

You are a mist
What is your life? You are a mist that appears for a little while and then vanishes.

'Show me, O LORD, my life's end and the number of my days; let me know how fleeting is my life.'—While people are saying, 'Peace and safety', destruction will come on them suddenly, as labour pains on a pregnant woman, and they will not escape. But you, brothers and sisters, are not in darkness so that this day should surprise you like a thief.

1 John 2:17. James 1:9–11; 4:14. Psalm 39:4. 1 Thessalonians 5:3–4.

Morning

When Christ, who is your life, appears, then you also will appear with him in glory.

'I am the resurrection and the life. He who believes in me will live, even though he dies.'—God has given us eternal life, and this life is in his Son. He who has the Son has life; he who does not have the Son of God does not have life.

For the Lord himself will come down from heaven, with a loud command, with the voice of the archangel and with the trumpet call of God, and the dead in Christ will rise first. After that, we who are still alive and are left will be caught up with them in the clouds to meet the Lord in the air. And so we will be with the Lord for ever. Therefore encourage each other with these words.

When he appears
But we know that when he appears, we shall be like him, for we shall see him as he is.

> Colossians 3:4. John 11:25. 1 John 5:11–12. 1 Thessalonians 4:16–18.
> 1 John 3:2.

Evening

Guide me in your truth and teach me.

'But when he, the Spirit of truth, comes, he will guide you into all truth.'—But you have an anointing from the Holy One, and all of you know the truth.

All Scripture is God-breathed
To the law and to the testimony! If they do not speak according to this word, they have no light of dawn.—All Scripture is God-breathed and is useful for teaching, rebuking, correcting and training in righteousness, so that God's servant may be thoroughly equipped for every good work. . . . The holy Scriptures . . . are able to make you wise for salvation through faith in Christ Jesus.

I will instruct you and teach you in the way you should go; I will counsel you and watch over you.

> Psalm 25:5. John 16:13. 1 John 2:20. Isaiah 8:20. 2 Timothy 3:16–17, 15.
> Psalm 32:8.

November 7

Morning

Let them give thanks to the LORD for his unfailing love and his wonderful deeds for human beings.

Taste and see that the LORD is good; blessed are those who take refuge in him. . . . How great is your goodness, which you have stored up for those who fear you.

'The people I formed for myself that they may proclaim my praise.'—He predestined us to be adopted as his children through Jesus Christ, in accordance with his pleasure and will—to the praise of his glorious grace, which he has freely given us in the One he loves.

The glorious splendour of your kingdom
The LORD is good to all; he has compassion on all he has made. All you have made will praise you, O LORD; your saints will extol you. They will tell of the glory of your kingdom and speak of your might, so that all people may know of your mighty acts and the glorious splendour of your kingdom.

> Psalms 107:8; 34:8; 31:19. Isaiah 43:21. Ephesians 1:5–6.
> Psalm 145:9–12.

Evening

We consider blessed those who have persevered.

We also rejoice in our sufferings, because we know that suffering produces perseverance; perseverance, character; and character, hope. And hope does not disappoint us, because God has poured out his love into our hearts by the Holy Spirit, whom he has given us.

Trial
Blessed are those who persevere under trial, because when they have stood the test, they will receive the crown of life that God has promised to those who love him.

In insults, in hardships
Therefore I will boast all the more gladly about my weaknesses, so that Christ's power may rest on me. That is why, for Christ's sake, I delight in weaknesses, in insults, in hardships, in persecutions, in difficulties. For when I am weak, then I am strong.

> James 5:11. Romans 5:3–5. James 12:2. 2 Corinthians 12:9–10.

Morning

Since we belong to the day, let us be self-controlled, putting on faith and love as a breastplate, and the hope of salvation as a helmet.

Stand firm then, with the belt of truth buckled around your waist, with the breastplate of righteousness in place. . . . In addition to all this, take up the shield of faith, with which you can extinguish all the flaming arrows of the evil one. Take the helmet of salvation and the sword of the Spirit, which is the word of God.

We trusted in him
He will swallow up death for ever. The Sovereign LORD will wipe away the tears from all faces; he will remove the disgrace of his people from all the earth. The LORD has spoken. In that day they will say, 'Surely this is our God; we trusted in him, and he saved us. This is the LORD, we trusted in him; let us rejoice and be glad in his salvation.'

1 Thessalonians 5:8. Ephesians 6:14, 16–17. Isaiah 25:8–9.

Evening

The Israelites camped opposite them like two small flocks of goats, while the Arameans covered the countryside.

'This is what the LORD says: "Because the Arameans think the LORD is a god of the hills and not a god of the valleys, I will deliver this vast army into your hands, and you will know that I am the LORD."' For seven days they camped opposite each other, and on the seventh day the battle was joined. The Israelites inflicted a hundred thousand casualties on the Aramean foot soldiers in one day.

You are from God
You, dear children, are from God and have overcome them, because the one who is in you is greater than the one who is in the world.

'I will rescue you'
'They will fight against you but will not overcome you, for I am with you and will rescue you,' declares the LORD.

1 Kings 20:27, 28–29. 1 John 4:4. Jeremiah 1:19.

November 9

Morning

'I have bestowed strength on a warrior; I have exalted a young man from among the people.'

For there is one God and one mediator between God and human beings, Christ Jesus.—'There is no other name under heaven given to people by which we must be saved.'

The very nature of a servant
Mighty God.—But made himself nothing, taking the very nature of a servant, being made in human likeness. And being found in appearance as a human being, he humbled himself and became obedient to death—even death on a cross! Therefore God exalted him to the highest place and gave him the name that is above every name.

But we see Jesus, who was made a little lower than the angels, now crowned with glory and honour because he suffered death, so that by the grace of God he might taste death for everyone.

Psalm 89:19. 1 Timothy 2:5. Acts 4:12. Isaiah 9:6. Philippians 2:7–9.
Hebrews 2:9.

Evening

'Gather to me my consecrated ones, who made a covenant with me by sacrifice.'

So Christ was sacrificed once to take away the sins of many people; and he will appear a second time, not to bear sin, but to bring salvation. . . . For this reason Christ is the mediator of a new covenant, that those who are called may receive the promised eternal inheritance.

'Father, I want those you have given me to be with me where I am.'—'And he will send his angels and gather his elect from the four winds, from the ends of the earth to the ends of the heavens.'

The LORD will bring you back
Even if you have been banished to the most distant land under the heavens, from there the LORD your God will gather you and bring you back.

Psalm 50:5. Hebrews 9:28, 15. John 17:24. Mark 13:27.
Deuteronomy 30:4.

Morning

Bearing fruit in every good work, growing in the knowledge of God.

Therefore, I urge you, brothers and sisters, in view of God's mercy, to offer your bodies as living sacrifices, holy and pleasing to God—this is your spiritual act of worship. Do not conform any longer to the pattern of this world, but be transformed by the renewing of your mind. Then you will be able to test and approve what God's will is—his good, pleasing and perfect will . . . Just as you used to offer the parts of your body in slavery to impurity and to ever-increasing wickedness, so now offer them in slavery to righteousness leading to holiness.

'My Father's glory'
'This is my Father's glory, that you bear much fruit, showing yourselves to be my disciples. . . . I chose you to go and bear fruit—fruit that will last. Then the Father will give you whatever you ask in my name. This is my command: Love each other.'

Colossians 1:10. Romans 12:1–2; 6:19. John 15:8, 16–17.

Evening

Wait for the L ORD; be strong and take heart and wait for the L ORD.

Return, O Israel, to the L ORD your God. Your sins have been your downfall! Take words with you and return to the L ORD. Say to him: 'Forgive all our sins and receive us graciously.'

When tempted, no-one should say, 'God is tempting me.' For God cannot be tempted by evil, nor does he tempt anyone; but each of you is tempted when, by your own evil desire, you are dragged away and enticed. Then, after desire has conceived, it gives birth to sin; and sin, when it is full-grown, gives birth to death. Don't be deceived, my dear brothers and sisters. Every good and perfect gift is from above, coming down from the Father of heavenly lights, who does not change like shifting shadows.

Find rest in God alone
My soul finds rest in God alone; my salvation comes from him. . . . Find rest, O my soul, in God alone; my hope comes from him.

Psalm 27:14. Hosea 14:1–2. James 1:13–17. Psalm 62:1, 5.

November 11

Morning

He guided them safely.

In all their distress he too was distressed, and the angel of his presence saved them. In his love and mercy he redeemed them; he lifted them up and carried them all the days of old.

It was not by their sword that they won the land, nor did their arm bring them victory; it was your right hand, your arm, and the light of your face, for you loved them.

Make straight your way before me
Lead me, O LORD, in your righteousness because of my enemies—make straight your way before me. . . . Send forth your light and your truth, let them guide me; let them bring me to your holy mountain, to the place where you dwell. Then will I go to the altar of God, to God, my joy and my delight. I will praise you with the harp, O God, my God.

Psalm 78:53. Isaiah 63:9. Psalms 44:3; 5:8; 43:3–4.

Evening

But you were washed, you were sanctified, you were justified.

The blood of Jesus, his Son, purifies us from all sin.

Christ loved the church and gave himself up for her by the washing with water through the word, and to present her to himself as a radiant church, without stain or wrinkle or any other blemish, but holy and blameless.

Our hearts sprinkled
Let us draw near to God with a sincere heart in full assurance of faith, having our hearts sprinkled to cleanse us from a guilty conscience and having our bodies washed with pure water.

Blessed are those whose transgressions are forgiven, whose sins are covered. Blessed are those whose sin the LORD does not count against them.

1 Corinthians 6:11. 1 John 1:7. Ephesians 5:25–27. Hebrews 10:22.
Psalm 32:1–2.

Morning

Godly sorrow brings repentance that leads to salvation and leaves no regret.

Then Peter remembered the word Jesus had spoken: 'Before the cock crows, you will disown me three times.' And he went outside and wept bitterly.—If we confess our sins, he is faithful and just and will forgive us our sins and purify us from all unrighteousness. . . . The blood of Jesus, his Son, purifies us from all sin.

You must return to your God
But you must return to your God; maintain love and justice, and wait for your God always.

A broken and contrite heart
The sacrifices of God are a broken spirit; a broken and contrite heart, O God, you will not despise . . . He heals the broken-hearted and binds up their wounds.

2 Corinthians 7:10. Matthew 26:75. 1 John 1:9, 7. Hosea 12:6.
Psalms 51:17; 147:3.

Evening

Beaten, and yet not killed; sorrowful, yet always rejoicing; poor, yet making many rich; having nothing, and yet possessing everything.

We are hard pressed on every side, but not crushed; perplexed, but not in despair; persecuted, but not abandoned; struck down, but not destroyed. We always carry around in our body the death of Jesus, so that the life of Jesus may also be revealed in our body.

We do not lose heart
Therefore we do not lose heart. Though outwardly we are wasting away, yet inwardly we are being renewed day by day. For our light and momentary troubles are achieving for us an eternal glory that far outweighs them all. So we fix not on what is seen, but on what is unseen.

Dear friend, I pray that you may enjoy good health and that all may go well with you, even as your soul is getting along well.

2 Corinthians 6:9–10; 4:8–10, 16–18. 3 John 2.

November 13

Morning

Christ loved the church and gave himself up for her to make her holy, cleansing her by the washing with water through the word.

For you have been born again, not of perishable seed, but of imperishable, through the living and enduring word of God.—'No-one can enter the kingdom of God without being born of water and the Spirit.'

Not because of righteous things we had done, but because of his mercy. He saved us through the washing of rebirth and renewal by the Holy Spirit.

Joy to the heart
The law of the LORD is perfect, reviving the soul. The statutes of the LORD are trustworthy, making wise the simple. The precepts of the LORD are right, giving joy to the heart. The commands of the LORD are radiant, giving light to the eyes.

Ephesians 5:25–26. 1 Peter 1:23. John 3:5. Titus 3:5. Psalm 19:7–8.

Evening

For through him we both have access to the Father by one Spirit.

'I in them and you in me. May they be brought to complete unity.'

'And I will do whatever you ask in my name, so that the Son may bring glory to the Father. You may ask me for anything in my name, and I will do it.'

One God and Father of all
There is one body and one Spirit—just as you were called to one hope when you were called—one Lord, one faith, one baptism; one God and Father of all, who is over all and through all and in all.

Therefore, brothers and sisters, since we have confidence to enter the Most Holy Place by the blood of Jesus, by a new and living way . . . let us draw near.

Ephesians 2:18. John 17:23; 14:13–14. Ephesians 4:4–6.
Hebrews 10:19–20, 22.

Morning

You are my help and my deliverer; O my God, do not delay.

The LORD makes firm the steps of those who delight in him; though they stumble, they will not fall, for the LORD upholds them with his hand.

Those who fear the LORD have a secure fortress, and for their children it will be a refuge.

'Be strong and courageous. Do not be afraid or terrified because of them, for the LORD your God goes with you; he will never leave you nor forsake you.'

You are my hiding place
But I will sing of your strength, in the morning I will sing of your love; for you are my fortress, my refuge in times of trouble. . . . You are my hiding place; you will protect me from trouble and surround me with songs of deliverance.

Psalms 40:17; 37:23–24. Proverbs 14:26. Deuteronomy 31:6.
Psalms 59:16; 32:7.

Evening

'When you pass through the waters, I will be with you; and when you pass through the rivers, they will not sweep over you.'

But we see Jesus, who was made a little lower than the angels, now crowned with glory and honour because he suffered death, so that by the grace of God he might taste death for everyone.

Your rod and your staff
Even though I walk through the valley of the shadow of death, I will fear no evil, for you are with me; your rod and your staff, they comfort me.

'The Living One'
'Do not be afraid. I am the First and the Last. I am the Living One; I was dead, and behold I am alive for ever and ever! And I hold the keys of death and Hades.'

Isaiah 43:2. Hebrews 2:9. Psalm 23:4. Revelation 1:17–18.

November 15

Morning

God, who has called you into fellowship with his Son Jesus Christ our Lord, is faithful.

Let us hold unswervingly to the hope we profess, for he who promised is faithful.—As God has said: 'I will live with them and walk among them, and I will be their God, and they will be my people.'—And our fellowship is with the Father and with his Son, Jesus Christ.

This love that surpasses knowledge
And I pray that you, being rooted and established in love, may have power, together with all the saints, to grasp how wide and long and high and deep is the love of Christ, and to know this love that surpasses knowledge—that you may be filled to the measure of all the fulness of God.

If anyone acknowledges that Jesus is the Son of God, God lives in them and they in God.

> 1 Corinthians 1:9. Hebrews 10:23. 2 Corinthians 6:16. 1 John 1:3.
> Ephesians 3:17–19. 1 John 4:15.

Evening

We are God's handiwork.

You also, like living stones, are being built into a spiritual house.

A dwelling in which God lives
Built on the foundation of the apostles and prophets, with Christ Jesus himself as the chief cornerstone. In him the whole building is joined together and rises to become a holy temple in the Lord. And in him you too are being built together to become a dwelling in which God lives by his Spirit.—Once you were not a people, but now you are the people of God.

God's building
You are . . . God's building.—Therefore, if anyone is in Christ, there is a new creation: the old has gone, the new has come!

> Ephesians 2:10. 1 Peter 2:5. Ephesians 2:20–22. 1 Peter 2:10.
> 1 Corinthians 3:9. 2 Corinthians 5:17.

Morning

'Sanctify them by the truth; your word is truth.'

'You are already clean because of the word I have spoken to you.'—Let the word of Christ dwell in you richly as you teach and admonish one another with all wisdom.

How can the young keep their way pure? By living according to your word. I seek you with all my heart· do not let me stray from your commands.

Understanding will guard you
For wisdom will enter your heart, and knowledge will be pleasant to your soul. Discretion will protect you, and understanding will guard you.

I have more insight than all my teachers, for I meditate on your statutes.— 'If you hold to my teaching, you are really my disciples. Then you will know the truth, and the truth will set you free.'

> John 17:17; 15:3. Colossians 3:16. Psalm 119:9–10. Proverbs 2:10–11.
> Psalm 119:99. John 8: 31–32.

Evening

Fellow-citizens with God's people.

All these people were still living by faith when they died. They did not receive the things promised; they only saw them and welcomed them from a distance. And they admitted that they were aliens and strangers on earth.

Our citizenship is in heaven
But our citizenship is in heaven. And we eagerly await a Saviour from there, the Lord Jesus Christ, who, by the power that enables him to bring everything under his control, will transform our lowly bodies, so that they will be like his glorious body.

The kingdom of the Son
The Father . . . has rescued us from the dominion of darkness and brought us into the kingdom of the Son he loves.

As aliens and strangers in the world, . . . abstain from sinful desires, which war against your soul.

> Ephesians 2:19. Hebrews 11:13. Philippians 3:20–21. Colossians 1:12–13.
> 1 Peter 2:11.

November 17

Morning

How profound your thoughts!

We have not stopped praying for you and asking God to fill you with the
knowledge of his will through all spiritual wisdom and understanding.—That
you, being rooted and established in love, may have power, together with all
the saints, to grasp how wide and long and high and deep is the love of Christ,
and to know this love that surpasses knowledge—that you may be filled to the
measure of all the fulness of God.

Wisdom and knowledge
Oh, the depth of the riches of the wisdom and knowledge of God! How
unsearchable his judgments, and his paths beyond tracing out!—'For my
thoughts are not your thoughts, neither are your ways my ways,' declares the
LORD. 'As the heavens are higher than the earth, so are my ways higher than
your ways and my thoughts than your thoughts.'

Psalm 92:5. Colossians 1:9. Ephesians 3:17–19. Romans 11:33.
Isaiah 55:8–9.

Evening

People reap what they sow.

Those who sow righteousness reap a sure reward.—Those who sow to please
the Spirit, from the Spirit will reap eternal life. Let us not become weary in
doing good, for at the proper time we will reap a harvest if we do not give up.
Therefore, as we have opportunity, let us do good to all people, especially to
those who belong to the family of believers.

A generous person will prosper
One gives freely, yet gains even more; another withholds unduly, but comes to
poverty. A generous person will prosper; the one who refreshes others will be
refreshed.—Whoever sows sparingly will also reap sparingly, and whoever
sows generously will also reap generously.

Galatians 6:7. Proverbs 11:18. Galatians 6:8–10. Proverbs 11:24–25.
2 Corinthians 9:6.

Morning

'I am with you and will save you,' declares the LORD.

He will not always accuse, nor will he harbour his anger for ever; he does not treat us as our sins deserve or repay us according to our iniquities.

God is faithful; he will not let you be tempted beyond what you can bear. But when you are tempted, he will also provide a way out so that you can stand up under it.—'Satan has asked to sift you as wheat. But I have prayed for you, Simon, that your faith may not fail.'

A shade from the heat
You have been a refuge for the poor, a refuge for the needy in their distress, a shelter from the storm and a shade from the heat. For the breath of the ruthless is like a storm driving against a wall.

Jeremiah 30:11. Psalm 103:9–10. 1 Corinthians 10:13. Luke 22:31–32.
Isaiah 25:4.

Evening

'I did not believe these things until I came and saw with my own eyes. Indeed, not even half was told me.'

'The Queen of the South will rise at the judgment with this generation and condemn it; for she came from the ends of the earth to listen to Solomon's wisdom, and now one greater than Solomon is here.'

We have seen his glory, the glory of the One and Only, who came from the Father, full of grace and truth.

The Spirit's power
My message and my preaching were not with wise and persuasive words, but with a demonstration of the Spirit's power, so that your faith might not rest on human wisdom, but on God's power. . . . However, as it is written: 'No eye has seen, no ear has heard, no mind has conceived what God has prepared for those who love him'—but God has revealed it to us by his Spirit. The Spirit searches all things, even the deep things of God.

1 Kings 10:7. Matthew 12:42. John 1:14. 1 Corinthians 2:4–5, 9–10.

November 19

Morning

'By their fruit you will recognise them.'

Can both fresh water and salt water flow from the same spring? My brothers and sisters, can a fig-tree bear olives, or a grapevine bear figs? Neither can a salt spring produce fresh water. Who is wise and understanding among you? Let them show it by their good life, by deeds done in the humility that comes from wisdom.

Live good lives
Live such good lives among the pagans that, though they accuse you of doing wrong, they may see your good deeds and glorify God on the day he visits us.
   'Make a tree good and its fruit will be good, or make a tree bad and its fruit will be bad, for a tree is recognised by its fruit. . . . Good people bring good things out of the good stored up in them, and evil people bring evil things out of the evil stored up in them.'

Matthew 7:20. James 3:11–13. 1 Peter 2:12. Matthew 12:33, 35.

Evening

That is what the LORD says: 'Heaven is my throne and the earth is my footstool.'

'I will shake all the nations'
'This is what the LORD Almighty says: "In a little while I will once more shake the heavens and the earth, the sea and the dry land. I will shake all nations, and the desired of all nations will come, and I will fill this house with glory," says the LORD Almighty . . . "The glory of this present house will be greater than the glory of the former house," says the LORD Almighty.'

'The dwelling of God is with human beings'
I saw a new heaven and a new earth, for the first heaven and the first earth had passed away, and there was no longer any sea. . . . And I heard a loud voice from the throne saying, 'Now the dwelling of God is with human beings, and he will live with them. They will be his people, and God himself will be with them and be their God.'

Isaiah 66:2. Haggai 2:6–7, 9. Revelation 21:1, 3.

Morning

Though I sit in darkness, the LORD will be my light.

'When you pass through the waters, I will be with you; and when you pass through the rivers they will not sweep over you. When you walk through the fire, you will not be burned; the flames will not set you ablaze. For I am the LORD, your God, the Holy One of Israel, your Saviour.'

'I will turn the darkness into light'
'I will lead the blind by ways they have not known, along unfamiliar paths I will guide them; I will turn the darkness into light before them and make the rough places smooth. These are the things I will do; I will not forsake them.'

I will not be afraid
When I am afraid, I will trust in you. In God, whose word I praise, in God I trust; I will not be afraid. What can mortals do to me?

Micah 7:8. Isaiah 43:2–3; 42:16. Psalm 56:3–4.

Evening

For there is one God and one mediator between God and human beings, Christ Jesus, himself human.

Moses stood in the breach
We have sinned, even as our fathers did; we have done wrong and acted wickedly. When our fathers were in Egypt, they gave no thought to your miracles; they did not remember your many kindnesses. . . . So he said he would destroy them—had not Moses, his chosen one, stood in the breach before him to keep his wrath from destroying them.

The apostle and high priest
Therefore, holy brothers and sisters, who share in the heavenly calling, fix your thoughts on Jesus, the apostle and high priest whom we confess. He was faithful to the one who appointed him, just as Moses was faithful in all God's house. Jesus has been found worthy of greater honour than Moses, just as the builder of a house has greater honour than the house itself.

1 Timothy 2:5. Psalm 106:6–7, 23. Hebrews 3:1–3.

November 21

Morning

'Whoever comes to me I will never drive away.'

'When he cries out to me, I will hear, for I am compassionate.'—'I will remember the covenant I made with you in the days of your youth, and I will establish an everlasting covenant with you.'

'Your sins are red as crimson'
'Come now, let us reason together,' says the LORD. 'Though your sins are like scarlet, they shall be as white as snow; though they are red as crimson, they shall be like wool.'

'Jesus, remember me when you come into your kingdom.' Jesus answered him, 'I tell you the truth, today you will be with me in paradise.'

A bruised reed he will not break, and a smouldering wick he will not snuff out.

John 6:37. Exodus 22:27. Ezekiel 16:60. Isaiah 1:18. Luke 23:42–43.
Isaiah 42:3.

Evening

The Son he loves.

'This is my Son, whom I love; with him I am well pleased.'—'Here is my servant, whom I uphold. My chosen one in whom I delight.'

This is how God showed his love among us: He sent his one and only Son into the world that we might live through him. This is love: not that we loved God, but that he loved us and sent his Son as an atoning sacrifice for our sins.

'I have given them the glory that you gave me, that they may be one as we are one: I in them and you in me. May they be brought to complete unity to let the world know that you sent me and have loved them even as you have loved me.'

Children of God
How great is the love the Father has lavished on us, that we should be called children of God!

Colossians 1:13. Matthew 3:17. Isaiah 42:1. 1 John 4:9–10.
John 17:22–23. 1 John 3:1.

Morning

Pray in the Holy Spirit.

'God is Spirit, and his worshippers must worship in spirit and in truth.'—For through him we both have access to the Father by one Spirit.

In the same way, the Spirit helps us in our weakness. We do not know what we ought to pray, but the Spirit himself intercedes for us with groans that words cannot express. And he who searches our hearts knows the mind of the Spirit, because the Spirit intercedes for the saints in accordance with God's will.

Ask according to his will
This is the assurance we have in approaching God: that if we ask anything according to his will, he hears us.

And pray in the Spirit on all occasions with all kinds of prayers and requests.

Jude 20. John 4:24. Ephesians 2:18. Romans 8:26–27. 1 John 5:14.
Ephesians 6:18.

Evening

At least there is hope for a tree: If it is cut down, it will sprout again, and its new shoots will not fail.

A bruised reed he will not break.—He restores my soul.—Godly sorrow brings repentance that leads to salvation and leaves no regret, but worldly sorrow brings death.

A remnant
'What has happened to us is a result of our evil deeds and our great guilt, and yet, our God, you have punished us less than our sins have deserved and have given us a remnant like this.'

Into the light
Do not gloat over me, my enemy! Though I have fallen, I will rise. Though I sit in darkness, the LORD will be my light. . . . He will bring me out into the light; I will see his justice.

Job 14:7. Isaiah 42:3. Psalm 23:3. 2 Corinthians 7:10. Ezra 9:13.
Micah 7:8–9.

November 23

Morning

'But whoever listens to me will live in safety and be at ease, without fear of harm.'

LORD, you have been our dwelling-place throughout all generations. . . . He who dwells in the shelter of the Most High will rest in the shadow of the Almighty. . . . His faithfulness will be your shield and rampart.

Your life is now hidden with Christ in God.—For whoever touches you touches the apple of his eye.—God is our refuge and strength, an ever present help in trouble. Therefore we will not fear.

But Jesus immediately said to them: 'Take courage! It is I. Don't be afraid.'

'Why do doubts rise in your minds?'
'Why are you troubled, and why do doubts rise in your minds? Look at my hands and my feet. It is I myself! Touch me and see; a ghost does not have flesh and bones, as you see I have.'

> Proverbs 1:33. Psalms 90:1; 91:1, 4. Colossians 3:3. Zechariah 2:8.
> Psalm 46:1–2. Matthew 14:27. Luke 24:38–39.

Evening

'My kingdom is not of this world.'

'In the future you will see the Son of Man sitting at the right hand of the Mighty One and coming on the clouds of heaven.'—For he must reign until he has put all his enemies under his feet.

God the only Ruler
He [God] raised him [Christ] from the dead and seated him at his right hand in the heavenly realms, far above all rule and authority, power and dominion, and every title that can be given, not only in the present age but also in the one to come. And God placed all things under his feet and appointed him to be head over everything for the church, which is his body, the fulness of him who fills everything in every way.—God, the blessed and only Ruler, the King of kings and Lord of Lords.

> John 18:36. Matthew 26:64. 1 Corinthians 15:25. Ephesians 1:20–23.
> 1 Timothy 6:15.

Morning

'My mother and brothers are those who hear God's word and put it into practice.'

But the one who makes people holy and those who are made holy are of the same family. So Jesus is not ashamed to call them brothers and sisters. He says, 'I will declare your name to my brothers and sisters; in the presence of the congregation I will sing your praises.'—For in Christ Jesus neither circumcision nor uncircumcision has any value. The only thing that counts is faith expressing itself through love.—'You are my friends if you do what I command.'

'Hear and obey'
'Blessed rather are those who hear the word of God and obey it.'—'Not everyone who says to me, "Lord, Lord," will enter the kingdom of heaven, but only those who do the will of my Father who is in heaven.'—'My food,' said Jesus, 'is to do the will of him who sent me.'

> Luke 8:21. Hebrews 2:11–12. Galatians 5:6. John 15:14. Luke 11:28.
> Matthew 7:21. John 4:34.

Evening

He knows the way I take.

O Lord, you have searched me and you know me. You know when I sit and when I rise; you perceive my thoughts from afar. You discern my going out and my lying down; you are familiar with all my ways. . . . Where can I go from your Spirit? Where can I flee from your presence? . . . If I rise on the wings of the dawn, if I settle on the far side of the sea, even there your hand will guide me, your right hand will hold me fast.

Whoever trusts in the Lord is kept safe
To fear anyone will prove to be a snare, but whoever trusts in the Lord is kept safe.—Though they stumble, they will not fall, for the Lord upholds them with his hand.—For though the righteous fall seven times, they rise again.

Let us not become weary in doing good, for at the proper time we will reap a harvest if we do not give up.

> Job 23:10. Psalm 139:1–3, 7, 9–10. Proverbs 29:25. Psalm 37:24.
> Proverbs 24:16. Galatians 6:9.

November 25

Morning

You have been set free from sin and have become slaves to righteousness.

'You cannot serve both God and Money.'—When you were slaves to sin, you were free from the control of righteousness. What benefit did you reap at that time from the things you are now ashamed of? Those things result in death! But now that you have been set free from sin and become slaves to God, the benefit you reap leads to holiness, and the result is eternal life. . . . Christ is the end of the law so that there may be righteousness for everyone who believes.

'Whoever serves me must follow me; and where I am, my servant also will be. My Father will honour the one who serves me.'

Your name alone do we honour
O LORD, our God, other lords besides you have ruled over us, but your name alone do we honour.

Romans 6:18. Matthew 6:24. Romans 6:20–22; 10:4. John 12:26.
Isaiah 26:13.

Evening

'And everyone who calls on the name of the Lord will be saved.'

Manasseh
[Manasseh] did evil in the eyes of the LORD, following the detestable practices of the nations the LORD had driven out before the Israelites. He rebuilt the high places his father Hezekiah had destroyed. . . . He bowed down to all the starry hosts and worshipped them. . . . In both courts of the temple of the LORD, he built altars to all the starry hosts. He sacrificed his own son in the fire, practised sorcery and divination, and consulted mediums and spiritists. He did much evil in the eyes of the LORD, provoking him to anger.

He humbled himself
In his distress he sought the favour of the LORD his God and humbled himself greatly before the God of his fathers. And when he prayed to him, the LORD was moved by his entreaty and listened to his plea. .

He is patient with you, not wanting anyone to perish.

Acts 2:21. 2 Kings 21:2–3, 5–6. 2 Chronicles 33:12–13. 2 Peter 3:9.

Morning

For the LORD will take delight in you.

This is what the LORD says—he who created you, . . . 'Fear not, for I have redeemed you; I have called you by name; you are mine.' . . . 'Can a mother forget her baby at her breast and have no compassion on the child she has borne? Though she may forget, I will not forget you! See, I have engraved you on the palms of my hands; your walls are ever before me.'

The LORD delights in those who fear him, who put their hope in his unfailing love.

Reconciled
Once you were alienated from God and were enemies in your minds because of your evil behaviour. But now he has reconciled you by Christ's physical body through death to present you holy in his sight, without blemish and free from accusation.

Isaiah 62:4. Isaiah 43:1; 49:15–16. Psalm 147:11. Colossians 1:21–22.

Evening

Worldly sorrow brings death.

A crushed spirit who can bear?

Is there no balm in Gilead? Is there no physician there? Why then is there no healing for the wound of my people?

Oil of gladness instead of mourning
The LORD has anointed me to preach good news to the poor. He has sent me to bind up the broken-hearted, to proclaim freedom for the captives and release for the prisoners, to proclaim the year of the LORD's favour and the day of vengeance of our God, to comfort all who mourn, and provide for those who grieve in Zion—to bestow on them a crown of beauty instead of ashes, the oil of gladness instead of mourning, and a garment of praise instead of a spirit of despair.

'Come to me, all of you who are weary and burdened, and I will give you rest. Take my yoke upon you and learn from me, for I am gentle and humble in heart, and you will find rest for your souls. For my yoke is easy and my burden is light.'

2 Corinthians 7:10. Proverbs 18:14. Jeremiah 8:22. Isaiah 61:1–3.
Matthew 11:28–30.

November 27

Morning

'I have given them the glory that you gave me.'

Isaiah
I saw the LORD seated on a throne, high and exalted, and the train of his robe filled the temple. Above him were seraphs, . . . And they were calling to one another: 'Holy, holy, holy is the LORD Almighty; the whole earth is full of his glory.'—Isaiah said this because he saw Jesus' glory and spoke about him.— Like the appearance of a rainbow in the clouds on a rainy day, so was the radiance around him. This was the appearance of the likeness of the glory of the LORD.

The face of Christ
No-one has ever seen God, but God the One and Only, who is at the Father's side, has made him known.—For God, who said, 'Let light shine out of darkness,' made his light shine in our hearts to give us the light of the knowledge of the glory of God in the face of Christ.

John 17:22. Isaiah 6:1–3. Ezekiel 1:28. John 1:18. 2 Corinthians 4:6.

Evening

My son, if sinners entice you, do not give in to them.

She took some [fruit] and ate. She also gave some to her husband, who was with her, and he ate it.—'Do not follow the crowd in doing wrong.'

The road to destruction
'For wide is the gate and broad is the road that leads to destruction, and many enter through it.'—For we do not live to ourselves alone.—You, my brothers and sisters, were called to be free. But do not use your freedom to indulge the sinful nature; rather, serve one another in love.

You sin against Christ
Be careful, however, that the exercise of your freedom does not become a stumbling-block to the weak. . . . When you sin against your brothers and sisters in this way and wound their weak conscience, you sin against Christ.

Proverbs 1:10. Genesis 3:6. Exodus 23:2. Matthew 7:13. Romans 14:7.
Galatians 5:13. 1 Corinthians 8:9, 12.

Morning

As the body without the spirit is dead, so faith without deeds is dead.

'Not everyone who says to me, "Lord, Lord," will enter the kingdom of heaven, but only those who do the will of my Father who is in heaven.'

Make your calling and election sure
Add to your faith goodness; and to goodness, knowledge; and to knowledge, self-control; and to self-control, perseverance; and to perseverance, godliness; and to godliness, mutual affection; and to mutual affection, love. For if you possess these qualities in increasing measure, they will keep you from being ineffective and unproductive in your knowledge of our Lord Jesus Christ. But if any of you do not have them, you are short-sighted and blind, and you have forgotten that you have been cleansed from your past sins.

James 2:26. Matthew 7:21. 2 Peter 1:5–10.

Evening

The sting of death is sin, and the power of sin is the law.

Thanks be to God! He gives us the victory through our Lord Jesus Christ.

We do not lose heart
Therefore we do not lose heart. Though outwardly we are wasting away, yet inwardly we are being renewed day by day. . . . Now we know that if the earthly tent we live in is destroyed, we have a building from God, an eternal house in heaven, not built by human hands. . . . Therefore we are always confident and know that as long as we are at home in the body we are away from the Lord. We live by faith, not by sight. We are confident, I say, and would prefer to be away from the body and at home with the Lord.

1 Corinthians 15:55, 57. 2 Corinthians 4:16; 5:1, 6–8.

November 29

Morning

We are filled with the good things of your house.

One thing I ask of the LORD, this is what I seek; that I may dwell in the house of the LORD all the days of my life, to gaze upon the beauty of the LORD and to seek him in his temple.

'Blessed are those who hunger and thirst for righteousness, for they will be filled.'

He satisfies the thirsty
For he satisfies the thirsty and fills the hungry with good things.—'I am the bread of life. Whoever comes to me will never go hungry, and whoever believes in me will never be thirsty.'

Unfailing love!
How priceless is your unfailing love! Both highborn and low find refuge in the shadow of your wings. They feast in the abundance of your house; you give them drink from your river of delights. For with you is the fountain of life; in your light we see light.

Psalms 65:4; 27:4. Luke 1:53. Psalm 107:9. John 6:35. Psalm 36:7–9.

Evening

'You believe at last!'

By faith Abraham
By faith Abraham, when God tested him, offered Isaac as a sacrifice. He who had received the promises was about to sacrifice his one and only son, even though God had said to him, 'It is through Isaac that your offspring will be reckoned.' Abraham reasoned that God could raise the dead.—Was not our ancestor Abraham considered righteous for what he did when he offered his son Isaac on the altar? . . . You see that people are justified by what they do and not by faith alone. . . . But those who look intently into the perfect law that gives freedom, and continue to do this, not forgetting what they have heard, but doing it—they will be blessed in what they do.

'By their fruit you will recognise them'
Thus, by their fruit you will recognise them. Not everyone who says to me, "Lord, Lord," will enter the kingdom of heaven, but only those who do the will of my Father who is in heaven.'

John 16:31. Hebrews 11:17–19. James 2:21, 24; 1:25. Matthew 7:20–21.

334

Morning

Now may the Lord of peace himself give you peace at all times and in every way. The Lord be with all of you.

Grace and peace to you from him who is, and who was, and who is to come.—The peace of God, which transcends all understanding, will guard your hearts and minds in Christ Jesus.

'Peace I leave with you'
Jesus himself stood among them and said to them, 'Peace be with you.'—'Peace I leave with you; my peace I give you. I do not give to you as the world gives. Do not let your hearts be troubled and do not be afraid. . . . The Counsellor . . . Spirit of truth.'

'My Presence will go with you, and I will give you rest.' Then Moses said to him, 'If your Presence does not go with us, do not send us up from here. How will anyone know that you are pleased with me and with your people unless you go with us?'

2 Thessalonians 3:16. Revelation 1:4. Philippians 4:7. Luke 24:36.
John 14:27; 15:26. Exodus 33:14–16.

Evening

We . . . rejoice in our sufferings.

If only for this life we have hope in Christ, we are to be pitied more than all people.—Sorrowful, yet always rejoicing.

Joy and peace
Rejoice in the Lord always. I will say it again: Rejoice!—The apostles left the Sanhedrin, rejoicing because they had been counted worthy of suffering disgrace for the Name.—May the God of hope fill you with all joy and peace as you trust in him.

Yet I will rejoice in the LORD
Though the fig-tree does not bud and there are no grapes on the vines, though the olive crop fails and the fields produce no food, though there are no sheep in the pen and no cattle in the stalls, yet I will rejoice in the LORD, I will be joyful in God my Saviour.

Romans 5:3. 1 Corinthians 15:19. 2 Corinthians 6:10. Philippians 4:4.
Acts 5:41. Romans 15:13. Habakkuk 3:17–18.

December 1

Morning

I call as my heart grows faint; lead me to the rock that is higher than I.

Since the children have flesh and blood, he too shared in their humanity.—'I and the Father are one.'

The shadow of the Almighty
He who dwells in the shelter of the Most High will rest in the shadow of the Almighty.—It will be a shelter and shade from the heat of the day, and a refuge and hiding-place from the storm and rain.—The LORD is your shade at your right hand; the sun will not harm you by day, nor the moon by night.

You are my hiding-place; you will protect me from trouble—You have been a refuge for the poor, a refuge for the needy in their distress, a shelter from the storm and a shade from the heat. For the breath of the ruthless is like a storm driving against a wall.

Psalm 61:2. Hebrews 2:14. John 10:30. Psalm 91:1. Isaiah 4:6.
Psalms 121:5–6; 32:7. Isaiah 25:4.

Evening

'Behold, I will create new heavens and a new earth.'

'As the new heavens and the new earth that I make will endure before me, . . . so will your name and descendants endure.'

The Holy City
Then I saw a new heaven and a new earth, for the first heaven and the first earth had passed away, and there was no longer any sea. I saw the Holy City, the new Jerusalem, coming down out of heaven from God, prepared as a bride beautifully dressed for her husband. And I heard a loud voice from the throne saying, 'Now the dwelling of God is with human beings, and he will live with them. They will be his people, and God himself will be with them and be their God. He will wipe every tear from their eyes. There will be no more death or mourning or crying or pain, for the old order of things has passed away.'

Isaiah 65:17; 66:22. Revelation 21:1–5.

Morning

But you have an anointing from the Holy One, and all of you know the truth.

'God anointed Jesus of Nazareth with the Holy Spirit and power.'—From the fulness of his grace we have all received one blessing after another.

His anointing teaches you
The anointing you received from him remains in you, and you do not need anyone to teach you. But as his anointing teaches you about all things and as that anointing is real, not counterfeit—just as it has taught you, remain in him.

'The Counsellor, the Holy Spirit, whom the Father will send in my name, will teach you all things and will remind you of everything I have said to you.'—The Spirit helps us in our weakness. We do not know what we ought to pray, but the Spirit himself intercedes for us with groans that words cannot express.

> 1 John 2:20. Acts 10:38. John 1:16. 1 John 2:27. John 14:26.
> Romans 8:26.

Evening

Having our hearts sprinkled to cleanse us from a guilty conscience.

The blood of goats and bulls and the ashes of a heifer sprinkled on those who are ceremonially unclean sanctify them so that they are outwardly clean. How much more, then, will the blood of Christ, who through the eternal Spirit offered himself unblemished to God, cleanse our consciences from acts that lead to death, so that we may serve the living God! . . . The sprinkled blood that speaks a better word than the blood of Abel.

Redemption through his blood
In him we have redemption through his blood, the forgiveness of sins, in accordance with the riches of God's grace.

In fact, the law requires that nearly everything be cleansed with blood, and without the shedding of blood there is no forgiveness.

> Hebrews 10:22; 9:13–14; 12:24. Ephesians 1:7. Hebrews 2:22.

December 3

Morning

Commit your way to the LORD; trust in him and he will do this.

Do not be anxious about anything, but in everything, by prayer and petition, with thanksgiving, present your requests to God.—Cast all your anxiety on him because he cares for you.

Hezekiah
Hezekiah received the letter from the messengers and read it. Then he went up to the temple of the LORD and spread it out before the LORD. And Hezekiah prayed to the LORD . . . 'Before they call I will answer; while they are still speaking I will hear.'—The prayer of a righteous person is powerful and effective.

I will call on him as long as I live
I love the LORD, for he heard my voice; he heard my cry for mercy. Because he turned his ear to me, I will call on him as long as I live.

Psalm 37:5. Philippians 4:6. 1 Peter 5:7. Isaiah 37:14–15; 65:24.
James 5:16. Psalm 116:1–2.

Evening

Our bodies washed with pure water.

'Make a bronze basin, with its bronze stand, for washing. Place it between the Tent of Meeting and the altar, and put water in it. Aaron and his sons are to wash their hands and feet with water from it. Whenever they enter the Tent of Meeting, they shall wash with water so that they will not die. Also, when they approach the altar to minister by presenting an offering made to the LORD by fire, they shall wash their hands and feet so that they will not die.'

Your body is a temple of the Holy Spirit, who is in you.

Your spiritual worship
Nothing impure will ever enter it.—Your eyes are too pure to look on evil; you cannot tolerate wrong.—Therefore, I urge you, brothers and sisters, in view of God's mercy, to offer your bodies as living sacrifices, holy and pleasing to God—this is your spiritual act of worship.

Hebrews 10:22. Exodus 30:18–21. 1 Corinthians 6:19. Revelation 21:27.
Habakkuk 1:13. Romans 12:1.

Morning

'But where can wisdom be found?'

If any of you lacks wisdom, you should ask God, who gives generously to all without finding fault, and it will be given you. But when you ask, you must believe and not doubt.—Trust in the LORD with all your heart and lean not on your own understanding; in all your ways acknowledge him, and he will make your paths straight.—The only God.—Do not be wise in your own eyes.

Jeremiah
'Ah, Sovereign LORD,' I said, 'I do not know how to speak; I am only a child.' But the LORD said to me, 'Do not say, "I am only a child." You must go to everyone I send you to say whatever I command you. Do not be afraid of them, for I am with you, and will rescue you,' declares the LORD.

> Job 28:12. James 1:5–6. Proverbs 3:5–6. 1 Timothy 1:17. Proverbs 3:7.
> Jeremiah 1:6–8.

Evening

I said, 'Oh, that I had the wings of a dove! I would fly away and be at rest.'

'I would hurry to my place of shelter, far from the tempest and storm.'

Our heavenly dwelling
Meanwhile we groan, longing to be clothed with our heavenly dwelling. . . . For while we are in this tent, we groan and are burdened, because we do not wish to be unclothed but to be clothed with our heavenly dwelling, so that what is mortal may be swallowed up by life.—I desire to depart and be with Christ, which is better by far.

Let us run with perseverance the race marked out for us. Let us fix our eyes on Jesus, the author and perfecter of our faith, who for the joy set before him endured the cross, scorning its shame, and sat down at the right hand of the throne of God. Consider him who endured such opposition from sinners, so that you will not grow weary and lose heart.

> Psalm 55:6, 8. 2 Corinthians 5:2, 4. Philippians 1:23. Hebrews 12:1–3.

December 5

Morning

It was good for me to be afflicted so that I might learn your decrees.

Although he was a son, he learned obedience from what he suffered.—We share in his sufferings in order that we may also share in his glory. I consider that our present sufferings are not worth comparing with the glory that will be revealed in us.

I will come forth as gold
But he knows the way that I take; when he has tested me, I will come forth as gold. My feet have closely followed his steps; I have kept to his way without turning aside.

Remember how the LORD your God led you all the way in the desert these forty years, to humble you and to test you in order to know what was in your heart, whether or not you would keep his commands. . . . Know then in your heart that as a man disciplines his son, so the LORD your God disciplines you. Observe the commands of the LORD your God, walking in his ways and revering him.

> Psalm 119:71. Hebrews 5:8. Romans 8:17–18. Job 23:10–11.
> Deuteronomy 8:2, 5–6.

Evening

'It is not by strength that one prevails.'

David
David said to the Philistine, 'You come against me with sword and spear and javelin, but I come against you in the name of the LORD Almighty, the God of the armies of Israel, whom you have defiled.' . . . Reaching into his bag and taking out a stone, he slung it and struck the Philistine on the forehead. The stone sank into his forehead, and he fell face down on the ground. So David triumphed over the Philistine with a sling and a stone.

In your hands are strength and power
No king is saved by the size of his army; no warrior escapes by his great strength. . . . But the eyes of the LORD are on those who fear him, on those whose hope is in his unfailing love.—Wealth and honour come from you; you are the ruler of all things. In your hands are strength and power to exalt and give strength to all.

> 1 Samuel 2:9; 17:45, 49–50. Psalm 33:16, 18. 1 Chronicles 29:12.

Morning

For it is God who works in you.

Not that we are competent to claim anything for ourselves, but our competence comes from God.—'A person can receive only what is given from heaven.' . . . 'No-one can come to me unless the Father who sent me draws them, and I will raise them up at the last day.'—'I will give them singleness of heart and action, so that they will always fear me.'

A kind of firstfruit
Don't be deceived, my dear brothers and sisters. Every good and perfect gift is from above, coming down from the Father of the heavenly lights, who does not change like shifting shadows. He chose to give us birth through the word of truth, that we might be a kind of firstfruits of all he created.—For we are God's handiwork, created in Christ Jesus to do good works, which God prepared in advance for us to do.

> Philippians 2:13. 2 Corinthians 3:5. John 3:27; 6:44. Jeremiah 32:39.
> James 1:16–18. Ephesians 2:10.

Evening

'The Spirit is willing, but the body is weak.'

Yes, LORD, walking in the way of your laws, we wait for you; your name and renown are the desire of our hearts. My soul yearns for you in the night; in the morning my spirit longs for you.

I see another law at work
I know that nothing good lives in me, that is, in my sinful nature. For I have the desire to do what is good, but I cannot carry it out . . . For in my inner being I delight in God's law; but I see another law at work in the members of my body, waging war against the law of my mind and making me a prisoner of the law of sin at work within my members.

I can do all things through him who gives me strength.—Our competence comes from God.

> Matthew 26:41. Isaiah 26:8–9. Romans 7:18, 22–23. Philippians 4:13.
> 2 Corinthians 3:5.

December 7

Morning

God made him who had no sin to be sin for us, so that in him we might become the righteousness of God.

The LORD has laid on him the iniquity of us all.—He himself bore our sins in his body on the tree, so that we might die to sins and live for righteousness; by his wounds you have been healed.—Just as through the disobedience of the one man many were made sinners, so also through the obedience of the one man the many will be made righteous.

Justified by his grace
But when the kindness and love of God our Saviour appeared, he saved us, not because of righteous things we had done, but because of his mercy. He saved us through the washing of rebirth and renewal by the Holy Spirit, whom he poured out on us generously through Jesus Christ our Saviour, so that, having been justified by his grace, we might become heirs having the hope of eternal life.

2 Corinthians 5:21. Isaiah 53:6. 1 Peter 2:24. Romans 5:19. Titus 3:4–7.

Evening

I will be like the dew to Israel.

The meekness and gentleness of Christ.—A bruised reed he will not break, and a smouldering wick he will not snuff out.

'The Spirit of the Lord is upon me, because he has anointed me to preach good news to the poor. He has sent me to proclaim freedom for the prisoners and recovery of sight for the blind, to release the oppressed, to proclaim the year of the LORD's favour.' . . . And he began by saying to them, 'Today this scripture is fulfilled in your hearing.' All spoke well of him and were amazed at the gracious words that came from his lips.

Like a shepherd
He tends his flock like a shepherd: He gathers the lambs in his arms and carries them close to his heart; he gently leads those that have young.

Hosea 14:5. 2 Corinthians 10:1. Isaiah 42:3. Luke 4:18–19, 21–22.
Isaiah 40:11.

Morning

Serve one another in love.

Brothers and sisters, if someone is caught in a sin, you who are spiritual should restore that person gently. But watch yourself, or you also may be tempted. Carry each other's burdens, and in this way you will fulfil the law of Christ.

Love one another deeply
My brothers and sisters, if one of you should wander from the truth and someone should bring that person back, remember this: Those who turn sinners from the error of their ways will save them from death and cover over a multitude of sins.—Now that you have purified yourselves by obeying the truth so that you have sincere mutual affection, love one another deeply, from the heart.

You who are younger, be submissive to those who are older. All of you, clothe yourselves with humility towards one another, because, 'God opposes the proud.'

Galatians 5:13; 6:1–2. James 5:19–20. 1 Peter 1:22; 5:5.

Evening

'For dust you are and to dust you will return.'

The body that is sown is perishable, it is raised imperishable; it is sown in dishonour, it is raised in glory; it is sown in weakness, it is raised in power; it is sown a natural body, it is raised a spiritual body. . . . The first man was of the dust of the earth, the second man from heaven.

I will see God
My body also will rest secure.—And after my skin has been destroyed, yet in my flesh I will see God.—The Lord Jesus Christ, who, by the power that enables him to bring everything under his control, will transform our lowly bodies so that they will be like his glorious body.

Teach us to number our days aright, that we may gain a heart of wisdom.

Genesis 3:19. 1 Corinthians 15:42–44, 47. Psalm 16:9. Job 19:26.
Philippians 3:20–21. Psalm 90:12.

December 9

Morning

To do what is right and just is more acceptable to the LORD than sacrifice.

'Does the LORD delight in burnt offerings and sacrifices as much as in obeying the voice of the LORD? To obey is better than to sacrifice, and to heed is better than the fat of rams.'

'To love him with all your heart, with all your understanding and with all your strength, and to love your neighbour as yourself is more important than all burnt offerings and sacrifices.'

'Only one thing is needed'
But you must return to your God; maintain love and justice, and wait for your God always.—Mary . . . sat at the Lord's feet listening to what he said. . . . 'But only one thing is needed. Mary has chosen what is better, and it will not be taken away from her.'

For it is God who works in you to will and to act according to his good purpose.

Proverbs 21:3. 1 Samuel 15:22. Mark 12:33. Hosea 12:6.
Luke 10:39, 42. Philippians 2:13.

Evening

The spirit returns to God who gave it.

With Christ is far better
We are always confident and know that as long as we are at home in the body we are away from the Lord. . . . We are confident, I say, and would prefer to be away from the body and at home with the Lord.—With Christ, which is better by far.

Brothers and sisters, we do not want you to be ignorant about those who fall asleep, or to grieve like the rest, who have no hope. We believe that Jesus died and rose again and so we believe that God will bring with Jesus those who have fallen asleep in him.

'I am going there to prepare a place for you. And if I go and prepare a place for you, I will come back and take you to be with me that you also may be where I am.'

Ecclesiastes 12:7. 1 Corinthians 15:45. 2 Corinthians 5:6, 8.
Philippians 1:23. 1 Thessalonians 4:13–14. John 14:2–3.

Morning

'No-one can snatch them out of my Father's hand.'

The Lord will rescue me from every evil attack and will bring me safely to his heavenly kingdom.

We are more than conquerors through him who loved us. For I am convinced that neither death nor life, neither the present nor the future, nor any powers, neither height nor depth, nor anything else in all creation, will be able to separate us from the love of God that is in Christ Jesus our Lord.

Inherit the kingdom
Has not God chosen those who are poor in the eyes of the world to be rich in faith and to inherit the kingdom he promised to those who love him?

May our Lord Jesus Christ himself and God our Father, who loved us and by his grace gave us eternal encouragement and good hope, encourage your hearts and strengthen you in every good deed and word.

> John 10:29. 2 Timothy 4:18. Romans 8:37–39. James 2:5.
> 2 Thessalonians 2:16–17.

Evening

Perfect law that gives freedom.

'Then you will know the truth, and the truth will set you free.' They answered him, 'We are Abraham's descendants and have never been slaves of anyone. How can you say that we shall be set free?' Jesus replied, 'I tell you the truth, everyone who sins is a slave to sin. . . . So if the Son sets you free, you will be free indeed.'

'Love your neighbour as yourself'
Stand firm, then, and do not let yourselves be burdened again by a yoke of slavery. . . . You, my brothers and sisters, were called to be free. But do not use your freedom to indulge the sinful nature; rather, serve one another in love. The entire law is summed up in a single command: 'Love your neighbour as yourself.'

You have been set free from sin and have become slaves to righteousness.

Through Christ Jesus the law of the Spirit of life set me free from the law of sin and death.

> James 1:25. John 8:32–34, 36. Galatians 5:1, 13–14. Romans 6:18; 8:2.

December 11

Morning

Avoid every kind of evil.

For we are taking pains to do what is right, not only in the eyes of the Lord but also in the eyes of others.

For it is God's will that by doing good you should silence the ignorant talk of foolish people. . . . If you suffer, it should not be as a murderer or thief or any other kind of criminal, or even as a meddler. However, if you suffer as a Christian, do not be ashamed, but praise God that you bear that name.

A stumbling block to the weak
Be careful, however, that the exercise of your freedom does not become a stumbling-block to the weak.—'But if any of you causes one of these little ones who believe in me to sin, it would be better for you to have a large millstone hung around your neck and to be drowned in the depths of the sea.' . . . 'Whatever you did for one of the least of these brothers and sisters of mine, you did for me.'

> 1 Thessalonians 5:22. 2 Corinthians 8:21. 1 Peter 2:15; 4:15–16.
> 1 Corinthians 8:9. Matthew 18:6; 25:40.

Evening

'Wake up, O sleeper, rise from the dead, and Christ will shine on you.'

Let us not be like others, who are asleep, but let us be alert and self-controlled. For those who sleep, sleep at night, and those who get drunk, get drunk at night. But since we belong to the day, let us be self-controlled, putting on faith and love as a breastplate, and the hope of salvation as a helmet.

'Arise, shine, for your light has come, and the glory of the LORD rises upon you. See, darkness covers the earth and thick darkness is over the peoples, but the LORD rises upon you and his glory appears over you.'

'Ready for service'
'Be dressed ready for service and keep your lamps burning, like those waiting for their master.'

> Ephesians 5:14. 1 Thessalonians 5:6–8. Isaiah 60:1–2. Luke 12:35–36.

Morning

The LORD, the King of Israel, is with you.

'So do not fear, for I am with you; do not be dismayed, for I am your God. I will strengthen you and help you; I will uphold you with my righteous right hand.' . . . Strengthen the feeble hands, steady the knees that give way; say to those with fearful hearts, 'Be strong, do not fear; your God will come, he will come with vengeance; with divine retribution he will come to save you.'

'He will quiet you with his love'
'The LORD your God is with you, he is mighty to save. He will take great delight in you, he will quiet you with his love, he will rejoice over you with singing.'—'Wait for the LORD; be strong and take heart and wait for the LORD.'

'He will wipe every tear from their eyes. There will be no more death or mourning or crying or pain.'

Zephaniah 3:15. Isaiah 41:10; 35:3–4. Zephaniah 3:17. Psalm 27:14.
Revelation 21:4.

Evening

But we prayed to our God and posted a guard day and night to meet this threat.

'Not everyone who says to me, "Lord, Lord," will enter the kingdom of heaven, but only those who do the will of my Father who is in heaven.'

'Anyone who chooses to do the will of God will find out whether my teaching comes from God or whether I speak on my own.'—Let us acknowledge the LORD; let us press on to acknowledge him.

Keep your spiritual fervour
'Watch and pray so that you will not fall into temptation.'—Be on your guard; stand firm in the faith; be courageous; be strong.—Never be lacking in zeal, but keep your spiritual fervour, serving the Lord.

Strengthen the feeble hands, steady the knees that give way; say to those with fearful hearts, 'Be strong, do not fear.'

Nehemiah 4:9. Matthew 7:21. John 7:17. Hosea 6:3. Matthew 26:41.
1 Corinthians 16:13. Romans 12:11. Isaiah 35:3–4.

December 13

Morning

Be strong in the grace that is in Christ Jesus.

Be strengthened with all power according to his glorious might. . . . So then, just as you received Christ Jesus as Lord, continue to live in him, rooted and built up in him, strengthened in the faith as you were taught, and overflowing with thankfulness.

Oaks of righteousness
They will be called oaks of righteousness, a planting of the LORD for the display of his splendour.—Built on the foundation of the apostles and prophets, with Christ Jesus himself as the chief cornerstone. In him the whole temple in the Lord is joined together and rises to become a holy temple in the Lord. And in him you too are being built together to become a dwelling in which God lives by his Spirit.

'Now I commit you to God and to the word of his grace, which can build you up and give you an inheritance among all those who are sanctified.'

2 Timothy 2:1. Colossians 1:11; 2:6–7. Isaiah 61:3. Ephesians 2:20–22.
Acts 20:32.

Evening

Surely you will reward everyone according to what they have done.

For we must all appear before the judgment seat of Christ, that everyone may receive what is due them for the things done while in the body, whether good or bad.

But when you give to the needy, do not let your left hand know what your right hand is doing, so that your giving may be in secret. Then your Father, who sees what is done in secret, will reward you. . . . 'After a long time the master of those servants returned and settled accounts with them.'

Our competence comes from God
Not that we are competent to claim anything for ourselves, but our competence comes from God.—LORD, you establish peace for us; all that we have accomplished you have done for us.

Psalm 62:12. 2 Corinthians 5:10. Matthew 6:3–4; 25:19.
2 Corinthians 3:5. Isaiah 26:12.

Morning

Sing to the glory of his name; offer him glory and praise!

'The people I formed for myself that they may proclaim my praise.'—Through Jesus, therefore, let us continually offer to God a sacrifice of praise—the fruit of lips that confess his name.

I will praise you, O Lord my God, with all my heart; I will glory your name for ever. For great is your love towards me; you have delivered my soul from the depths of the grave.

I will praise God's name in song
'Who among the gods is like you, LORD? Who is like you—majestic in holiness, awesome in glory, working wonders?'—I will praise God's name in song and glorify him with thanksgiving.

[They] sang the song of Moses the servant of God and the song of the Lamb: 'Great and marvellous are your deeds, Lord God Almighty.'

Psalm 66:2. Isaiah 43:21. Hebrews 13:15. Psalm 86:12–13.
Exodus 15:11. Psalm 69:30. Revelation 15:3.

Evening

Like the rest, we were by nature objects of wrath.

At one time we too were foolish, disobedient, deceived and enslaved by all kinds of passions and pleasures. We lived in malice and envy, being hated and hating one another.—'You should not be surprised at my saying, "You must be born again." '

Surely I have been a sinner from birth, sinful from the time my mother conceived me.—He testified concerning him [David]: 'I have found David son of Jesse a man after my own heart; he will do everything I want him to do.'

The Spirit gives birth to spirit
Even though I was once a blasphemer and a persecutor and a violent man, I was shown mercy because I acted in ignorance and unbelief.—Flesh gives birth to flesh, but the Spirit gives birth to spirit.

Ephesians 2:3. Titus 3:3. John 3:7. Psalm 51:5. Acts 13:22.
1 Timothy 1:13. John 3:6.

December 15

Morning

Carry each other's burdens, and in this way you will fulfil the law of Christ.

Each of you should look not only to your own interests, but also to the interests of others. Your attitude should be the same as that of Christ Jesus. . . . [He] made himself nothing, taking the very nature of a servant.

'A ransom for many'
'Even the Son of man did not come to be served, but to serve, and to give his life as a ransom for many.'
  Rejoice with those who rejoice; mourn with those who mourn.

Be sympathetic
All of you live in harmony with one another; be sympathetic, love one another, be compassionate and humble. Do not repay evil with evil or insult with insult, but with blessing, because to this you were called so that you may inherit a blessing.

Galatians 6:2. Philippians 2:4–5, 7. Mark 10:45. Romans 12:15.
1 Peter 3:8–9.

Evening

'Son, go and work today in the vineyard.'

So you are no longer slaves, but God's children; and since you are his children, God made you also heirs.
  In the same way, count yourselves dead to sin but alive to God in Christ Jesus. Therefore do not let sin reign in your mortal body so that you obey its evil desires. Do not offer the parts of your body to sin, as instruments of wickedness, but rather offer yourselves to God.
  As obedient children, do not conform to the evil desires you had when you lived in ignorance. But just as he who called you is holy, so be holy in all you do.—Made holy, useful to the Master and prepared to do any good work.

Let nothing move you
Therefore, my dear brothers and sisters, stand firm. Let nothing move you. Always give yourselves fully to the work of the Lord, because you know that your labour in the Lord is not in vain.

Matthew 21:28. Galatians 4:7. Romans 6:11–13. 1 Peter 1:14–15.
2 Timothy 2:21. 1 Corinthians 15:58.

Morning

Having loved his own who were in the world, he now showed them the full extent of his love.

'I pray for them, I am not praying for the world, but for those you have given me, for they are yours. All I have is yours, and all you have is mine. And glory has come to me through them. . . . My prayer is not that you take them out of the world but that you protect them from the evil one. They are not of the world, even as I am not of it.'

'You are my friends'
'As the Father has loved me, so have I loved you. Now remain in my love. . . . Greater love has no-one than this, to lay down one's life for one's friends. You are my friends if you do what I command.'
   'A new commandment I give you: Love one another. As I have loved you, so you must love one another.'

John 13:1; 17:9–10, 15–16; 15:9, 13–14; 13:34.

Evening

God has revealed it to us by his Spirit.

'The knowledge of the secrets of the kingdom of heaven has been given to you.'
   We have not received the spirit of the world but the Spirit who is from God, that we may understand what God has freely given us.

Power through his Spirit
For this reason I kneel before the Father, from whom his whole family in heaven and on earth derives its name. I pray that out of his glorious riches he may strengthen you with power through his Spirit in your inner being, so that Christ may dwell in your hearts through faith. And I pray that you, being rooted and established in love, may have power, together with all the saints, to grasp how wide and long and high and deep is the love of Christ, and to know this love that surpasses knowledge—that you may be filled to the measure of all the fulness of God.

1 Corinthians 2:10. Matthew 13:11. 1 Corinthians 2:12.
Ephesians 3:14–19.

December 17

Morning

Revive us, and we will call on your name.

The Spirit gives life.—In the same way, the Spirit helps us in our weakness. We do not know what we ought to pray, but the Spirit himself intercedes for us with groans that words cannot express. And he who searches our hearts knows the mind of the Spirit, because the Spirit intercedes for the saints in accordance with God's will.

Pray in the Spirit
And pray in the Spirit on all occasions with all kinds of prayers and requests. With this in mind, be alert and always keep on praying for all the saints.

I will never forget your precepts, for by them you have renewed my life.— 'The flesh counts for nothing. The words I have spoken to you are spirit and they are life.'—For the letter kills, but the Spirit gives life.

And no-one can say, 'Jesus is Lord,' except by the Holy Spirit.

Psalm 80:18. John 6:63. Romans 8:26–27. Ephesians 6:18. Psalm 119:93.
John 6:63. 2 Corinthians 3:6. 1 Corinthians 12:3.

Evening

Have nothing to do with the fruitless deeds of darkness, but rather expose them.

Do not be misled: 'Bad company corrupts good character.' . . . I have written to you in my letter not to associate with sexually immoral people—not at all meaning the people of this world who are immoral, or the greedy and swindlers, or idolaters. In that case you would have to leave this world. But now I am writing to you that you must not associate with any who call themselves believers but are sexually immoral or greedy, idolaters or slanderers, drunkards or swindlers. With such persons do not even eat.

Become blameless and pure
So that you may become blameless and pure, children of God without fault in a crooked and depraved generation in which you shine like stars in the universe.

Ephesians 5:11. 1 Corinthians 15:33; 5:9–11. Philippians 2:15.

Morning

Let us then approach the throne of grace with confidence, so that we may receive mercy and find grace to help us in our time of need.

Do not be anxious about anything, but in everything, by prayer and petition, with thanksgiving, present your requests to God. And the peace of God, which transcends all understanding, will guard your hearts and your minds in Christ Jesus.

'Abba, *Father*'
For you did not receive a spirit that makes you a slave again to fear, but you received the Spirit of sonship. And by him we cry, '*Abba*, Father.'

'*The Lord is my helper*'
Let us draw near to God with a sincere heart in full assurance of faith, having our hearts sprinkled to cleanse us from a guilty conscience and having our bodies washed with pure water. . . . So we say with confidence, 'The Lord is my helper; I will not be afraid. What can human beings do to me?'

Hebrews 4:16. Philippians 4:6–7. Romans 8:15. Hebrews 10:22; 13:6.

Evening

'Then you will know the truth, and the truth will set you free.'

Where the Spirit of the Lord is, there is freedom.—'So if the Son sets you free, you will be free indeed.'

Justified by faith
Know that a person is not justified by observing the law, but by faith in Jesus Christ. So we, too, have put our faith in Christ Jesus that we may be justified by faith in Christ and not by observing the law, because by observing the law no-one will be justified.

Christ has set us free
But those who look intently into the perfect law that gives freedom, and continue to do this, not forgetting what they heard, but doing it—they will be blessed in what they do.—It is for freedom that Christ has set us free. Stand firm, then, and do not let yourselves be burdened again by a yoke of slavery.

John 8:32. 2 Corinthians 3:17. John 8:36. Galatians 2:16. James 1:25.
Galatians 5:1.

December 19

Morning

Even in darkness light dawns for the upright.

Though they stumble, they will not fall, for the LORD upholds them with his hand.—For these commands are a lamp, this teaching is a light.

The LORD will be my light
Do not gloat over me, my enemy! Though I have fallen, I will rise. Though I sit in darkness, the LORD will be my light. Because I have sinned against him, I will bear the LORD's wrath, until he pleads my case and establishes my right. He will bring me out into the light; I will see his justice.

'The eye is the lamp of the body. If your eyes are good, your whole body will be full of light. But if your eyes are bad, your whole body will be full of darkness. If then the light within you is darkness, how great is that darkness!'

Psalm 112:4; 37:24. Proverbs 6:23. Micah 7:8–9. Matthew 6:22–23.

Evening

He tends his flock like a shepherd: He gathers the lambs in his arms and carries them close to his heart; he gently leads those that have young.

'I have compassion for these people; they have already been with me three days and have nothing to eat. I do not want to send them away hungry, or they may collapse on the way.'

People were bringing little children to Jesus to have him touch them, . . . And he took the children in his arms, put his hands on them and blessed them.

'For the Son of Man came to seek and to save what was lost.'—For you were like sheep going astray, but now you have returned to the Shepherd and Overseer of your souls.

I myself will tend my sheep
'Do not be afraid, little flock, for your Father has been pleased to give you the kingdom.'—I myself will tend my sheep and make them lie down, declares the Sovereign LORD.

Isaiah 40:11. Matthew 15:32. Mark 10:13, 16. Luke 19:10. 1 Peter 2:25.
Luke 12:32. Ezekiel 34:15.

Morning

For he chose us in him before the creation of the world to be holy and blameless in his sight.

From the beginning God chose you to be saved through the sanctifying work of the Spirit and through belief in the truth. He called you to this through our gospel, that you might share in the glory of our Lord Jesus Christ.

For those God foreknew he also predestined to be conformed to the likeness of his Son, that he might be the firstborn among many brothers and sisters. And those he predestined, he also called; those he called, he also justified; those he justified, he also glorified.

A new heart and a new spirit
'I will give you a new heart and put a new spirit in you; I will remove from you your heart of stone and give you a heart of flesh.'—For God did not call us to be impure, but to live a holy life.

Ephesians 1:4. 2 Thessalonians 2:13–14. Romans 8:29–30. Ezekiel 36:26.
1 Thessalonians 4:7.

Evening

'Look, even if the LORD should open the floodgates of the heavens, could this happen?'

'Have faith in God.'—Without faith it is impossible to please God.—'With God all things are possible.'
'Was my arm too short to ransom you? Do I lack the strength to rescue you?'

'Test me'
'Test me in this,' says the LORD Almighty, 'and see if I will not throw open the floodgates of heaven and pour out so much blessing that you will not have room enough for it.'

We rely on God
We might not rely on ourselves but on God, who raises the dead.

2 Kings 7:2. Mark 11:22. Hebrews 11:6. Matthew 19:26. Isaiah 50:2.
Malachi 3:10. 2 Corinthians 1:9.

December 21

Morning

'And your days of sorrow will end.'

'In this world you will have trouble.'—We know that the whole creation has been groaning as in the pains of childbirth right up to the present time. Not only so, but we ourselves, who have the firstfruits of the Spirit, groan inwardly as we wait eagerly for our adoption, the redemption of our bodies.

'Springs of living water'
'These are they who have come out of the great tribulation; they have washed their robes and made them white in the blood of the Lamb. Therefore they are before the throne of God and serve him day and night in his temple; and he who sits on the throne will spread his tent over them. Never again will they hunger; never again will they thirst. The sun will not beat upon them, nor any scorching heat. For the Lamb at the centre of the throne will be their shepherd; he will lead them to springs of living water. And God will wipe away every tear from their eyes.'

Isaiah 60:20. John 16:33. Romans 8:22–23. Revelation 7:14–17.

Evening

'Teacher, don't you care if we drown?'

The LORD is good to all; he has compassion on all he has made.

God heard the boy
The LORD is good, a refuge in times of trouble. He cares for those who trust in him.—God heard the boy crying, and the angel of God called to Hagar from heaven and said to her, 'What is the matter, Hagar? Do not be afraid; God has heard the boy crying as he lies there.' . . . Then God opened her eyes and she saw a well of water. So she went and filled the skin with water and gave the boy a drink.

'So do not worry, saying, "What shall we eat?" or "What shall we drink?" or "What shall we wear?" . . . Your heavenly Father knows that you need them.'—Hope in God, who richly provides us with everything for our enjoyment.

Mark 4:38. Psalm 145:9. Nahum 1:7. Genesis 21:17, 19.
Matthew 6:31–32. 1 Timothy 6:17.

Morning

Your work produced by faith.

'The work of God is this: to believe in the one he has sent.'—Faith by itself, if it is not accompanied by action, is dead.—Faith expressing itself through love. . . . Those who sow to please their sinful nature, from that nature will reap destruction; those who sow to please the Spirit, from the Spirit will reap eternal life.

For we are God's handiwork, created in Christ Jesus to do good works, which God prepared in advance for us to do.

Your faith is growing
We ought always to thank God for you, brothers and sisters, and rightly so, because your faith is growing more and more, and the love every one of you has for each other is increasing. . . . With this in mind, we constantly pray for you, that our God may count you worthy of his calling, and that by his power he may fulfil every good purpose of yours and every act prompted by your faith.

1 Thessalonians 1:3. John 6:29. James 2:17. Galatians 5:6; 6:8.
Ephesians 2:10. 2 Thessalonians 1:3, 11.

Evening

'Where is this "coming" he promised?'

Enoch, the seventh from Adam, prophesied about these men: 'See, the Lord is coming with thousands upon thousands of his holy ones to judge everyone, and to convict all the ungodly of all the ungodly acts they have done in the ungodly way, and of all the harsh words ungodly sinners have spoken against him.'

Look, he is coming with the clouds, and every eye will see him, even those who pierced him, and all the peoples of the earth will mourn because of him.

The Lord himself will come
For the Lord himself will come down from heaven, with a loud command, with the voice of the archangel and with the trumpet call of God, and the dead in Christ will rise first. After that, we who are still alive and are left will be caught up with them in the clouds to meet the Lord in the air. And so we will be with the Lord for ever.

2 Peter 3:4. Jude 14–15. Revelation 1:7. 1 Thessalonians 4:16–17.

December 23

Morning

'Let them come to me for refuge; let them make peace with me.'

'For I know the plans I have for you,' declares the LORD, 'plans to prosper you and not to harm you, plans to give you hope and a future.'—'There is no peace,' says the LORD, 'for the wicked.'—But now in Christ Jesus you who once were far away have been brought near through the blood of Christ. For he himself is our peace.

Through faith in his blood
God presented him as a sacrifice of atonement, through faith in his blood. He did this to demonstrate his justice, because in his forbearance he had left the sins committed beforehand unpunished—he did it to demonstrate his justice at the present time, so as to be just and the one who justifies those who have faith in Jesus.

Trust in the LORD for ever, for the LORD, the LORD, is the Rock eternal.

Isaiah 27:5. Jeremiah 29:11. Isaiah 48:22. Ephesians 2:13–14.
Romans 3:24–26. Isaiah 26:4.

Evening

God has given us eternal life, and this life is in his Son.

'For just as the Father raises the dead and gives them life, even so the Son gives life to whom he is pleased to give it.'

'I am the resurrection and the life'
'I am the resurrection and the life. Those who believe in me will live, even though they die; and whoever lives and believes in me will never die.'

'I am the good shepherd'
'I am the good shepherd. The good shepherd lays down his life for the sheep . . . I lay down my life—only to take it up again. No-one takes it from me, but I lay it down of my own accord. I have authority to lay it down and authority to take it up again. This command I received from my Father.' . . . 'No-one comes to the Father except through me.'

Those who have the Son have life; those who do not have the Son of God do not have life.

1 John 5:11. John 5:21; 11:25–26; 10:11, 17–18; 14:6. 1 John 5:12.

Morning

For if you live according to the sinful nature, you will die; but if by the Spirit you put to death the misdeeds of the body, you will live.

The acts of the sinful nature are obvious: sexual immorality, impurity and debauchery; . . . and the like. I warn you, as I did before, that those who live like this will not inherit the kingdom of God. But the fruit of the Spirit is love, joy, peace, patience, kindness, goodness, faithfulness, gentleness and self-control. Against such things there is no law. Those who belong to Christ Jesus have crucified the sinful nature with its passions and desires. Since we live by the Spirit, let us keep in step with the Spirit.

Live self-controlled lives
For the grace of God that brings salvation has appeared to all people. It teaches us to say 'No' to ungodliness and worldly passions, and to live self-controlled, upright and godly lives in this present age, while we wait for the blessed hope—the glorious appearing of our great God and Saviour, Jesus Christ.

Romans 8:13. Galatians 5:19, 21–25. Titus 2:11–13.

Evening

For we are the temple of the living God.

If you are insulted because of the name of Christ, you are blessed, for the Spirit of glory and of God rests on you. If you suffer, it should not be as a murderer or thief or any other kind of criminal, or even as a meddler.

Live good lives
Do not allow what you consider good to be spoken of as evil.—Live such good lives among the pagans.

God called you out of darkness
But you are a chosen people, a royal priesthood, a holy nation, a people belonging to God, that you may declare the praises of him who called you out of darkness into his wonderful light.

1 Corinthians 6:16. 1 Peter 4:14–15. Romans 14:16. 1 Peter 2:12, 9.

December 25

Morning

When the kindness and love of God our Saviour appeared.

'I have loved you with an everlasting love.'—This is how God showed his love among us: He sent his one and only Son into the world that we might live through him. This is love: not that we loved God, but that he loved us and sent his Son as an atoning sacrifice for our sins.

But when the time had fully come, God sent his Son, born of a woman, born under the law, to redeem those under the law, that we might receive adoption as God's children.

He appeared in a body
The Word became flesh and made his dwelling among us. We have seen his glory, the glory of the One and Only, who came from the Father, full of grace and truth.—Beyond all question, the mystery of godliness is great: He appeared in a body, was vindicated by the Spirit.

Titus 3:4. Jeremiah 31:3. 1 John 4:9–10. Galatians 4:4–5. John 1:14.
1 Timothy 3:6.

Evening

Thanks be to God for his indescribable gift!

Shout for joy to the LORD, all the earth. Serve the LORD with gladness; come before him with joyful songs. . . . Enter his gates with thanksgiving and his courts with praise; give thanks to him and praise his name.

Prince of Peace
For to us a child is born, to us a son is given, and the government will be on his shoulders. And he will be called Wonderful Counsellor, Mighty God, Everlasting Father, Prince of Peace.

A son, whom he loved
He . . . did not spare his own Son, but gave him up for us all.—'He had one left to send, a son, whom he loved.'

2 Corinthians 9:15. Psalm 100:1–2, 4. Isaiah 9:6–7. Romans 8:32.
Mark 12:6.

Morning

'But whoever stands firm to the end will be saved.'

Stand firm. Let nothing move you. Always give yourselves fully to the work of the Lord, because you know that your labour in the Lord is not in vain.

Rooted and built up in him
So then, just as you received Christ Jesus as Lord, continue to live in him, rooted and built up in him, strengthened in the faith as you were taught, and overflowing with thankfulness.

Do good to all people
Those who sow to please their sinful nature, from that nature will reap destruction; those who sow to please the Spirit, from the Spirit will reap eternal life. Let us not become weary in doing good, for at the proper time we will reap a harvest if we do not give up. Therefore, as we have opportunity, let us do good to all people, especially to those who belong to the family of believers.

Matthew 24:13. 1 Corinthians 15:58. Colossians 2:6–7.
Galatians 6:8–10.

Evening

He is able to save completely those who come to God through him.

'I am the way and the truth and the life. No-one comes to the Father except through me.'—'Salvation is found in no-one else, for there is no other name under heaven given to people by which we must be saved.'

'My sheep listen to my voice; I know them, and they follow me. I give them eternal life, and they shall never perish; no-one can snatch them out of my hand.'

The only God our Saviour
To him who is able to keep you from falling and to present you before his glorious presence without fault and with great joy—to the only God our Saviour be glory, majesty, power and authority, through Jesus Christ our Lord, before all ages, now and for evermore! Amen.

Hebrews 7:25. John 14:6. Acts 4:12. John 10:27–28. Jude 24–25.

December 27

Morning

We fix our eyes not on what is seen, but on what is unseen. For what is seen is temporary, but what is unseen is eternal.

For here we do not have an enduring city. . . . You knew that you yourselves had better and lasting possessions.

'Do not be afraid, little flock, for your Father has been pleased to give you the kingdom.'—For a little while you may have had to suffer grief in all kinds of trials.—There the wicked cease from turmoil, and there the weary are at rest.

No more mourning
For while we are in this tent, we groan and are burdened.—'He will wipe every tear from their eyes. There will be no more death or mourning or crying or pain, for the old order of things has passed away.'

> 2 Corinthians 4:18. Hebrews 13:14; 10:34. Luke 12:32. 1 Peter 1:6.
> Job 3:17. 2 Corinthians 5:4. Revelation 21:4.

Evening

He himself is our peace.

God was reconciling the world to himself in Christ, not counting people's sins against them . . . God made him who had no sin to be sin for us, so that in him we might become the righteousness of God.—And through him to reconcile to himself all things, whether things on earth or things in heaven, by making peace through his blood, shed on the cross. Once you were alienated from God and were enemies in your minds because of your evil behaviour. But now he has reconciled you by Christ's physical body through death to present you holy in his sight, without blemish and free from accusation.

'My peace I give you'
'Peace I leave with you; my peace I give you. I do not give to you as the world gives. Do not let your hearts be troubled and do not be afraid.'

> Ephesians 2:14. 2 Corinthians 5:19, 21. Colossians 1:20–22. John 14:27.

Morning

'Son, your sins are forgiven.'

'For I will forgive their wickedness and will remember their sins no more.'—'Who can forgive sins but God alone?'

'I, even I, am he who blots out your transgressions, for my own sake, and remembers your sins no more.'

Blessed are those whose transgressions are forgiven, whose sins are covered. Blessed are those whose sin the LORD does not count against them. Who is a God like you, who pardons sin and forgives the transgression?

Set free from sin
As far as the east is from the west, so far has he removed our transgressions from us.—For sin shall not be your master, because you are not under law, but under grace. . . . You have been set free from sin and have become slaves to righteousness.

> Mark 2:5. Jeremiah 31:34. Mark 2:7. Isaiah 43:25. Psalm 32:1–2.
> Micah 7:18. Psalm 103:12. Romans 6:14, 18.

Evening

'We would like to see Jesus.'

Yes, LORD, walking in the way of your laws, we wait for you; your name and renown are the desire of our hearts.—The LORD is near to all who call on him, to all who call on him in truth.

'I will be with you always'
'For where two or three come together in my name, there am I with them.'—'I will not leave you as orphans; I will come to you.'—'And surely I will be with you always, to the very end of the age.'

Face to face
Let us run with perseverance the race marked out for us. Let us fix our eyes on Jesus, the author and perfecter of our faith.—Now we see but a poor reflection; then we shall see face to face.—I desire to depart and be with Christ, which is better by far.

> John 12:21. Isaiah 26:8. Psalm 145:18. Matthew 18:20. John 14:18.
> Matthew 28:20. Hebrews 12:1–2. 1 Corinthians 13:12. Philippians 1:23.

December 29

Morning

Understand what the Lord's will is.

It is God's will that you should be holy.—'Now this is eternal life; that they may know you, the only true God, and Jesus Christ, whom you have sent.'

We have not stopped praying for you and asking God to fill you with the knowledge of his will through all spiritual wisdom and understanding.

The Spirit of wisdom and revelation
I keep asking that the God of our Lord Jesus Christ, the glorious Father, may give you the Spirit of wisdom and revelation, so that you may know him better. I pray also that the eyes of your heart may be enlightened in order that you may know the hope to which he has called you, the riches of his glorious inheritance in the saints, and his incomparably great power for us who believe.

Ephesians 5:17. 1 Thessalonians 4:3. John 17:3. Colossians 1:9.
Ephesians 1:17–19.

Evening

Come near to God and he will come near to you.

Enoch walked with God.—Do two walk together unless they have agreed to do so?—But as for me, it is good to be near God.

In their distress
The LORD is with you when you are with him. If you seek him, he will be found by you, but if you forsake him, he will forsake you . . . In their distress they turned to the LORD, the God of Israel, and sought him, and he was found by them.

'Plans to prosper you'
'For I know the plans I have for you,' declares the LORD, 'plans to prosper you and not to harm you, plans to give you hope and a future. Then you will call upon me and come and pray to me, and I will listen to you. You will seek me and find me when you seek me with all your heart.'

James 4:8. Genesis 5:24. Amos 3:3. Psalm 73:28. 2 Chronicles 15:2, 4.
Jeremiah 29:11–13.

Morning

Blameless on the day of our Lord Jesus Christ.

Once you were alienated from God and were enemies in your minds because of your evil behaviour. But now he has reconciled you by Christ's physical body through death to present you holy in his sight, without blemish and free from accusation—if you continue in your faith, established and firm, not moved from the hope held out in the gospel.

So that you may become blameless and pure, children of God without fault in a crooked and depraved generation, in which you shine like stars in the universe.

Blameless and at peace
So then, dear friends, since you are looking forward to this, make every effort to be found spotless, blameless and at peace with him.—Pure and blameless until the day of Christ.

1 Corinthians 1:8. Colossians 1:21–23. Philippians 2:15. 2 Peter 3:14.
Philippians 1:10.

Evening

He will guard the feet of his saints.

If we claim to have fellowship with him yet walk in the darkness, we lie and do not live by the truth. But if we walk in the light, as he is in the light, we have fellowship with one another, and the blood of Jesus, his Son, purifies us from all sin.—'Those who have had a bath need only to wash their feet; their whole body is clean.'

The way of wisdom
I guide you in the way of wisdom and lead you along straight paths. When you walk, your steps will not be hampered; when you run, you will not stumble.

The Lord will rescue me from every evil attack and will bring me safely to his heavenly kingdom. To him be glory for ever and ever. Amen.

1 Samuel 2:9. 1 John 1:6–7. John 13:10. Proverbs 4:11–12.
2 Timothy 4:18.

December 31

Morning

'Thus far has the LORD helped us.'

'I carried you on eagles' wings and brought you to myself.'—In all their distress he too was distressed, and the angel of his presence saved them. In his love and mercy he redeemed them; he lifted them up and carried them all the days of old.

Like an eagle
Like an eagle that stirs up its nest and hovers over its young, that spreads its wings to catch them and carries them on its pinions. The LORD alone led him; no foreign god was with him.

God is our God for ever
'Even to your old age and grey hairs I am he, I am he who will sustain you. I have made you and I will carry you; I will sustain you and I will rescue you.'— For this God is our God for ever and ever; he will be our guide even to the end.
    Cast your cares on the LORD and he will sustain you.

1 Samuel 7:12. Exodus 19:4. Isaiah 63:9. Deuteronomy 32:11–12.
Isaiah 46:4. Psalms 48:14; 55:22.

Evening

'There are still very large areas of land to be taken over.'

Not that I have already obtained all this, or have already been made perfect, but I press on to take hold of that for which Christ Jesus took hold of me.

'Be perfect'
'Be perfect.'—Make every effort to add to your faith goodness; and to goodness, knowledge; and to knowledge, self-control; and to self-control, perseverance; and to perseverance, godliness; and to godliness, mutual affection; and to mutual affection, love.
    And this is my prayer: that your love may abound more and more in knowledge and depth of insight.—'No eye has seen, no ear has heard, no mind has conceived what God has prepared for those who love him'—but God has revealed it to us by his Spirit.

Joshua 13:1. Philippians 3:12. Matthew 5:48. 2 Peter 1:5–7.
Philippians 1:9. 1 Corinthians 2:9–10.

Morning

They cried to the LORD in their trouble, and he saved them from their distress. Let them give thanks to the LORD for his unfailing love and his wonderful deeds for human beings.

'Were not all ten cleansed? Where are the other nine?'—Forget not all his benefits.—God, who answered me in the day of my distress.

I sought the LORD, and he answered me; he delivered me from all my fears.

My heart leaps for joy
My heart trusts in him, and I am helped. My heart leaps for joy and I will give thanks to him in song.

'Call upon me in the day of trouble; I will deliver you, and you will honour me. He who sacrifices thank-offerings honours me.'

Psalm 107:19, 21. Luke 17:17. Psalm 103:2. Genesis 35:3.
Psalms 34:4; 28:7; 50:15, 23.

Evening

Those who hope in me will not be disappointed.

'Did I not tell you that if you believed, you would see the glory of God?'

'Daniel, servant of the living God, has your God, whom you serve continually, been able to rescue you from the lions?' . . . No wound was found on him, because he had trusted in his God.

'My heart rejoices in the LORD'
'I prayed . . . and the LORD has granted me what I asked of him.—My heart rejoices in the LORD.'—Come and listen, all you who fear God; let me tell you what he has done for me.

Let them give thanks to the LORD for his unfailing love.—Blessed are those who take refuge in him.

Isaiah 49:23. John 11:40. Daniel 6:20, 23. 1 Samuel 1:27; 2:1.
Psalm 66:16. Psalms 107:31; 34:8.

For a Birthday

Morning

The LORD bless you and keep you.

May the LORD, the Maker of heaven and earth, bless you.—God our Father.—God, who richly provides us with everything for our enjoyment.

'Your heavenly Father knows that you need them.'—'The Father himself loves you.'

No good thing does he withhold from those whose walk is blameless.—He holds victory in store for the upright, he is a shield to those whose walk is blameless.

Peace at all times
The LORD will be your confidence and will keep your foot from being snared.—The LORD of peace himself give you peace at all times and in every way.

> Numbers 6:24. Psalm 134:3. 2 Thessalonians 2:16. 1 Timothy 6:17.
> Matthew 6:32. John 16:27. Psalm 84:11. Proverbs 2:7; 3:26.
> 2 Thessalonians 3:16.

Evening

The LORD your God will be with you wherever you go.

The land you are crossing the Jordan to take possession of is a land of mountains and valleys . . . a land the LORD our God cares for; the eyes of the LORD your God are continually on it from the beginning of the year to its end.

God's field
You are God's field.—Created in Christ Jesus to do good works, which God prepared in advance for us to do.

The shelter of the Most High
How great is your goodness, which you have stored up for those who fear you.—Whoever dwells in the shelter of the Most High will rest in the shadow of the Almighty.

> Joshua 1:9. Deuteronomy 11:11, 12. 1 Corinthians 3:9. Ephesians 2:10.
> Psalms 31:19; 91:1.

Marriage

Jesus and his disciples had also been invited to the wedding.

Marriage should be honoured by all.—The LORD God said, 'It is not good for the man to be alone.'—Everything God created is good, and nothing is to be rejected if it is received with thanksgiving, because it is consecrated by the word of God and prayer.

Love and compassion
The blessing of the LORD brings wealth, and he adds no trouble to it.—God, who richly provides us with everything for our enjoyment.— And crowns me with love and compassion. He satisfies my desires with good things.

Christ loved the church and gave himself up for her.—You are not your own.—Set your minds on things above.

John 2:2. Hebrews 13:4. Genesis 2:18. 1 Timothy 4:4–5. Proverbs 10:22.
1 Timothy 6:17. Psalm 103:4–5. Ephesians 5:25. 1 Corinthians 6:19.
Colossians 3:2.

The New Home

I will walk in my house with blameless heart.

As for me and my household, we will serve the LORD.

'Seek first his righteousness'
'Seek first his kingdom and his righteousness, and all these things will be given to you as well.'—'No servant can serve two masters. . . . You cannot serve both God and Money.'

Heirs . . . of the gracious gift of life, so that nothing will hinder your prayers.—Two are better than one, . . . if one falls down, his friend can help him up.—Let us consider how we may spur one another on towards love and good deeds.

Husbands, love your wives.—Not easily angered.—Be kind and compassionate to one another, forgiving each other, just as in Christ God forgave you.

Psalm 101:2. Joshua 24:15. Matthew 6:33. Luke 16:13. 1 Peter 3:7.
Ecclesiastes 4:9–10. Hebrews 10:24. Colossians 3:19. 1 Corinthians 13:5.
Ephesians 4:32.

For Times of Anxiety

Morning

Teach me to do your will, for you are my God.

Lead me, O LORD, in your righteousness, make straight your way before me.—My times are in your hands.

If any of you lacks wisdom, you should ask God, who gives generously to all without finding fault, and it will be given to you. But when you ask, you must not doubt.

Put your hope in God
When anxiety was great within me, your consolation brought joy to my soul.—Why are you downcast, O my soul? Why so disturbed within me? Put your hope in God.

Jesus said to his disciples, 'Why are you so afraid? Do you still have no faith?'—Now faith is being . . . certain of what we do not see.

> Psalms 143:10; 5:8; 31:15. James 1:5–6. Psalms 94:19; 42:5. Mark 4:40.
> Hebrews 11:1.

Evening

'Do not fear; I will help you.'

'Come to me, all you who are weary and burdened, and I will give you rest.'

You call upon me, and I will answer you; I will be with you in trouble.—'I have made you and I will carry you; I will sustain you and I will rescue you.'— 'I will be with you.'

Do not be anxious about anything
Do not be anxious about anything, but in everything, by prayer and petition, with thanksgiving present your requests to God. And the peace of God, which transcends all understanding, will guard your hearts and your minds in Christ Jesus.

I will instruct you and teach you in the way you should go; I will counsel you and watch over you.

'Do not be afraid. I am the First and the Last.'

> Isaiah 41:13. Matthew 11:28. Psalm 91:15. Isaiah 46:4; 43:2.
> Philippians 4:6–7. Psalm 32:8. Revelation 1:17.

Affliction

Save me, O God, for the waters have come up to my neck.

'My Father, if it is possible, may this cup be taken from me. Yet not as I will, but as you will.'—Being in anguish.—Jesus wept.

Surely he took up our infirmities and carried our sorrows.—We do not have a high priest who is unable to sympathise with our weaknesses, but we have one who has been tempted in every way, just as we are—yet was without sin. Let us then approach the throne of grace with confidence, so that we may find grace to help in our time of need.

'Never will I forsake you'
He cares for you.—'When you pass through the waters, I will be with you; and when you pass through the rivers, they will not sweep over you.'—'Never will I leave you; never will I forsake you.'

Psalm 69:1. Matthew 26:39. Luke 22:44. John 11:35. Isaiah 53:4.
Hebrews 4:15–16. 1 Peter 5:7. Isaiah 43:1–2. Hebrews 13:5.

For Sickness

'Lord, the one you love is sick.'

Surely he took up our infirmities and carried our sorrows.—'He took up our infirmities and carried our diseases.'—Yet he was merciful.—As a father has compassion on his children, so the LORD has compassion on those who fear him; for he knows how we are formed.

Who shall separate us from the love of Christ? Shall trouble or hardship?— We know that in all things God works for the good of those who love him.

'My power is made perfect in weakness'
The Lord said to me, 'My grace is sufficient for you, for my power is made perfect in weakness.' Therefore I will boast all the more gladly about my weaknesses, so that Christ's power may rest on me.

John 11:3. Isaiah 53:4. Matthew 8:17. Psalms 78:38; 103:13–14.
Romans 8:35, 28. 2 Corinthians 12:9.

Bereavement

Morning

'Father, I want those you have given me to be with me where I am.'

I am torn between the two: I desire to depart and be with Christ, which is better by far.—Whether we live or die, we belong to the Lord.

You knew that you yourselves had better and lasting possessions.—What we will be has not yet been made known. But we know that when he appears, we shall be like him, for we shall see him as he is.—Now we see but a poor reflection; then we shall see face to face.—In righteousness I shall see your face; when I awake, I shall be satisfied with seeing your likeness.

Encourage each other
So we will be with the Lord for ever. Therefore, encourage each other with these words.

> John 17:24. Philippians 1:23. Romans 14:8. Hebrews 10:34. 1 John 3:2.
> 1 Corinthians 13:12. Psalm 17:15. 1 Thessalonians 4:17–18.

Evening

Asleep.

Fallen asleep.—Those who have fallen asleep in Jesus.—Asleep in Christ.

'Our friend Lazarus has fallen asleep.'—Jesus had been speaking of his death.—They were stoning Stephen . . . and . . . he fell asleep.—He grants sleep to those he loves.

Victory through our Lord Jesus Christ
Death has been swallowed up in victory. Where, O death, is your victory? Where, O death, is your sting? The sting of death is sin, and the power of sin is the law. But thanks be to God! He gives us the victory through our Lord Jesus Christ. Therefore, my dear brothers and sisters, stand firm. Let nothing move you. Always give yourselves fully to the work of the Lord, because you know that your labour in the Lord is not in vain.

> 1 Thessalonians 4:13. 1 Corinthians 15:6. 1 Thessalonians 4:14.
> 1 Corinthians 15:18. John 11:11, 13. Acts 7:59–60. Psalm 127:2.
> 1 Corinthians 15:54–58.

Morning

The LORD keep watch between you and me when we are away from each other.

I urge you to pray
Pray . . . I particularly urge you to pray so that I may be restored to you soon.—But, brothers and sisters, when we were torn away from you for a short time (in person, not in thought), out of our intense longing we made every effort to see you. For we wanted to come to you—certainly I, Paul, did, again and again—but Satan stopped us.

'I will be with you always'
God has said, 'Never will I leave you; never will I forsake you.' So that we may boldly say, 'The Lord is my helper; I will not be afraid. What can human beings do to me?'—'Surely I am with you always, to the very end of the age.'

Genesis 31:49. Hebrews 13:18–19. 1 Thessalonians 2:17–18.
Hebrews 13:5–6. Matthew 28:20.

Evening

'I will not leave you as orphans; I will come to you.'

They went up out of Egypt and came to their father Jacob in the land of Canaan. They told him, 'Joseph is still alive! In fact, he is ruler of all Egypt.' Jacob was stunned; he did not believe them. But when they told him everything Joseph had said to them, and when he saw the carts Joseph had sent to carry him back, the spirit of their father Jacob revived. And Israel said, 'I'm convinced! My son Joseph is still alive. I will go and see him before I die.'

He knelt down and prayed
'Now I know that none of you among whom I have gone about preaching the kingdom will ever see me again.' . . . When he had said this, he knelt down with all of them and prayed. They all wept as they embraced him and kissed him. What grieved them most was his statement that they would never see his face again. Then they accompanied him to the ship.

John 14:18. Genesis 45:25–28. Acts 20:25, 36–38.

Reunion

Morning

'I will see you again.'

Israel said to Joseph, 'I never expected to see your face again, and now God has allowed me to see your children too.'

When the LORD brought back the captives to Zion, we were like those who dreamed. Our mouths were filled with laughter, our tongues with songs of joy. Then it was said among the nations, 'The LORD has done great things for them.' The LORD has done great things for us, and we are filled with joy. . . . He who goes out weeping, carrying seed to sow, will return with songs of joy, carrying sheaves with him.

'I will come back'
'I am going . . . to prepare a place for you. And if I go and prepare a place for you, I will come back and take you to be with me that you may be where I am.'—For in just a very little while, 'He who is coming will come and will not delay.'

John 16:22. Genesis 48:11. Psalm 126:1–3, 6. John 14:2–3.
Hebrews 10:37.

Evening

Sorrow and sighing will flee away.

God sent me here ahead of you
Joseph . . . made himself known to his brothers. . . . He said, 'I am your brother Joseph, the one you sold into Egypt! And now, do not be distressed and do not be angry with yourselves for selling me here, because it was to save lives that God sent me ahead of you. Tell my father about all the honour accorded me in Egypt . . . And bring my father down here quickly.'

The Lord brought him out of prison
Peter was kept in prison, but the church was earnestly praying to God for him. . . . He described how the Lord had brought him out of prison.

Isaiah 35:10. Genesis 45:1, 4–5. Acts 12:5, 17.

Recovery from Sickness

'I am the LORD who heals you.'

Praise the LORD, O my soul, and forget not all his benefits. He forgives all my sins and heals all my diseases.

Hezekiah

In those days Hezekiah became ill and was at the point of death. Hezekiah . . . prayed to the LORD, 'Remember, O LORD, how I have walked before you faithfully and with wholehearted devotion and have done what is good in your eyes.' And Hezekiah wept bitterly. Then the word of the LORD came to Isaiah: 'Go and tell Hezekiah, "This is what the LORD, the God of your father David, says: I have heard your prayer and seen your tears; I will add fifteen years to your life."'

Cured of his leprosy

A man with leprosy came and knelt before him and said, 'Lord, if you are willing, you can make me clean.' Jesus reached out his hand and touched the man. 'I am willing,' he said. 'Be clean!' Immediately he was cured of his leprosy.

Exodus 15:26. Psalm 103:2–3. Isaiah 38:1–5. Matthew 8:2–3.

Convalescence

Be still before the LORD and wait patiently for him.

He said to them, 'Come with me by yourselves to a quiet place and get some rest.'

An angel touched him

He lay down under the tree and fell asleep. All at once an angel touched him and said, 'Get up and eat.' He looked around, and there by his head was a cake of bread baked over hot coals, and a jar of water. He ate and drank and then lay down again. The angel of the LORD came back a second time and touched him and said, 'Get up and eat, for the journey is too much for you.' So he got up and ate and drank. Strengthened by that food, he travelled for forty days and forty nights until he reached Horeb, the mountain of God.

The LORD is my shepherd, I shall lack nothing. He makes me lie down in green pastures, he leads me beside quiet waters, he restores my soul.

Psalm 37:7. Mark 6:31. 1 Kings 19:5–8. Psalm 23:1–3.

Disappointed Hopes

When times are bad, consider.

If you falter in times of trouble, how small is your strength!—See, I have refined you, though not as silver; I have tested you in the furnace of affliction.—'We must go through many hardships to enter the kingdom of God.'

Though the fig-tree does not bud and there are no grapes on the vines, though the olive crop fails and the fields produce no food, though there are no sheep in the pen and no cattle in the stalls, yet I will rejoice in the LORD, I will be joyful in God my Saviour.

The God of all comfort
Praise be to the God and Father of our Lord Jesus Christ, the Father of compassion and the God of all comfort, who comforts us in all our troubles, so that we can comfort those in any trouble with the comfort we ourselves have received from God.

Ecclesiastes 7:14. Proverbs 24:10. Isaiah 48:10. Acts 14:22.
Habakkuk 3:17–18. 2 Corinthians 1:3–4.

Days of Prosperity

When times are good, be happy.

The LORD was with Joseph and he prospered.—'The LORD be exalted, who delights in the well-being of his servant.'

Like trees planted by streams
Blessed are those who do not walk in the counsel of the wicked or stand in the way of sinners or sit in the seat of mockers. But their delight is in the law of the LORD, and on his law they meditate day and night. They are like trees planted by streams of water, which yield their fruit in season and whose leaves do not wither. Whatever they do prospers.

Meditate
Do not let this book of the Law depart from your mouth; meditate on it day and night, so that you may be careful to do everything written in it. Then you will be prosperous and successful.—And the LORD was with him; he was successful in whatever he undertook.

Ecclesiastes 7:14. Genesis 39:2. Psalms 35:27; 1:1–3. Joshua 1:8.
2 Kings 18:7.

Morning

Though your riches increase, do not set your heart on them.

Remember the LORD your God, for it is he who gives you the ability to produce wealth.—The blessing of the LORD brings wealth and he adds no trouble to it.—Riches . . . surely sprout wings and fly off.

God provides
Command those who are rich in this present world not to be arrogant nor to put their hope in wealth, which is so uncertain, but to put their hope in God, who richly provides us with everything for our enjoyment.

Honour the LORD with your wealth
Honour the LORD with your wealth, with the firstfruits of all your crops; then your barns will be filled to overflowing, and your vats will brim over with new wine.

> Psalm 62:10. Deuteronomy 8:18. Proverbs 10:22. Proverbs 23:5.
> 1 Timothy 6:17. Proverbs 3:9–10.

Evening

'Do whatever he tells you.'

'Apart from me you can do nothing.'
  When he had finished speaking, he said to Simon, 'Put out into deep water, and let down the nets for a catch.' Simon answered, 'Master, we've worked hard all night and haven't caught anything. But because you say so, I will let down the nets.' When they had done so they caught such a large number of fish that their nets began to break. So they signalled to their partners in the other boats to come and help them, and they came and filled both boats so full that they began to sink. When Simon Peter saw this, he fell at Jesus' knees and said, 'Go away from me, Lord; I am a sinful man!' For he and all his companions were astonished at the catch of fish they had taken.

Your labour in the Lord is not in vain
Therefore, my dear brothers and sisters, stand firm. Let nothing move you. Always give yourselves fully to the work of the Lord, because you know that your labour in the Lord is not in vain.

> John 2:5; 15:5. Luke 5:4–9. 1 Corinthians 15:58.

The Birth of a Child

Morning

'I prayed for this child, and the LORD has granted me what I asked of him.'

Children are a heritage from the LORD, offspring a reward from him.—A little child will lead them.—Train children in the way they should go, and when they are old they will not turn from it.—Your children will be like olive shoots round your table.

'Let the little children come to me'
He took a little child whom he placed among them. Taking the child in his arms, he said to them, 'Whoever welcomes one of these little children in my name welcomes me; and whoever welcomes me does not welcome me but the one who sent me.'—Jesus . . . said . . . 'Let the little children come to me, and do not hinder them, for the kingdom of God belongs to such as these.'

1 Samuel 1:27. Psalm 127:3. Isaiah 11:6. Proverbs 22:6. Psalm 128:3.
Mark 9:36–37; 10:14.

Evening

Thanks be to God for his indescribable gift!

This is how God showed his love among us: He sent his one and only Son into the world that we might live through him.

She gave birth
And she gave birth to her firstborn, a son. She wrapped him in cloths and placed him in a manger, because there was no room for them in the inn. And there were in the same country shepherds . . . keeping watch over their flocks at night. An angel of the Lord appeared to them, and the glory of the Lord shone around them, and they were terrified. But the angel said to them, 'Do not be afraid. I bring you good news of great joy that will be for all the people. Today in the town of David a Saviour has been born to you; he is Christ the Lord. This will be a sign to you: You will find a baby wrapped in cloths and lying in a manger.' Suddenly a great company of the heavenly host appeared with the angel, praising God and saying, 'Glory to God in the highest, and peace on earth to those on whom his favour rests.'

2 Corinthians 9:15. 1 John 4:9. Luke 2:7–14.

Morning

Is not wisdom found among the aged? Does not long life bring understanding?

The length of our days is seventy years—or eighty, if we have the strength; yet their span is but trouble and sorrow, for they quickly pass, and we fly away.

Even to your grey hairs
Even to your old age and grey hairs I am he, I am he who will sustain you. I have made you and I will carry you; I will sustain you and I will rescue you.— Grey hair is the splendour of the old.

Blessed are those who find wisdom
Blessed are those who find wisdom, those who gain understanding, for she is more profitable than silver and yields better returns than gold. She is more precious than rubies; nothing you desire can compare with her. Long life is in her right hand; in her left hand are riches and honour.

Job 12:12. Psalm 90:10. Isaiah 46:4. Proverbs 20:29; 3:13–16.

Evening

They will still bear fruit in old age.

Whoever dwells in the shelter of the Most High will rest in the shadow of the Almighty . . . 'With long life will I satisfy you and show you my salvation.'

Show respect for the elderly
Rise in the presence of the aged, show respect for the elderly and revere your God. I am the LORD.—That you may love the LORD your God, listen to his voice, and hold fast to him. For the LORD is your life, and he will give you many years.

Trust in the LORD with all your heart and lean not on your own understanding; in all your ways acknowledge him and he will make your paths straight.—The path of the righteous is like the first gleam of dawn, shining ever brighter till the full light of day.

Psalms 92:14; 91:1, 16. Leviticus 19:32. Deuteronomy 30:20.
Proverbs 3:5–6; 4:18.

The End of the Journey

Morning

You guide me with your counsel, and afterwards you will take me into glory.

In your unfailing love you will lead the people you have redeemed. In your strength you will guide them to your holy dwelling.

My shepherd to this day
Not one of all the good promises the LORD your God gave you has failed. Every promise has been fulfilled; not one has failed.—The God who has been my shepherd all my life to this day.—You will fill me with joy in your presence, with eternal pleasures at your right hand.—Surely goodness and love will follow me all the days of my life, and I will dwell in the house of the LORD for ever.

Simeon
'Sovereign Lord, as you have promised, you now dismiss your servant in peace. For my eyes have seen your salvation.'

Psalm 73:24. Exodus 15:13. Joshua 23:14. Genesis 48:15.
Psalms 16:11; 23:6. Luke 2:29–30.

Evening

'In my Father's house are many rooms.'

Teach us to number our days aright, that we may gain a heart of wisdom.

A rich welcome
And you will receive a rich welcome into the eternal kingdom of our Lord and Saviour Jesus Christ.—For we know in part and we prophesy in part, but when perfection comes, the imperfect disappears. . . . Now we see but a poor reflection . . . then we shall see face to face. Now I know in part; then I shall know fully, even as I am fully known.

He will wipe every tear from their eyes. There will be no more death or mourning or crying or pain, for the old order of things has passed away.

We will all be changed
Listen, I tell you a mystery: We will not all sleep, but we will all be changed.— We shall be like him, for we shall see him as he is.

John 14:2. Psalm 90:12. 2 Peter 1:11. 1 Corinthians 13:9–10. 12.
Revelation 21:4. 1 Corinthians 15:51. 1 John 3:2.